PARTY AUTONOMY IN EU PRIVATE INTERNATIONAL LAW

European Family Law Series

PARTY AUTONOMY IN EU PRIVATE INTERNATIONAL LAW

Choice of Court and Choice of Law in Family Matters and Succession

Jacqueline Gray

INTERSENTIA

Cambridge – Antwerp – Chicago

Intersentia Ltd
8 Wellington Mews
Wellington Street | Cambridge
CB1 1HW | United Kingdom
Tel: +44 1223 736 170
Email: mail@intersentia.co.uk
www.intersentia.com | www.intersentia.co.uk

Distribution for the UK and
Rest of the World (incl. Eastern Europe)
NBN International
1 Deltic Avenue, Rooksley
Milton Keynes MK13 8LD
United Kingdom
Tel: +44 1752 202 301 | Fax: +44 1752 202 331
Email: orders@nbninternational.com

Distribution for Europe
Lefebvre Sarrut Belgium NV
Hoogstraat 139/6
1000 Brussels
Belgium
Tel: +32 (0)800 39 067
Email: mail@intersentia.be

Distribution for the USA and Canada
Independent Publishers Group
Order Department
814 North Franklin Street
Chicago, IL 60610
USA
Tel: +1 800 888 4741 (toll free) | Fax: +1 312 337 5985
Email: orders@ipgbook.com

Party Autonomy in EU Private International Law. Choice of Court and Choice of Law in Family Matters and Succession

ISBN 978-1-78068-974-6
D/2021/7849/5
NUR 822

British Library Cataloguing in Publication Data. A catalogue record for this book is available from the British Library.

ACKNOWLEDGEMENTS

'Standing on the shoulders of giants', the well-known quote attributed to Bernard of Chartres (and, more recently, the tagline of Google Scholar), is the phrase that springs to mind when I look back on this research project. For in as much as writing this book has been my own personal challenge, it seems to me that the key to success lies equally in having a network of supportive people who are willing to provide wisdom, collaboration and encouragement throughout the highs and lows that are inevitable on such a journey.

First and foremost, I would like to express my deep gratitude to my supervisor, Prof. Katharina Boele-Woelki. Whilst her insight and innovation helped to establish an invaluable foundation from which to launch this research, the combination of guidance and freedom that she provided throughout created the ideal environment in which to pursue this project. Furthermore, I want to take this opportunity to thank the head of Utrecht Centre for European Research into Family Law (UCERF), Prof. Wendy Schrama, who was ready to offer her support and expertise on a wide range of topics whenever it was required. I also wish to convey my appreciation to the members of the Assessment Committee for their acceptance of this role and for taking the time to provide constructive critique that has aided in the completion of the final version of this manuscript.

I am especially grateful for the diverse opportunities that being part of UCERF and the wider Molengraaff Institute for Private Law has brought me during these past years. Undertaking this research in a setting which seamlessly combines an interdisciplinary focus with an international outlook has irrefutably broadened my horizons. However, it is the people who truly make a place, and I am particularly thankful for the many working relationships that have blossomed into wonderful friendships, both in the Netherlands and further afield (most prominently, my two paranymphs during the defence ceremony: Evelien van Wijk-Verhagen and Maximilian Strutz).

Finally, I would like to take the time to acknowledge the unwavering support of my family, in particular my parents, during the course of this research. I am also grateful to my husband, Martin (my own 'international' spouse), who has been there to provide an encouraging voice and a listening ear whenever it was needed. Last, but certainly not least, I wish to thank my daughter, Emilie, whose entrance into my life has provided perspective, challenge and motivation in the delivery of this paper 'baby'.

Jacqueline Gray
July 2020

CONTENTS

LIST OF ABBREVIATIONS

Brussels I Regulation	Council Regulation (EC) No 44/2001 of 22 December 2000 on jurisdiction and the recognition and enforcement of judgments in civil and commercial matters [2001] OJ L 12/1
Brussels I Recast Regulation	Council Regulation (EC) No 1215/2012 of 12 December 2012 on jurisdiction and the recognition and enforcement of judgments in civil and commercial matters (Recast) OJ L 351/1
Brussels II bis Regulation	Council Regulation (EC) No 2201/2003 of 27 November 2003 concerning jurisdiction and the recognition and enforcement of judgments in matrimonial matters and the matters of parental responsibility [2003] L 338/1
Brussels IIa (Recast) Regulation	Council Regulation (EU) 2019/1111 of 25 June 2019 on jurisdiction, the recognition and enforcement of decisions in matrimonial matters and the matters of parental responsibility, and on international child abduction [2019] OJ L 178/1 [in force from 1 August 2022]
CJEU	Court of Justice of the European Union
ECHR	European Convention on Human Rights
ECtHR	European Court of Human Rights
EU	European Union
EU Charter of Fundamental Rights	Charter of Fundamental Rights of the European Union
Hague Maintenance Protocol	Hague Protocol of 23 November 2007 on the Law Applicable to Maintenance Obligations
Maintenance Regulation	Council Regulation (EC) No. 4/2009 of 18 December 2008 on jurisdiction, applicable law, recognition and enforcement of decisions and cooperation in matters relating to maintenance obligations [2009] OJ L 7/1

Matrimonial Property Regulation	Council Regulation (EU) 2016/1103 of 24 June 2016 implementing enhanced cooperation in the area of jurisdiction, applicable law and the recognition and enforcement of decisions in matters of matrimonial property regimes [2016] OJ L 183/1
Partnership Property Regulation	Council Regulation (EU) 2016/1104 of 24 June 2016 implementing enhanced cooperation in the area of jurisdiction, applicable law and the recognition and enforcement of decisions in matters of the property consequences of registered partnerships [2016] OJ L 183/30
Property Regulations	Collective reference to both the Partnership Property Regulation and the Matrimonial Property Regulation (above)
Rome I Regulation	Council Regulation (EC) No. 593/2008 of the European Parliament and of the Council of 17 June 2008 on the law applicable to contractual obligations (Rome I) [2008] OJ L 177/6
Rome II Regulation	Council Regulation (EC) No. 864/2007 of the European Parliament and of the Council of 11 July 2007 on the law applicable to non-contractual obligations (Rome II) [2007] OJ L 199/40
Rome III Regulation	Council Regulation (EU) No. 1259/2010 of 20 December 2010 implementing enhanced cooperation in the area of the law applicable to divorce and legal separation [2010] L 343/10
Succession Regulation	Regulation (EU) No. 650/2012 of the European Parliament and of the Council of 4 July 2012 on jurisdiction, applicable law, recognition and enforcement of decisions and acceptance and enforcement of authentic instruments in matters of succession and on the creation of a European Certificate of Succession [2012] L 201/107
TEU	Treaty on European Union
TFEU	Treaty on the Functioning of the European Union

LIST OF CASES

SUPRANATIONAL JURISPRUDENCE

CJEU

ECtHR

NATIONAL JURISPRUDENCE

ENGLAND AND WALES

BELGIUM

CZECH REPUBLIC

FRANCE

NETHERLANDS

SPAIN

LIST OF TREATIES AND LEGISLATION

PRIMARY INSTRUMENTS

INTERNATIONAL TREATIES

EU PRIMARY LEGISLATION

HAGUE CONFERENCE INSTRUMENTS

SECONDARY INSTRUMENTS

EU DIRECTIVES

EU REGULATIONS

EU PROPOSED INSTRUMENTS

NATIONAL LEGISLATION

ENGLAND AND WALES

NETHERLANDS

UNITED STATES

PART I

CONCEPT AND OBJECTIVES

CHAPTER 1
INTRODUCTION

1.1. PREMISE

During the course of the past 20 years, the EU has undertaken the ambitious task of unifying – 'Europeanising'[1] – private international law rules on a supranational level. As part of this mission to create 'a genuine European area of justice'[2] for those that make use of their free movement rights within the Union, several instruments have been introduced that specifically address family matters (matrimonial matters, parental responsibility, property relations and maintenance) and succession. The process of unifying private international law rules on a Union level is distinguished not only by its ambitious scale, but also by its tendency towards novelty.

Arguably one of the most prominent of such developments is the widespread inclusion of party autonomy in the EU's instruments concerning family matters and succession.[3] Although party autonomy is not unheard of within Member States' own jurisdictional and conflict-of-laws rules on these topics, its appearance has until now been sporadic between states and subject areas. Its large-scale introduction within the realm of cross-border family matters and succession in Europe provides considerable scope for examination. Most notably, there has been to date little scrutiny concerning the purpose and validity of its introduction in the European Union context.

This book pursues an examination of the party autonomy provisions[4] established within the EU's instruments on family matters and succession in view of the status of such rules as measures of Union law. This involves identifying the particular values that the EU attaches to party autonomy, as well as the more general objectives behind legislative action in the Union setting, and evaluating the coherence of these provisions with the established parameters.

---

1 For usage of this term see, for instance, K. Boele-Woelki, 'For Better or for Worse: The Europeanization of International Divorce Law' (2010) 12 *Yearbook of private international law* 1–26.

2 Tampere European Council Conclusions 1999, at para.28.

3 At times, hereinafter, collectively referred to as the 'relevant instruments'.

4 At times, hereinafter, referred to as 'relevant provisions'.

The conclusions that are generated will present a valuable critique of the 'state of affairs' following the flurry of legislative activity that has taken place over the past two decades.

1.2. DELINEATION OF PARTY AUTONOMY

In concise terms, the concept of party autonomy refers to the opportunity for parties to make a choice of court or choice of law agreement (or, in the case of a succession, a *professio juris*) in the private international law context.[5] It should be distinguished from the related (but distinct) notion of private autonomy in substantive law.[6] The present term essentially equates to an active[7] expression of will by parties that has the effect of electing the jurisdiction or applicable law that will govern a (future) proceeding. Within the EU private international law framework relating to family matters and succession, such a designation is made on the ground of a close connection or connection to the corresponding law or jurisdiction that governs the same matter.

At the same time, 'subsidiary choice of court provisions', that lay at (or arguably, beyond[8]) the limits of what might be considered to be an exercise of party autonomy in private international law, will also be addressed. This category includes mechanisms that require a jurisdiction to be 'accepted' rather than designated, or agreement to a court's competence to be demonstrated by merely entering an appearance in that jurisdiction. In such instances, whilst the consent of the party whose agreement is required is decisive to the successful assumption of jurisdiction, it is by no means the instigating or sole factor in this process.

Such provisions have been included within the scope of this book in view of the special requirements that accompany family matters and succession; for instance, the need to safeguard the best interests of the child in processes concerning parental responsibility, or to provide additional opportunities for the facilitation of access to justice. Furthermore, as will become apparent in later chapters, party autonomy in this context presents a sliding scale in terms

5 The remit of 'court' and 'applicable law' for the purposes of making such agreements will be examined in Chapter 5: 'The Focus of Choice'.

6 F. Maultzsch, 'Party Autonomy in European Private International Law: Uniform Principle or Context-Dependent Instrument' (2009) 12(3) *Journal of Private International Law* 466, at p.476. By way of example, see the arrangement of property through agreements between spouses or registered partners in accordance with a country's domestic law.

7 This book will not extend to consider indirect forms of party autonomy, such as informal agreements between parties to act in an orchestrated manner (e.g. to seise a certain court with jurisdiction). It is solely concerned with action taken by parties according to prescribed rules.

8 A. Mills, *Party Autonomy in Private International Law* (Cambridge University Press, Cambridge, 2018), at pp.17–19, paras.1.3.2–1.3.3.

of the nature of the participation of the parties. Beyond the mainstream brand of party autonomy discussed above, it would be hard to draw a dividing line without appearing somewhat arbitrary. Lastly, examination of such mechanisms provides a useful point of comparison against which to consider the form and function of the choice of court and choice of law provisions that form the bulk of this evaluation.

1.3. DEVELOPMENT IN EU PRIVATE INTERNATIONAL LAW

The usage of party autonomy as a device in cross-border legal relations has a complex history, with various influences contributing towards its emergence (and, in the case of contractual relations, its dominance) on the European stage.[9] The historic underpinnings of this principle are explored below, first generally, and then more specifically to the present family and succession law context.

It is difficult to identify the exact point in time at which a construction resembling party autonomy as it is known today first emerged in the sphere of cross-border legal relations. Around 120-118 B.C., it has been said that a decree was issued in Hellenistic Egypt providing that contracts written in Egyptian would be subject to Egyptian jurisdiction and Egyptian law, and contracts written in Greek would be adjudged by the Greek jurisdiction and Greek law.[10] However, this method was rather far removed from the present conception of party autonomy, given that it balanced upon a generic perception, rather than the actual intentions of the parties.

The genesis of a concept that comes close to that seen within the current private international law framework occurred much closer to the present day. Starting with the jurisdictional context, it can be seen that up until the nineteenth century, connection with the forum in civil and common law traditions was generally based on territorial or personal connections[11] and, crucially, was a matter for the state to determine.[12] This *status quo* gradually began to be eroded in common law during the course of that century by judgments that allowed the courts to decline jurisdiction where the parties had agreed for a foreign court or

9 Ibid., at p.65, para.2.2.3.

10 See, in this regard, S. Symeonides, 'Party autonomy in Rome I and II: an outsiders perspective' (2010) 28(2) *Nederlands Internationaal Privaatrecht* 191 at p.191, fn.1.

11 See historical discussion of Roman law connections for determining jurisdiction in various scenarios (the place of domicile or nationality of the defendant; place where the contract performed or relevant act took place; place where property located). In common law, such connections were the place of the location of relevant acts or events, or place of the location of the defendant. See Mills (n.8), at pp.32–33, para.2.2.1.

12 Mills (n.8 above), at pp.31–33, para.2.2.1.

arbitral tribunal to hear the matter. However, in such instances, the courts were empowered, but not obliged to stay their proceedings.[13]

During this period in time, the German jurist Savigny also proposed an argument in favour of 'voluntary submission' whereby the parties, by opting to enter a contract that would be performed in a certain place, were seen to choose a 'seat' for proceedings concerning their contract in the place of obligation.[14] However, it should be pointed out that this theory balanced on a tacit expression of the parties' will, rather than active consent, and thus remains distinguishable from the modern conception of party autonomy.

Ultimately, it was a 1920 amendment of the Rules of the Supreme Court in England that provided a catalyst for a shift in the previous paradigm.[15] This revision established that the English courts could give permission for claimants to instigate proceedings within their remit against defendants outside this jurisdiction if, *inter alia*, the parties agreed that the English court could have jurisdiction for claims arising under their contract. The courts could assume jurisdiction on the basis of such an agreement even where there was no connection between the circumstances and England.[16]

Due to a tendency to view jurisdiction as a matter of public law under the control of governmental authorities, European countries with civil law traditions were more reluctant to accept party autonomy in the jurisdictional context.[17] However, there was nevertheless a trend towards recognition of 'choice of court' agreements in such jurisdictions during the course of the twentieth century.[18] This shift was reflected in the supranational action taken by the Hague Conference,[19] which introduced instruments allowing for a choice of court in the international sale of goods (1958[20]) and for a general choice of court (1965[21]).

---

13 *Law v. Garrett* (1878) LR 8 Ch D 26 (CA). See also earlier cases of *Giener v. Meyer* (1796) 126 ER 726 and *Johnson v. Machielsne* (1811) 170 ER 1300 that introduced a similar concept in maritime law. See commentary in Mills (n.8 above), pp.33–36, para.2.2.1.

14 F.K. von Savigny, *Private International Law. A Treatise on the Conflict of Laws, and the Limits of Their Operation in Respect of Place and Time* (translated by W. Guthrie) (T. & T. Clark, Edinburgh; Stevens and Sons, London, 1869), at pp.152–153. See commentary of this influence in Mills (n.8 above), at p.35, para.2.2.1.

15 Rule 2a of Order XI of the Rules of the Supreme Court 1920.

16 *Unterweser Reederei GmbH v. Zapata Off-Shore Company* [1968] 2 Lloyd's Rep 158. See discussion of these developments in Mills (n.8 above), at p.38, para.2.2.1.

17 P. Nygh, *Autonomy in international contracts* (Clarendon Press, Oxford, 1999), at pp.21–22.

18 Although this occurred in a more fragmented manner: for instance, until 1995, Italian courts would not recognise derogation of jurisdiction by agreement if one or more of the parties were resident Italian nationals (See Article 2 of the Italian Code of Civil Procedure 1942), whilst the French courts used a legal fiction in the form of the 'deemed' domicile of the parties ascertained through the contractual agreement in order to establish jurisdiction (See Article 111 of the French Civil Code). See Nygh (ibid.), at p.22 and Mills (n.8 above), at p.43, para.2.2.1.

19 See Mills (n.8 above).

20 Article 2 of the Hague Convention of 15 April 1958 on the Jurisdiction of the Selected Forum in the Case of International Sales of Goods.

21 Article 1 of the Hague Convention of 25 November 1965 on the Choice of Court.

It should, however, be noted that neither of these conventions ever entered into force.[22] More tangible success was achieved by the Brussels Convention of 1968[23] (between EEC Contracting States) and the Lugano Convention of 1988[24] (between the EEC and EFTA Contracting States) which provided, subject to one or more of the parties being domiciled in a Contracting State, that such parties could designate the courts of one of the Contracting States to decide on disputes arising out of their relationship. The 2000 Brussels I Regulation superseded the earlier Brussels Convention, establishing that any Member State court could be prorogued for proceedings concerning civil and commercial matters within the scope of this instrument.[25]

In a similar manner to the determination of jurisdiction (see above), the connections that existed immediately prior to the emergence of party autonomy in the choice of law context could also be broadly categorised as 'personal' and 'territorial'.[26] To further elaborate upon this, emerging from the late medieval statutist theory,[27] the prevailing judicial treatment of contracts followed an approach whereby the applicable law was determined according to whether the subject matter of the contract was deemed 'personal' in nature (the law of the place where the parties were citizens), concerned property (the law of the place where the object was situated), or related to acts (the law of either the place of contracting or performance).[28] The focus was firmly set on the sovereignty of individual states, and their right to impose obligations upon those whose activities were deemed to attach to their territory.[29]

It was during the sixteenth century that the French jurist Charles Dumoulin proposed an alternative to this *status quo*, whereby the intention of the parties

---

22 It should be noted that the later Hague Convention of 30 June 2005 on Choice of Court agreements did however enter into force.

23 See Article 17 of the Brussels Convention of 27 September 1968 on jurisdiction and the enforcement of judgments in civil and commercial matters [1968] OJ L 299.

24 See Article 17 of the Lugano Convention of 16 September 1988 on jurisdiction and the enforcement of judgments in civil and commercial matters [1988] OJ L 319. Superseded by the Lugano Convention of 30 October 2007 on jurisdiction and the enforcement of judgments in civil and commercial matters [2007] OJ L 339/3.

25 See Article 23 of Council Regulation (EC) No 44/2001 of 22 December 2000 on jurisdiction and the recognition and enforcement of judgments in civil and commercial matters [2001] OJ L 12/1. Subsequent recast: see Article 25 of Council Regulation (EC) No 1215/2012 of 12 December 2012 on jurisdiction and the recognition and enforcement of judgments in civil and commercial matters (recast) OJ L 351/1.

26 Mills (n.8 above), at p.46, para.2.2.2.

27 Ibid.

28 See, for elaboration on this approach, the work of the fourteenth-century statutist Bartolus, *Bartolus on the Conflict of Laws*, J. Beale (trans), 3rd edn (The Lawbook Exchange Ltd., Clark, NJ, 2003), at pp.17–20, 29, 31. For discussion, see: Nygh (n.17 above), at pp.3–4; O. Lando, 'Contracts' in R. David et al. (eds.), *International Encyclopedia of Comparative Law (Private International Law: Volume 2)* (Mohr Siebeck, Tübingen / Martinus Nijhoff, Leiden, 2011), at para.24.9; Mills (n.8 above), at p.46, para.2.2.2.

29 Nygh (n.17 above), at p.4.

to a contract should be used to determine the governing law.[30] Due to his apparent emphasis on the will of the parties, Dumoulin has been penned as the 'father' of modern-day party autonomy.[31] However, such an assertion can be viewed as slightly premature, since Dumoulin subscribed to a doctrine of implied intention,[32] which he gauged from the circumstances surrounding the agreement (e.g. the place of contracting and the domicile of the parties, as well as other considerations) rather than a reflection of the actual will of the parties.[33] As has already been discussed above, a similar critique can be levelled at Savigny and his use of 'voluntary submission' in order to locate a relationship in a particular legal system.[34]

Notwithstanding such critique, by the nineteenth century a process of political liberalisation and the emergence of the free market economy was beginning to give rise to an evolution in the notion of the freedom of contract within English law, from an obligation placed on the parties by the law as a result of their transaction, to an obligation created by the parties themselves. Within this altered conception, parties could choose for themselves the content of their contracts, considering their own interests as they saw fit, with the law merely serving to protect against impediments such as fraud and duress.[35]

This changing perception of the freedom of the parties in the domestic setting slowly began to spill over into conflict of laws. In the 1870s, the Italian jurist Mancini pronounced support for an express choice of applicable law in contracts. Against the general backdrop of general party choice in international contract law, he held that in matters where the parties are free to regulate their own legal relations through contract, they should be permitted to choose the applicable law – territoriality should only play a role in public policy.[36] Around the same period, the English judiciary began to allude to the possibility of direct party autonomy in their reasoning.[37] However, it was not until 1939 that the UK Privy Council took the pivotal step of actually asserting the parties' freedom to

[30] Ibid. and Lando (n.28 above), at para.24.10.

[31] For example, M. Zhang, 'Party Autonomy and Beyond: An International Perspective of Contractual Choice of Law' (2006) 20 *Emory International Law Review* 511, at pp.516–517.

[32] Nygh (n.17 above), at p.4.

[33] Lando (n.28 above), at para.24.10, Mills (n.8 above), at pp.46–48, para.2.2.2. and M. Hook, *The Choice of Law Contract* (Hart Publishing, Oxford, 2016), at p.20.

[34] Savigny (n.14 above), at pp.89–92 and 175–176. See for commentary: Mills (n.8 above), at p.52, para.2.2.2 and Hook (n.33 above), at p.20.

[35] Nygh (n.17 above), at pp.7–8 and Mills (n.8 above), at pp.62–63, para.2.2.2.

[36] P. Mancini, 'De l'Utilite de Rendre Obligatoires pour Tous les Etats …', (1874) 5(1) *Journal du Droit International Privé et de la Jurisprudence Comparée* 221, at p.295. For commentary see: Nygh (n.17), at p.8.

[37] *Peninsula and Oriental Steam Navigation Co. v. Shand* (1865) 3 Moo. N.S. 272, 16 E.R. 103, and *Lloyd v. Guibert* (1865) L.R. 1 Q.B. 115. For discussion, see Lando (n.28 above), at paras.24.27–24.31.

expressly choose the law that applies to a contract.[38] In this regard, Lord Wright stated:

> Where there is an express statement by the parties of their intention to select the law of the contract, it is difficult to see what qualifications are possible, provided the intention expressed is bona fide and legal, and provided there is no reason for avoiding the choice on the ground of public policy.[39]

Acceptance of the exercise of express party autonomy also emerged in civil law jurisdictions from the latter part of the nineteenth century[40] and during the course of the twentieth century.[41] The consensus in favour of its adoption is evidenced in the agreement of the 1955 Hague Convention on the Law Applicable to the International Sale of Goods, which provides that a sale is governed by the internal law of the country indicated by the parties.[42] On an EU level, the opportunity to make an explicit, generally unlimited choice of law in contractual matters was firmly established in the Rome I Convention[43] (later the Rome I Regulation[44]), and expanded to include non-contractual obligations (Rome II Regulation[45]), and, crucially for the present purposes, it was also introduced in the Union's instruments that concerned family matters and succession.

Taking a step back, although it is clear that the development of party autonomy in family matters and succession is certainly not as well evidenced as its rise to prominence in contractual matters, its appearance on the EU stage in this context was by no means a novelty for all Member States. As far back as the sixteenth century, Dumoulin postulated in favour of recognising the implied choice of the parties in the context of matrimonial property.[46] This provided the

---

38 *Vita Food Products Inc. v. Unus Shipping Co Ltd.* [1939] AC 277.

39 Ibid. at para.290.

40 See, for example, the choice of law rule in the 1865 civil code in Italy – see Mills (n.8 above), at pp.63–64, para.2.2.2.

41 For example, see the French Cour de Cassation judgment in *American Trading Co. v. Quebec Steamship Co.* Cass. (civ.) 5 December 1910, S. 1911. I. 129; the Belgian Cour de Cassation judgment in *SA Antwerpia v. Ville d'Anvers*, Cass. 24 February 1938, *Revue critique de droit international privé* (1938), 661, 662; and the Dutch Hoge Raad judgement in *Alnati*: Hoge Raad, 13 May 1966, *Nederlandse Jurisprudentie* (1967) no.3. For elaboration of this context, see Lando (n.28 above), at paras.24.34–24.44 and 24.51–24.55.

42 Article 2 of the Hague Convention of 15 June 1955 on the Law Applicable to International Sales of Goods. See also Nygh (n.17 above), at pp.12–13.

43 Article 3 of the Rome I Convention on the Law Applicable to Contractual Obligations of 9 October 1980 [1980] OJ L 266

44 Article 3 of Council Regulation (EC) No 593/2008 of the European Parliament and of the Council of 17 June 2008 on the law applicable to contractual obligations (Rome I) [2008] OJ L 177/6.

45 Article 14 of Council Regulation (EC) No 864/2007 of the European Parliament and of the Council of 11 July 2007 on the law applicable to non-contractual obligations (Rome II) [2007] OJ L 199/40.

46 See description of Dumoulin's exemplified case concerning party autonomy in matrimonial property law: J. Basedow, *The Law of Open Societies – Private Ordering and Public Regulation*

basis for the development of the French approach towards conflict of laws in this context, whereby priority was first given to the express choice of the parties, and in the absence of this choice, the first common matrimonial domicile was viewed as having been tacitly chosen by the spouses. Although this approach is said to have strongly influenced the French judiciary's approach towards identifying the applicable law to matrimonial property regimes, the Member States that have introduced a choice of law in such matters closer to the present day have disregarded tacit choice in favour of the grounds of 'close connection' found within the EU and Hague Convention instruments on family matters and succession.[47]

The emergence of party autonomy in the context of the law applicable to succession[48] and divorce[49] in Member States' jurisdictions was mainly concentrated at the end of the last century and the beginning of the current one. At the other end of this scale is the field of maintenance obligations, which did not entertain any possibility for party autonomy in the Member States until the EU and the Hague Conference adopted instruments that unified the private international law rules in this field at the start of this century (see below).[50]

The first foray into party autonomy in family matters and succession on a supranational level was brought about (with very limited success) by the 1978 Hague Convention on the Law Applicable to Matrimonial Property Regimes,[51] which was only ratified by France, Luxembourg and the Netherlands, and the 1989 Hague Convention on the Law Applicable to Succession to the Estates of Deceased Persons,[52] which never came into force in the signatory states.[53]

---

of International Relations (Brill Nijhoff, Leiden, 2015), at pp.236–238, paras.385–386. He opined that the neglect by a married couple to make a designation of a property regime in accordance with the law of the territory in which they had been living meant that they had tacitly chosen the property regime of their common domicile to extend to assets located outside of this territory.

47 Ibid., at pp.238–240, at paras.387–389. Most prominently, Germany (1986), Belgium (2004) and Bulgaria (2005).

48 E. Castellanos Ruiz, 'Article 22: Choice of Law' in A. Calvo Caravaca et al. (eds.), *The EU Succession Regulation: A Commentary* (Cambridge University Press, Cambridge, 2016), at p.325, para.2: An opportunity for a *professio juris* was brought about in Germany in 1986 and Italy in 1995; Basedow (n.46 above), at p.266, para.424: The Netherlands (1996), as well as the non-signatory states of Belgium (2004), Finland (2001) and Poland (2011) embraced the connecting factors for a *professio juris* established in the Hague Convention of 1 August 1989 on the Law Applicable to Succession to the Estates of Deceased Persons.

49 Basedow (n.46 above), at pp.251–253, paras.405–406. The Netherlands was the first country to allow for a choice of law for divorce in 1981, and some other Member States subsequently followed suit (e.g. Germany – 1986 and Belgium – 2004).

50 Ibid., at p.259, para.414.

51 Article 3 of the Hague Convention of 14 March 1978 on the Law Applicable to Matrimonial Property Regimes.

52 Article 5 of the Hague Convention of 1 August 1989 on the Law Applicable to Succession to the Estates of Deceased Persons.

53 Argentina, Luxembourg, Switzerland and the Netherlands. Only the Netherlands ratified this convention.

The Brussels II Regulation was the first EU instrument to be introduced that specifically concerned the realm of family matters (matrimonial matters and parental responsibility). Emulating the prorogation mechanism established in Article 10 of the 1996 Hague Convention on Jurisdiction, Applicable Law, Recognition, Enforcement and Co-operation in Respect of Parental Responsibility and Measures for the Protection of Children (hereinafter: the Hague Convention on Child Protection),[54] Article 3(2) of the Brussels II Regulation[55] offered the possibility for the spouses to agree to link jurisdiction for matters of parental responsibility relating to their child to the Member State court which was competent for their divorce, legal separation or marriage annulment. The prorogation rule was developed and expanded in Article 12 of the 2003 Brussels II bis Regulation, relaxing its remit to include situations in which only one of the spouses in the proceedings concerning matrimonial matters was the parent of the child.[56]

Next in this legislative timeline was the EU Maintenance Regulation in 2008.[57] Prior to its introduction, party autonomy in maintenance obligations in the choice of court context was provided for in the 2000 Brussels I Regulation. Whilst the Maintenance Regulation provided jurisdictional rules, it deferred to the 2007 Hague Protocol on the Law Applicable to Maintenance Obligations (hereinafter: the Hague Maintenance Protocol)[58] for the determination (and designation) of the applicable law.[59]

In 2010, after a turbulent legislative process,[60] the Rome III Regulation[61] was passed through enhanced cooperation between 14 Member States

54 Hague Convention of 19 October 1996 on Jurisdiction, Applicable Law, Recognition, Enforcement and Co-operation in respect of Parental Responsibility and Measures for the Protection of Children.

55 Council Regulation (EC) No 1347/2000 of 29 May 2000 on jurisdiction and the recognition and enforcement of judgments in matrimonial matters and in matters of parental responsibility for children of both spouses [2000] L 160/19.

56 Council Regulation (EC) No 2201/2003 of 27 November 2003 concerning jurisdiction and the recognition and enforcement of judgments in matrimonial matters and the matters of parental responsibility [2003] L 338/1. See also S. Francq, 'Parental responsibility under "Brussels II"' (2003) 4(1) *ERA-Forum* 54 at pp.56–57 and P. McEleavy, 'Current Developments: I. Brussels II bis: Matrimonial Matters, Parental Responsibility and Mutual Recognition' (2004) 53(2) *International and Comparative Law Quarterly* 503, at p.507, fn.27.

57 Articles 4 and 5 of the Council Regulation (EC) No 4/2009 of 18 December 2008 on jurisdiction, applicable law, recognition and enforcement of decisions and cooperation in matters relating to maintenance obligations [2009] OJ L 7/1.

58 Articles 7 and 8 of the Hague Protocol of 23 November 2007 on the Law Applicable to Maintenance Obligations.

59 Article 15 of the Maintenance Regulation.

60 K. Boele-Woelki, 'To Be, Or Not to Be: Enhanced Cooperation in International Divorce Law within the European Union' (2008) 39(4) *Victoria University Wellington Law Review* 779, at pp.783–786, para.3 and Kruger, 'Rome III and Parties' Choice' (January 2014) *Family and Law*, at para.1, available at: http://www.familyandlaw.eu/tijdschrift/fenr/2014/01/FENR-D-13-00010.

61 Council Regulation (EU) No 1259/2010 of 20 December 2010 implementing enhanced cooperation in the area of the law applicable to divorce and legal separation [2010] L 343/10, Article 5.

(now 17 Member States[62]). It provides conflict of laws rules (including the possibility for a choice of law) for cross-border divorce and legal separation in participating Member States. Six years later, after a similarly difficult process of negotiations, enhanced cooperation was again used to bring about the joint regulations on matrimonial property regimes[63] and the property consequences of registered partnerships[64] (hereinafter referred to as the Matrimonial Property Regulation, Partnership Property Regulation and, collectively, the Property Regulations).

Originally binding upon 18 Member States (now 19 Member States[65]), the regulations provided both unified conflict of laws and jurisdictional rules, with party autonomy permitted in both areas.[66] It is interesting to note that this was not originally the case, and that party autonomy was only permitted in the Partnership Property Regulation towards the end of the long-winded process of drafting.[67]

The 2012 Succession Regulation,[68] like the Property Regulations, is a comprehensive instrument that provides for party autonomy in the determination of both jurisdiction and applicable law. However, it is distinguished from the concurrent legislative activity by the fact that it was adopted on a Union-wide basis, helped (at least in part) by the fact that succession falls within the scope of the ordinary legislative procedure that only requires a qualified majority (rather than unanimity) within the Council.[69]

---

62 Commission Decision (EU) 2016/1366 of 10 August 2016 confirming the participation of Estonia in enhanced cooperation in the area of the law applicable to divorce and legal separation [2016] OJ L 216.

63 Council Regulation (EU) 2016/1103 of 24 June 2016 implementing enhanced cooperation in the area of jurisdiction, applicable law and the recognition and enforcement of decisions in matters of matrimonial property regimes [2016] OJ L 183/1.

64 Council Regulation (EU) 2016/1104 of 24 June 2016 implementing enhanced cooperation in the area of jurisdiction, applicable law and the recognition and enforcement of decisions in matters of the property consequences of registered partnerships [2016] OJ L 183/30.

65 European Council of the European Union, *Press release: 18 EU countries agree to clarify rules on property regimes for international couples* (9 June 2016), available at: http://www.consilium.europa.eu/en/press/press-releases/2016/06/09/property-regimes-for-international-couples. In this press release, it was announced that Estonia intended to be the 19th participant following the adoption of the regulations.

66 For party autonomy in the jurisdictional context: see Articles 7 and 8 of the Property Regulations; with regard to applicable law, see Article 22 of the Property Regulations.

67 Party autonomy was not permitted under the original 2011 draft proposal for the Partnership Property Regulation: Proposal for a Council Regulation on jurisdiction, applicable law and recognition and enforcement of decisions regarding the property consequences of registered partnerships, COM(2011) 127 final.

68 Regulation (EU) No. 650/2012 of the European Parliament and of the Council of 4 July 2012 on jurisdiction, applicable law, recognition and enforcement of decisions and acceptance and enforcement of authentic instruments in matters of succession and on the creation of a European Certificate of Succession [2012] L 201/107.

69 Whilst Article 81(3) of the Consolidated version of the Treaty on the Functioning of the European Union [2016] OJ C 202 (TFEU) requires Council unanimity for legislative acts concerning family matters (maintenance, matrimonial matters, parental responsibility and property relations), according to Article 81(2) of this treaty other measures can be adopted using the Qualified Majority Voting (QMV) procedure. See also Article 294 TFEU for

1.4. OUTLINE OF APPROACH

This book pursues a critical examination of party autonomy within the EU private international law framework relating to family matters and succession in light of the status of such rules as measures of Union law. This narrow focus allows the relevant choice of court and choice of law provisions to be considered against the backdrop of the environment from which these rules emerged. Within this paradigm, the functional value of party autonomy in the Union context is brought to the forefront, with such measures being evaluated against the justifications that provided the impetus for legislative action in this realm.

In order to set the scene, the next two chapters are dedicated to establishing the objectives that underlie the introduction of party autonomy into the EU's unified private international law rules concerning family matters and succession. In pursuit of this, Chapter 2 will consider the manifestation of, and the value attributed to, the exercise of free will within the current EU framework. Following on from this, Chapter 3 will serve to discuss party autonomy in its function as an EU measure.

The main chapters will follow a concurrent (rather than successive) approach to evaluating the provisions that allow for a choice of court or choice of law in the EU private international framework relating to family matters and succession. This method is employed in view of the high level of symmetry and intertwinement between the relevant instruments. The relevant party autonomy provisions will be critiqued, compared and contrasted at logical common stages in order to present an in-depth analysis of the various aspects that a choice entails in this context. In addition, the gaps within the framework that have become apparent during the course of this investigation will be highlighted and preliminary recommendations on how to remedy such issues will be proposed.

Particular regard will also be given to the cohesion that may be achieved through coordination of related provisions of the relevant instruments within this framework. This aspect concerns both (i) cohesion between the provisions that determine the competent court and the applicable law that governs a particular proceeding ('vertical cohesion') and (ii) cohesion between the competent court and/or the laws that govern proceedings involving related areas of family and succession law ('horizontal cohesion'[70]). The existence and consequences of

a detailed description of the ordinary legislative procedure. In this instance, Malta voted against the final draft of the Succession Regulation, but this did not hinder its adoption.

70 For these purposes, related legal proceedings can be broadly divided into two groupings: those that are connected with the dissolution of a marriage by divorce or legal separation or the dissolution of a registered partnership (proceedings dissolving the relationship, in conjunction with the dissolution of the couple's property regime, matters of maintenance and/or parental responsibility), and those that arise upon the death of a spouse or registered partner (succession proceedings in conjunction with the couple's dissolution the property regime).

cohesion within the framework (or the lack thereof) will be assessed according to the same values by which the whole of this evaluation is conducted.

The preliminary elements that underpin party autonomy in this field will firstly be delineated: the *subject matter* over which such a choice can be exercised (Chapter 4) and the *focus* of this choice – the competent court or the applicable law (Chapter 5). Secondly, the main content of this book will be examined: the connections through which a choice of court or law can be made within the EU private international framework relating to family matters and succession. The three chapters that compose this Part concern *direct connections* (Chapter 6), *coordinating provisions* (Chapter 7) and *subsidiary party autonomy provisions* (Chapter 8). Finally, the considerations that impact upon the ultimate success of a choice of court or law in this realm will be addressed: the formal and material requirements that determine its validity (Chapter 9) and the variables that hold the potential to alter or extinguish choice at the stage of enforcement (Chapter 10). Chapter 11 concludes by establishing a macro synthesis that brings together the various strands of this examination and reconsiders its findings in view of the baseline values that are attached to party autonomy in the Union context.

CHAPTER 2

CONCEPTUALISING FREE WILL IN EU PRIVATE INTERNATIONAL LAW RELATING TO FAMILY MATTERS AND SUCCESSION

2.1. INTRODUCTION

In embarking upon this examination of party autonomy within the EU private international law framework relating to family matters and succession, the next two chapters of this book are dedicated to establishing the factors through which this analysis will be guided. This chapter will focus upon the role of free will in the context of party autonomy, with the eventual goal of presenting the preliminary values attached to this concept within the present realm.

The chapter is divided into three stages. Firstly, the intrinsic value attached to the exercise of free will shall be analysed, with particular attention paid to the weight that can be attributed to it in private international law (2.2.). Secondly, this investigation will be brought into the present EU setting, in which the values attached to free will within the European human rights framework and CJEU case law will be presented (2.3.). Finally, the examination will narrow in upon the particular context around which this book revolves – the EU private international law relating to family matters and succession – through establishing the preliminary significance of free will in this setting and the caveats that exist in this regard (2.4.).

2.2. THE INTRINSIC VALUE OF FREE WILL IN THE PARTY AUTONOMY CONTEXT

The first step in this exploration of the value of free will in the exercise of party autonomy in this present EU private international law realm involves stepping back to examine its essential components and its placement within the legal framework. This will necessitate establishing the requisite elements that compose the exercise of free will in this setting (2.2.1.), presenting the purported rationale for attaching intrinsic value to the exercise of free will in this context (2.2.2.), and considering the hierarchy between will of the parties and the law (2.2.3.).

2.2.1. REQUISITE ELEMENTS OF FREE WILL

Autonomy takes its roots from the Ancient Greek word *autonomia* – literally meaning *self* (auto-) *law* (nomos) – the exercise of self-determination or self-governance – the freedom to choose one's own path. It applies on a variety of different levels (from the governmental to the individual) and in a multitude of different spheres (e.g. medical ethics, religion, education, contract law and, of course, for these present purposes, private international law).

Launching from the root of autonomy set out above, it is firstly asserted that this concept necessarily involves a reflection of self. It has been stated that party autonomy presupposes that the will of the parties has been freely expressed.[71] In this regard, *authenticity* must be demonstrated to the extent that a choice is based on a party's own preferences and not simply a channel for the desires of others. Consent is impaired either where a party has been induced to make a choice or agreement on the basis of false information, or where they have been coerced to do so.[72] In this latter regard, efforts by one party to overcome the will of another could amount to a direct use of force or threat,[73] or may be more insidious, such as the exertion of improper pressure.[74] Such conduct can be exerted in any interaction, but it is close relationships containing a degree of dependency that specifically foster this potential.[75] It should, however, be emphasised that a party

71 S. Symeonides, 'The Hague Principles on Choice of Law for International Contracts: Some Preliminary Comments' (2013) 61(4) *The American Journal of Comparative Law* 873 at p.878.

72 E.A Farnsworth, 'Comparative Contract Law' in M. Reimann and R. Zimmerman, *The Oxford Handbook of Comparative Law* (Oxford University Press, Oxford, 2006), at p.911: 'The two most common kinds of abuse are those which arise from conduct that is *misleading* and from conduct that is coercive' (emphasis added).

73 E.A. Kramer and T. Probst, 'Defects in the contracting process' in A.T. von Mehren (ed.), *International Encyclopedia of Comparative Law* (Mohr Siebeck, Tübingen / Martinus Nijhoff, Leiden, 2008), at paras.390–394 (force), 395–400 (threat of force), 205–208 (economic duress); H.G. Beale, 'Duress and undue influence' in H.G. Beale (ed.), *Chitty on Contracts*, 30th edn. (Sweet and Maxwell, London, 2008), at para.7-011 (duress of person), 7-012 (duress of goods) and 7-014 (economic duress); E. McKendrick, *Contract Law: Text, Cases, and Materials* 5th edn. (Oxford University Press, Oxford, 2012), at pp.627–632 (duress of the person), 632–634 (duress of goods), and 634–649 (economic duress).

74 Kramer and Probst (ibid.), at p.213 *et seq.* See definition of English law concept of 'undue influence' in *Allcard v. Skinner* (1887) 36 Ch D 145, at p.181: 'Some unfair and improper conduct, some coercion from the outside, some overreaching, some form of cheating, and generally, though not always, some personal advantage obtained by the donee placed in some close and confidential relation to the donor'.

75 See, e.g. *Barclays Bank plc v. O'Brien* [1993] UKHL 6, a UK House of Lords judgment in which the relevance of relationships of 'trust and confidence' (in this case, between a husband and wife) was emphasised in the context of a finding of undue influence.

may well take into account another's opinion in an exercise of autonomy; it is only where they have been manipulated through falsehood or force to such an extent that they are merely projecting the will of others that their decision can no longer be deemed to be authentic.

Beyond this, in order for a party to form their own preferences, they have to be armed with *sufficient information* concerning the consequences of their choice. The type of information required to make an informed decision is dependent on the subject matter at hand. In the medical context, an individual would seek to be informed regarding the significant risks that are involved in the procedure in question.[76] In making an agreement with a spouse concerning the division of matrimonial property, information as to the content and consequences of the marital contract is often a prerequisite.[77]

In the present setting, sufficient knowledge of the content of the available legal systems, as well as the relevant consequences that flow from a particular choice, is considered to be a necessity. Furthermore, if a choice is made in advance of proceedings taking place, regard should be had to the potential impact of changing circumstances over time. The intricacies involved in such enquiries require that advice be sought from (preferably specialised) independent legal professionals. This need to obtain impartial advice is particularly important in view of the propensity for power imbalances to arise from close family relationships (see discussion at 2.4.2.).

Besides the requirement to be sufficiently informed regarding the content and consequences of choice, an additional prerequisite to autonomy is the presence of an individual's own *capacity* to undertake the decision-making process. This, of course, has to be assessed on a case-by-case basis, but necessarily involves the presence of the ability to understand the relevant information, retain that information, and use or weigh it up as part of a decision-making process.[78] However, it is most important to note that the actual thought process and manner in which decisive factors are weighed cannot be regulated. To quote a key principle of the Mental Capacity Act 2005 (England and Wales): 'a person is not to be treated as unable to make a decision merely because he makes an unwise decision'.[79]

---

76 See, for example, *Chester v. Afshar* [2004] UKHL 41.

77 A requirement imposed upon notaries to inform parties regarding the content and consequences of a chosen matrimonial property regime exists in a number of European jurisdictions (e.g. Austria, Belgium, France, and the Netherlands). See J.M. Scherpe (ed.), *Marital Agreements and Party Autonomy in Comparative Perspective* (Hart Publishing, Oxford and Portland OR, 2012), at pp.58 (Austria), 78–79 (Belgium and France), 248 (the Netherlands), 493 (comparative perspective).

78 For elucidation of these criteria see, for example, Section 3 of the Mental Capacity Act 2005 (England and Wales).

79 Section 1(4), ibid.

Attempts could be made to establish additional, more profound prerequisites for the exercise of autonomy. Kant, for instance, required that it be the manifestation of *rational* will, not simply a reflection of the inclinations or desires of the parties.[80] Others have adopted a focus on a high standard of *authenticity*, holding that a true act of autonomy ought to be based on convictions or principles that are rooted in the individual's character.[81] However, as stated above, whilst it is possible to dwell upon an analysis of motivational integrity, this is not especially useful to the present context. Persons may select or agree upon a particular choice of law or court for any number of reasons, including emotional ties, if they so wish. To vet the process of decision-making against a high standard of rationality or entrenchment of personal values would set an impossibly high bar for the formation of choice in this context.

2.2.2. FREEDOM AS AN INTRINSIC JUSTIFICATION FOR PARTY AUTONOMY

Having established the requisite elements that constitute a full exercise of free will, the next matter to be tackled is exactly *why* prestige ought to be pinned to the will of the parties in this context. Can legitimacy for sidestepping the application of uniform rules be drawn directly from the free will of the parties?

Despite its now-prevalence within the private international law setting, the sources of inner legitimacy for the exercise of free will have been subject to relatively little scrutiny.[82] Some have criticised the unquestioning promotion and acceptance of party autonomy as being based on a 'foundational myth',[83] whilst others have dismissed its usage as merely a 'stop gap', serving as a pragmatic tool used to remedy the shortcomings of other legal methods within the cross-border context.[84] This leads to the question: can party autonomy be justified on the basis of individual freedom?

80 I. Kant, *Groundwork on the Metaphysics of Morals*, M. Gregor, (ed.) (Cambridge University Press, Cambridge, 1996), at paras.4:400–4:401.

81 E.g. L. Hinchman, 'Autonomy, individuality, and self-determination' in J. Schmidt (ed.), *What is Enlightenment? Eighteenth-century Answers and Twentieth-century Questions* (University of California Press, Oakland CA, 1996), at p.488.

82 Mills (Chapter 1, n.8), at p.67, para.2.3. and Basedow (Chapter 1, n.46), at p.115, paras.183–184.

83 H. Muir-Watt, '"Party autonomy" in international contracts: from the makings of the myth to the requirements of global governance' (2010) 6(3) *European Review of Contract Law* 250, at pp.256–257.

84 M. Lehmann, 'Liberating the Individual from Battles Between States: Justifying Party Autonomy in Conflicts of Laws' (2008) 41(2) *Vanderbilt Journal of Translational Law*381 at p.394.

The starting point for this is the notion that the individual will is something which is inherently valuable and, framed in this manner, that interference with autonomy (rather than autonomy itself) must be subject to justification.[85] In support of this view, reference could be made to the emphasis on individual freedom and liberty that permeates the international human rights framework. In this regard, The UN Universal Declaration of Human Rights of 1948 opens with the proclamation: 'All human beings are born free and equal in dignity and rights',[86] before going on to state: 'Everyone has the right to life, liberty and the security of person'.[87] Support for this standpoint can also be drawn from the emphasis on freedom and natural will postulated by enlightenment philosophers such as Locke,[88] Rousseau[89] and Kant.[90] To quote the last of these three authors:

> there is only one innate right. Freedom (independence from being constrained by another's choice), insofar as it can coexist with the freedom of every other in accordance with a universal law, is the only original right belonging to every man by virtue of his humanity.[91]

Notwithstanding the resonance of the above rhetoric in terms of its linkage to the basic nature of man, the breadth of its appeal makes it difficult to contextualise within the present framework. This argumentation appears to be more appropriate as a basis for protecting individuals from interference with their essential liberties (e.g. freedom from slavery) rather than for shaping a positive right to organise the conditions to which an individual's legal relations are exposed.[92]

---

85 See this explanation of 'deontological libertarianism' in Mills (Chapter 1, n.8), at p.70, para.2.3.1.1.

86 Article 1.

87 Article 3. See also discussion of the '*a priori*' conception of party autonomy in Basedow (Chapter 1, n.46), at pp.125–127, paras.199–203.

88 J. Locke, *The Second Treatise of Civil Government*, T. Hollis (ed.), 6th edn (A. Millar et al. London, 1764 [1689])at s.4: 'we must consider, what state all men are naturally in, and that is, a state of perfect freedom to order their actions, and dispose of their possessions and persons, as they think fit, within the bounds of the law of nature, without asking leave, or depending upon the will of any other man'.

89 J.J. Rousseau, *The Social Contract*, D.G.H. Cole (trans.), 1st edn (J.M. Dent & Sons, London and Toronto / E.P. Dutton & Co., New York, 1913), at ch.4: '[on children] they are born men, and free; their freedom belongs to them, and nobody except them has a right to dispose of it'.

90 Kant (n.80 above), at p.30, para.6:238. See commentary on Locke, Rousseau and Kant's approaches in Basedow (Chapter 1, n.46), at pp.242–243, paras.239–240.

91 Kant (n.80 above), at p.30, para.6:238. However, doubt has been cast upon the viability of this endorsement in the context of corporate activity, since Kant's notion of autonomy focused on *individual* moral agency: see Mills (Chapter 1, n.8), at p.70, para.2.3.1.1.

92 For instance, Rousseau considered freedom in the context of slavery. See also discussion in context of UN Declaration in Basedow (Chapter 1, n.46), at p.146, para.249.

In view of the above critique, a few more specific justifications for attaching value to free will in the party autonomy setting can be presented. Firstly, there is the notion that individuals have access to information concerning their own situation, welfare, beliefs and preferences that is unavailable to others.[93] Based on this, it might be argued that it is the parties themselves, rather than the legislators, who are best placed to make decisions concerning their legal conditions.[94]

Alternatively, a utilitarian stance could be adopted towards this question, asserting that parties should be allowed to make their own decisions concerning the legal conditions to which their relationships are subject on the basis that this generates the greatest amount of happiness for those involved. This could be understood both in terms of the act of making the decision (which can be seen as fulfilling in itself), or the positive consequences that flow from a person's own decision-making (linking back with the primary justification discussed above).[95]

However, the problem with the above assertions is that they are essentially subjective. How can it concretely be stated that personal choice is always best for an individual, or that the freedom to choose is necessarily a positive experience? Indeed, strong counter-arguments can be raised with regard to the benefits of pursuing legal paternalism,[96] or the negative consequences of being oversaturated by choice.[97] Although the attributes of autonomy highlighted above may serve as *functional* justifications for its introduction onto the EU stage (as elaborated upon in later sections[98]), these values cannot be asserted in absolute terms.

2.2.3. RECONCILING THE WILL OF THE PARTIES WITH THE LAW

In order to complete this examination of the value to be attributed to the free will of the parties in the present context, it is necessary to consider its positioning *vis-à-vis* the law.

---

93 G. Rühl, 'Choice of law by the parties' in J. Basedow et al. (eds.), *Max Planck Encyclopedia of European Private Law* (Oxford University Press, Oxford, 2012), at p.33 and G. Rühl, 'Party Autonomy in the Private International Law of Contracts: Transatlantic Convergence and Economic Efficiency', *CLPE Research Paper 4/2007* 1, at pp.32–34 (2007).

94 See reflections of this argument in the context of efficiency in Basedow (Chapter 1, n.46), at p.141, para.237.

95 See S. Darwall, 'The value of autonomy and autonomy of the will' (2006) 116(2) *Ethics* at pp.265–266.

96 A principal example would clearly be to prevent the making of potentially detrimental choices by the parties.

97 For instance, parties may feel burdened by information overload and face choice 'paralysis' in the face of a multitude of options.

98 See 2.3. and 2.4.

Starting with its most abstract conception, party autonomy can be viewed as assuming a free-floating quality, existing outside and above national or supranational legal systems.[99] This links back to the discussion of the freedom and natural will discussed in the previous section, focusing upon the 'natural capacity of individuals to determine the applicable law for themselves, irrespective of the confines of any legal system'.[100] The will of the parties in this setting is viewed as truly autonomous – they are free to choose any law they wish to govern their relationship, or even no law at all.[101] From this viewpoint, the will of the parties is viewed as sovereign, rather than subject to the sovereignty of the state.[102] This conception is particularly attractive in the cross-border context whereby a relationship might naturally situate itself outside any single legal system.

By extension to the above notion, the independent will of the parties can also be framed as assuming legislative force, replacing the law itself.[103] This is the notion of *contrat sans loi*, whereby self-made 'law' becomes manifested through the agreement of the parties.[104] *Contrat sans loi* enjoyed a degree of recognition in French jurisprudence on choice of law in contracts for a short period in the early twentieth century.[105] Perhaps unsurprisingly, this usage of the above device did not ultimately take hold. To understand party autonomy as entirely independent of any legal system lends legitimacy to an argument that favours almost unlimited scope for individuals to design their own legal conditions. This is a situation that would be untenable in the face of state sovereignty (as well as with regard to the need to ensure the functioning of an efficient judiciary).

At the opposite end of the spectrum, there is the belief that party autonomy merely serves to incorporate the rules of another legal system into an agreement or declaration. This so-called 'incorporation theory' garnered a degree of support in continental Europe and the United States during the twentieth century.[106]

---

99 Nygh (Chapter 1, n.17), at p.31.

100 Basedow (Chapter 1, n.46), at p.125, para.199.

101 Nygh (Chapter 1, n.17), at pp.31–32 and C.I. Nagy, 'What Functions May Party Autonomy Have in International Family and Succession Law? An EU Perspective' (2012) 4 *Nederlands Internationaal Privaatrecht* 576, at p.578. See also Basedow's description of the 'pre-governmental' right in this context in Basedow (Chapter 1, n.46), at p.146, paras.248–253.

102 Mills (Chapter 1, n.8), at p.72, para.2.3. and Zhang (Chapter1, n.31), at p.553.

103 Lehmann (n.84 above), at p.390 and K. Kroll, *Die Rolle der Parteiautonomie im Europäischen Kollisionsrecht* (Mohr Siebeck, Heidelberg, 2013), at pp.156–158, on the 'Autocratie contractuelle'.

104 Kroll (ibid.), at pp.158–163.

105 See, for example, the French case cited in Kroll's description (n.103 above) of this conception of party autonomy in: *American Trading Co. v. Quebec Steamship Co.*, Cour de Cassation, 5.12.1910, Clunet (39) 192, 1156 ff.

106 Lehmann (n.84 above), at pp.391–392. See, for instance, the parallel drawn between wording of Article 187(1) of the Restatement (Second) of Conflict of Laws (1971) and the incorporation theory by Lehmann (n.84 above, at p.391).

From this perspective, party autonomy is constrained by any mandatory requirements of the otherwise applicable law that the state wishes to impose.

An approach assimilating to the incorporation theory was exemplified in the Hague Convention on the Law Applicable to Succession (1989). According to the Explanatory Report, under Article 6 of this instrument, the testator may incorporate a foreign law into their authentic instrument, which will then be subject to the mandatory rules of the default applicable law.[107] However, this approach (which was actually framed as a substantive law reference, rather than a conflict-of-laws rule[108]) appears to be an anomaly within the wider framework. Such a construction (the substantive law reference and the subjugation to mandatory requirements) has not been carried forward in the later EU regulations concerning this field or, indeed, any other relevant EU or Hague Conference instrument.[109]

The incorporation theory has been criticised for unduly downplaying the status of party autonomy.[110] In particular, the exercise of autonomy in EU private international law relating to family matters and succession necessitates a cross-border element, and this lends parties the legitimacy to bypass the mandatory requirements of national law that would be imposed in a purely domestic situation.[111] However, notwithstanding the above critique, the crux of the incorporation theory – the ultimate subordination of the will of the parties to the law – rings true when examining the current EU private international law framework.

It is to be acknowledged that the (national and supranational) judicial and regulatory bodies play a decisive role in lending legitimacy to the exercise of party autonomy. This becomes particularly apparent in view of the fact that Member States still have public policy and overriding mandatory rules at their disposal. Such rules can be seen to take on an analogous role to mandatory rules in the domestic setting, ultimately subordinating the application of the chosen law to the particular standards set by the forum. In the event of incompatibility, judicial discretion can be used to reject the choice that has been made.

Upon closing this exploration of the manifestation of free will in the party autonomy context, it is clear that despite the attractiveness of the rhetoric surrounding natural will and the sovereign nature of autonomy in the private international law context, this is a utopian ideal. Whilst free will is the guiding

---

107 D. Waters, *Explanatory Report on the 1989 Hague Succession Convention* (HCCH Publications, the Hague, 1990), at para.27.

108 See explanation in Waters, ibid., at p.561, para.70.

109 Although it can be seen, for instance, in the Rome I Regulation that consumers cannot be deprived of the protection afforded to them by their law of habitual residence (Article 6(2)), this is based on a different rationale to the incorporation theory.

110 Lehmann (n.84 above), at pp.391–392.

111 Ibid.

force behind the exercise of party autonomy, it is clear that its exercise is only permitted so far as the legal framework will allow.[112] The breadth of choice provided may be almost unlimited, or comparatively restrictive. However, either way, the positive force of the legal rules cannot be denied: the law is the ultimate gatekeeper.

2.3. THE VALUE ATTACHED TO FREE WILL IN THE EU SETTING

The preceding section established that free will in private international law is to be considered as constrained by the legal framework in which it exists. However, this is not to claim that free will holds no worth in the present context. As has been established, underpinnings for this concept can be identified within the human rights framework and enlightenment notions based on natural law. This section proceeds further along this line of examination, outlining the values ascribed to free will within the European human rights context (2.3.1.) and by the Court of Justice of the European Union (CJEU) (2.3.2.).

2.3.1. EUROPEAN HUMAN RIGHTS FRAMEWORK

As discussed in the previous section (2.2.1.), the protection of individual liberty has strong ties to the *a priori*[113] view of party autonomy. The proclamations contained in the UN's Universal Declaration of Human Rights of 1948[114] have already been outlined above. For the purposes of the European context, a similar sentiment is echoed in the European Convention on Human Rights,[115] the EU Charter of Fundamental Rights[116] and Treaty on the European Union.[117]

Can this overarching emphasis on freedom within human rights frameworks be taken to apply to the private international law context? There have indeed

---

112 See analysis of the limits of modern-day party autonomy in Nygh (n.17 above), at pp.33.34. See also Muir Watt (n.83 above), at pp.257–258 and T. Yetano, 'The Constitutionalisation of Party Autonomy in European Family Law' (2010) 6(1) *Journal of Private International Law* 155, at p.191: critiques the notion of *contrat sans loi* as merely a rhetorical advice, since party autonomy is 'a creature of the law'.

113 Basedow (Chapter 1, n.46), at p.125, para.199.

114 Article 1: 'All human beings are born free and equal in dignity and rights'.

115 Article 5 of the European Convention on Human Rights (1950) (ECHR).

116 See Preamble, noting the 'universal values of human dignity, freedom, equality and solidarity' on which the Union is founded, and Article 6 of the Charter of Fundamental Rights of the European Union [2012] OJ C 326 (EU Charter of Fundamental Rights).

117 Article 2 of the Consolidated version of the Treaty on European Union [2016] OJ C 202 (TEU).

been suggestions of such a link. In 1991, the Institut de Droit International issued a resolution recognising that 'party autonomy is one of the basic principles of private international law', and paying heed to the 'freedom of the individual as recognized by the conventions and resolutions of the United Nations'.[118]

However, as argued in 2.2.2 above, there ought to be a degree of caution in reading too much into the broad language of these instruments. It is apparent that the primary purpose of such provisions is to safeguard the individual against undue interference with their liberty (e.g. unlawful detention). Drawing on the protection of freedom in this context in order to support a positive right to make a choice of law or court appears misplaced. That being said, the general emphasis on the freedom of the individual could be viewed as lending *support* to the development of party autonomy.

Article 8 of the European Convention on Human Rights (and Article 7 of the EU Charter of Fundamental Rights) may also be referred to in support of the opportunity for an individual to cultivate their own legal conditions. In the context of the freedom of contract, Snijders has argued that Article 8 ECHR comfortably encompasses a specific 'right to personal autonomy'.[119] Pursuant to this, he particularly draws upon the ECtHR's judgment in *Pretty v. UK*,[120] in which the Court stated that it 'considers that the notion of personal autonomy is an important principle underlying the interpretation of its guarantees'.[121]

However, there should again be vigilance against attributing an overly generous interpretation to this statement. The aforementioned case concerned a specific set of circumstances: a woman's request to have her husband help end her life without subsequent prosecution. In drawing upon self-determination, the Court was not alluding to a general right of action, but rather considering whether to allow an individual to give effect to her desire to die with dignity without state interference. It stated that autonomy *underlies* the interpretation of the convention's guarantees; at no point did it say that this *was* a guarantee. The individual in question argued that her right to die formed part of her right to a private life;[122] her autonomy was framed as auxiliary to this.

The 2007 ECtHR judgment in *Wagner v. Luxembourg*[123] appears to have presented a much stronger support for party autonomy in European human rights context. The case concerned Luxembourg's non-recognition of a foreign adoption concluded under Peruvian law on the basis that adoption by unmarried

---

118 E. Jayme, 'Rapport definitif' (1991) 64(1) *Annuaire de l'Institut de Droit International* 62, at pp.64 and 77. Translations provided by Basedow (Chapter 1, n.46), at pp.148–149, para.255, fn.448.

119 H.J. Snijders, 'Privacy of Contract' in K. Ziegler (ed.), *Human Rights and Private Law: Privacy as Autonomy* (Hart Publishing, Oxford, 2007), at p.106.

120 *Pretty v. UK* (Application no.2346/02), ECtHR (29 July 2002).

121 Ibid., at para.61.

122 Ibid., at para.58.

123 *Wagner and J.M.W.L. v. Luxembourg* (Application no.76240/01), ECtHR (28 September 2007).

persons is not permitted under the Luxembourgish conflict-of-laws rules, and the ECtHR found that this refusal to recognise this legal status contravened Article 8 ECHR.[124] Although the Court primarily employed arguments based on 'social reality' in presenting its judgment,[125] the circumstances of this case appear to involve a person who went abroad in order to adopt under a more permissive foreign law than in her country of origin.[126] In finding a contravention of Article 8, the ECtHR seemed to give effect to her apparent 'choice' of applicable law.[127]

Although no reference is actually made to autonomy or the exercise of free will in *Wagner*, the outcome of this judgment leans more towards supporting the use of positive choice by parties than in the aforementioned case of *Pretty*. Of particular relevance for the present purposes is the involvement of the cross-border context and the seemingly positive choice by the party to subject him- or herself to a foreign law. Such circumstances coincide with those addressed by the CJEU cases that will be considered in the next subsection.

2.3.2. CJEU CASE LAW

In addition to its entwinement with individual liberty in the human rights context, a regard for free will permeates the exercise of the EU's fundamental freedoms. Although the evolution and characterisation of such rights will be considered more specifically in the next chapter,[128] it is also fitting to consider here the particular value placed upon autonomy in CJEU jurisprudence.

Given that the present focus is upon private parties in family matters and succession, starting this analysis in the realm of company law might seem somewhat misplaced. However, it is in this area that party autonomy has most frequently been evidenced in CJEU jurisprudence. A regard for an individual's freedom to choose their own legal conditions can be extracted from the CJEU's approach to the incorporation theory in connection with the freedom of establishment, most notably in its judgments in *Centros*,[129] *Überseering*[130] and *Inspire Art*.[131]

---

124 Ibid., at paras.123 and 135–136.

125 Ibid., at para.132.

126 Yetano (n.112 above), at p.165.

127 Ibid.

128 In which the status of party autonomy as a measure of EU law will be fully explored.

129 Case C-212/97 *Centros Ltd v. Erhvervs- og Selskabsstyrelsen*. Reference for a preliminary ruling: Højesteret – Denmark [1999] ECR 1-1459.

130 Case C-208/00 *Überseering BV v. Nordic Construction Company Baumanagement GmbH (NCC)*. Reference for a preliminary ruling: Bundesgerichtshof – Germany [2002] ECR I-09919.

131 Case C-167/01 *Kamer van Koophandel v. Fabrieken voor Amsterdam and Inspire Art Ltd*. Reference for a preliminary ruling: Kantongerecht te Amsterdam – the Netherlands [2003] ECR I-10155.

These three cases involved situations in which companies, despite being strongly linked with one Member State,[132] had intentionally incorporated in another Member State in order to avoid the imposition of more restrictive rules. When the companies came into contact with the authorities of the Member States to which they were more closely connected (either in order to register a branch or, in the instance of *Überseering*, to take part in a court case), they were met with resistance (respectively refusal to recognise the branch, the imposition of additional requirements for registration or denial of legal standing).

The companies challenged the stance of the respective Member State authorities, and the cases found their way before the CJEU by way of references for preliminary rulings. In all three instances, the Court ruled that the companies' freedom of establishment had been restricted,[133] and that the actions taken by the Member States could not be justified by overriding reasons in the public interest.[134]

Although Member States are permitted to introduce measures designed to combat the use of EU provisions as a way of undertaking improper or fraudulent activities or improperly circumventing national rules,[135] incorporating in another Member State solely in order to avoid restrictive rules is not, in itself, considered to be an abuse of the freedom of establishment.[136] This rationale has subsequently been adapted to cover cross-border conversions, whereby a company may undertake such a conversion in accordance with the law of the 'receiving' Member State regardless of whether it continues to conduct its main

---

132 For instance, the UK-incorporated company *Centros* was established by two Danes and exclusively traded in Denmark; in *Überseering* all the directors of the company were German, whilst it was incorporated in the Netherlands; and in *Inspire Art* the company had been established by a Dutchman under the laws of England and Wales.

133 *Centros* (n.129 above), at paras.15–22; *Überseering* (n.130 above), at paras.78–82; *Inspire Art* (n.131 above), at paras.95–105.

134 *Centros* (n.129), at paras.23–39; *Überseering* (n.130 above), at paras.83–94; *Inspire Art* (n.131), at paras.131–143. See commentary on these cases in J.-J. Kuipers, 'Cartesio and Grunkin-Paul: Mutual Recognition as a Vested Rights Theory Based on Party Autonomy in Private Law' (2009) 2(2) *European Journal of Legal Studies* 66, at pp.69–71 and T. Szabados, 'Companies in EU Private International Law – An EU Law Perspective' in M. Király and T. Szabados (eds.), *Perspectives of Unification of Private International Law in the European Union* (Eötvös University Press, Budapest, 2018), at pp.89–91.

135 E.g. *Centros* (n.129 above), at para.24. This stance has become more nuanced in later cases, most notably those concerning tax: Case C-196/04 *Cadbury Schweppes plc and Commissioners of Inland Revenue*. Reference for a preliminary ruling: Special Commissioners of Income Tax, London – United Kingdom [2006] ECR 1-7995, at para.51 and Case C-524/04 *Test Claimants in the Thin Cap Group Litigation v. Commissioners of Inland Revenue*. Reference for a preliminary ruling: High Court of Justice (England & Wales), Chancery Division – United Kingdom [2007] ECR I-02107, at para.74: whilst the freedom of establishment can indeed be used to take advantage of more favourable national rules, it has been found to be permissible for Member States to introduce measures designed to tackle wholly artificial arrangements aimed solely at evading otherwise applicable laws. See also Kuipers (n.134 above), at p.81.

136 *Centros* (n.129 above), at para.27; *Inspire Art* (n.131 above), at para.121.

operations in the Member State from which it 'departed'.[137] It is important to note, however, that Member States retain the power to define the connecting factor through which the national law applicable to a company's incorporation is determined.[138]

A somewhat similar approach to that developed in the CJEU's jurisprudence on incorporation has been adopted towards the issue of cross-border name law. In the case of *Garcia Avello*,[139] the facts of the case involved the refusal of the Belgian authorities to accept a request to change the surname of two children living in Belgium who held dual Belgian-Spanish nationality (by virtue of their father and mother). The parties wished to change to a double-barrelled surname that comprised both the father and mother's surnames (in accordance with Spanish custom) and had been registered with the Spanish embassy. However, Belgian name law only permitted children to be registered with their father's surname.

In answer to the request for a preliminary ruling by the Belgian court, the CJEU stated that the case came within the scope of Community law by virtue of the fact that the children were EU citizens[140] who held dual nationality.[141] It held that the principle of non-discrimination (Article 12 EC) denotes that dual nationals such as the children in this instance may assert a right to be treated differently from persons who only hold Belgian nationality in this context. Drawing on the specific inconveniences of the discrepancy in surname in this case,[142] and in the absence of a valid justification for the refusal of the Belgian authorities to register the double-barrelled name,[143] the CJEU found that a refusal to grant the surname change for the two children was contrary to Article 12 and 17 EC.

The 2008 case of *Grunkin-Paul*[144] involved a refusal by the German authorities to register a double-barrelled surname of a German child who had

---

137 Case C-106/16 *Proceedings brought by Polbud – Wykonawstwo sp. z o.o.* Request for a preliminary ruling from the Sąd Najwyższy – Poland [2017] ECLI:EU:C:2017:804. See Szabados (n.134 above), at pp.90–92.

138 See Case C-210/06 *Cartesio Oktató és Szolgáltató bt.* Reference for a preliminary ruling: Szegedi Ítélőtábla – Hungary [2008] ECR I-09641, at paras.109–112: although this power cannot be used to prevent a company incorporating or converting under the law of another Member State. See Szabados (n.134), at p.93.

139 Case C-148/02 *Carlos Garcia Avello v. État belge.* Reference for a preliminary ruling: Conseil d'État – Belgium [2003] ECR I-11613.

140 Bringing Article 17 EC into the scope of this situation: ibid. at para.21.

141 Ibid., at paras.26–27.

142 Ibid., at paras.35–36: for instance, a difference in surnames could result in diplomas from one Member State not being easily recognised in the other.

143 Ibid., at para.41.

144 Case C-353/06 *Stefan Grunkin and Dorothee Regina Paul.* Reference for a preliminary ruling: Amtsgericht Flensburg – Germany [2008] ECR I-7639.

been born and registered[145] under that name in Denmark. Unlike under Belgian law (see above), German law would have allowed the double-barrelled name to be registered if the child had been a dual national; however, this was not the scenario here. A request for a preliminary reference was made to the CJEU on this matter. The Court found that the matter came within the scope of EU law by virtue of the fact that the child was a national of one Member State (Germany) and was living in another (Denmark).[146] On the basis of Article 18 EC (the right to free movement for EU citizens), employing a somewhat similar line of reasoning to that in *Garcia Avello*,[147] the Court found that the discrepancy in surnames that would arise from this refusal held a strong potential to restrict the enjoyment of this right,[148] and that the reasons provided by the government were not sufficient to justify this restriction.[149]

As discussed previously in the context of the CJEU's jurisprudence on incorporation, Member States can restrict the enjoyment of fundamental freedoms in certain circumstances on the basis of their own public policy, provided the measure pursues a legitimate and proportionate objective. In the present name law context, this has been exemplified in the pursuit of protecting a national language (*Runevič-Vardyn*[150]) or in view of the constitutional abolition of nobility (*Sayn-Wittgenstein*[151]).

The incorporation and name law cases have been collectively framed as evidence of an entrenchment of the principle of party autonomy in the context of the EU's fundamental freedoms.[152] With echoes of the ECtHR's judgment in *Wagner* (see 2.3.1. above), the request for recognition in one state of a status created in another could be viewed as a functional choice of law by the parties (although it is never referred to as such in the actual judgments). However, in comparison to the incorporation law cases, the connection of the name law

145 Or, to express it in more detail, the child had his surname changed to Grunkin-Paul in Denmark following his birth: M. Lehmann, 'What's in a Name? *Grunkin-Paul* and Beyond' (2008) 10 *Yearbook of Private International Law* 135, at p.143.

146 *Grunkin-Paul* (n.144 above), at paras.15–18.

147 Although the Court in *Garcia Avello* considered the impact of such inconveniences in the context of EU citizenship under Article 17 EC. It should also be noted that unlike in the previous case, there was no possibility to invoke a claim of discrimination on the grounds of nationality (Article 12 EC) in Grunkin-Paul.

148 *Grunkin-Paul* (n.144 above), at paras.23–24.

149 Ibid., at paras.30–38.

150 Case C-391/09, *Malgožata Runevič-Vardyn and Łukasz Paweł Wardyn v. Vilniaus miesto savivaldybės administracija and Others*. Reference for a preliminary ruling: Vilniaus miesto 1 apylinkės teismas – Lithuania [2011] ECR I-03787, at para.86. Although, in this instance, the CJEU found that it was for the national court to determine whether the restriction on registration was proportionate to the aim pursued (at paras.77–78).

151 Case C-208/09 *Ilonka Sayn-Wittgenstein v. Landeshauptmann von Wien*. Reference for a preliminary ruling: Verwaltungsgerichtshof – Austria [2010] ECR I-13693, at paras.88–89, 93–94.

152 See Lehmann (n.145 above), at pp.159–161 and Nagy (n.101 above), at pp.581–582, para.3.2.1. and pp.583–584, para.3.2.3.

cases to the exercise of autonomy appears more tenuous. In *Garcia Avello* and *Grunkin-Paul*, the parties pursued the registration of double-barrelled surnames in order maintain a consistent identity (and, in the case of the former, retain cultural considerations) throughout the Union. Whilst it has been argued that the decision in the name law cases equated to an obligation upon one Member State to recognise the parties' 'choice' of name law,[153] these cases seem to lack the element of forward planning that accompanies the actions of companies that purposefully incorporate in one Member State in order to avoid the imposition of the more restrictive rules of another.[154]

Above all, both the incorporation and name law cases (along with *Wagner*) appear principally to involve a need to maintain a status (or, perhaps a 'vested right'[155]) across borders rather than a choice of law in the context in which it is being considered here. In other words, such instances seemingly focus upon the question of the effects of the application of another law being recognised, rather than the law itself being applied.

As a closing note, it is interesting to contrast the position in the above case law with the reasoning adopted by the CJEU in the recent *Coman* judgment.[156] With regard to the (non-)recognition of a same-sex marriage for the purposes of an EU citizen's right to free movement and the residency rights of a third country spouse, the Court appeared to place a lesser emphasis on the pre-existing nature of the couple's status, instead primarily concentrating on the impact of non-recognition upon the free movement rights of the EU citizen spouse and his right to a family life. With regard to this politically sensitive realm, the CJEU's restrictive wording created comparatively little scope for discussion of a choice of law or even a vested rights approach in this context.[157]

2.4. FREE WILL IN EU CROSS-BORDER FAMILY MATTERS AND SUCCESSION

Having established the character and intrinsic value attached to the exercise of free will in both the wider and EU contexts, this third and final stage of the present chapter involves considering the *prima facie* nature of free will in the

---

153 See Kuipers (n.134 above), at pp.84–85, which frames the CJEU's approach in *Grunkin-Paul* as involving a 'choice of law made by the parties' in the context of vested rights.

154 Although, it should be noted that it was the children (rather than their parents) in the case of *Garcia Avello* who wished to have their name changed to align with Spanish cultural practice: Yetano (n.112 above), at p.159.

155 A topic that will be discussed with regard to enforcement of choice, in Chapter 10. See framing of these cases in this manner in Kuipers (n.134 above).

156 Case C-673/16 *Coman and Others v. Romania*. Reference for a preliminary ruling from the Curtea [2018] ECLI:EU:C:2018:385.

157 See further discussion of the CJEU's reasoning in *Coman* at 4.3.2., 4.5.2 and 10.6.1.

specific realm of the EU private international law rules relating to family matters and succession. In pursuit of this, two facets of its distinctive character will be set out, namely the restricted character of choice in cross-border family matters and succession (2.4.1.) and the additional regard for the position of specific parties in the exercise of autonomy in this realm (2.4.2.).

2.4.1. RESTRICTED CHARACTER

The boundaries of the law are narrowly demarcated in the realm of cross-border family matters and succession, where choice is significantly constrained, with parties generally only being permitted to select a law or Member State court having a close connection to themselves or the relationship. This sits in sharp contrast to the EU regulations that provide for a choice of law or choice of court in (non)contractual obligations, under which parties may generally select an unconnected applicable law or Member State court to govern their proceedings.[158]

A number of reasons can be identified for this comparative constraint. First and foremost, family and succession matters strike at the heart of the personal lives of individuals. In contrast to the relatively neutral setting of contract law (and, to a lesser extent, non-contractual obligations), family relationships and succession matters involve a mix of legal, emotional, religious and moral considerations. The parties involved in such interactions are often not dealing with one another 'at arm's length', due to emotional and financial interdependency.[159] Unfettered private ordering in the realms of family and succession may appear to be inappropriate or risky.

Despite the private nature of family matters and succession, this is also a realm that the state demonstrates a particular interest in regulating. The unique juxtaposition of law and society gives rise to legal rules that reflect cultural trends or religious influences predominant in the relevant state.[160] Peari,[161] drawing

---

[158] Subject to caveats, see, for instance, the protection of specific weaker parties under the Rome I and Rome II Regulations, the limitation of choice for matters concerning rights *in rem* under Article 4(1)(c) of Rome I and the restriction of choice prior to an event under Rome II unless the situation involves commercial activity (Article 14(1)(b) of Rome II).

[159] N. Dethloff, 'Contracting in Family Law: A European Perspective' in K. Boele-Woelki et al. (eds.), *The Future of Family Property in Europe* (Intersentia, Antwerp, 2011), at para.3.2.1. and P. Wautelet, 'Party Autonomy in International Family Relationships: A Research Agenda' in C. Cauffman and J.M. Smits (eds.), *The Citizen in European Private Law* (Intersentia, Antwerp, 2016), at para.16.

[160] For example, a contrast is seen between divorce law in predominantly Catholic Ireland, which imposes a mandatory waiting period of four years' separation before a divorce may be granted, versus the comparatively liberal society of the Netherlands, in which no waiting period is imposed for divorce.

[161] S. Peari, 'Choice-of-law in family law: Kant, Savigny and the parties' autonomy principle', (2012) 4 *Nederlands Internationaal Privaatrecht* 597–604.

upon the work of Savigny, attempts to explain the comparatively limited nature of party autonomy in family law by reference to its 'mixed' structure (involving moral and legal considerations), which contrasts with the purely legal nature of contract and property law. Entrenched within the community and spirit of the forum state, family law is seen to necessitate the application of the *lex fori*.

Unsurprisingly, the limited nature of party autonomy in cross-border family and succession matters does not go unchallenged. For instance, it can be seen that comparatively greater scope to organise legal relations is permitted with regard to the domestic arrangement of matrimonial property (in civil law countries), the disposal of property upon succession, and, to a lesser extent, the agreement of maintenance obligations.[162] Given that family law, both domestic and international, entails a similar interplay between legal and societal elements, why is there greater scope for private ordering in the national setting?

An attempt to explain this discrepancy may be made on the basis of the rationale that domestic law retains the means to safeguard parties' interests, as well as national values, by imposing mandatory rules. However, in the private international law setting, it must be recalled that fundamental values of national law (e.g. non-discrimination) can be ensured through the use of the public policy exception.[163]

Solutions have been proposed by several authors that counter the framing of restricted autonomy as the only means of protecting the 'weaker party'. For instance, it has been suggested that a much wider range of jurisdictional links could be offered, with a higher degree of judicial discretion available in ensuring an actual close connection between the jurisdiction and the parties,[164] or that the focus should more be placed upon ensuring adequate safeguards in the exercise of choice (e.g. the requirement for adequate professional information) rather than limiting the choice itself.[165]

Notwithstanding the above points of discussion, the fact nevertheless remains that accepting party autonomy requires the relinquishment of sovereignty in exchange for comity and mutual trust between states. Arguably, the EU provides a favourable setting for such a shift in priorities. However, it is clear from the turbulent process of negotiating EU instruments on family matters and succession that Member States certainly do not part with their sovereignty easily, particularly in the sensitive realm of family matters.[166] It is here, at the

---

162 Yetano (n.112 above), at p.180.

163 Ibid., at p.192.

164 L. Walker, 'Party Autonomy, Inconsistency and the Specific Characteristics of Family Law in the EU' (2018) 14(2) *Journal of Private International Law* 225, at p.255.

165 T. Kruger and L. Samyn, 'Brussels II bis: Successes and Suggested Improvements' (2016) 12(1) *Journal of Private International Law* 132, at p.145.

166 For example, certain Member States such as Sweden and Finland were reluctant to accept the choice of law set out in the Rome III Regulation because they feared having to impose a

interplay between law and society, that states are especially resistant to foreign influence. For this reason, the current limited form of party autonomy appears to be a fixture for the foreseeable future.

2.4.2. ADDRESSING THE NEEDS OF SPECIFIC PARTIES

As briefly touched upon above, parties in long-term family relationships are not dealing with one another 'at arms' length'. It must therefore be acknowledged that general power imbalances may readily arise in their interactions. The necessity to seek out impartial legal advice regarding the content of an individual's choices and the consequences that flow from them is brought to the forefront as a starting point for safeguarding fullness of free will for all parties in this context (see the conditions set out in 2.2.1.). Moving beyond this general dependency that arises during the normal course of relationships, there are also those parties who, as a result of their inherent characteristics, are considered to be in a weaker position.

In the realm of (non-)contractual relations[167] such parties may be exemplified as passengers, consumers, insurance policy-holders and employees.[168] Protective limitations upon party autonomy in these fields include the inability to derogate by agreement from mandatory provisions of the law of the weaker party's habitual residence,[169] a limited choice of the connecting factors that determine choice of law[170] (akin to the standard practice in the rules on cross-border family law and succession), and the upholding of jurisdictional agreements only where they allow the weaker party to bring proceedings before a forum which would not otherwise be available.[171]

---

more restrictive divorce law than their own. For commentary in this regard see: Boele-Woelki (Chapter 1, n.1), at p.22.

167 See the Rome I Regulation: Articles 5(2) (carriage of passengers), 6 (consumer contracts), 7(3) (insurance contracts), 8 (individual employment contracts), and Recital 23 and Brussels I Recast: Articles 10–23 (insurance, consumer and individual employment contracts) and Recital 18. The Rome II Regulation protects types of torts (e.g. product liability – Article 5), however, it does not have specific provisions aimed at certain categories of victims. Despite this, it could be argued that protections for specific torts also protect the victims of that tort (e.g. the consumer); see regard for weaker party protection in Recital 31. See also discussion in G. van Calster, *European Private International Law* (Hart Publishing, Oxford and Portland, second edition, 2016), at paras.2.2.8.1., 3.2.5, and 4.6.

168 J.M. Carruthers, 'Party Autonomy in the Legal Regulation of Adult Relationships: What Place for Party Choice in Private International Law?' (2012) 61(4) *International and Comparative Law Quarterly* 881, at p.908; E. Lein, 'The new Rome I / Rome II / Brussels I synergy' (2008) 10 *Yearbook of Private International Law* 177, at pp.186–188; V. Lazić, 'Procedural Justice for "Weaker Parties" in Cross-Border Litigation under the EU Regulatory Scheme' (2014) 10(4) *Utrecht Law Review* 100–117; and Basedow (Chapter 1, n.46), p.136–139, paras.226–232.

169 See Article 6(2) of the Rome I Regulation.

170 See Article 5(2) (carriage of passengers) and Article 7(2) (insurance contracts) of the Rome I Regulation.

171 See Article 19(2) of Brussels I Recast (consumers).

It has been said that 'generically' weak parties, such as the ones discussed above, are difficult to identify in cross-border family and succession relations.[172] Nevertheless, for the purposes of this evaluation, a number of categories of parties that merit specific protection in the exercise of a choice of law or court in these fields can be discerned.

Firstly, and perhaps unsurprisingly, there is a strong need for protectionism in the EU's private international law rules involving children. Since the legal relationships of minors tend to be organised by adults, and minors generally do not have capacity to enter into contracts, a clear weakness can be seen to arise from the fact that children are unable to significantly influence or represent themselves in decisions that have an impact upon their lives. The exercise of their free will is performed by others who may or may not hold competing interests to those of the child. It is thus for the legal framework to ensure that the best interests of the child are served in all decisions that concern a minor.[173] Vulnerable adults who lack capacity and are not in a position to protect their own interests are another group whose vulnerability arises from the fact that decision-making might have to be undertaken on their behalf. In view of this, there is a necessity for the legal framework to safeguard their interests from the whims of pragmatism.

Another notable category of weaker party is that of the spousal/child maintenance creditor.[174] This group's vulnerability emerges from the fact that the creditor is looking to obtain payment from the debtor in order to sustain him or herself – the necessity of action is unilateral. Furthermore, since the creditor is seeking payment in the first place, they are likely to be in a financially weaker position than the debtor, and thus less able to access specialist legal advice or travel to attend proceedings. The position of the creditor may arise from a 'structural power imbalance'[175] that existed within the relationship that gave rise to the maintenance obligation, for instance, due to inequality between the parties with regard to childcare and participation in the workforce.[176] This imbalance in bargaining power, as well as the interdependence inherent in such family relationships, could arguably affect the authenticity of consent to an agreement with the other party.[177]

---

172 Carruthers (n.168 above), at p.909.

173 In line with Article 3(1) of the UN Convention on the Rights of the Child (1989): 'In all actions concerning children, whether undertaken by public or private social welfare institutions, courts of law, administrative authorities or legislative bodies, the best interests of the child shall be a primary consideration' and Article 24(2) of the EU Charter of Fundamental Rights. See also Recitals 12 and 13 of Brussels II bis.

174 See regard for the position of the creditor in Recitals 9, 15, 26, and 27 of the Maintenance Regulation.

175 See discussion in: Walker (n.164 above), at pp.246–250.

176 Ibid., at p.248.

177 Ibid., at pp.247–249.

Finally, there are those parties whose vulnerability arises from the fact that, although they hold a fundamental interest in the outcome of proceedings, they sit outside of the primary legal process. The first of these categories are beneficiaries of an estate, whose vulnerability arises from the fact that the organisation of the estate is primarily a task that belongs exclusively to the testator prior to his/her death. This category primarily suffers from practical hindrances to accessing justice and lack of affinity with the applicable law due to being 'locked out' of the organisation of succession proceedings.[178] Secondly, there are third parties who, although they are not directly involved in a relationship or legal arrangement, are nonetheless affected by changes that occur within it. In this setting, the full consent of the third parties in legal relations with the main parties to the relationship or legal arrangement might be compromised by not being informed as to changes in, most prominently, the applicable law.[179]

178 See regard for the position of beneficiaries in Recitals 7, 16, 32 and 38 of the Succession Regulation. See also Explanatory Memorandum accompanying the Proposal for a regulation of the European Parliament and of the Council on jurisdiction, applicable law, recognition and enforcement of decisions and authentic instruments in matters of succession and the creation of a European Certificate of Succession, COM(2009) 154 final, at p.2, para.1.2., p.5, para.4.2., and p.7, para.4.3.

179 See regard for position of third parties in the Recitals 46, 51–52 of the Matrimonial Property Regulation and Recitals 45 and 50–51 of the Partnership Property Regulation. See also the Proposal for a Council Regulation on jurisdiction, applicable law and the recognition and enforcement of decisions in matters of matrimonial property regimes, COM(2016) 106 final and the Proposal for a Council Regulation on jurisdiction, applicable law and the recognition and enforcement of decisions in matters of the property consequences of registered partnerships, COM(2016) 107 final, at p.10, para.5.3.

CHAPTER 3

THE OBJECTIVES BEHIND THE UNIFICATION OF PRIVATE INTERNATIONAL LAW ON FAMILY MATTERS AND SUCCESSION

3.1. INTRODUCTION

The previous chapter addressed the intrinsic value of free will within the present context of party autonomy in the EU private international law relating to family matters and succession. It was established that although free will holds value as the guiding force that drives party autonomy, for the present purposes the concept is essentially restricted by the legal system and context in which it is set.

There are other justifications that have been proposed for the usage of party autonomy in private international law besides that which focuses on its inherent value; for instance those based upon the beneficial impact of party autonomy to the parties themselves, as well as wider society.[180] However, this examination specifically focuses upon the underpinnings of this principle in relation to its status as a unified measure of EU law. In order to do this, the specific goals behind the EU's unification of private international law rules on family matters and succession must be presented.

This chapter begins by presenting the context in which such unification is embedded by illustrating the ideological and legal changes that have taken place over the past 25 years in order to accommodate private international law measures on family matters and succession (3.2.). Leading on from this, the aims of party autonomy in its role as an EU measure that purports to facilitate

---

[180] See, for instance, Basedow (Chapter 1, n.46), at pp.139–142, paras.235–238, concerning the efficiency brought about through choice of law exercised by private actors; Maultzsch (Chapter 1, n.6), at p.477 on efficiency and the promotion of competition between national substantive law regimes; Mills (Chapter 1, n.8), at pp.74–78, para.2.3.1.2. on 'private consequentialist libertarianism', concerning the beneficial impact of party autonomy on the individual in the context of efficiency, and at pp.79–84, para.2.3.2. on 'public consequentialist libertarianism: public-systematic justifications', focusing on the societal benefits of party autonomy; and Rühl (Chapter 2, n.93, (2007)), at pp.32–34 on efficiency.

the free movement of persons will be considered by setting out the potential obstacles that people face in cross-border family matters and succession, namely legal uncertainty (3.3.), a lack of affinity with the applicable law (3.4.), and practical hindrances to accessing justice (3.5.) Along with the exercise of free will as defined in the previous chapter, these identified obstacles will make up the elements through which the evaluation carried out in this book will be conducted.

3.2. THE EUROPEANISATION OF PRIVATE INTERNATIONAL LAW ON FAMILY MATTERS AND SUCCESSION

To set the scene for considering the objectives of EU action to introduce unified measures for private international law in family matters and succession, the manner in which the Union came to be involved in this field must first be considered.[181]

This section will begin by outlining the evolution of the right to free movement in the EU, from one that was once solely concerned with economically active persons, to today's embracive right of all citizens of Member States to move freely around the Union (3.2.1.). Following on from this, the emergence of the sphere in which private international law measures are contained – the area of freedom, security and justice – will be detailed (3.2.2.). Finally, the process of establishing a suitable legal basis for the Union to introduce measures on family matters and succession will be outlined (3.2.3.).

3.2.1. THE CHANGING NATURE OF FREE MOVEMENT

In establishing the context of the EU's involvement in private international law, the dramatic evolution that has taken place over the past 25 years in terms of the Union's ideology ought first to be examined. The scope of EU action has considerably expanded, breaking away from its original remit of simply facilitating the free movement of economically active persons[182] (e.g. workers[183]),

181 For extended commentary on the subject matter of this section, see this author's article: J. Gray, 'Identifying the Impetus behind the Europeanization of the Private International Law Rules on Family Matters and Succession' (2015) 17(2) *European Journal of Law Reform* 341.

182 C. Barnard, *The Substantive Law of the EU: The Four Freedoms*, 3rd edn. (Oxford University Press, Oxford, 2010), at p.224.

183 Articles 49–51 of the Treaty establishing the European Economic Community [1992] OJ C 224 (EEC).

to embody a much wider set of aims, designed to safeguard the right of all EU citizens to move freely within the European Union.

The first stage of this transformation can be linked to two developments that emerged in the early 1990s. It was at this point that the Community gradually began to turn its attention towards enabling non-economic actors to benefit from the free movement rights contained in the Treaty. The CJEU (or ECJ, as it was then known) developed a precedent for allowing the families of workers to accompany them in their exercise of free movement,[184] and directives were introduced that offered a right of movement and residence within the EU to retired persons,[185] students,[186] and those of independent means.[187]

During this same period, the concept of EU citizenship was first introduced into the Community setting. Building upon a 1990 proposal by the Spanish government entitled 'The Road to European Citizenship',[188] the Maastricht Treaty of 1992 formally recognised this concept, establishing the right of all persons holding the nationality of a Member State: 'to move and reside freely within the territory of the Member States, subject to the limitations and conditions laid down in this Treaty and by the measures adopted to give it effect'.[189]

Whilst the CJEU initially appeared to regard the new citizenship rights as merely an addendum to the existing economic-based rights,[190] it steadily began to recognise the status of citizenship in itself (e.g. the right of non-economically active persons to collect social security[191]). In 2004, the Citizenship Directive[192] was adopted, which consolidated the case law and piecemeal legislation in order

184 Case C-370/90 *R v. Immigration Appeal Tribunal and Surinder Singh, ex parte Secretary of State for Home Department*. Reference for a preliminary ruling: High Court of Justice, Queen's Bench Division – United Kingdom [1992] ECR I-4265.

185 Council Directive 90/365/EEC of 28 June 1990 on the right of residence for employees and self-employed persons who have ceased their occupational activity [1990] OJ L 180/28.

186 Council Directive 90/366/EEC of 28 June 1990 on the right of residence for students [1990] OJ L 180/30.

187 Council Directive 90/364/EEC of 28 June 1990 on the right of residence [1990] OJ L 180/20.

188 See the Spanish Delegation to the Intergovernmental Conference on Political Union: 'The Road to European Citizenship' (24 September 1990), unpublished Council document SN 3940/90.

189 See Part II, Article 8a of the Treaty on European Union of the 7 February 1992 [1992] OJ C 191.

190 For example, Case C-193/94 *Criminal proceedings against Sofia Skanavi and Konstantin Chryssanthakopoulos*. Reference for a preliminary ruling: Amtsgericht Tiergarten, Berlin – Germany [1996] ECR I-6193, at para.22.

191 For example, Case C-85/96 *María Martínez Sala v. Freistaat Bayern*. Reference for a preliminary ruling: Bayerisches Landessozialgericht – Germany [1998] ECR I-2691 and Case C-184/99 *Rudy Grzelczyk v. Centre public d'aide sociale d'Ottignies-Louvain-la-Neuve*. Reference for a preliminary ruling: Tribunal du travail de Nivelles – Belgium [2001] ECR I-6193.

192 Directive 2004/38/EC on the right of citizens of the Union and their family members to move and reside freely within the territory of the Member States [2004] OJ L 158/77.

to bring about a raft of rights designed to facilitate the free movement of citizens and their families throughout the Union. The free movement of EU citizens had now emerged as a fifth freedom, alongside and independent of the free movement rights relating to goods, services, capital and workers.[193]

3.2.2. THE EMERGENCE OF THE AREA OF FREEDOM, SECURITY AND JUSTICE

The development in the conception of the free movement of persons and the introduction of citizenship undoubtedly extended the EU's remit well beyond economic concerns. However, the question remains as to the significance of citizenship to the Union's involvement in civil matters, and, more specifically, what was its impetus to unify private international law rules on family matters and succession? In answer to this, there is a final piece to this puzzle: the establishment of the area of freedom, security and justice.

The Treaty of Amsterdam, signed in 1997, established the new goal of giving 'citizens a common sense of justice throughout the Union',[194] and taking steps to 'simplify and facilitate the judicial environment in which they live in the European context'.[195] In order to bring this into action, a meeting was held in 1999 by the European Council in Tampere, during which *the area of freedom, security and justice* (AFSJ) was formally created.

The conclusions which resulted from the Tampere meeting established that steps should be taken towards a 'genuine European area of justice', in which individuals (citizens, as well as third country nationals[196]) 'should not be prevented or discouraged from exercising their rights by the incompatibility or complexity of legal and administrative systems in the Member States'.[197] The implementation of this AFSJ called for proposals to be submitted on a variety of civil and criminal law matters, among which were included family and succession matters.[198]

---

193 M. Fallon, 'Constraints of Internal Market Law on Family Law' in J. Meeusen et al. (eds.), *International Family Law for the European Union* (Intersentia, Antwerp, 2007), at pp.151–152.

194 Action plan of the Council and the Commission on how best to implement the provisions of the Treaty of Amsterdam on an area of freedom, security and justice [1999] OJ C 19, at para.15.

195 Ibid.

196 Tampere Conclusions (Chapter 1, n.2), at para.18.

197 Ibid., para.28.

198 Hague Programme: Strengthening Freedom, Security and Justice in the European Union, [2005] OJ C 53/1, at para.3.4.2. and the Stockholm Programme: An open and secure Europe, serving and protecting citizens, [2010] OJ C 115/1, at para.3.1.2.

3.2.3. THE DEVELOPMENT OF A SUITABLE LEGAL BASIS

Although somewhat surprisingly given the current raft of legislation, EU law and private international law were, for a long time, regarded as 'uneasy bedfellows'.[199] In fact, prior to 1999, the Union had no specific competence in the Treaty to legislate in the field of private international law. However, a limited number of instruments were nevertheless created before this time, taking the form of conventions, and brought about on the basis of intergovernmental cooperation between the Member States.[200] Whilst negotiations concerning these instruments were facilitated within the framework of the treaties,[201] this was not actually necessary for their conclusion.

The Maastricht Treaty of 1992 introduced an opportunity for limited involvement of the EU institutions in legislative action in this field.[202] However, it was not until judicial cooperation in civil matters was *communitised* by the Treaty of Amsterdam, and brought within the scope of the newly-created Title IV on 'visa, asylum, immigration and other policies related to the free movement of persons', that the Union became competent to adopt private international law measures of its own accord.[203]

The following years gave rise to a surge in legislative activity in the field of private international law.[204] The new legal basis, Article 65 EC, served as a means of communitarising several existing conventions (e.g. the Brussels I Regulation and Rome I Regulation), bringing about entirely new measures (e.g. the Maintenance Regulation and Rome II Regulation), and resurrecting a number of instruments which had never entered into force under the previous system[205]

---

199 J. Meeusen, '"What Has it Got to Do Necessarily with the European Union?": International Family Law and European (Economic) Integration' (2006–2007) 9 *Cambridge Yearbook of European Legal Studies* 329, at p.329.

200 See the 1968 Brussels Convention and the 1980 Rome Convention.

201 Article 220 served as an underlying basis upon which negotiations on the Brussels Convention were based.

202 The Council and Commission had the right of initiative, whilst the Parliament could be consulted and provide recommendations.

203 K. Boele-Woelki, 'Unification and Harmonisation of Private International Law in Europe' in E. Hondius and F.W. Grosheide (eds.), *International Contract Law 2003: Articles on Various Aspects of Transnational Contract Law* (Intersentia, Antwerp, 2004), at pp.325–326, and K. Boele-Woelki and R.H. van Ooik, 'The Communitization of Private International Law', ibid., at pp.344–345.

204 Partly helped by the alterations to the voting requirements brought about by the Treaty of Nice amending the Treaty on European Union, the Treaties establishing the European Communities and certain related acts [2001] OJ L 80/1: see A. Fiorini, 'The Evolution of European Private International Law' (2008) 57(4) *International and Comparative Law Quarterly* 969, at p.974.

205 See Council Regulation (EC) No 1346/2000 of 29 May 2000 on insolvency proceedings [2000] OJ L 160/1 and Council Regulation (EC) No 1348/2000 of 29 May 2000 on the service in the Member States of judicial and extrajudicial documents in civil or commercial matters [2000] OJ L 160/37.

(e.g. the Brussels II Regulation, which was based on the unratified Brussels II Convention of 1998).

In the space of less than a decade, Union involvement in private international law increased dramatically, and the first successful instruments concerning family matters had emerged. Despite this, issues remained as to the formal suitability of Article 65 for such purposes. This provision established that measures should be taken in the field of judicial cooperation in civil matters 'in so far as necessary for the proper functioning of the *internal market*' (emphasis added). If the internal market is to be viewed as concerning purely economic integration (in line with its definition in Article 14 EC),[206] questions arise as to how differences between legal systems with regard to family and succession law affect economically active persons *in particular* (as opposed to all citizens who exercise their right to free movement within the Union).[207]

It could be argued that once a person crosses a national border, friction may occur from the imposition of foreign legal system, which may in turn harm the functioning of the internal market.[208] However, this treatment of the internal market requirement is unconvincing. Whilst providing uniform private international law rules on family matters and succession may well benefit the internal market, this is incidental to the wider goal of promoting conditions for all internationally active persons within the Union.[209] According to the Court of Justice, the EU legislator cannot use bases such as this to adopt measures that merely have the ancillary effect of harmonising the internal market.[210]

As a means of resolving this tension, an attempt could be made to reconcile the emergence of the AFSJ with a change in the conception of the internal market. The AFSJ could be envisaged as a deepening of the internal market; a level of further integration going beyond purely economic concerns. Indeed, the absence of express reference to the 'internal market' in the Tampere Conclusions

---

206 Meeusen (n.199 above), at p.336; G. Straetmans, 'Non-economic Free Movement of EU Citizens and Family Law Matters' in J. Meeusen et al. (eds.), *International Family Law for the European Union* (Intersentia, Antwerp, 2007), at p.235.

207 Meeusen (n.199 above).

208 For this view, see N.A. Baarsma, *The Europeanisation of International Family Law* (T.M.C. Asser Press, The Hague, 2011), at p.131; T. Wiedmann, 'Artikel 65 EGV' in J. Schwarze (ed.) *EU-Kommentar* (Nomos, Baden-Baden, 2007), at p.877. See also, J. Basedow, 'The Communitarisation of the Conflict of Laws under the Treaty of Amsterdam' (2000) 37 *Common Market Law Review* 687, at p.703: 'The point of departure should be the implicit recognition, by Article 65 (b), that the compatibility of conflict rules is necessary for the proper functioning of the internal market'; and S. Schmahl, 'Artikel 65 EGV' in A. Bardenhewer-Rating et al. (eds.), *Kommentar zum Vertrag über die Europäische Union und zur Gründung der Europäischen Gemeinschaft* (Nomos, Baden-Baden, 2003), at p.1868, fn.4.

209 Meeusen (n.199 above), p.338.

210 See, for example, Case C-376/98 *Federal Republic of Germany v. European Parliament and Council of the European Union* [2000] ECR I-8419, at para.33; Case C-187/93 *Parliament v. Council* [1994] ECR I-2857, at para.25; and Case C-84/94 *United Kingdom v. Council* [1996] ECR I-5755, at para.45.

may be taken to signify a desire on the part of the Union to evolve beyond the limitations placed on its actions in the field of civil justice by this concept.[211] However, there is also strong evidence to the contrary: for instance, within Article 3 TEU, the two concepts are clearly enumerated as separate goals.[212] In the absence of further clarification, it cannot be assumed that the concept of 'internal market' contained within the context of Title IV ('visas, asylum, immigration and other policies related to the free movement of persons') carried a different meaning compared with the rest of the Treaty.[213]

This critique aside, following the signing of the Lisbon Treaty in 2007, Article 81 TFEU replaced Article 65 EC, and brought with it a reformulated provision stating that measures concerning civil matters with cross-border implications could be adopted '*particularly* when necessary for the proper functioning of the internal market' (emphasis added).[214] The replacement of the phrase 'in so far as' with the words 'particularly when' means that measures adopted under this provision are no longer *required* to meet the internal market criterion.[215] Instead, this has been transformed into exemplification of one of a number of aims that private international law provisions should pursue.[216] The formal scope of Union competence to act in this field is now visibly expanded,[217] and the question of the relevance of measures concerning cross-border family matters and succession to the proper functioning of the internal market has become markedly less crucial.

With the removal of the internal market imperative by Article 81 TFEU, the creation of the AFSJ has gained greater legitimacy and moved to the forefront as a justification for EU action in the field of civil justice. This chiefly pursues the aim of making everyday life simpler for EU citizens by introducing measures designed to tackle the problems that occur from encountering different legal systems when exercising the right to free movement.[218] The remainder of this chapter will be dedicated to defining and contextualising this broad goal by outlining the potential obstacles that internationally active persons may face in the specific context of cross-border family and succession matters, namely: legal

211 J. Israel, 'Conflicts of Law and the EC after Amsterdam: A Change for the Worse?' (2000) 7(1) *Maastricht Journal of European and Comparative Law* 81, at p.95.

212 Article 3(2) TEU – area of freedom, security and justice; Article 3(3) TEU – internal market.

213 Meeusen (n.199 above), at p.336 and Straetman (n.206 above), at p.235.

214 Article 81(2) TFEU.

215 G.-R. de Groot and J.-J. Kuipers, 'The New Provisions on Private International Law in the Treaty of Lisbon' (2008) 15(1) *Maastricht Journal of International and Comparative Law* 109, at pp.111–112.

216 Although, the use of the word 'particularly' instead of, for example, 'such as', would indicate that the proper functioning of the internal market is still formally placed at the top of the hierarchy of goals which should be pursued in judicial cooperation in civil matters.

217 Fiorini (n.204 above), at p.976.

218 Tampere Conclusions (Chapter 1, n.2), at para.28; Hague Programme (n.198 above), at para 3.4.1.

uncertainty (3.3.), a lack of affinity with the law which is applied to their legal relations or proceedings (3.4.) and practical barriers to accessing justice (3.5.).

3.3. OBSTACLE I: LEGAL UNCERTAINTY

The promotion of legal certainty for EU citizens who exercise their right of free movement has been cited by the Commission as one of the main purposes behind the creation of a European judicial area.[219] The pursuit of this goal is also cited as a primary justification for EU action in the respective regulations on divorce,[220] maintenance,[221] property relations[222] and succession.[223] However, the question remains as to what exactly legal certainty actually entails. In EU documentation, there is little light shed on the definition of this principle or the specific problems relating to legal uncertainty that arise in cross-border family matters and succession.

In pursuit of elaborating upon this key goal that underlies EU legislative action in cross-border family matters and succession, the following subsections will provide a theoretical and legal background to the principle of legal certainty by discussing its origins and the relevant elements of which it is composed (3.3.1.). The specific drivers behind legal uncertainty in cross-border family matters and succession in the European Union will then be discussed in light of this conception (3.3.2.).

3.3.1. EXTRICATING THE ELEMENTS OF LEGAL CERTAINTY

The principle of legal certainty is a complex, multi-faceted concept.[224] In basic terms, it is understood as requiring that the law must be clear and predictable.[225] However, this principle is employed in a wide range of contexts and manners.

219 See European Commission, Communication from the Commission to the European Parliament, the Council, the European Economic and Social Committee and the Committee of the Regions, *Bringing legal clarity to property rights for international couples*, COM(2011) 125/3, at pp.1–3, 5–6, 8–9.

220 See Recitals 9, 15, 21, 23 and 29 of the Rome III Regulation. The Brussels II bis Regulation does not, however, mention either legal certainty or predictability.

221 See Recital 19 of the Maintenance Regulation.

222 See Recitals 15, 36, 43, 47, 49 and 72 of the Matrimonial Property Regulation and Recitals 15, 37, 42, 46, 48 and 70 of the Partnership Property Regulation.

223 See Recital 37 and 48 of the Succession Regulation.

224 J. Raitio, *The Principle of Legal Certainty in EC Law* (Kluwer, Dordrecht, 2003), at p.125.

225 J. Raitio, 'The Principle of Legal Certainty as a General Principle of EU Law' in U. Bernitz et al., *General Principles of EC Law in a Process of Development* (Kluwer, Alphen aan den Rijn, 2008), at pp.53–54.

Legal certainty underlies all areas and hierarchies of law,[226] and has been recognised as an EU general principle.[227] In this latter regard, it has been applied in a variety of settings by the European Union Court of Justice, ranging from ensuring the clarity of EU measures,[228] to supporting the full enforcement of EU law,[229] and securing unity and coherence within the EU legal order.[230]

However, despite the prevalence of its usage by the Court of Justice, the exact meaning of legal certainty remains difficult to pin down.[231] It is not defined in any of the Union's Treaties, the EU Charter of Fundamental Rights, or in secondary legislation. Given this fluid nature, its meaning can best be ascertained by reference to the principles with which it is associated.[232] The following paragraphs will therefore set out a number of the principles with which legal certainty has been closely linked.

Legal certainty can be seen to emerge as one of the components of the rule of law. This relationship will act as a starting point from which to conduct this examination into the meaning of legal certainty (3.3.1.1.). This will be followed by a discussion of two of the components of legal certainty: predictability (3.3.1.2.) and legitimate expectations (3.3.1.3.). It should be emphasised that legal certainty does encompass other aspects beyond the two listed above;[233] however, for the sake of this analysis, these are to be considered the principal elements.

---

226 J. Schwarze, *European Administrative Law*, 1st revised edn. (Sweet and Maxwell, London, 2006) at pp.868–869: 'The principle of legal certainty is widely recognised in the Member States of the Community as a general legal principle'.

227 See, for example, Case C-345/06 *Gottfried Heinrich*. Reference for a preliminary ruling: Unabhängiger Verwaltungssenat im Land Niederösterreich –Austria [2009] ECR I-1659, at para.44: individuals must be able to ascertain the content of the rights and obligations that are imposed upon them.

228 See, for example, Case 169/80 *Administration des douanes v. Société anonyme Gondrand Frères and Société anonyme Garancini*. Reference for a preliminary ruling: Cour de cassation – France [1981] ECR 1931, at paras.17–18.

229 See, for example, Case 29/84 *Commission of the European Communities v. Federal Republic of Germany* [1985] ECR 1661.

230 See, for example, Case 314/85 *Foto-Frost v. Hauptzollamt Lübeck-Ost*. Reference for a preliminary ruling: Finanzgericht Hamburg – Germany. [1987] ECR 4199, at para.15.

231 T. Tridimas, *The General Principles of EC Law* (Oxford University Press, Oxford, 1999), at p.164: 'Legal certainty is by its nature diffuse, perhaps more so than any other general principle, and its precise content is difficult to pin down' and T. Kruger, 'The Quest for Legal Certainty in International Civil Cases' in *Collected Courses of the Hague Academy of International Law, Volume 380* (Brill Nijhoff, Leiden, 2016) 281, at p.295, describing the use of the term legal certainty as 'fluid'.

232 See H. Schermers and D.F. Waelbroeck, *Judicial Protection in the European Union*, 6th edn (Kluwer, The Hague, 2001), at pp.64–87.

233 See Kruger (n.231 above), at p.297: 'accessibility of legal rules, general nature, clarity, transparency, rationality, publication, time limitations, expectations of the parties, predictability, foreseeability, the protection of vested rights, the protection of legitimate expectations, non-retroactivity, doctrinal uniformity among courts, simplicity'.

3.3.1.1. *The Rule of Law*

The rule of law, much like legal certainty, is by its nature as an underlying legal principle, difficult to succinctly describe.[234] In general terms, it comprises a raft of different elements that serve to guard against arbitrary rule and limit the use of power by those who govern.[235] It is a principle that is present, in a variety of manifestations, in all European legal systems.[236]

There is no decisive list of the elements of which the rule of law is said to be composed: however, recurring themes include legal certainty, as well as the legality principle, equality of all individuals before the law, and adherence to substantive and procedural standards of justice (e.g. the right to an effective remedy and the right to a fair trial).[237]

Lord Diplock expressed the direct association between the rule of law and legal certainty in the English case *Black Clawson Ltd. v. Papierwerke AG*, in which he stated that

> the acceptance of the rule of law as a constitutional principle requires that a citizen, before committing himself to any course of action, should be able to know in advance what are the legal consequences which flow from it.[238]

This assertion strikes at the very heart of the rationale underlying the principle of legal certainty: the belief that a person should be armed with prior knowledge of the law and its consequences in order to plan his or her actions accordingly.

3.3.1.2. *Securing a Predictable Outcome*

EU documentation frequently cites the furtherance of *predictability* alongside *legal certainty* as underlying rationales for legislative action in the fields of cross-border family matters and succession. These concepts appear often at times to be so closely associated that the question may be raised as to whether the two are in fact interchangeable.[239] However, despite the fact that the relationship and

234 Raitio (n.224 above), at p.134.

235 Parliamentary Assembly of the Council of Europe, *Report: The Principle of the Rule of Law*, Doc.11343 (2007), at para.5.

236 See discussion of the British conception of the *rule of law* versus the German *Rechtsstaat* and the French *Etat de droit* in the Report, ibid., at Appendix I, Section I.

237 See the Report, ibid., at para.12; I. Brownlie, *The Rule of Law in International Affairs. International Law at the Fiftieth Anniversary of the United Nations* (Martinus Nijhoff Publishers, The Hague/London/Boston MA, 1998), at pp.213–214; and A.V. Dicey, *Introduction to the Study of the Law and the Constitution* (Macmillan Press, London, 1959), at ch.4.

238 *Black-Clawson International Ltd v Papierwerke Waldhof Aschaffenburg* [1975] AC 591, at p. 638.

239 It could, however, be questioned whether the Commission intended a deep meaning to be construed from the position of terminology: given the multiple times in which legal certainty

distinction between these two terms are not well delineated in the texts,[240] they are nevertheless to be treated as two separate entities, with predictability as an (albeit dominant) component of legal certainty.

It has been stated that predictability involves the requirement that 'the law must be clear, stable and understandable, allow parties to ascertain, with relative accuracy, the legal consequences of their actions and the outcome of legal proceedings.[241] Within the wider context of legal theory, it has been suggested that predictability falls into the category of formal (or objective) legal certainty,[242] whereby the parties can determine the possible outcomes of their actions.[243] However, at the same time, it has also been argued that predictability also comes within the scope of subjective legal certainty, since it also concerns the ability of parties to gauge their own individual legal outcomes from the rules provided.[244]

3.3.1.3. The Protection of Legitimate Expectations

The second element of legal certainty that is to be employed here – the protection of legitimate expectations – has been well developed by the case law of the Court of Justice,[245] as well as utilised to varying degrees in the Member State jurisdictions.[246] It serves to safeguard certain expectations that the law has created. To draw upon Lord Diplock's assertion in the *Black-Clawson Ltd.* case: where parties have planned their actions according to legal rules, they should not suffer as a result of the disappointment of these expectations.[247] In contrast to predictability, by concentrating on the impact that the observation of the law has had upon the parties, this element clearly veers towards the subjective conceptualisation of legal certainty.

---

and predictability are used in the texts without further elaboration, it could be argued that these terms primarily function as rhetorical devices in the documentation.

240 For example, Recital 21 of the Rome III Regulation states that harmonised conflict of laws rules should be introduced 'with a view to guaranteeing legal certainty and predictability' (emphasis added), whilst Recital 15 of the Property Regulations establishes that its rules should be covered by a single instrument in order to provide couples with 'legal certainty as to their property and offer them a degree of predictability'.

241 E. Paunio, 'Beyond Predictability – Reflections on Legal Certainty and the Discourse Theory of Law in the EU Legal Order' (2009) 10(11) *German Law Journal* 1469, at p.1469.

242 As opposed to *factual* or *subjective* legal certainty (see 3.3.1.3. below). See Raitio (n.224 above), at pp.372–376.

243 Kruger (n.231 above), at p.297.

244 Ibid., at pp.300–301.

245 See case law discussed at nn.248–250 below.

246 See, with specific regard to administrative and constitutional law, Schwarze (n.226 above), at ch.6, particularly pp.869–870. In these fields, the protection of legitimate expectations finds its most clear expression in German and Dutch law, but exists in the law of many other Member States, such as Italy, Belgium and the United Kingdom.

247 Raitio (n.225 above), at p.54.

In the European Union setting, the protection of legitimate expectations has several applications, but primarily concerns the limitation placed upon both the retroactive application of the law,[248] and the immediate application of the law to pre-existing legal relationships or processes.[249] It also serves to safeguard certain expectations arising from prior legislation.[250]

This principle can therefore be seen to extend legal certainty backwards through time, safeguarding expectations created through the making of an administrative or judicial decision, or the attribution of a particular right or status. In this way, it applies even where a new set of rules establishes clear and foreseeable outcomes; in such situations, a right or status legitimately acquired under a former set of rules may nevertheless merit recognition.

The protection of legitimate expectations has been distinguished from legal certainty proper by some commentators in a temporal sense:[251] whilst a strict interpretation of legal certainty requires that the rules which apply *at a given time* must be clear and precise, the protection of legitimate expectation denotes that the authorities must exercise their powers over a period of time to ensure that the relationships which are created through the law are not affected in a way 'which could not be foreseen by a diligent person'.[252]

However, moving beyond this rather stringent construction, this protection can be seen to reflect a more flexible approach to legal certainty. As discussed in the previous subsection, predictability is the factual manifestation of legal certainty. In contrast, the protection of legitimate expectations is more subjective in nature, with ascertainment of legitimacy dependent on context and circumstance.[253]

---

248 See, for example, Case 232/81 *Agricola commerciale olio Srl and others v. Commission of the European Communities* [1984] ECR 3881 and Case 264/81 *SpA Savma v. Commission of the European Communities* [1984] ECR 3915.

249 See, for example, Case T-472/93 *Campo Ebro Industrial and Others v. Council* [1995] ECR II-421, at para.42.

250 See, for example, the milk quota cases: Case 120/86 *J. Mulder v. Minister van Landbouw en Visserij*. Reference for a preliminary ruling: College van Beroep voor het Bedrijfsleven – Netherlands [1988] ECR 2321, at para.23 and Case C-189/89 *Karl Spagl v. Hauptzollamt Rosenheim*. Reference for a preliminary ruling: Finanzgericht München – Germany [1990] ECR I-4539, at para.28.

251 Tridimas (n.231 above), at p.170 and H. Schermers and D.F. Waelbroeck, *Judicial Protection in the European Union*, 6th edn. (Kluwer, The Hague, 2001), at p.80.

252 See Opinion of AG Cosmas in Case C-63/93 *Duff and Others v. Minister for Agriculture and Food, Ireland, and the Attorney General* [1996] ECR I-572, at para.25. For further discussion see Tridimas (n.231 above), at p.170.

253 This protection is based on ensuring the stability of the law in light of real circumstances: it is coined by Raitio as 'factual' legal certainty (in contrast to the 'formal' legal certainty associated with predictability). See Raitio (n.224 above), at pp.372–376.

It should be emphasised that not all expectations can be viewed as legitimate: an expectation will not be classed as such unless it is reasonable. It must be ascertained whether, given the circumstances, a prudent person would have held such an expectation.[254] Furthermore, even if an expectation is seen as legitimate, this protection is not absolute: it must be balanced against overriding public interest considerations[255] (e.g. pressing economic reasons[256]).

Particular protection is attributed to the related concept of *vested* or *acquired* rights – a status, benefit or right conferred upon an individual.[257] The protection accorded to the expectations arising from such rights is much more absolute because of the specific nature of their conferral.[258] The propensity for the frustration of such entrenched expectations in the current context will be outlined later on in this section (see 3.3.2.4.).

3.3.2. SOURCES OF LEGAL UNCERTAINTY IN EU CROSS-BORDER FAMILY MATTERS AND SUCCESSION

The above subsections have established a framework for understanding the concept of legal certainty. Turning now to place this in context, the question arises: what forms of legal uncertainty are faced by those involved in cross-border family or succession matters? The European Commission has drawn

---

254 Joined Cases 95 to 98/74, 15 and 100/75 *Union nationale des coopératives agricoles de céréales and others v. Commission and Council of the European Communities* [1975] ECR 1615 and Case 78/77 *Johann Lührs v. Hauptzollamt Hamburg-Jonas*. Reference for a preliminary ruling: Finanzgericht Hamburg – Germany [1978] ECR 169. See also for commentary: T.C. Hartley, *The Foundations of European Union Law*, 7th edn. (Oxford University Press, Oxford, 2010), at p.163.

255 See, for example, Case 78/77 *Johann Lührs v. Hauptzollamt Hamburg-Jonas*. Reference for a preliminary ruling: Finanzgericht Hamburg – Germany [1978] ECR 177, at para. 6. See also: Case 98/78 *A. Racke GmbH & Co. v. Hauptzollamt Mainz*. Reference for a preliminary ruling: Bundesfinanzhof – Germany [1979] ECR 69, at para.20: 'Although in general the principle of legal certainty precludes a community measure from taking effect from a point in time before its publication, it may exceptionally be otherwise where the purpose to be achieved so demands and where the legitimate expectations of those concerned are duly respected'.

256 See, for example, C-37/70 *Rewe-Zentrale des Lebensmittel-Großhandels GmbH v. Hauptzollamt Emmerich*. Reference for a preliminary ruling: Finanzgericht Düsseldorf – Germany [1971] ECR 36, at paras.15–16.

257 For reason of their similar nature, the concepts of vested rights and the protection of legitimate expectations are frequently confused. However, the principle of legitimate expectation should only be brought into play when vested rights cannot be identified (since the protection afforded to vested rights is more absolute). See J. Mertens de Wilmars, 'The Case-law of the Court of Justice in relation to the review of the legality of economic policy in mixed-economy systems' (1982) 9 *Legal Issues of European Integration* 1, at pp.15–16.

258 See ibid., pp.15–16.

heavily upon the enhancement of legal certainty in order to justify the adoption of measures in the field of private international law concerning family matters and succession.[259] However, it may not be immediately apparent how uncertainty arises in cross-border family matters and succession. The following subsections seek to shed light on a number of drivers behind legal uncertainty in this regard.

These sources of legal uncertainty for those in cross-border family matters and succession can be divided into four layers, which can be seen to range from outwardly appreciable (3.3.2.1.) to highly subjective (3.3.2.4.).

3.3.2.1. The Complexity of the Private International Law Framework

The outermost layer of legal uncertainty for those involved in cross-border family and succession matters involves the lack of predictability that arises as a result of the complexity of the private international law framework.

This complexity can be seen to emerge from the multiplicity of legal sources that exist amongst the EU Member States. The various countries each have their own private international law rules, that not only vary in terms of the grounds through which the jurisdiction can be seised,[260] but also in the content of their conflict-of-laws rules[261] (e.g. differences can be seen in the connecting factors that are provided for[262] and their respective approaches to *renvoi*[263]). This, alongside a piecemeal ratification of Hague Conference instruments,[264] creates a fragmentary framework that even private international law specialists may find

259 See, for example, the Communication from the Commission to the European Parliament, the Council, the European Economic and Social Committee and the Committee of the Regions: 'Bringing legal clarity to property rights for international couples', COM(2011) 125/3, at pp.1–3, 5–6, 8–9; Recital 21 of the Rome III Regulation, which states that harmonised conflict-of-laws rules should be introduced 'with a view to guaranteeing legal certainty and predictability'; and Recital 19 of the Maintenance Regulation: 'In order to increase legal certainty, predictability … this Regulation should enable the parties to choose the competent court by agreement'.

260 See elaboration of this problem in the area of cross-border matrimonial property in European Policy Evaluation Consortium, *Impact Assessment on Community Instruments concerning matrimonial property regimes and property of unmarried couples with transnational elements* (EPEC, 2009), at pp.91–92.

261 See discussion of divergent development in conflict of laws connections in Basedow (Chapter 1, n.46), at pp.233–235, paras.382–383.

262 For instance, compare the first connecting factors for determining the law applicable to divorce under Estonian and Lithuanian conflict-of-laws rules (common residence and domicile respectively) with Portugal and Spain (common nationality). For a full overview of Member States' connecting factors in this area (circa 2006) see European Policy Evaluation Consortium, *Study to inform a subsequent Impact Assessment on the Commission proposal on jurisdiction and applicable law on divorce matters* (EPEC, 2006), at p.45.

263 See the example regarding the impact of differing national approaches towards *renvoi* upon the determination of applicable law: Box 2.8. in EPEC (n.260 above), at p.98.

264 See, for example, the 1978 Hague Convention on the Law Applicable to Matrimonial Property Regimes, which was only ratified by France, Luxembourg and the Netherlands.

hard to navigate.[265] As established in the last subsection, legal certainty requires that the law be understandable, so that its consequences can be ascertained with a relative degree of accuracy.

The complexity of the private international law framework can be seen to form the *superficial* layer of uncertainty in cross-border family and succession relations, since it involves the problems that are likely to be faced by parties upon first encountering such rules, and are easily appreciable to those on the outside.

3.3.2.2. *The Indefinite Nature of the Private International Law Framework*

The second layer of uncertainty steps beyond the difficulties experienced in striving to understand the complex private international law framework, by concentrating upon the uncertainty that is intrinsic to the functioning of the private international law rules themselves.

Firstly, uncertainty may arise from the availability of multiple fora to be seised by parties within the private international law framework. Although the existence of alternative jurisdictions can be seen to increase access to justice,[266] it also holds the potential for a 'rush to court', whereby the parties in a dispute (e.g. divorce) may compete to seise the jurisdiction which best caters towards their individual needs.[267] This element of competition means that the ultimate forum that will decide the case will be hard to predict until the 'race' is won.[268]

Secondly, the outcome of the private international law rules might be indefinite for the parties involved. Such rules may only assess the connecting factor at the time of proceedings (e.g. the law of the habitual residence of the parties *at the time the court is seised*). Parties therefore are not able to definitively ascertain the legal system which will apply to their relationships(s) until the proceedings have actually been instigated. This lack of predictability may especially impact upon those who frequently make use of their free movement rights, since it could be very hard for such people to pinpoint in which country they will be habitually resident when future proceedings begin.

---

265 T.M.C. Asser Institute, *Étude sur les régimes matrimoniaux des couples mariés et sur le patrimoine des couples non mariés dans le droit international privé et le droit interne des États membres de l'Union Européenne: Analyse comparative des rapports nationaux et propositions d'harmonisation* (2003), at p.32, para.1.2.1.4. See also: Kruger (n.231 above), at p.303.

266 A choice of multiple jurisdictions may offer the parties a greater possibility to seise a court that is most convenient to them.

267 EPEC (n.262 above), at p.7, para.1.4.

268 I. Viarengo and F.C. Villata (eds.), 'Final Study' in Università degli Studi di Milano et al., (eds.), *Planning the future of cross-border families: a path through coordination* (2017), at pp.130–132, available at: http://www.eufams.unimi.it/wp-content/uploads/2017/12/EUFams-Final-Study-v1.0.pdf.

3.3.2.3. *Expectations that have Arisen under a Previously Applicable Legal System*

The third layer of uncertainty concerns the potential for the frustration of expectations connected to decision-making that has taken place under a previously applicable legal system. As parties move throughout the European Union, differences between Member States' private international law rules[269] along with changes in their own circumstances (e.g. a new habitual residence), may equate to a shift in the legal regime that governs their relationships or legal processes.

Each respective set of national private international law rules can be seen to create an expectation concerning the law and jurisdiction that will be applied to a relationship. This expectation helps shape the way in which the parties organise their lives (e.g. the knowledge of the applicable law in the event of divorce and the division of matrimonial property may influence the manner in which they organise their finances). However, when a new legal regime becomes applicable, this can entail the application of rules that the parties had not anticipated in their prior decision-making regarding the organisation of their relationship. It may not even have been clear to the parties that their situation merited a shift in legal regime in the first place.[270]

As has been discussed, the principle of legal certainty denotes that those subject to the law must be able to know what the law is so they are able to plan their actions.[271] To draw once more upon Lord Diplock: 'a citizen, before committing himself to any course of action, should be able to know in advance what are the legal consequences which flow from it'.[272] In line with this, legal uncertainty not only emerges from the mere inability to ascertain an outcome upon being presented with a set of rules, but also from the frustration of expectations built around a previously applicable legal system.[273]

Unanticipated changes in legal systems may be particularly detrimental in matters relating to family and succession, since such relationships are not

---

269 For instance, a couple who share a nationality would have the law of that common nationality applied to a divorce by Spanish courts but, if they moved to Estonia, would instead have the law of their habitual residence govern. See Table 6.7. in EPEC (n.262), at p.45, para.6.2.1.

270 The internationality of a party's situation may take them by surprise: see discussion in Utrecht University and University of Vienna, 'Moving to Another Country in the EU? This is what you need to know about the legal implications for your family', *Empowering European Families* (2019), available at: https://www.europeanlawinstitute.eu/fileadmin/user_upload/p_eli/Projects/EEF/EEF_Information_Sheet_for_Couples.pdf.

271 Tridimas (n.231 above), at p.163.

272 Black-Clawson (n.238 above), at p.638.

273 See, in this regard, Th. de Boer, 'The Purpose of Uniform Choice-of-law Rules' (2009) 56(3) *Netherlands International Law Review* 295, at pp.304–305: 'Any uniform choice-of-law rule, however unsophisticated, will allow the parties to know with certainty which law will be applicable and to predict the outcome of litigation. But it may not provide the *equitable* solution the parties have a right to expect' (at p. 305).

one-off occurrences; they are long-term undertakings through which legal decisions that are made in the past are designed to bind the present. This is particularly the case with matrimonial property or the property consequences of registered partnerships, since such relationships encompass transactions (e.g. the disposal of property by one of the parties) that may have taken place many years previously, under an entirely different legal system. Should the property regime subsequently become subject to a connecting factor that casts a new law over the entirety of the relationship, this can understandably be seen as an affront to the legitimate expectations of the parties involved.[274]

As discussed above, in order for an expectation to be classed as legitimate, it has to be reasonable. Frustration of an expectation should not be capable of being foreseen by a prudent party. It could be argued that cross-border parties, having taken the conscious step to leave one country for another, ought to have a certain degree of foresight regarding the application of a new set of private international law rules upon their relations. However, family relationships are usually long-running ventures, and it may, in many instances, not be apparent during the course of the relationship that the parties will exercise their right to free movement. Furthermore, if the Union is to be regarded as a single common area of justice,[275] the question of which country created the expectation is of less relevance to ascertaining its reasonableness. It could therefore be argued that legitimate expectations created in one jurisdiction should be accorded protection regardless of the movements of parties between Member State borders.

This third level of uncertainty, dependent on the individual circumstances and knowledge of the parties, can be seen to be more subjective in nature than the previous two types discussed above. In this way, although it holds the potential to be highly detrimental, it is less susceptive to appreciation by those outside the relationship.

3.3.2.4. *Entrenched Expectations as to the Effects of a Relationship*

Finally, there is the inner core of legal uncertainty, which represents the entrenched expectations that the parties carry across borders concerning the legal effects of a relationship. Although parties, after moving between Member States, may know that their relationship is subject to the rules of a new legal system, they could nevertheless presume that certain key aspects of their relationship will be upheld regardless of their movements. This could be because they are unaware of the (at times significant) substantive differences that

274 See examples of mutable connecting factors cited by Basedow in the national private international law rules concerning property relations in Slovenia, Bulgaria, Italy, Romania and Poland: Basedow (Chapter 1, n.46), at pp.288–289, para.388.

275 In accordance with the creation of the Area of Freedom, Security and Justice. See Tampere Conclusions (Chapter 1, n.2), at para.28.

exist between the Member States' family and succession laws.[276] For instance, spouses might hold the (erroneous) belief that the community of matrimonial property regime that was previously applicable under Dutch law would be taken into account in the dissolution of their property regime by the Irish courts.[277] Although expectations may lose their foundation due to the movement of the parties from one jurisdiction to another,[278] they may continue to shape their relationship according to these beliefs.[279]

Certain Member State jurisdictions have attempted to mitigate the frustration of such entrenched expectations by giving effect to the good-faith intentions of parties under the concept of 'acting under the wrong law' (*Handeln unter falschem Recht*). This comes into play in circumstances in which a party holds the good faith assumption that the law of Country A is applicable to a particular proceeding, when in fact it is the law of Country B which governs it. In order to remedy the frustration of the expectations of the party based on this mistaken belief, the court may attempt to interpret the law of Country A and translate it into the law of Country B in order to give effect to the party's intentions.[280]

---

276 Alongside the example below in the text, the reader can look to the restrictive divorce laws found in Poland or Ireland that bear little resemblance to the liberal, 'fast-track' manner of marriage dissolution in the Nordic states: EPEC, *Study to inform a subsequent Impact Assessment on the Commission proposal on jurisdiction and applicable law on divorce matters* (n.262 above), at p.6, para.1.4. and Table 6.2., at p.37, para.6.3.1. In succession law, divergence can be seen between the Member States, for example, in terms of the size of the share of the estate given to family members, and the possibility of a compulsory share of the estate for close family members: European Commission, Commission staff working document accompanying the Proposal for a Regulation of the European Parliament and the Council on jurisdiction, applicable law, recognition and enforcement of decisions and authentic instruments in matters of succession on the introduction of a European Certificate of Inheritance: Impact Assessment, Sec(2009) 153, at: https://eur-lex.europa.eu/legal-content/EN/TXT/?uri=CELEX:52009SC0153, at p.9.

277 The Irish courts apply the *lex fori* to the distribution of a couple's property, and the law does not allow for the possibility to choose a matrimonial property regime: Couples in Europe, *Republic of Ireland: Which law applies?* Available at: http://www.coupleseurope.eu/en/ireland/topics/1-which-law-applies.

278 For more discussion of the loss or change of legal position across borders see: N. Dethloff, 'Arguments for the Unification and Harmonisation of Family Law in Europe' in K. Boele-Woelki (ed.), *Perspectives for the Unification and Harmonisation of Family Law in Europe* (Intensentia, Antwerp, 2003), at pp.43–50.

279 This subtly contrasts with the scenarios discussed in 3.2.2.3. above, in which a legitimate expectation arises due to a decision that was made in the past based upon the rule of a legal system which was applicable at that time.

280 In situations in which a person appears to have acted, in good faith, in accordance with the 'wrong' law that they perceive to be applicable, the German courts have attempted to take the putative law into account in applying the actually applicable law. See, for analysis of *Handeln unter falschem Recht* in family matters and succession: Nagy (Chapter 2, n.101), at pp.580–581 and E. Jayme, 'Party Autonomy in International Family and Succession Law: New Tendencies' (2009) 11 *Yearbook of Private International Law* 1, at pp.5–7. See also the Dutch approach to parties who, in good faith, erroneously assume the wrong law is applicable to their relationship. In that jurisdiction, the 'conflicts approach' is used in cases where the parties

Parties may also maintain faith in the continuity of their relationship and its effects on the basis that this is a fundamental status that has been bestowed upon them (e.g. marriage or registered partnership). However, given the highly fragmentary recognition of same-sex marriage and registered partnership amongst the Member States,[281] such beliefs are particularly susceptible to frustration.

These entrenched expectations arguably carry greater weight because they are derived from statuses or rights that have been conferred upon the parties in a previously applicable legal system. In the context of private international law, a number of authorities have postulated in favour of the sustainability of vested rights across borders.[282] In this regard, Dicey opined that rights that have been duly acquired in a foreign civilised system should be recognised and, in general, enforced, by the (English) courts,[283] whilst *Pillet* proposed that rights acquired in one sovereign state should be enforceable in another as a corollary of mutual respect between nations.[284]

A regard for vested rights has recently been seen to emerge in the EU private international law setting. In the conflict of laws context, the protection of vested rights imposes a duty on a state to accommodate foreign rights in its own legal system.[285] As discussed in the previous chapter,[286] vested rights appear to have been recognised by the EU Court of Justice in company law[287] and name law.[288] In the latter instance, non-recognition of a surname acquired under a foreign law was seen as constituting a barrier to the freedom of every citizen of the Union to move and reside in the territory of the Member States.

have behaved as though another law is applicable to their relationship (Zimbabwe-arrest, Hoge Raad, 19 maart 1993, NJ 1994, 187, LJN ZC0897). The Dutch court applies the conflicts rules of the putatively applicable law in order to remedy the frustration of expectations. This approach is now codified under the *fait accompli* exception: Burgerlijk Wetboek 10:9.

281 As of 2019, same-sex marriage is provided for in 14 out of the 28 Member States, and registered partnership is established in 21 Member States (although some of these Member States, such as Sweden and Denmark, no longer pronounce new registered partnerships following same-sex marriage being introduced). See overview of Member States in: European Commission, *Property of International Couples (Marriages and Registered Partnerships)*, available at: https://ec.europa.eu/info/policies/justice-and-fundamental-rights/civil-justice/family-law/property-international-couples-marriages-and-registered-partnerships_en#registeredpartnership.

282 For further discussion of this topic see G. Kaeckenbeeck, 'The protection of vested rights in international law' (1936) 17 *British Yearbook of International Law* 1, at pp.5–8.

283 A.V. Dicey, *Conflict of Laws*, 5th edn (Sweet and Maxwell, London, 1932), at p.17.

284 A. Pillet, *Principes de Droit International privé* (Perdone, Paris, 1903) at p.515, para.284.

285 J.-J. Kuipers, *EU Law and Private International Law: The Interrelationship in Contractual Obligations* (Martinus, Nijhoff Publishers, Leiden/Boston MA, 2012), at p.306.

286 See 2.3.2.

287 See, for example, *Centros* (Chapter 2, n.129) and *Inspire Art* (Chapter 2, n.131).

288 See *Garcia Avello* (Chapter 2, n.139) and *Grunkin-Paul* (Chapter 2, n.144). For further discussion, see Kuipers (n.285 above), at p.306.

In view of such judgments, it has been suggested that the entrenched concept of civil status may also merit protection as a vested right.[289] Along this line of argumentation, the expectation of same-sex spouses as to the continued validity of their marriage,[290] or the belief of registered partners concerning the original characterisation of their relationship,[291] may be seen as particularly vindicated.

There ought, however, to be a degree of caution when interpreting the concept of legitimate expectations in the field of family relationships. In order for expectations to be legitimate, they should be based on situations that have at least existed at one time, and are capable of verification.[292] In commercial relations, since parties are likely to found their expectations upon inspection of relevant legal provisions and information, their subsequent conduct based on these expectations is well vindicated.[293] In contrast, in the context of family relationships, the parties are less likely to seek expert legal advice and information without a specific purpose (e.g. for the arrangement of a legal relationship). It is not that legal advice is needed in order for expectations to be vindicated; it is, however, necessary that entrenched expectations were based on actual knowledge of the rules that were once applicable.

This inner layer of uncertainty is the most subjective, since continued beliefs that lack a present foundation may be very difficult for others to appreciate. However, the ingrained nature of such expectations holds the potential to be most damaging, since the parties themselves are unaware of their erroneous nature, and therefore little can be done in advance to correct this.

3.4. OBSTACLE II: LACK OF AFFINITY WITH THE APPLICABLE LAW

Upon exercising the right to free movement within the Union, relationships and property may become, through the application of conflict of laws and jurisdictional rules, subject to shifts in legal regime. As has been discussed above in 3.3., such changes can result in considerable legal uncertainty for parties, particularly in terms of the frustration of legitimate expectations.

---

289 Kuipers (n.285 above), at p.310.

290 For example, it would not be possible for a same-sex couple to have their marriage dissolved by the Polish courts. Thus so-called 'limping relationships' may emerge.

291 P. Wautelet, 'Private International Law Aspects of Same-sex Marriages and Partnerships in Europe' in K. Boele-Woelki and A. Fuchs (eds.), *Legal Recognition of Same-sex Relationships in Europe*, 2nd edn. (Intersentia, Antwerp, 2012) at p.36.

292 A. Shapira, 'Territorialism, National Parochialism, Universalism and Party Autonomy: How Does One Square the Choice-of-law Circle?' (2000) 26(1) *Brooklyn Journal of International Law* 199, at p.203.

293 Ibid., at pp.203–204.

Beyond this, moving between EU Member States may also give rise to the application of a law that does not reflect an individual's life circumstances and/or relationships, and the expectations that rise therefrom. In light of this, the EU legislator, in seeking to unify private international law rules on cross-border family matters and succession, pursues the aim of ensuring that a law of 'close connection' applies to proceedings concerning family matter or succession.[294]

The following subsection will first set out a number of considerations that play a role in the forming of an affinity with a particular legal system (3.4.1.). After this, the problems that those who move within the European Union may face in aligning their relationships with a legal system of close connection will be explored (3.4.2.).

3.4.1. THE COMPONENTS OF CLOSE CONNECTION

As parties move throughout the Union, the law that applies to their family relationships or property may be seen to shift from one legal system to another. In this way, a legal connection is made between the parties and the new applicable law. However, the mere existence of a legal connection is not the same as an affinity with a legal system. This latter concept represents the actual ties that bind parties with a particular state's legal system.

The forming of affinity with a national legal system is based on a number of considerations – familiarity with the law of a state and entrenched expectations that arise in this regard, as well integration in the society and the holding of shared values with the state in question. Accordingly, legal expectations may be based upon the knowledge and acceptance of the rules that are used in the particular Member State, and/or the principles that the state and its laws reflect.

Given the strong link between the society within a country, its values, and the nature of its family or succession law, the existence of affinity can be viewed as more important in the family or succession law setting than in other areas of private international law (e.g. contractual obligations). These are areas that strike at the heart of personal values, and the law that applies ought to reflect these values accordingly.

The considerations involved in forming such an affinity (*knowledge of the law*, *entrenched expectations*, *integration in society* and *shared values*) may be based on a particular state and its law – either the state in which their everyday

[294] This aim is pursued both with regard to the provisions relating to party autonomy, and those which apply in the absence of choice. See Recital 14 of the Rome III Regulation, Recitals 23–25 of the Succession Regulation, Recitals 43, 45 and 49 of the Matrimonial Property Regulation and Recitals 42, 44 and 48 of the Partnership Property Regulation. A similar goal is also pursued with regard to contractual obligations: see Recital 21 of the Rome I Regulation.

life is situated, or where their culture and/or origins originate. In addition to this *personal affinity*, there is also another type of connection – *situational affinity* – that can be seen to link a particular relationship or property (rather than the parties themselves), to a certain legal system.[295]

From the outset, it should be noted that when looking at the general population, the place where a person lives is, on the balance of probabilities, likely to be the place they identify with in terms of origin and culture, and where their relationships are concentrated. However, this analysis is focused on those persons with cross-border aspects to their relationships. As such, this means that their affinities have a higher likelihood of being split between Member States, with one connection being significantly stronger than the other(s) (e.g. a person may have stronger ties with the place in which their everyday life is situated than where their culture originates from).

The creation of one tie does not extinguish the other(s); there is a possibility that parties may enjoy a close connection with a number of Member States. Furthermore, it may be the case that a person holds affinities with different states depending on the relationship in question (e.g. they may hold a strong tie with France for the purposes of their marriage, but retain an entrenched link with Spain, where their property is located, for the purposes of succession).

3.4.1.1. *Everyday Life*

It has been stated that a person tends to live according to the rules that exist within his or her environment.[296] However, the question arises: how is such an environment to be defined? The first answer to this would probably be the place where a person lives on a regular basis. This is where his or her family ties, property and work are likely to be located – it is the epicentre of their everyday life.

Accordingly, the law of the place where a party's everyday life is concentrated sets out the rules that they are most likely to interact with on an everyday basis. Knowledge of these rules will have a bearing upon the making of legal arrangements, such as (where applicable) the type of matrimonial property regime selected by spouses, and manner in which assets are allocated in a will. Such knowledge will also create entrenched expectations as to the validity and consequences of relationships.

---

295 This distinction is similar to the juridical indicators cited by S. Peari, 'The Choice-Based Perspective of Choice-of-Law' (2013) 43 *Duke Journal of Comparative & International Law* 477, at p.489. In this article the author sets *territorial* indicators (e.g. place of transaction) apart from *personality* indicators (e.g. nationality or the place of business).

296 D. Martiny, 'Objectives and Values of EU Private International Law in Family Law' in J. Meeusen et al. (eds.), *International Family Law for the European Union* (Intersentia, Antwerp, 2007), at p.85.

Furthermore, it can be perceived that a legal system usually arises organically from the society that it serves (e.g. a very liberal society, such as Sweden, gives rise to a liberal family law, and vice-versa). Thus, if the parties identify with the values of the society in which they live, they are more likely to accept the consequences of that legal system. In this way, parties not only base their expectations merely on being subject to the rules that the legal system produces, but also on the values that they themselves hold, and which the legal system reflects.

3.4.1.2. Origin and Culture

The state in which everyday life is concentrated may, in certain instances, not be the main influence upon the way in which parties lead their lives and base their legal expectations. Instead, the legal rules, and societal norms, of the state from which they originate, or have family ties, could have a decisive influence upon their expectations concerning the consequences of relationships.[297]

Take, for example, Northern European expats who retire to live in the warmer climate of the south of Spain. Such persons, although they now live on Spanish soil, may actually integrate most fully within the sizeable expat community of their compatriots. In this way, their relocation could change little in terms of their values and expectations of their relationships: their 'environment' remains largely influenced by the place from which they originate.

The influence of origins and culture may be particularly apparent where there is a significant divergence between the laws, values and beliefs of the state of origin or familiar links, and the state in which the parties live. For instance, parties originating from a state with a religious or conservative culture (e.g. Poland or Ireland) may retain the belief that divorce should be a long-winded procedure, long after they have moved to a more liberal jurisdiction.

3.4.1.3. Situational Affinity

Moving beyond considerations relating to the personal ties of the parties, it can be seen that, in certain circumstances, a source of affinity might emerge from the embedding of a particular relationship or asset in a certain country. This is based on the rationale that, since the law of this country gave rise to the status and effects of the relationship or asset in question, this state's legal system has a decisive influence upon the expectations that parties attach to the relationship or property in question.

One example would be the place in which a relationship was legally created (celebrated or registered). Since the relationship was created from the law of that

297 Ibid., at p.85.

state, it can be presumed that there is a complementary legal framework set up around the relationship in question. Application of the law of this legal system would help avoid situations where certain consequences of the relationship are 'lost in translation'. This benefit is particularly relevant to situations in which a relationship is not universally recognised throughout the Union (most prominently, same-sex marriage and registered partnership).

Another example of such a tie could be found where the property consequences that emanate from a particular relationship (e.g. matrimonial property or a person's own estate) are located. Arguably, given the long-term nature of property relations, having the state where the assets are located apply its own law to proceedings would serve to meet the expectations of those involved (e.g. not only the owners, but also third parties and beneficiaries).

It could be argued that the latter two determinants (*integration in society* and *shared values*) do not play a role in establishing situational affinity. Whilst these considerations are certainly of less relevance than they are to personal affinity, the role of such determinants cannot be excluded with regard to ties based on the attribution of certain fundamental statuses. If a couple is permitted to get married or register their partnership in a certain jurisdiction, this can be viewed as societal acceptance of the formalisation of their relationship.

3.4.2. DIFFICULTY IN SECURING A LAW OF CLOSE CONNECTION

Traditionally, Member States' conflict-of-laws rules have been designed to direct a relationship towards a particular legal system, based on the legislator's perception of where the relationship is most likely to be closely connected to. However, there is no uniform consensus amongst the jurisdictions as to what should be the dominant link in establishing close connection for those who cross borders in the European Union. For instance, whilst some Member States place an emphasis on the origins of the parties, others concentrate on their everyday environment.[298] Furthermore, there are some jurisdictions that instead tend towards applying the *lex fori* when their courts are seised to govern proceedings concerning family matters or succession.[299]

---

298 In a study of 14 Member States that apply a hierarchy of objective connecting factors, it was found that the first connecting factor was common nationality for 12 out of the 14 Member States, whilst two applied habitual residence or domicile. However, after this point, the differences became much more stark, with a wide variety of approaches being used to connect the relationship with a jurisdiction (e,g. *lex fori*, cumulative application of the laws of nationality, common habitual residence, etc.). See Table 6.7. in EPEC (n.262 above), at p.45, para.6.2.1.

299 For example, in divorce proceedings, the UK, Ireland, Cyprus, Malta, Denmark, Sweden, Finland, Latvia, and Slovakia apply the *lex fori*. See Annex 2 of European Commission,

Above all, the real problem lies in the fact that connecting factors contained in the conflict-of-laws rules tend to be composed on an objective, hierarchical basis that captures the state of play at a moment in time (e.g. common nationality at the time a court is seised or, failing that, their last common habitual residence at the time a court is seised, etc.[300]). This results in a one-size-fits-all approach to adjudging connection that permits little flexibility.[301]

At the same time, affinity in cross-border situations is hard to ascertain. As stated previously, the affinities held by those who do not cross borders are likely to remain within their state of origin. However, upon exercising their right to free movement within the Union, a party's ties are more likely to diverge (e.g. they may live in one Member State, have cultural ties to another and, perhaps, even hold property somewhere else). Depending upon the level of integration, a party may not hold the same level of affinity with one state as with the other (e.g. they could be considerably more integrated in the state of origin than the state where their everyday life takes place). Further, affinity may remain with a place long after objective ties have been extinguished (e.g. if a party lives in a location for many years, only to subsequently move on).

The rigid nature of objective conflict-of-laws rules does not lend itself to tackling these nuances. The complex nature of cross-border situations means that affinity can only be truly ascertained on an individual basis (since integration and values are, by their very nature, subjective). Furthermore, since such objective rules usually base their ascertainment upon the 'state of affairs' at a particular point in time (e.g. the moment when a court is seised of proceedings), they fail to take into account the longevity and depth of connections, past and present.

3.5. OBSTACLE III: PRACTICAL HINDRANCES TO ACCESSING JUSTICE

The primary goal of the development of the area of freedom, security and justice is to make everyday life simpler for persons who exercise their right to free movement within the Union.[302] As has been discussed, the EU aims

Commission staff working document – Annex to the proposal for a Council Regulation amending Regulation (EC) No 2201/2003 as regards jurisdiction and introducing rules concerning applicable law in matrimonial matters – Impact assessment, SEC(2006) 949.

300 Drawn from examples of Spanish conflict-of-laws rules provided in: See Table 6.7. in EPEC (n.262 above), at p.45, para.6.2.1.

301 Notwithstanding the fragmented possibility for party autonomy in the national private international law rules in some Member States, especially the opportunity to make a choice of law in divorce and succession (e.g. in the Netherlands and Belgium). See extended discussion in 1.3., as well as Castellanos Ruiz (Chapter 1, n.48), at p.325, para.2 and Basedow (Chapter 1, n.46), at p.266, para.424 and pp.251–253, paras.405–406.

302 Tampere Conclusions (Chapter 1, n.2), at para.28; Hague Programme (n.199 above), at para.3.4.1. See also discussion in 3.2.2. above.

to facilitate the legal processes that emanate from cross-border family and succession relationships by reducing legal uncertainty for the parties, and by striving to ensure that a legal system of close connection to them applies to their relationships. The third and final aspect of this drive to simplify concerns the removal of obstacles to justice that parties face as a consequence of the cross-border nature of their proceedings.

This section will begin by outlining the definition attached to access to justice in this cross-border context (3.5.1.), before turning to establish the specific drivers that place those in cross-border situations in a disadvantaged position with regard to obtaining justice in family or succession matters (3.5.2.).

3.5.1. ACCESS TO JUSTICE FOR PARTIES IN CROSS-BORDER SITUATIONS

The right of access to justice is intended to enable access to court, the effective enforcement of rights and, if necessary, the obtaining of redress.[303] The protection that this right offers falls within the scope of the 'right to a fair trial' as provided by Article 6 ECHR and Article 47 of the EU Charter of Fundamental Rights. This right should be enjoyed equally by all, and may require additional measures to ensure a level playing-field.[304]

The European Council highlighted access to justice as one of the main goals in creating the area of freedom, security and justice.[305] In doing so, it drew upon the importance of removing additional burdens (e.g. financial, informational, lingual or travel-related[306]) for those who wish to enforce their rights in a cross-border setting, so that they can access justice on an equal footing to those in purely internal situations.

Whilst the European Council's exemplification generally focused upon facilitating access to justice in the consumer or victim's rights context, this rhetoric can be seen to equally apply in the civil law setting.[307] The right to obtain a divorce, claim maintenance payments, or enforce a right to property, unhindered by the additional obstacles or inconveniences that arise due to a

---

303 See Figure 1 in Fundamental Rights Agency, *Access to Justice in Europe: An Overview of Challenges and Opportunities* (2010), at: https://fra.europa.eu/sites/default/files/fra_uploads/1520-report-access-to-justice_EN.pdf, at p.16.

304 For example, in the form of legal aid to those who cannot afford to pay the fees for legal representation. See ibid., at p.47 *et seq.*

305 See Tampere Conclusions (Chapter 1, n.2), at paras.29–32 and the Stockholm Programme (n.198 above), at paras.3 and 3.4.1.

306 Stockholm Programme (n.198 above), para.3.4.1.

307 Article 67(4) TFEU: 'The Union shall facilitate access to justice, in particular through the principle of mutual recognition of judicial and extrajudicial decisions in civil matters'.

person's cross-border situation, can be seen to embody the fundamental aims behind the creation of a European area of justice.

3.5.2. BARRIERS TO ACCESSING JUSTICE IN THE PRIVATE INTERNATIONAL LAW SETTING

As a result of the functioning of jurisdictional and conflict of laws rules, parties in cross-border situations face an increased likelihood of experiencing hindrances to accessing justice with regard to legal aspects of family matters or succession. This can be seen to emerge from the greater possibility they face of having to travel to attend court (3.5.2.1.), the potential for longer, more complex proceedings to arise (3.5.2.2.), and the risk of disadvantageous outcomes resulting from incompatible interaction between the governing laws and/or fora (3.5.2.3.).

3.5.2.1. The Necessity to Travel to Attend Proceedings

The first obstacle to justice faced by those in cross-border situations lies in the possibility that they may have to travel to attend proceedings concerning their family or succession matters. The multiplicity of jurisdictions that might be available to be seised of proceedings (along with the possibility of completing jurisdictional interests cumulating in a 'rush to court') means that there could well arise circumstances in which one or both of the parties have to travel to attend proceedings located in state other than that in which their everyday life is situated.[308] A similar need to travel would emerge where different courts are seised to deal with closely related proceedings (e.g. divorce and maintenance).

Time spent away from home not only detrimentally impacts upon social and family obligations of the parties in question (e.g. the care of young children), but is also likely to generate considerable additional expense (from the act of travelling abroad itself, as well as a possible loss of income from employment). Such practical, temporal and financial expenditure can be seen to make it harder for those with cross-border aspects to their lives to access court in order to enforce the effects of their relationships.

3.5.2.2. Complex Proceedings

Proceedings that involve a cross-border element may, for a number of reasons, also hold an increased tendency to be longer and more complex than purely

308 See, with regard to detrimental consequences of cross-border matrimonial property matters, the 'problem tree' outlined in EPEC (n.260 above), at p.8.

internal cases.[309] Firstly, linking back to the possibility of a 'rush to court' where multiple jurisdictions are available to be seised, discussed above,[310] it can be proposed that this has a negative impact upon the convenience and cost-minimisation during proceedings, since it has a negative impact on consensus between the parties and reduces the likelihood of Alternative Dispute Resolution (ADR) being used in, most notably, divorce proceedings.[311]

Beyond this, parties may also struggle to adequately understand the functioning of a legal system in cases that include a cross-border element, usually as a result of proceedings being held in a state with which they do not have close links. For instance, they could be unfamiliar with the (legal) culture from which the legal system originates, or may not understand the language in which the legislation and procedural paperwork is written. Such problems in comprehending a 'foreign' legal system hold the potential to impinge upon the parties' ability to effectively plan their actions. In order to counteract this, the expertise of (bi-lingual) legal professionals and/or interpreters would have to be heavily relied upon during proceedings, resulting in additional time and monetary costs for the parties. The additional monetary burden could also lead to financial discrimination against those parties who do not have the resources to afford the aforementioned expertise.[312]

Complexity might additionally emerge from the increased likelihood of a court having to apply foreign law in proceedings involving parties with cross-border aspects to their relationships. A jurisdiction, when called upon to apply the law of another state, may have to spend a greater amount of time scrutinising the foreign legislation and jurisprudence in order to administer it correctly.[313] In this regard, it could have particular difficulty in applying a law that originates from a legal system that is far removed from its own: it may not be entirely clear which provisions of the foreign law should be applied to a certain relationship, and in what manner this should be carried out.[314]

---

309 EPEC (n.260 above), at p.8.

310 See 3.3.2.2. for discussion of negative consequences in light of legal certainty.

311 Walker (Chapter 2, n.164), at p.228.

312 See EPEC (n.260 above), at pp.98–99. Particular regard should be had for the financial position of the maintenance creditor: see 2.4.2.

313 I. Viarengo and F. Marchetti (eds.), 'EU FAM's Policy Guidelines' in Università degli Studi di Milano et al., (eds.), *Planning the future of cross-border families: a path through coordination* (2017), at pp.8-9, available at: http://www.eufams.unimi.it/wp-content/uploads/2017/12/EUFAMS-Policy-Guidelines-v1.0.pdf.

314 See the preliminary question referred to the Court of Justice in Case C-220/95 *Antonius van den Boogaard v. Paula Laumen* (Reference for a preliminary ruling: Arrondissementsrechtbank Amsterdam - Netherlands) [1997] ECR I-1147, in which the Dutch national court asked whether the English law concept of ancillary relief was more likely to relate to maintenance, or matrimonial property It was ultimately, after a great deal of deliberation, ascertained as maintenance (at para.27).

Even small differences between the law of the jurisdiction, and that which the court is asked to apply, will be enough to generate greater time and monetary costs for those involved in proceedings. These are incurred not only through the increased time and money spent on lengthier proceedings,[315] but also as a result of the needs of the judge, and other legal professionals involved in the case to consult additional specialist expertise in the foreign law at hand. Whilst some of the costs may be borne by the legal system itself, the costs of consulting experts tend to be viewed as litigation costs, and therefore are paid by the parties themselves.[316] Furthermore, although Member States' legal aid may cover such costs, this tends to be available only to those who have a low income.

Finally, where different Member State fora are seised to decide on linked matters (e.g. the dissolution of a matrimonial property regime and divorce) separate legal representation will likely have to be hired in the respective jurisdictions.[317] Similarly, if divergent national laws are found to apply to related disputes, the parties may have to rely on either separate legal expertise for each case, or attempt to find a (probably more expensive) legal representative who is specialised in the laws of the multiple jurisdictions concerned. Such requirements will inevitably place an additional financial burden upon those with cross-border aspects to their relations, which is not usually experienced by those in purely internal situations.

3.5.2.3. Incompatible Interactions

The final obstacle to obtaining justice for parties in cross-border family or succession matters is the possibility for disadvantageous outcomes to arise as a result of incompatibility between laws(s) and/or fora that govern proceedings. This can be seen to emerge in situations in which, through the functioning of private international law rules, different courts and/or applicable laws govern proceedings.

Firstly, as discussed above, judges and other legal professionals may encounter difficulties in applying foreign law. Whilst efforts are made to apply foreign law as precisely as possible, inaccuracies can nevertheless arise from the lack of experience that the jurisdiction has in dealing with the foreign law, the absence of an inherent understanding of the background from which the

315 In an empirical study that asked legal professionals about the application of foreign law in civil matters, 57% stated cost as a problem in consulting foreign legal experts, and 20% cited time as a problem in this same regard. However, it ought to be kept in mind that this study did not take into account the views of the parties to the proceedings: the Swiss Institute of Comparative Law, *The Application of Foreign Law in Civil Matters and its Application for the Future*, JLS/2009/JCIV/PR/0005/E4, at pp.54–55.

316 Swiss Institute of Comparative Law (ibid.), at p.35.

317 Walker (n.164 above), at p.240.

law originates,[318] as well as problems with regard to the quality of resources concerning the foreign legal system.[319] Such unfamiliarity could lead to a different legal outcome than if the law had been applied by the jurisdiction from which it originated. In addition, in the specific context of an applicable law that addresses 'non-traditional' relationships such as same-sex marriage or registered partnership, it can be observed that the potential for non-recognition by the forum gives rise to the ultimate example of an irreconcilable interaction in this regard.

Secondly, if laws from different states are found to govern factually related proceedings, problems could emerge from the fact that the respective laws do not 'fit' well together. Laws that originate from the same legal system are often drafted with one another in mind, and may serve to complement each other.[320] However, if divergent national laws are applied to proceedings concerning related matters, the parties would not benefit from the cohesive functioning of this interaction.

In order to illustrate this problem, a study carried out by the EPEC on cross-border matrimonial property put forward the scenario in which divergent applicable laws govern the dissolution of matrimonial property and succession respectively. In certain instances, each applicable law holds that provision for the surviving spouse is regulated under the other law (e.g. the law that governs succession provides that the rights of the surviving spouse are regulated under the rules on matrimonial property, and vice versa). Such contradiction could result in the complete denial of justice – a limping relationship.[321]

Less extreme examples could include a reduction in the compensatory effect that the law on one area would have vis-à-vis the other within the same legal system. Drawing on the example of matrimonial property and maintenance, it may be the case that where a legal system favours a complete separation of property between spouses, the substantive law of maintenance functions to redress any inequity between the spouses which may result from the functioning

318 EPEC (n.260 above), at p.98.

319 For example, in the above-mentioned empirical study, the respondents stated that official sources on the internet were their most frequently used way of obtaining information on foreign law (50% used such resources frequently). However, 35% of the respondents stated that the quality of the resources was a problem. In addition, the language and interpretation of such sources were also identified as possible problem areas: the Swiss Institute of Comparative Law (n.316 above), at pp.54–55.

320 J. Gray and P. Quinzá Redondo, 'Stress-Testing the EU Proposal on Matrimonial Property Regimes: Co-operation between EU Private International Law Instruments on Family Matters and Succession', *Family and Law*, at para.4. (November 2013), available at: http://www.familyandlaw.eu/tijdschrift/fenr/2013/11/FENR-D-13-00008.

321 See examples of incompatible interaction in this regard set out in: EPEC (n.260 above), at pp.106–107.

of this system.[322] If divergent national laws were to be applied to proceedings concerning the dissolution of a matrimonial property regime and maintenance in such a situation, the parties would not benefit from the compensatory functioning of this interaction.

Thirdly, disadvantageous outcomes may also arise where divergent fora are responsible for linked proceedings. These could emerge from inconsistencies in the manner in which the respective jurisdictions interpret and apply the same applicable law.[323] Take the example of two different courts, competent to decide respectively on the dissolution of a couple's property regime and succession. The same law is applied to these related proceedings, but for one court this is its own national law, whilst for the other it is foreign law. Although courts strive to apply foreign law in the most accurate manner possible, differences may nevertheless emerge. As discussed above, applicable laws from the same legal system are often drafted to complement one another. Thus, if there is a difference in the manner in which the law is applied in the respective jurisdictions, this compensatory effect may be hindered.

Beyond considerations relating to the actual application of law, it could furthermore be suggested that the court that is seised to decide on the first legal process has the benefit of already being familiar with the facts of the case. Given this, such a court is arguably better suited to deciding on proceedings that are related to this case, having experience in the circumstances of the parties from the onset. In contrast, should a new jurisdiction be asked to decide on a related proceeding, it may not have such a natural 'feel' for the situation at hand, resulting in less equitable outcomes for the parties. This argumentation is particularly relevant where there is a degree of discretion involved in proceedings (e.g. the ascertainment of the level of maintenance in light of the dissolution of the matrimonial property regime) and/or where there is a compensatory relationship between the linked proceedings.

---

322 For example, although Irish law provides for a separation of property, it also gives judges considerable discretion to make financial orders to return the spouses to their standard of living had the divorce not occurred. Ancillary relief (as it is known) can take many forms such as the redistribution of property, periodic payments and lump-sum payments.

323 Utrecht University and University of Vienna, 'Toolkit for advising European families: Married couples', *Empowering European Families* (2019), available at: https://backend.univie.ac.at/fileadmin/user_upload/p_eli/Projects/EEF/Toolkit_A_for_Advising_European_Families_Married_Couples.pdf, at fn.42.

PART II
PRELIMINARIES OF CHOICE

CHAPTER 4

MATERIAL AND PERSONAL SCOPE

4.1. INTRODUCTION

As the first step to evaluating the party autonomy provisions within the EU framework of unified rules on family matters and succession, this chapter will establish and analyse the parameters that underpin a choice of court or choice of law in the present setting.

In establishing the material and personal remit of agreements in the present realm, this chapter will begin by considering the prerequisite elements that underlie all situations that fall within the scope of the EU's unified rules on cross-border family matters and succession (4.2.), before proceeding to delineate the particular subject matters and parties that the respective instruments concern. Matrimonial matters will be considered first (4.3.), followed by the other major area involving adult relationships: property relations between spouses and registered partners (4.4.). Maintenance obligations (4.5) and parental responsibility (4.6.) will be dealt with next, before finally turning to consider succession (4.7.).[324] By way of exception to the simultaneous approach that is pursued in this book, this present chapter will establish the material and personal scopes of the respective areas of law addressed here on a successive basis.[325]

This chapter will consider the following questions in conjunction with the factors of evaluation established in Chapters 2 and 3: (i) Firstly, how well are the subject areas delineated? What matters are expressly included / excluded in the scope of the respective instruments? And are there any grey areas? (ii) Secondly, what are the connections between the subject areas concerned, and is there any risk of overlap? (iii) Are there any notable absences with regard to the subject matter that need to be addressed? The answers to these questions will be brought together in the synthesis (4.8.).

---

[324] This order of treatment has been selected based on the possibilities for linkage through party autonomy between matrimonial matters and the areas of property relations (between spouses), maintenance and parental responsibility. Succession, as a distinct issue within the EU framework (e.g. measures in this field can be adopted using the ordinary legislative procedure), is the final topic to be discussed here.

[325] Since this chapter seeks to establish the diverse subject areas, a simultaneous approach would not be appropriate an appropriate way of presenting the subject matter in this setting.

4.2. PRELIMINARY OBSERVATIONS

Before proceeding with the presentation and examination of the respective material and personal scope of the relevant instruments that unify the EU's private international law rules on family matters and succession, it is necessary to outline a number of overarching elements which permeate all aspects of the subject matter. As such, the following subsections will address the autonomous meaning to be attributed to provisions of EU law (4.2.1.), delineate the meaning of term 'civil matters' in the context of the EU regulations (4.2.2.), and consider the 'cross-border' requirement that underlies legislative action in this field (4.2.3.).

4.2.1. THE AUTONOMOUS MEANING OF CONCEPTS IN EU LAW

As a starting point to this analysis, it should be emphasised that where a provision of EU law makes no reference to the law of a Member State for the purposes of determining its meaning and scope, an autonomous and uniform meaning must be attached, having regard to the wording, context and objectives of the instrument in question.[326] This point is crucial for the forthcoming analysis, since this means that national conceptions of a particular subject area might well diverge from its meaning on an EU level. The development of an autonomous meaning by the CJEU for concepts addressed by EU law brings with it legal certainty for those who make use of the EU regulations, who can rely on a concrete definition, rather than national conceptions that are prone to variance across borders.

4.2.2. CIVIL MATTERS

As discussed in the previous chapter, the unified rules form part of a broader impetus for the EU to address civil matters on a Union level in order to remove the everyday legal obstacles that parties face when they cross borders in Europe. Reference to civil law is thus ubiquitous within the texts of the relevant EU instruments. It has been established that the term 'civil matters' ought to be

326 For example, Case C-558/16 *Doris Margret Lisette Mahnkopf*. Reference for a preliminary ruling: Kammergericht Berlin [2018] ECLI:EU:C:2018:138, at para.32; Case C-435/06 *C*. Reference for a preliminary ruling: Korkein hallinto-oikeus – Finland [2007] ECR I-10141, at paras.41–46; and Case C-135/15 *Republik Griechenland v. Grigorios Nikiforidis*. Reference for a preliminary ruling: Bundesarbeitsgericht [2016] ECLI:EU:C:2016:774, at para.28.

interpreted broadly, with a view to achieving the objectives and aims of the relevant instrument.[327] A crucial point to stress is that, since civil matters are to be treated as an autonomous concept of EU law,[328] it is irrelevant if a certain subject matter is considered to be public law in the national law of a Member State.[329] As will be discussed below in 4.6.1., this emphasis is of particular relevance in the field of parental responsibility, where there are a number of grey areas in which the distinction between private law and public law becomes blurred.

4.2.3. INTERNATIONAL CHARACTER

Whilst the EU regulations make reference to their goal of addressing subject matter with 'cross-border implications' in their recitals, the Hague Maintenance Protocol only mentions in passing the 'international' character of this instrument.[330] However, it is not the cross-border nature of these unified rules that are at stake here (since the legislative purposes of both the EU and the Hague Conference in introducing these instruments are manifest in this regard[331]), but the actual limits of what would be viewed as a cross-border situation in this setting.

Although there does not appear to have been large-scale research performed into the precise characteristics of the 'international' population within the European Union, a number of statistics have been offered in order to support legislative action in this present field. To this effect, for instance, it is proffered that 13 per cent of new marriages and 19 per cent of new registered partnerships

327 Case C-215/15 *Vasilka Ivanova Gogova v. Ilia Dimitrov Iliev*. Reference for a preliminary ruling: Varhoven kasatsionen sad [2015] ECLI:EU:C:2015:710 at paras.26–28 and *C* (n.326 above), at paras.45–46. In the wider EU context (insolvency proceedings), see Case C-251/12 *Christian Van Buggenhout and Ilse Van de Mierop v. Banque Internationale à Luxembourg S.A.* Request for a preliminary ruling from the tribunal de commerce de Bruxelles [2013] ECLI:EU:C:2009:474, at para.26.

328 *Gogova* (n.327 above.), at para.26 and *C* (n.326 above), at paras.45–46.

329 European Commission, *Practice Guide for the application of the Brussels IIa Regulation* (2014), at pp.19–20, para.3.1.1.3, available at: https://e-justice.europa.eu/fileDownload.do?id=b1f086c0-8d5b-4cb9-ad0e-85e38d528c7a. See also Case C-523/07 *A*. Reference for a preliminary ruling: Korkein hallinto-oikeus – Finland [2009] ECR I-2805, at paras.21–29 and *C.* (n.326 above), at paras.45–53.

330 See Article 20 of the Hague Maintenance Protocol.

331 See EU documentation describing their intent towards the private international law aspects of the family and succession law fields discussed here, for instance: X. Kramer et al., European Parliament Study: *A European Framework for Private International Law: Current Gaps and Future Perspectives* (2012) PE 462.487. See also Article 1 of the 1955 Statute of the Hague Conference on Private International Law: describing the purpose of the HCCH as being to 'work for the progressive unification of the rules of private international law'.

in the Union are international in character[332] whilst one in ten successions are seen to have an international aspect.[333]

In the search to identify the potential compositions of such situations, clear examples would be spouses who have different nationalities to one another and/or are living in a state other than that of which they are nationals, or a deceased person who was living outside of their country of nationality at the time of their death. Another inclusion that can readily be accepted in the context of property relations or succession would be the ownership of assets (e.g. a holiday home) located outside a person's country of nationality.

However, there also arise a number of scenarios whereby there may be hesitation in ascertaining whether a cross-border element exists. Would a situation in which a couple hold shares in a company incorporated in a foreign Member State qualify as falling within the scope of the Property Regulations?[334] Or could a couple who have formerly had a cross-border aspect to their relationship (e.g. they have previously worked abroad) nevertheless make a choice of law according to Rome III upon instigating proceedings?[335] Above and beyond this debate, the parties' own awareness of the international situation (or a lack thereof) may be particularly key in such instances.

It has been queried whether the validity of an agreement for the purposes of its usage within the EU private international law framework ought to be adjudged on the basis of the positive presence of a requisite cross-border element, or merely on the absence of a purely domestic situation. It has been argued that in the absence of a precise obligation for the subject matter to be cross-border in nature,[336] the latter approach is more appropriate, since a presumption of validity on this basis will improve legal certainty for the parties.[337]

In closing this discussion, one further point to mention is that provided an international element is identified in a particular situation, parties living in a third country can make use of the relevant instruments,[338] subject to fulfilment of the connection criteria established therein.[339] One caveat in this regard is that

---

332 Notaries of Europe, *European couples are changing, but their need for legal certainty is not*, available at: http://www.notaries-of-europe.eu/index.php?pageID=226.

333 Notaries of Europe, *The New EU Regulation 650/2012 on International Successions*, available at: http://www.notaries-of-europe.eu//index.php?pageID=9836.

334 Gray / Quinzá Redondo (Chapter 3, n.320), at para.2.2.1.

335 See Boele-Woelki (Chapter 1, n.1), at pp.28–29 for argumentation in support of this view.

336 Reference is only made in the recitals of the relevant EU instruments to the legislative need to address the cross-border situation.

337 See discussion of teleological reduction in the context of a choice of court under the Maintenance Regulation in: M. Abendroth, 'Choice of court in matters relating to maintenance obligations' in P. Beaumont et al. (eds.), *The Recovery of Maintenance in the EU and Worldwide* (Hart Publishing, Oxford, 2014), at p.470.

338 Viarengo / Villata (Chapter 3, n.268), at pp.29–30.

339 For instance, where an instrument's jurisdictional or conflict of laws rules permit, on the basis of the party's nationality.

where a child is habitually resident in a third country that is a contracting state of the 1996 Hague Convention on Child Protection, the jurisdictional rules of the convention will prevail over those contained in Brussels II bis.[340]

4.3. MATRIMONIAL MATTERS

The first subject matter to be dealt with here is that of 'matrimonial matters': the term employed by the EU instruments to describe divorce and legal separation (and also, in the context of the Brussels II bis Regulation, marriage annulment). For these present purposes, party autonomy, in the form of an opportunity to make a choice of applicable law for proceedings involving divorce and legal separation, is currently only provided for in the Rome III Regulation.

Neither the Brussels II bis Regulation nor the new recast of this instrument that was introduced in June 2019 (Brussels IIa (Recast)) gives an opportunity to make a choice of court agreement in matrimonial matters. There is, however, a residual regard for matrimonial matters in the context of the choice (or 'prorogation') of the court which is competent for such matters to deal with related issues of parental responsibility.[341] In addition to this, reference to matrimonial matters also arises for the purposes of coordinating proceedings under the Matrimonial Property Regulation,[342] Maintenance Regulation[343] and the Hague Maintenance Protocol.[344]

At the outset of this examination into the material and personal scope of the Rome III Regulation, it should be noted that the substantive scope of this instrument is to be treated as the same as that of Brussels II bis[345] (with the exception of marriage annulment,[346] to which Rome III does not apply). Thus, despite the general exclusion of party autonomy from the scope of matrimonial matters under Brussels II bis, case law and literature concerning the material scope of this instrument will be involved in the following discussion.

---

340 *EC Practice Guide* (n.329 above), at p.90, para.8.3.4.

341 Article 12(1) of Brussels II bis (see 7.2.3.). Although the revised provision contained in Article 10 of Brussels IIa does not itself refer to linkage with the court of matrimonial matters, this purpose is mentioned in Recital 23 of this instrument. Council Regulation (EU) 2019/1111 of 25 June 2019 on jurisdiction, the recognition and enforcement of decisions in matrimonial matters and the matters of parental responsibility, and on international child abduction [2019] OJ L 178/1.

342 Article 5 of the Matrimonial Property Regulation. See 7.2.1.

343 Article 4(1)(c)(i) of the Maintenance Regulation (2201/2003), Chapter 1, n.56. See 7.2.2.

344 Articles 8(1)(d) of the Hague Maintenance Protocol. See 7.3.1.

345 See, for instance, the CJEU's statement to this effect and its use of Brussels II bis in the context of considering the material scope of the Rome III Regulation: Case C-372/16 *Soha Sahyouni v. Raja Mamisch*. Reference for a preliminary ruling: Oberlandesgericht München [2017] ECLI:EU:C:2017:988, at paras.40–41.

346 Recital 10 and Article 1(2)(c).

4.3.1. MATERIAL SCOPE

As discussed above, Rome III serves to unify the conflict-of-laws rules in participating Member States with regard to the dissolution or loosening of marriage ties through divorce and legal separation respectively.[347] For these present purposes, the former process can be simply defined as involving a decision by a judicial or administrative authority[348] that results in the termination of a marriage.[349] An important point that was recently clarified in the context of Rome III is that its rules do not extend to cover 'private' religious divorce (in the case at hand, under Sharia law).[350] Only divorces pronounced by the national court or under its supervision come within the scope of matrimonial matters in this context.[351]

Legal separation essentially constitutes a weakening of the marriage bond, through a decision by a judicial or administrative authority, that leads to the spousal duties (e.g. to live together) and consequences of marriage (e.g. the division of property) being redefined.[352] Unlike divorce, legal separation is not present in all Member States, and tends to arise in legal traditions that emerged from the Romanic legal family and where the influence of canon law is strong.[353] In certain Member States, such as Italy, it is in fact a requisite step to obtaining divorce.[354]

In line with the position taken in Brussels II bis,[355] it is made clear from the presence of Article 9 that the conversion of legal separation to divorce also comes within the ambit of Rome III. The law applicable to a legal separation is applied to the subsequent conversion to divorce, unless an additional designation is made otherwise, or the law that has been applied to the legal separation does not provide for conversion to divorce (in which case Article 9(2) provides that the applicable law will be determined by Article 8).[356]

---

347 Recital 10 and Article 1(1).

348 The statement in Article 1(1) of Brussels II bis: 'whatever the nature of the court or tribunal', has been taken by multiple sources to mean judicial or administrative authority: see the Explanatory Memorandum accompanying the Proposal for Regulation 1347/2000 (Brussels II Regulation), COM(1999) 220 final, at p.11, para.4.3: 'Administrative procedures officially recognised in a Member State are therefore included'. See also M.N. Shúilleabháin, *Cross-border divorce law: Brussels II Bis* (Oxford University Press, Oxford, 2010), at pp.123–124, paras.3.61–3.62 and W. Pintens, 'Chapter I: Scope and definitions' in U. Magnus and P. Mankowski (eds.), *Brussels IIbis Regulation* (Sellier, Munich, 2012), at p.52, para.4.

349 See K. Boele-Woelki, *European Parliament Note: The Proposal for enhanced cooperation in the area of cross-border divorce (Rome III)* (2010), PE 432.730, at p.13 and K. Boele-Woelki (Chapter 1, n.1), at p.28.

350 *Sahyouni* (n.345 above).

351 Ibid., at para.39.

352 See Pintens (n.348 above), at p.69, para.47.

353 Ibid, at pp.69–70, para.48.

354 Ibid.

355 See Pintens (n.348 above), at p.68, para.42.

356 For commentary on the application of Article 9 of Rome III in Member State courts, see: I. Viarengo, 'The Rome III Regulation in Legal Practice: Case Law and Comments' (2014) 15(4) *ERA Forum* 547, at p.558.

Recital 10 and Article 1(2) serve to establish the outer limits of the material scope of Rome III by establishing a number of exclusions:

(a) the legal capacity of natural persons;
(b) the existence, validity or recognition of a marriage;
(c) the annulment of a marriage;
(d) the name of the spouses;
(e) the property consequences of the marriage;
(f) parental responsibility;
(g) maintenance obligations;
(h) trusts or successions.

In view of the above list, a number of points for discussion can be highlighted:

1. It can be seen from this concise list that the determination of the capacity of the spouses and the existence of the marriage itself are expressly excluded, along with commonly related matters that are largely addressed in other EU instruments.[357] Since there is little question of overlap between the material scope of divorce and legal separation and that of these related issues, further examination of the interrelationship between these areas is not necessary for these purposes.
2. One express exclusion that is markedly absent from the above list is the dissolution of registered partnership. There has in fact been at least one recorded instance in which a Czech court applied the rules of Brussels II bis to a registered partnership.[358] However, given that there is nothing in the wording of this instrument to indicate that it is to be applied to this type of relationship,[359] and the CJEU has expressly stated that registered partnership cannot be assimilated to marriage simply because it is treated as such by certain Member States' national rules,[360] it has to be concluded that the aforementioned instance should be treated as an analogous extension of EU rules by a Member State court. Notwithstanding this, in light of the new

[357] With the exclusion of trusts and name law.

[358] District Court of Rokycany No. 6 C 59/2011 of 20.9.2011. See the European Commission, *Study on the assessment of Regulation (EC) No 2201/2003 and the policy options for its amendment: Final report, analytical annexes* (2018), at p.118. See also T.M.C. Asser Institute et al., *Regulation Brussels IIbis Guide for Application*: Chapter 1 (2018), at p.7, para.2.1.1.3., available at: http://www.asser.nl/media/4649/m-5796-ec-justice-cross-border-proceedings-in-family-law-matters-10-publications-02-guide-for-application-chapter-1.pdf, in which a Greek national reporter also stated that since registered partnership for same-sex couples has been introduced in Greece, it is considered to fall within the scope of the Brussels II bis Regulation.

[359] The sole reference to 'spouses' and the designation of the subject area as concerning 'divorce and legal separation' appears to definitively exclude this possibility.

[360] Joined cases C-122/99P and C-125/99 P *D and Kingdom of Sweden v. Council of the European Union* [2001] ECR I-4319, at paras.29–41.

regulation on the property relations between registered partners that generally provides for similar rules to married couples, it might be useful if a stance were to be pronounced as to the application of Rome III in this regard.[361]

3. A more general point of critique which can be levelled against the EU instruments that contain a list of exclusions[362] relates to the question of whether the standard list of exclusions that are established is exhaustive in nature. Conflicting views have been expressed in this regard. For instance it has been argued, in the context of the Succession Regulation, that the absence of the qualification 'in particular' (as is the case with the parallel list of inclusions in this instrument) would indicate that such lists are to be treated as closed.[363] However, it has also been opined (this time in respect of Brussels II bis) that despite the omission of this term, it can be construed from the scope and aims of the instrument that there are additional topics that can be excluded.[364] Given this need to take account of the scope and aims of an instrument in considering its material breadth, a finite list could be seen to form an inflexible barrier to the ascertainment of whether particular matter of national law falls within the scope of an instrument.

4.3.2. PERSONAL SCOPE

Rome III determines the law that applies to the dissolution or weakening of a marriage – in short, a legally recognised union between *spouses*. The existence of a marriage between the parties is a fundamental issue, since this is a preliminary question at the outset of proceedings concerning matrimonial matters.[365] However, unlike the institution of registered partnership,[366] no EU instrument provides a definition of marriage or spouse for the purposes of its application. This raises the question of how 'non-traditional' forms of marriage that are not recognised in every Member State – chiefly marriage between members of the same sex,[367] but also polygamous marriage and marriage involving transgender persons – are to be treated within this context.

---

361 Although it should be emphasised that the wording of the current instrument, with its sole reference to 'spouses' and the processes of divorce and legal separation, would appear to exclude such an application.

362 All relevant EU instruments apart from the Maintenance Regulation.

363 R. Frimston, 'Chapter I: Scope and definitions' in U. Bergquist et al. (eds.), *EU Regulation on Succession and Wills* (Otto Schmidt, Cologne, 2015), at p.40, para.6.

364 Pintens (n.348 above), at p.78, para.73: for instance, rights of asylum and immigration, or public measures of a general nature on education or health (see Recital 10 of Brussels II bis).

365 See Viarengo / Villata (Chapter 3, n.268), at p.24.

366 See Article 3(1)(a) of the Partnership Property Regulation, and discussion in 4.4.2. below.

367 Same-sex marriage will be treated as the principal 'non-traditional' marriage here, since it is by far the most predominant form of marriage that is not universally recognised throughout the Union.

Whilst it has not been expressly enunciated whether or not marriage, for the purposes of this instrument (or the other relevant regulations) is to be autonomously defined, the presence of Article 13 of Rome III would indicate that it is to be interpreted on a Member State level.[368] In this regard, it has been demonstrated in a recent study that whilst Member States that provided for same-sex marriage in their national law tended towards including same-sex marriage within the scope of the instrument, the opposite was true where there was no provision in national law for this form of marriage.[369] Since only 14 out of the 28 Member States currently provide for same-sex marriage in their domestic laws,[370] this inevitably leads to difficulty in safeguarding the legal effects of such relationships across borders.

Notwithstanding the above discussion, evidence of a subtle shift in the EU's 'hands-off' approach has been demonstrated in the CJEU's recent *Coman* judgment,[371] in which it was established, in consideration of an EU citizen's right to free movement (Article 21 TFEU applied with analogy to Directive 2004/38) and the residency rights of a third country spouse, that a Member State could not rely on its own national legislation to refuse to recognise a same-sex marriage concluded in another state. However, it should be emphasised that this does not translate into a general requirement upon Member States to recognise foreign same-sex marriages in all areas covered by EU law.[372] The language employed by the Court focused primarily on the EU citizen's right to free movement and the enjoyment of his right to a family life, rather than the recognition of a status lawfully created in another Member State.[373]

---

368 The court of a participating Member State may refuse to pronounce a divorce or legal separation on the basis that according to its own law, the marriage in question is not considered to be valid. See examination of this provision in K. Boele-Woelki (Chapter 1, n.1), at pp.37–38.

369 Whilst national reporters from a number of countries that catered towards same-sex marriage in their domestic law – Spain, France, Ireland, the Netherlands and Portugal – indicated that their courts applied Brussels II bis to same-sex marriage, the reporters from Bulgaria, Greece, Hungary, Italy, Latvia, Lithuania, Poland and Romania, which are jurisdictions in which same-sex marriage is not provided for, indicated that Brussels II bis did not apply in this context. See commentary in T.M.C. Asser Institute et al. (n.358 above), at p.6, para.2.1.1.2.

370 Belgium, Denmark, Finland, France, Germany, Malta, Ireland, Luxembourg, the Netherlands, Portugal, Spain, Sweden, United Kingdom, Austria (2019). See also Chapter 10, Table 6 at 10.6.1.

371 *Coman v. Romania* (Chapter 2, n.156), at para.36. See also the recent ruling in *Orlandi and Others v. Italy*, Applications no.26431/12, 26742/12, 44057/12 and 60088/12, ECtHR (14 December 2017), in which the ECtHR concluded that the refusal of the Italian authorities to attribute any form of legal recognition to same-sex marriages contracted abroad was a violation of Article 8 ECHR.

372 See B. Rudevska, 'The "Coman" Case (C-673/16): Some reflections from the point of view of private international law' (2 July 2018), available at: http://conflictoflaws.net/2018/the-coman-case-c-673-16-some-reflections-from-the-point-of-view-of-private-international-law.

373 Contrast with the CJEU cases concerning name law and the incorporation theory at 2.3.2. See further discussion at 10.6.1. in the context of the enforcement of choice.

Even though there are possible indications of a change in attitude on the EU stage towards the recognition of same-sex marriage, it would be premature to say there has been any material change at this point in time. Thus, for now, the approach indicated by Article 13 of Rome III prevails. Whilst this is by no means satisfactory in terms of providing same-sex spouses with predictability and protecting their expectations concerning the status of their marriages, a degree of predictability has, however, been achieved through the articulation of the means through which participating Member State courts might deal with such relationships. This is a topic that will be returned to in the context of the enforcement of choice in Chapter 10.[374]

4.4. PROPERTY RELATIONS BETWEEN SPOUSES AND REGISTERED PARTNERS

Following naturally on from discussion of matrimonial matters are the two most recent regulations to enter the sphere of EU private international law: the joint regulations on matters of matrimonial property regimes and on the property consequences of registered partnerships.

In contrast to the Rome III Regulation, these instruments are 'comprehensive' in nature, providing rules that address both choice of court and choice of applicable law. Although the present two regulations clearly concern different types of relationships, through the long-winded drafting process, the two instruments were brought largely in line with one another in terms of the provision of choice.[375]

4.4.1. MATERIAL SCOPE

By their very nature, the joint regulations concerning the property relations between spouses, and those between registered partners, present less immediate clarity with regard to material scope than, for instance, the straightforward delineation set out in Rome III. The decisions concerning property relations between spouses or registered partners serve a broad range of purposes, which are subject to national variation (particularly in the case of those relations that exist between registered partners).

---

374 See 10.6.

375 See the Matrimonial Property Regulation (Chapter 1, n.63) and the Partnership Property Regulation (Chapter 1, n.64) of 2016. Party autonomy was not permitted under the 2011 Proposal for a Council Regulation on jurisdiction, applicable law and the recognition and enforcement of decisions regarding the property consequences of registered partnerships, COM(2011) 127 final.

The regulations themselves depart with the stipulation that the property relations with which they are concerned involve

> a set of rules concerning the property relationships between the spouses [of the partners, between themselves] and in their relations with third parties, as a result of marriage or its dissolution [as a result of the legal relationship created by the registration of the partnership or its dissolution].[376]

This definition is purposefully broad in order to cater for the various conceptions of property relations in the Member States.

The above assertion reflects the breadth of definition previously established for rights arising out of the matrimonial property relationship in the context of the Brussels Convention in the CJEU case of *de Cavel v. de Cavel (No.1)*,[377] in which the Court stated that this: 'included not only property arrangements specifically and exclusively envisaged by certain national legal systems in the case of marriage, but also any proprietary relationships resulting directly from the matrimonial relationship or the dissolution thereof'.

The regulations are designed to apply broadly, encompassing decisions on the daily management of the property regime, as well as those that arise upon separation, or upon the death of one of the spouses or partners.[378] It is useful at this stage to point out that, in the context of a choice of court, the opportunities for party autonomy vary between the subject areas, with no possibility for a direct choice of court provided for the dissolution of a property regime upon the death of one of the spouses or partners.

Although the two regulations are generally uniform in their approach to delineating the breadth of the subject matter which they cover, they diverge with regard to the elaboration provided of Articles 3(1)(a) and 3(1)(b) respectively, with only the regulation on property relations between spouses providing for a broad, autonomous interpretation to be given to the concept of the matrimonial property regime (according to Recital 18 thereof):

> [The regulation] should encompass not only rules from which the spouses may not derogate but also any optional rules to which the spouses may agree in accordance with the applicable law, as well as any default rules of the applicable law. It includes not only property arrangements specifically and exclusively envisaged by certain national legal systems in the case of marriage but also any property relationships, between the spouses and in their relations with third parties, resulting directly from the matrimonial relationship, or the dissolution thereof.

---

376 Article 3(1)(a) of the Matrimonial Property Regulation, 2016/1103 and Article 3(1)(b) of the Partnership Property Regulation, 2016/1104.

377 Case 143/78 *Jacques de Cavel v. Louise de Cavel.* Reference for a preliminary ruling: Bundesgerichtshof – Germany [1979] ECR 1055.

378 See Article 3(1)(a) and 3(1)(b) respectively.

The absence of a parallel elaboration in the Introduction to the Partnership Property Regulation signifies that the property relations with which this instrument is concerned are to be interpreted on a Member State level. There thus arises a risk of inconsistent interpretation by the Member States of the extent of the property relations between registered partners. However, the opportunity to select both the court and applicable law under this instrument allows the parties to purposefully avoid the potential frustration of expectations that might arise from such a scenario.

In line with the format which will be seen in the majority of the relevant EU instruments that address the conflict of laws (with the exception of Rome III), a further layer of definition is added by Article 27 of both regulations, which sets out a non-exhaustive list of subject matter that the applicable law determined by both instruments covers:

> (a) the classification of property of either or both spouses [partners] into different categories during and after marriage;
> (b) the transfer of property from one category to the other one;
> (c) the responsibility of one spouse for liabilities and debts of the other spouse [partner];
> (d) the powers, rights and obligations of either or both spouses [partners] with regard to property;
> (e) the dissolution of the matrimonial property regime and the partition, distribution or liquidation of the property [the partition, distribution or liquidation of the property upon dissolution of the registered partnership];
> (f) the effects of the matrimonial property regime [property consequences of registered partnerships] on a legal relationship between a spouse [partner] and third parties; and
> (g) the material validity of a matrimonial property agreement [partnership property agreement].

The delineation of the content of matrimonial property regimes and the property relations between registered partners has been improved considerably by the adding of this list of inclusions, as it was sorely lacking in the draft regulations that were first presented in 2011.[379] The list itself is extensive and straightforward in nature. One point to note relates to the inclusion of the material validity of matrimonial property agreements / partnership property agreements (see Article 27(g)) within this scope. It can also be seen that the applicable law extends to cover any formal validity requirements of such documents (Article 25(3)).

379 For a critique of the 2011 Proposal for a Council Regulation on jurisdiction, applicable law and recognition and enforcement of decisions in matters of matrimonial property regimes, COM (2011) 126 final, see: Gray / Quinzá Redondo (Chapter 3, n.320).

The list of inclusions contained in Article 27 is complemented by an enumeration of express exclusions from the scope of the instruments set out in Article 1(2) of both regulations:

(a) the legal capacity of spouses [partners];
(b) the existence, validity or recognition of a marriage [registered partnership];
(c) maintenance obligations;
(d) the succession to the estate of a deceased spouse [partner];
(e) social security;
(f) the entitlement to transfer or adjustment between spouses [partners], in the case of divorce, legal separation or marriage annulment [in the case of dissolution or annulment of the registered partnership], of rights to retirement or disability pension accrued during marriage [registered partnership] and which have not generated pension income during the marriage [registered partnership];
(g) the nature of rights *in rem* relating to a property; and
(h) any recording in a register of rights in immoveable or moveable property, including the legal requirements for such recording, and the effects of recording or failing to record such rights in a register.

Several points merit further elaboration with regard to these exclusions to the scope of the texts:

1. Firstly, the lists contained in Article 1(2) mirror the exclusions that were set out in the 1978 Hague Convention on the Law Applicable to Matrimonial Property Regimes (legal capacity of the spouses, and maintenance obligations[380] and succession rights between spouses[381]), but extend far beyond the basic delineation in this earlier instrument. In line with the trend of other EU instruments considered here, questions concerning the existence of the relationship are not included within the scope of the regulations.
2. Questions concerning the entitlement to transfer rights to retirement or disability pensions are excluded from consideration under these instruments, even where such pensions were contributed to during the marriage or partnership. However, Recital 23 of each regulation stresses that this is to be interpreted strictly, and classification of retirement or disability pensions, and the amount of pension that has already been paid out to one spouse [partner] during the marriage [registered partnership] (as well as possible compensation in this regard) does fall within the scope of the regulations.

380 The relationship (and potential overlap between) property relations and maintenance obligations will be considered in the next subsection (4.5.1.).

381 See Article 1 of the 1978 Hague Convention on the Law Applicable to Matrimonial Property Regimes.

3. The category of the 'nature of rights *in rem*' to property is classified as excluded according to the above list, on the rationale that a Member State should not be required to recognise a right *in rem* over property located within its territory that is unknown in its own law.[382] According to Article 29, along with Recitals 25 and 26 of both regulations, the possibility remains for a Member State court to adapt rights *in rem* found in the applicable law that are unknown in the law of the Member State in which that property is located to the closest equivalent under this latter law. The CJEU has also recently taken steps to clarify the scope of the exclusion of the nature of rights *in rem*, in the context of the similar provision in the Succession Regulation, stating that the method by which rights *in rem* are transferred is not covered by such an exclusion.[383] Given the complexity in categorising the various aspects involved with rights *in rem*, it can be anticipated that this will not be the last time that a question regarding this area will come before the EU court.[384]
4. Finally, one area that has not been adequately clarified in the instruments is the question of whether 'personal effects' of marriage or registered partnership (e.g. cohabitation, faithfulness and assistance) are excluded. This exclusion was actually present in the 2011 draft proposal concerning registered partnership,[385] but was subsequently removed. Although personal effects would, in any case, appear to be excluded by the definitions of matrimonial property regimes and property consequences of registered partnerships provided in Article 3(1)[386] (which solely mention 'property'), it has been suggested that confusion as to characterisation may still arise with regard to rights and duties with a secondary property element.[387]

4.4.2. PERSONAL SCOPE

Party autonomy can be exercised under these parallel instruments by spouses and registered partners respectively. The former category has already been described above. For the sake of uniformity between instruments within the same framework, it is assumed that the same definition is to be employed in this

---

382 See Recitals 24 of both Property Regulations.

383 Case C-218/16 *Aleksandra Kubicka v. Przemysława Bac*. Reference for a preliminary ruling: Sąd Okręgowy w Gorzowie Wielkopolskim – Poland [2017] ECLI:EU:C:2017:755, at paras.48–49. See 4.7.1. below.

384 See observation with regard to the similar exclusion in the Succession Regulation (see also 4.7.1.): Frimston (n.363 above), at p.49, para.66.

385 Article 1(3)(a).

386 See Article 3(1)(a) and 3(1)(b) respectively.

387 I. Viarengo, 'The EU Proposal on Matrimonial Property Regimes' (2011) 13 *Yearbook of Private International Law* 199, at p.204.

context. The regulation on matrimonial property regimes further supports the aforementioned view held here that marriage is to be interpreted on a Member State level, by expressly excluding the recognition of the marital relationship from the scope of its application in Article 1(2)(b)[388] and stating in Recital 17 that it does not define marriage.

Turning now to focus upon the institution of registered partnership, it is seen to be readily distinguishable from marriage when considered on the European stage, both in the sense that it is not a universal institution between the Member States[389] (being a relatively novel form of relationship[390]), and it varies in its conception (form, function and effects) between the Member States that do provide for it.

Such unions may be intended as a substitute for marriage for same-sex couples in jurisdictions that do not provide for the latter to be concluded between same-sex couples, and which either holds a similar function and effects to marriage (e.g. Slovenia[391]) or represents a weaker union in terms of function and effects, primarily aiming to provide same-sex couples with a route to officiating their relationship (e.g. Czech Republic[392]). There are also jurisdictions that offer one or the other of the two broad categories of partnership discussed above, but open such relationships up to opposite-sex couples too. For instance, whilst the Netherlands establishes a substitute to marriage with regard to the effects of registered partnership,[393] Belgium offers it as a form of marriage-'lite'.[394]

---

388 See also Recital 21 of the Matrimonial Property Regulation.

389 Currently 21 Member States provide for some form of registered partnership in their legislation: the Netherlands, France, Belgium, Luxembourg, Czech Republic, Slovenia, Greece, Hungary, Austria, Malta, Sweden, Denmark, Germany, Ireland, Malta, Spain, Croatia, Cyprus, Estonia, Italy, and the United Kingdom, although some of these countries, such as Sweden and Denmark, no longer pronounce new registered partnerships following same-sex marriage being introduced.

390 First emerging in the second half of the 20th century.

391 In this jurisdiction a registered partnership has the same property consequences for the partners as marriage for opposite-sex spouses. See Couples in Europe, *Slovenia: what does the law provide for the property of registered and non-registered partners?* Available at: http://www.coupleseurope.eu/en/slovenia/topics/8-what-does-the-law-provide-for-the-property-of-registered-and-non-registered-partners/.

392 Czech law does not provide any specific property regime for registered partners, whilst a statutory property regime is provided for spouses. See Couples in Europe, *Czech Republic: Is there a statutory matrimonial property regime and if so, what does it provide?* Available at: http://www.coupleseurope.eu/en/czech-republic/topics/2-is-there-a-statutory-matrimonial-property-regime-and-if-so-what-does-it-provide/; and Couples in Europe, *Czech Republic: What does the law provide for the property of registered and non-registered partners?* Available at: http://www.coupleseurope.eu/en/czech-republic/topics/8-what-does-the-law-provide-for-the-property-of-registered-and-non-registered-partners/.

393 K. Boele-Woelki et al, *Commission on European Family Law: Property relationship between spouses – The Netherlands* (September 2008), available at: http://ceflonline.net/wp-content/uploads/Netherlands-Property.pdf, at p.5, Question 4.

394 W. Pintens et al, *Commission on European Family Law: Property relationship between spouses – Belgium* (August 2008), available at: http://ceflonline.net/wp-content/uploads/Belgium-Property.pdf, at p.3, Question. 4. For further discussion of these contrasts,

A subsidiary point to note is that is appears that registered partnership, at least to the extent that is established as a substitute for marriage between same-sex couples, is on the decline. In recent years, several states, such as Germany, the Republic of Ireland and Denmark have removed this institution in conjunction with the introduction of same-sex marriage into their legal systems.

Unlike marriage (which the EU instruments have, until now, refrained from defining), this relationship is defined by Article 3(a) as being 'the regime governing the shared life of two people which is provided for in law, the registration of which is mandatory under that law and which fulfils the legal formalities required by that law for its creation'. The broadness of this delineation can be seen to encompass the variety of formations discussed above.

In view of the divergent conceptions of registered partnership seen amongst the participating Member States, and in line with the parallel exclusion of recognition of a registered partnership from the regulation's scope, laid out in Article 1(2)(b), it is asserted here that the validity of such a relationship is, like marriage, to be ascertained according to Member States' own laws (including private international laws) in the present context. Linking back to the variation that is seen amongst the Member States with regard to the recognition and conceptions of this form of relationship, it is accordingly submitted that potential for the frustration of parties' expectations may arise in this setting.[395]

4.5. MAINTENANCE OBLIGATIONS

Party autonomy in the area of maintenance obligations is provided comprehensively by the choice of court and choice of law laid out in the Maintenance Regulation and the Hague Protocol on the Law Applicable to Maintenance Obligations respectively. The Union's decision to collectively ratify the Hague Maintenance Protocol and simply refer to its provisions within its own regulation[396] reflects a shared desire on the part of the Hague Conference on Private International Law and the EU to create a comprehensive regime dealing with all private international law aspects relating to maintenance obligations.[397]

---

see E. Goossens, 'Different regulatory regimes for registered partnership and marriage: outdated or indispensible? A European perspective on the Belgian model' in A. Verbeke et al (eds.), *Confronting the Frontiers of Family and Succession Law: Liber amicorum Walter Pintens* (Intersentia, Antwerp, 2012), at pp.364–368. See also for more extensive comparative analysis on this subject area: I. Curry-Sumner, *All's Well that Ends Registered?* (Intersentia, Antwerp, 2005).

395 See 10.7.

396 See Article 15 of the Maintenance Regulation.

397 Originally the EU intended to include its own conflict of laws regime in the regulation, see wider discussion in: M. Župan, 'Innovations of the 2007 Hague Maintenance Protocol' in P. Beaumont et al. (eds.), *The Recovery of Maintenance in the EU and Worldwide* (Hart Publishing, Oxford, 2014), at pp.312–315.

4.5.1. MATERIAL SCOPE

Maintenance obligations are commonly understood to involve the provision of support (usually financial) from one party to another.[398] In line with the default trend followed by the EU instruments, the Maintenance Regulation expressly provides that an autonomous meaning is to be attached to 'maintenance obligations' within its context.[399] Both the regulation and the Protocol establish application to obligations arising from a broad range of links, including those emerging from 'a family relationship, parentage, marriage or affinity'.[400] By mirroring the same departing premise, it would appear that the essential material scope of both instruments is to be viewed as the same. However, a more compelling argument in support of this approach arises from the fact that since it is the Member State (as designated by the Maintenance Regulation) that applies the law determined by the Hague Maintenance Protocol, the material scope of the regulation has priority.

In a similar manner to the other instruments that have already been discussed in this chapter, it is left to the Member States themselves to establish the existence of the relationship from which the claim for maintenance is derived.[401] This being said, it can be observed that the more loosely delineated category of 'family relationships' upon which an obligation can be founded introduces a potential for flexibility in the treatment of relationships that are not generally recognised by the national law of the forum.[402] Notwithstanding this, it is highlighted that the remaining risk for the non-recognition of a relationship, and the consequent impediment to conducting proceedings on this basis, gives rise to a particularly detrimental situation in view of the need for provision that lies at the heart of a request for maintenance in the first place.

---

398 Viarengo / Villata (Chapter 3, n.268), at p.43.

399 See Recital 11 of the Maintenance Regulation.

400 Article 1(1) of the Maintenance Regulation and Article 1(1) of the Hague Maintenance Protocol. The latter also includes the addendum: '... including a maintenance obligation in respect of a child regardless of the marital status of the parents'. On an additional note, for the purposes of clarity, 'related by affinity' refers to a family relationship brought about through marriage: see example provided in A. Bonomi, *Explanatory Report on the Hague Protocol of 23 November 2007 on the Law Applicable to Maintenance Obligations* (HCCH Publications, the Hague, 2013), at para.56.

401 See Recital 21 of the Maintenance Regulation. See also Bonomi (ibid.), at para.31, L. Walker, *Maintenance and Child Support in Private International Law* (Hart Publishing, Oxford, 2015), at pp.37–39, B. Hess and S. Spancken, 'Setting the scene – the EU Maintenance Regulation' in P. Beaumont et al. (eds.), *The Recovery of Maintenance in the EU and Worldwide* (Hart Publishing, Oxford, 2014), at p.333 and J. Halliday, 'Characterisation as Maintenance or Succession' in P. Beaumont et al. (eds.), *The Recovery of Maintenance in the EU and Worldwide* (Hart Publishing, Oxford, 2014), at pp.455–456.

402 See Halliday (ibid.), at p.456.

The propensity for a limping relationship to emerge in this manner is becoming increasingly irreconcilable with the recent judgment in *Coman*,[403] as well as other jurisprudence from the CJEU and ECtHR.[404] Furthermore, it is proposed that where a maintenance obligation concerns a minor, the lack of recognition of the relationship upon which this claim was based ought to be balanced against consideration of the child's best interests.[405]

The Maintenance Regulation does not provide any further elaboration as to the characterisation of its subject matter. In contrast, the Hague Maintenance Protocol goes on to further illustrate its boundaries in terms of the type of decisions over which the applicable law will apply, by setting out a non-exhaustive list of inclusions[406] in Article 11:

(a) whether, to what extent and from whom the creditor may claim maintenance;
(b) the extent to which the creditor may claim retroactive maintenance;
(c) the basis for calculation of the amount of maintenance, and indexation;
(d) who is entitled to institute maintenance proceedings, except for issues relating to procedural capacity and representation in the proceedings;
(e) prescription or limitation periods;
(f) the extent of the obligation of a maintenance debtor, where a public body seeks reimbursement of benefits provided for a creditor in place of maintenance

The scope of applicable law is conceived as fairly broad, and finds its basis in the parallel provision in the Hague Convention of 2 October 1973 on the Law

403 *Coman* (Chapter 2, n.156).

404 See, for instance, C-267/06 *Tadao Maruko v. Versorgungsanstalt der deutschen Bühnen.* Reference for a preliminary ruling: Bayerisches Verwaltungsgericht München – Germany [2008] ECR I-1788, in which it was established that the German authorities' denial of a widower's pension to a registered partner of the same sex was in contravention of Directive 2000/78/EC, which forbids discrimination on the grounds of sexual orientation with regard to employment-related benefits; Case C-267/12 *Frédéric Hay v. Crédit agricole mutuel de Charente-Maritime et des Deux-Sèvres.* Request for a preliminary ruling from the Cour de cassation (France) [2013] ECLI:EU:C:2013:823, in which it was found that an employee who was in a same-sex registered partnership should receive the same benefits as a married employee (as long as a registered partnership is the highest level of status that same-sex couples can access in the jurisdiction in question). It was opined that opposite-sex spouses and same-sex partners were in a comparable situation in these circumstances, and that the company had directly discriminated on the grounds of sexual orientation in not providing the same employee benefits for both groups; *Pajić v. Croatia*, Application no.68453/13, ECtHR (23 February 2016) in which contravention of Article 14 in conjunction with Article 8 ECHR was identified in view of the difference in treatment of the applicant on the grounds of sexual orientation with regard to family reunification and immigration law; *E and Others v. Italy*, Application no.26431/12, ECtHR (2017), in which the ECtHR concluded that the refusal of the Italian authorities to attribute any form of legal recognition to same-sex marriages contracted abroad was a violation of Article 8 ECHR; and *Orlandi and Others v. Italy* (n.371 above). See further discussion of relevant jurisprudence in: Viarengo / Villata (Chapter 3, n.268), at pp.46–50.

405 See further discussion in the context of holders of parental responsibility – 4.6.2.2. below

406 Bonomi (n.400 above), at para.166.

Applicable to Maintenance Obligations,[407] with a number of points of further elaboration.[408] Notably for the present context, the applicable law determines the existence of the relationship that gives rise to maintenance (including the manifestations and derivatives of the parent-child relationship[409]), which gives the parties a means of maintaining the existence of their decisive bond through making a choice of law.

In contrast to the other regulations examined here, neither instrument provides a list of specific exclusions to the scope of maintenance obligations. This lack of delineation inevitably gives rise to uncertainty regarding the limits of 'maintenance obligations' for these purposes. However, it can be proposed that such a list was purposefully exempted in order to provide as broad a material scope of application as is permitted in the Member State / Contracting State context in order to provide the maintenance creditor with much needed definitional flexibility in pursuing their claim.

Notwithstanding the above, a number of points of exclusion can be identified in view of the texts and the relationship of maintenance with other subject areas:

1. In view of the Protocol's Explanatory Report[410] and Recital 21 of the Maintenance Regulation, it can be seen that the law applicable to a maintenance obligation is to be principally treated as separate from that which applies to the determination of the existence of a relationship (a question that is to be determined according to the national law of the Member States, including their rules of private international law.[411] This aligns with established practice of the other relevant instruments in the present field. However, it should be noted that if such a question is preliminary to the determination of maintenance, states may nevertheless opt to also apply the designated applicable law under this instrument (although this solution is not binding – the forum is free to apply its own conflict-of-laws rules to the determination of the existence of a relationship).[412]
2. Another exclusion is established by Article 8(4) of the Protocol, which provides that the question of whether the creditor can renounce his or her right to maintenance is to be determined by the law of the habitual residence of the creditor at the time of designation. Accordingly, a choice

407 See Article 10 of this instrument. See Bonomi (n.400 above), at para.165.

408 Article 11(b), (c) and (e). See also Article 11(e) for differences in format 'except for issues relating to procedural capacity and representation in the proceedings'. Note that Article 10(2) of the 1973 Hague Convention follows slightly different wording that somewhat emulates Article 11(e) of the Protocol.

409 E.g. obligations arising from a stepparent-child relationship. See Walker (n.401 above), at pp.37–39.

410 Bonomi (n.400 above), at para.31.

411 Ibid., at para.31.

412 Ibid., at para.24.

of law cannot impact upon this aspect. This measure is to be seen as a protective one which is designed to shield the creditor from suffering the negative consequences of agreeing to a particularly unprotective law.[413] It should be noted that the awarding of a lump sum does not constitute a renunciation of ongoing maintenance rights within the meaning of this rule.[414]

3. Whilst in many instances it will be clear that a particular case concerns a maintenance obligation (e.g. a simple request from one party to another for periodic financial support), there is a degree of overlap with the realm of property relations between spouses or registered partners. For instance, under the national law of the Republic of Ireland,[415] which lacks the conception of 'matrimonial property regimes' found in civil law systems, it may be hard to define whether a distribution of property or lump sum payment upon divorce is to be regarded as relating to maintenance or to matrimonial property for the purposes of the Maintenance Regulation.[416]

For the purpose of drawing a distinction between these subject areas, a number of CJEU judgments on the Brussels Convention can be presented. Leading on from the autonomous definition of matrimonial property that is provided for the purposes of differentiating these two fields in 143/78 *de Cavel v. de Cavel (No.1)*,[417] the Court stated in 120/79 *de Cavel v de Cavel (No.2)*[418] that maintenance obligations between divorced spouses include 'any financial obligations between former spouses after divorce which are fixed on the basis of their respective needs and resources'.[419]

However, it was not until more recently, in 1997, that the CJEU set out specific criteria designed to help distinguish between maintenance and matrimonial property in Member States. This was established in the case of

413 Ibid., at para.147.

414 Ibid., para.148.

415 A similar assertion can be made with regard to the UK, although this is of minimal relevance given its impending exit from the EU.

416 M. Torga, 'Drawing a demarcating line between spousal maintenance obligations and matrimonial property in the context of the new instruments of European Union private international law' in P. Beaumont et al. (eds.), *The recovery of maintenance in the EU and worldwide* (Hart Publishing, Oxford, 2014), at pp.425–426.

417 *De Cavel I* (n.377 above), at para.7 'not only property arrangements specifically and exclusively envisaged by certain national legal systems in the case of marriage, but also any proprietary relationships resulting directly from the matrimonial relationship or the dissolution thereof'. See also discussion with regard to property relations in the preceding section.

418 Case 120/79 *Louise de Cavel v. Jacques de Cavel*. Reference for a preliminary ruling: Bundesgerichtshof – Germany [1980] ECR 731.

419 Ibid., at para.5.

Van den Boogaard v. Laumen,[420] in which the CJEU was requested to examine how an order for ancillary relief under English law should be characterised. It was held here that the form of order (periodic payment, lump sum, or transfer of property) was irrelevant for determining its character.[421] An order will be categorised as involving maintenance if the reasoning of the decision shows that it was intended to allow a party to provide for him- or herself, or if the respective needs and resources of the parties were taken into consideration in determining the amount. An order purely concerned with the division of property owned by the parties will be categorised as involving matrimonial property.[422] It may also be that a case can involve both aspects, if correspondence between these respective aims and different parts of the provision can be shown.[423]

It has furthermore been proposed that due to the more efficient recognition and enforcement procedure set out in the Maintenance Regulation compared with the Matrimonial Property Regulation (in particular, the abolition of the exequatur procedure established in the former), and in view of the specific objectives of the EU legislator in drafting an instrument on maintenance obligation (e.g. securing a free flow of judgments so that creditors can claim effectively against debtors in cross-border situations),[424] the scope of subject matter addressed in the Maintenance Regulation ought to be interpreted broadly in borderline cases.[425] A similar argument can be made given the specific protections, acknowledging the weakened position of the creditor, that are built into the private international law framework relating to maintenance,[426] but absent in the more neutral instrument on matrimonial property.

4.5.2. PERSONAL SCOPE

Choice of court and choice of law agreements formed under the Maintenance Regulation and the Hague Protocol are concluded between a creditor (person owed maintenance) and debtor,[427] linked together by a family relationship, parentage, marriage or affinity. As mentioned in the previous subsection, it is left to the Member States to define the relationships that fall into these categories (although entire categories may not be excluded completely).

---

420 *Van den Boogaard v Laumen* (Chapter 3, n.314).
421 Ibid., at paras.23 and 25.
422 Ibid., at para.22.
423 Ibid., at para.22.
424 See Recital 22 of the Maintenance Regulation.
425 Torga (n.416 above), at pp.431–432 and 434–435.
426 In particular, the protections established in the Hague Protocol: see, for example, Article 8(4).
427 Terminology employed by Maintenance Regulation and Protocol, respectively – the person who owes maintenance.

4.5.2.1. *Debtor*

The role of the debtor is fairly self-explanatory in this context. To use the definition employed by the Maintenance Regulation: 'the person who purportedly owes the creditor an obligation to pay maintenance: any individual who owes or who is alleged to owe maintenance'.[428] One clarification that might be necessary is that although in most cases the 'debtor' and 'defendant' are one and the same (particularly in an initial claim for maintenance), the two terms are not entirely synonymous. For instance, a debtor might assume the role of applicant in order to request that a maintenance order be varied.

4.5.2.2. *Creditor*

Employing the concise terminology of the Maintenance Regulation once more, the creditor is to be defined as: 'any individual to whom maintenance is owed or is alleged to be owed'.[429] As discussed in Chapter 2, this is a category of party that can be seen as generically weak, paralleling the categories of consumers and employees in (non-)contractual obligations.[430] The creditor's vulnerability emerges from the fact that he or she is looking to obtain payment from the debtor in order to sustain him or herself – the necessity is unilateral. And, since the creditor is seeking payment in the first place, they are likely to be in a financially weaker position than the debtor, which could also be indicative of an imbalance of power that already existed during their relationship. Such characteristics generally make it more difficult for the creditor to recover maintenance from a debtor situated abroad – given the need to pay for foreign legal representation – and, more specifically in view of the present context, place the maintenance creditor in a weaker bargaining position than the debtor when an agreement on a choice of court or law is made.

Minors (children under the age of 18 for these purposes) are a category of creditors that experience a specifically low level of bargaining power because they generally lack the capacity to exercise party autonomy directly, even though they bear the consequences of the proceedings that are organised through such agreements.[431] Furthermore, conflicts of interest are perceived as more likely to arise for those representing the children in such proceedings, because such persons are usually the children's own parents, who are bound to provide for them.[432] In response to this, the Maintenance Regulation does not permit choice

---

428 Article 2(11) of the Maintenance Regulation.

429 Article 2(110).

430 See discussion of weaker parties in 2.4.2.

431 Abendroth (n.337 above), at p.468.

432 Bonomi (n.400 above), at paras.127–128.

of court agreements to be made with respect to maintenance obligations owed to minors.[433] However, a very limited possibility for party autonomy is permitted under Article 7 (selection of the *lex fori*) of the Hague Protocol.

Notwithstanding the clear weaknesses inherent in a minor's bargaining position, this general exclusion of the possibility for a choice of court in situations involving minors under the Maintenance Regulation can be criticised on the basis of a lack of consistency in approach with the wider framework. Such an exclusion did not exist in the context of choice of court agreements for maintenance under Article 23 of the Brussels I Regulation,[434] and prorogation of the court and participation in the transfer of court is permitted for matters of parental responsibility under the Brussels II bis Regulation. The absence of a possibility for jurisdictional party autonomy in instances involving child maintenance also means that there is no opportunity for the parties to agree to coordinate related proceedings (most prominently concerning matrimonial matters and parental responsibility) through the exercise of choice.

This exclusion also contrasts with the active encouragement within EU Member States' domestic legal systems of the formation of agreements between parties concerning the amount of child maintenance to be paid. The drafters of the Maintenance Regulation seemingly neglected to acknowledge circumstances in which prorogation of the court that decides upon maintenance obligations may well be in the best interests of the child.[435] It is argued here that a similar 'best interests consideration' to that set out in Articles 12 and 15 of Brussels II bis[436] could have been used in the Maintenance Regulation in order to guard against the potential risks that arise from conflicts of interests while preserving the valuable flexibility of party autonomy.[437]

Notwithstanding the discussion above, an anomalous exception to the general exclusion of party autonomy in situations involving minors under the Maintenance Regulation arises from the apparent (in the absence of specification to the contrary) omission to set an age-limit limit for participation in the subsidiary choice of court mechanism that is contained in Article 5 (jurisdiction by submission of the defendant). Although the debtor will most likely be the defendant in cases involving a request for maintenance, it is not precluded that the creditor might assume this role if the debtor is applying for a variation of

433 Article 4(3) of the Maintenance Regulation.

434 Walker (Chapter 2, n.164), at pp.231–232.

435 M. Hellner, 'The Maintenance Regulation: a critical assessment of the Commission's Proposal' in K. Boele-Woelki and T. Sverdrup (eds.), *European Challenges in Contemporary Family Law* (Intensentia, Antwerp, 2008), at p.349. Hellner states that, to his knowledge, this possibility under Brussels I did not give rise to any known problems.

436 See discussion in 7.2.3. and 8.2.1.–8.2.2. of the best interests criterion in these provisions.

437 Viarengo / Marchetti (Chapter 3, n.313), at pp.55–56.

a maintenance order.[438] Thus, a situation might conceivably arise in which a minor creditor (or the party who acts on his or her behalf) accepts jurisdiction through submission according to Article 5, a mechanism that arguably seems more susceptible to risk than the established grounds for a choice of court under Article 4 of the Maintenance Regulation.[439] The inclusion of this residual possibility will be explored in further detail in 8.3.2.

One further area of contrast between the Maintenance Regulation and the Hague Protocol is seen in their treatment of vulnerable adults (with an impairment or insufficiency of mental faculties[440]). Whilst the Protocol generally excludes party autonomy in situations involving such individuals except where a choice for the *lex fori* is made under Article 7 (in line with its approach towards minors),[441] no such protection is apparent under the Maintenance Regulation. It should therefore be presumed that choice of court agreements relating to the maintenance obligations involving vulnerable adults are permitted under Article 4. The reasons for this inconsistency in treatment are not immediately apparent,[442] since such persons often also lack capacity to form agreements. Notwithstanding the argument above in favour of loosening the blanket exclusion of prorogation of court in maintenance cases involving children, a degree of protection should nevertheless be in place for both minors and vulnerable adults who are incapable of exercising consent in this context.

4.6. PARENTAL RESPONSIBILITY

Moving onto the area of parental responsibility, it is seen that a limited choice of court is established under Article 12 of the Brussels II bis Regulation, as well as the residual opportunity to participate in a transfer of jurisdiction under Article 15 of the same instrument. It should be noted that there is presently no possibility to make a choice of *law* in this realm.[443]

Notwithstanding the opportunity to link jurisdiction with related matrimonial proceedings, in order to ensure equality amongst differently circumstanced

438 See discussion in the context of the role of debtor in 4.5.2.1. above.

439 For instance, the jurisdiction can be entirely disconnected from the creditor. See Walker (Chapter 2, n.164), at pp.232–233.

440 As defined by Article 1(1) of the Hague Convention of 13 January 2000 on the International Protection of Adults: 'Adults who, by reason of an impairment or insufficiency of their personal faculties, are not in a position to protect their interests'. See also Bonomi (n.400 above), at para.127.

441 Article 8(3) of the Hague Maintenance Protocol.

442 This decision was said to be based on 'legislative history': see Abendroth (n.337 above), at p.468.

443 The private international law rules on applicable law in the realm of parental responsibility are provided by the 1996 Hague Convention on Child Protection.

children in its application,[444] the Brussels II bis Regulation principally provides that questions of parental responsibility are to be considered independently of such matters.[445]

4.6.1. MATERIAL SCOPE

The term 'matters of parental responsibility' is, like the other subject matters dealt with in this chapter, limited to civil law.[446] Given the intersection of this particular field and public law, it must be reiterated that civil law[447] is to be interpreted autonomously and broadly in this context in view of the context and objectives of the instrument[448] (amongst which include the furtherance of the best interests of the child[449]).

In the present instance, matters that are listed as inclusions under Article 1(2) (see below), but which are defined as public law within national law, are to fall within the scope of the regulation.[450] By adhering to a distinct, uniform meaning of civil matters in the context of Community law, it is intended that discrimination between children in different states will be avoided.[451]

As a starting point to establishing the scope of matters of 'parental responsibility' for the purposes of the regulation, reference can be made to Article 2(8), which states that it should be taken to mean:

> All rights and duties relating to the person or the property of a child which are given to a natural or legal person by judgment, by operation of law or by an agreement having legal effect. The term shall include rights of custody and rights of access.

---

444 See Recital 5 of the Brussels II bis Regulation and Case C-92/12 *Health Service Executive v. S.C. and A.C.* Reference for a preliminary ruling from the High Court (Ireland) [2012] ECLI:EU:C:2012:255, at para.64.

445 Ensuring equality between children under the Regulation regardless of the marital status of those that hold parental responsibility. This was not the case under the Brussels II Regulation, which only addressed matters of parental responsibility in connection with the dissolution of a marriage.

446 See Article 1 of Brussels II bis.

447 See 4.2.2.

448 *Gogova* (n.327 above), at para.27 and *C* (n.326 above), at paras.45–49.

449 See references in Recitals 12 and 13, Articles 12 and 15 of Brussels II bis.

450 See the example of public law rules relating to child protection (removal of children and placement in foster care) provided in *C* (n.326 above), at paras.45, 51 and 53 and Case C-428/15 *Child and Family Agency (CAFA) v J.D.* Request for a preliminary ruling from the Supreme Court (Ireland) [2016] ECLI:EU:C:2016:819, at para.33. See also EC Practice Guide (n.329 above), at pp.19–20, para.3.1.1.3. In addition, see the Dutch case in which a parental application made under public law rules fell within the scope of application of the Regulation, since the particular purpose of the rule was to be a measure relating to parental responsibility: Rechtbank Den Haag, 11-07-2013, nr. C/09/443928 FA RK 13-4125.

451 *C* (n.326 above), at para.47.

This broad summation is carried forth and elucidated upon by the non-exhaustive list of inclusions set out in Article 1(2):

(a) rights of custody and rights of access;
(b) guardianship, curatorship and similar institutions;
(c) the designation and functions of any person or body having charge of the child's person or property, representing or assisting the child;
(d) the placement of the child in a foster family or in institutional care;
(e) measures for the protection of the child relating to the administration, conservation or disposal of the child's property.

Beyond the well-known usage of parental responsibility in areas such as custody, rights of access and guardianship, a number of topics on this list of inclusions can be highlighted for further discussion:

1. Firstly, in addition to addressing all proceedings involving custody and rights of access between parents, the interpretation of Brussels II bis is also to be extended to include decisions on the rights of access of third persons such as grandparents or siblings.[452] The CJEU has also clarified that penalty payments intended to ensure the effectiveness of access rights fall within the scope of this instrument.[453]
2. With regard to the placement of the child in a foster family or in institutional care, the CJEU has held that this inclusion extends to encompass therapeutic and educational care entailing deprivation of liberty for the child's own protection, provided that such a measure is not intended to punish the child (see exclusion contained in Article 1(3)(g) below).[454]
3. Decisions involving the assistance or representation of a child with regard to their property only fall within the scope of Brussels II bis by virtue of Article 1(2)(c) when made in pursuit of the protection of the child. According to Recital 9, this is to be understood as the designation and functions of any person or body having charge of the child's property, representing or assisting the child, or the administration, conservation or disposal of the child's property.[455] Matters relating to the general organisation of the child's

[452] Case C-335/17 *Neli Valcheva v. Georgios Babanarakis*. Request for a preliminary ruling from the Varhoven kasatsionen sad (Bulgaria) [2018] ECLI:EU:C:2018:359. See also Pintens (n.348 above), at pp.76–77, para.70.

[453] Case C-4/14 *Christophe Bohez v. Ingrid Wiertz*. Request for a preliminary ruling from the Korkein oikeus (Finland) [2014] ECLI:EU:C:2015:563, at paras.34–35, 47–53.

[454] *Health Service Executive v. S.C. and A.C.* (n.444 above), at paras.56–66.

[455] The stated example included in this recital is of a dispute between parents regarding the administration of the child's property.

property are instead dealt with by the Brussels I Regulation.[456] It is left to the judge to decide which category a measure falls into.[457]

In line with the format of the majority of EU instruments in this field, a parallel list of excluded topics is established in Article 1(3):

(a) the establishment or contesting of a parent-child relationship;
(b) decisions on adoption, measures preparatory to adoption, or the annulment or revocation of adoption;
(c) the name and forenames of the child;
(d) emancipation;
(e) maintenance obligations;
(f) trusts or succession;
(g) measures taken as a result of criminal offences committed by children.

Turning to examine the specific elements of these exclusions, a number of comments can be made:

1. It is firstly seen that there is a potential for overlap between the excluded matter of adoption and the inclusion of foster care in Article 1(2)(d). In order to delineate the inevitably blurred boundaries between these categories, it has been proposed that placement with a foster family in preparation for a later adoption is excluded from the regulation's scope of application.[458] However, given the often-uncertain nature of the road from foster care to adoption, it may be difficult to impose this exclusion in practice.
2. Notwithstanding the exclusion of succession matters by Article 1(3)(f),[459] the CJEU has found that an application for a Member State court to approve an agreement for the sharing-out of an estate concluded by a guardian *ad litem* on behalf of minor children constitutes a measure relating to the exercise of parental responsibility within the meaning of Article 1(1)(b) of Brussels II bis.[460] It stated that the need to obtain approval from the court dealing with guardianship matters is directly connected with the status and capacity of the minor children, and constitutes a protective measure for the child relating to the administration, conservation or disposal of the child's property in the exercise of parental responsibility according to Article 1(2)(e) of the Brussels II bis.[461] The CJEU recalled the

456 *EC Practice Guide* (n.329 above), at.pp.20–21, at para.3.1.1.4.
457 Ibid., at.pp.20–21, at para.3.1.1.4.
458 Pintens (n.348 above), at p.78, para.72.
459 With such matters generally falling instead within the scope of the Succession Regulation.
460 Case C-404/14 *Proceedings brought by Marie Matoušková*. Request for a preliminary ruling from the Nejvyšší soud České republiky [2015] ECLI:EU:C:2015:653.
461 Ibid., at para.31.

aforementioned reasoning[462] in the recent case of *Saponaro*,[463] in which the Court adjudged that a request from the parents of minor children to renounce inheritance concerned the status and capacity of these children and did not fall within the law of succession.[464]

3. It is stated that decision-making concerning maintenance obligations is excluded from the scope of this regulation. However, a connection is made between proceedings involving the subject matter covered by Brussels II bis and the Maintenance Regulation by way of the alternative objective grounds set out in Article 3(c) and (d) of the latter instrument. These provisions establish that if the application for maintenance is ancillary to proceedings involving either the separation or weakening of a marital link, or a matter of parental responsibility, the Member State court which is competent to rule on one of the latter matters shall have jurisdiction. It should be noted that where both of the aforementioned proceedings occur in tandem in different Member States, the Member State in which proceedings concerning parental responsibility are being conducted is competent to rule on the ancillary maintenance matter involving the minor.[465] Although Article 3 of the Maintenance Regulation sits outside the scope of this present investigation, it nevertheless offers a mitigating consideration when looking at the general exclusion of party autonomy in maintenance obligations involving minors (see also the discussion at 4.5.2.2. above).
4. On a closing note, it should be remarked that there have been some reported difficulties in interpreting parental responsibility in Member States' domestic courts. For instance, it has been highlighted that since there is no equivalent to this concept in French or Polish domestic law, and national judges are not familiar with the notion that persons other than the parents (or guardians) can be holders of parental responsibility, there is a risk that the term be confused with the more restrictive concept of 'parental authority'. It has also been stated that problems in interpretation may arise in the Finnish legal system as a result of the mismatch between parental responsibility and the concepts of custody and guardianship that are used in domestic law.[466] However, given the high degree of elaboration already provided in Article 1(2) and (3), it has to be concluded that such difficulties are more due to a lack of judicial familiarity with Brussels II bis than poor drafting of the instrument itself.

462 *Saponaro* (n.463 below), at para.17.

463 Case C-565/16 *Alessandro Saponaro and Kalliopi-Chloi Xylina*. Request for a preliminary ruling from the Eirinodikeio Lerou (Greece) [2018] ECLI:EU:C:2018:265.

464 Ibid., at para.18.

465 Case C-184/14 *A. v. B.* Request for a preliminary ruling from the Corte suprema di cassazione [2015] ECLI:EU:C:2015:479.

466 Asser Institute (n.358 above), at p.31, para.3.9.

4.6.2. PERSONAL SCOPE

The distinct forms of party autonomy in matters of parental responsibility found under Brussels II bis clearly focus upon the child, but potentially involve the participation of a broad range of individuals or bodies.

4.6.2.1. Child

Although the child is not technically a participant in the exercise of party autonomy in matters of parental responsibility, he or she nevertheless holds a pivotal place at the centre of proceedings. Unlike the 1996 Hague Convention on Child Protection, which sets the age of majority at 18 years old (Article 2), the exact limits of minority remain undefined for the purposes of Brussels II bis. The question of whether the matter of parental responsibility concerns a minor is left to the applicable national law.[467]

4.6.2.2. Holders of Parental Responsibility

Article 12(1) requires that the spouses involved in a request for a divorce, legal separation or marriage annulment express their consent to the prorogation of the same court to decide on related matters of parental responsibility. In contrast to Article 3(1) of the Brussels II Regulation, which necessitated that both spouses be the parent of the child,[468] Article 12(1) only requires that one spouse is a holder of parental responsibility (meaning that a stepparent of a child may also participate in this process[469]). This brings the regulation into line with the contemporary prevalence of composite families in Europe.

In addition to this, in order for a prorogation of court to succeed under Article 12(1), the prorogued jurisdiction also has to be accepted by any other party who holds parental responsibility over the child (e.g. the ex-partner of the spouses). This is a necessary inclusion, given that the spouses are not necessarily *both* holders of parental responsibility; nor are they always the *sole* holders of parental responsibility. Such additional holders of parental responsibility could include ex-partners of one of the spouses, grandparents, or even local authorities.[470] Requiring the agreement of these interested parties ensures that the forum is also convenient for them and that their access to justice is not impeded through

[467] *EC Practice Guide* (n.329 above), at.p.19, para.3.1.1.1. and E. Pataut, 'Chapter II – Jurisdiction, Section 2 – Parental Responsibility' in U. Magnus and P. Mankowski (eds.), *Brussels IIbis Regulation* (Sellier, Munich, 2012), at pp.75–76, para.65.

[468] Francq (Chapter 1, n.56), at pp.56–57.

[469] McEleavy (Chapter 1, n.56), at p.507, fn.27.

[470] Under Article 2(7), the Regulation states that a holder of parental responsibility can be a natural or legal person. See also *EC Practice Guide* (n.329 above), at p.19, para.3.1.1.2.

prorogation. In addition, their consent may be taken as additional evidence in favour of adjudging prorogation of court to be in the best interests of the child; unlike the spouses, they do not have an interest in concentrating matrimonial and parental responsibility proceedings in the same jurisdiction.

One further point for discussion concerns the treatment of parties who hold parental responsibility in one Member State, but whose status might be refused on the grounds of rules and/or public policy in another Member State that does not recognise the relationship between the holder of parental responsibility and the child. This might prominently arise in the case of a non-biological same-sex parent, but also with regard to parents who have acquired their status through surrogacy. In contrast to married couples (see 4.3.2. above), in these cases a decision to recognise a parental bond will also have to take into account the additional principle of the primary or paramount consideration for the best interests of the child.[471] Thus, it is even less clear how 'non-traditional' holders of parental responsibility would be treated in the cross-border context. This topic will be addressed further with regard to the enforcement of choice in Chapter 10.[472]

4.6.2.3. *Parties to the Proceedings*

Prorogation according to Article 12(3) and the transfer of jurisdiction under Article 15 involve the possibility for involvement of a much wider group of participants. Both mechanisms require, to different extents,[473] the contribution of the parties to the proceedings. A slight terminological difference can be seen between the two provisions, with Article 12(3) referring to 'parties to the proceedings', whilst Article 15 only uses the term 'parties'. However, it is proposed here that in the absence of qualification to the contrary, it would be logical to assume that no difference in the composition of such groups is intended.

---

471 Framed as a primary consideration in Article 3(1) of the UN Convention on the Rights of the Child (1989) and Article 24(2) of the EU Charter of Fundamental Rights, and as a paramount or primary consideration in ECtHR cases concerning adoption/surrogacy in the context of Article 8 ECHR. See Wagner (Chapter 2, n.123), at paras.133–134; *Mennesson v. France*, Application no. 65192/11, ECtHR (26 June 2014), at paras.81 and 84; *Labassee v. France*, no.65941/11, ECHR (26 June 2014), at para.60; and *Paradiso and Campanelli v. Italy*, Application no. 25358/12, ECtHR Grand Chamber (24 January 2017), at paras.127 and 208. See also L. Bracken, 'Assessing the best interests of the child in cases of cross-border surrogacy: inconsistency in the Strasbourg approach?' (2017) 39(3) *Journal of Social Welfare and Family Law* 368–379 and R. Blauwhoff and L. Frohn, 'International Commercial Surrogacy Arrangements: The Interests of the Child as a Concern of Both Human Rights and Private International Law' in C. Paulussen et al. (eds.), *Fundamental Rights in International and European Law* (T.M.C. Asser Press, the Hague, 2016), at pp.219–227, para.10.3.

472 See 10.6.1.

473 See discussion of functioning of both provisions in 8.2.1. and 8.2.2.

There is a degree of variation in the literature as to how this provision ought to be interpreted. Some authors suggest that this requirement only extends to those parties who are actually involved in proceedings. This means that interested parties who do not hold parental responsibility (e.g. grandparents) should be consulted if they are participating in proceedings, and, conversely, the agreement of holders of parental responsibility is not necessary if they are not involved in the case.[474] However, others take a more expansive approach, stating that the agreement of all those who hold parental responsibility is required.[475]

The former interpretation lends itself to minimising complexity, since the requirement to seek out the agreement of all those with parental responsibility may place an undue burden on both the court and the parties directly involved in the case. However, it ought to be acknowledged that this more restrictive interpretation does risk 'surprising' the holder of parental responsibility who is not party to the proceedings, and later finds out about a case concerning their child which has taken place, in their absence, in a state other than their habitual residence.[476] As a means of mediating this potential problem, it has been suggested that consideration of the best interests of the child may be used in order to adjudge, in the light of circumstances, including the position of those who hold parental responsibility, whether the court is indeed suitably placed to hear the case.[477]

The term 'all the parties to the proceedings' which is used in Article 12(3) has been the subject of clarification in the recent CJEU judgment in *Saponaro*.[478] The Court held the opinion that the term was formulated in a broad manner in order to encompass the meaning of such a grouping within the context of national law.[479] Although the CJEU did not improve clarity with regard to the composition of such a category (since this appeared to be wholly delegated to national law), this is in line with the apparent approach of the EU towards delineating the relationships that participate in party autonomy in this context. It should also be noted that this stance towards determining the identity of participating parties on the basis of national law has been explicitly cemented in the recent Brussels IIa (Recast) Regulation.[480]

---

474 Pataut (n.467 above), at p.157, para.53.

475 D. van Iterson, *Ouderlijke verantwoordelijkheid en kinderbescherming* (Maklu, Apeldoorn/Antwerp, 2011), at p.151, para.265.

476 Pataut (n.467 above), at p.157, para.53.

477 Ibid.

478 *Saponaro* (n.463 above).

479 Ibid., at para.28. See wider discussion of this case in Walker (Chapter 2, n.164), at p.230.

480 See Recital 23 of the Brussels IIa Regulation (n.341 above): 'According to the case-law of the Court of Justice, anyone other than the parents who, *according to national law*, has the capacity of a party to the proceedings commenced by the parents, should be considered a party to the proceedings for the purposes of this Regulation' (emphasis added).

4.7. SUCCESSION

Finally, the material and personal scope of the Succession Regulation is brought into focus. This realm is technically considered to be separate from the other areas discussed in this book, as it was introduced through a different legislative procedure.[481] However, it clearly belongs in the same family of regulations, being as it is legislatively intertwined with the Property Regulations, and sharing the same restrictive approach to party autonomy as other instruments discussed here. Still, as will become apparent, succession is at the same time distinct in nature, with its unique balance between the autonomy of the deceased prior to his or her death, and that of the parties concerned with his or her succession.

4.7.1. MATERIAL SCOPE

Article 2(1) of the Succession Regulation outlines the premise that its material scope includes

> succession to the estate of a deceased person and covers all forms of transfer of assets, rights and obligations by reason of death, whether by way of a voluntary transfer under a disposition of property upon death or a transfer through intestate succession.

The regulation sets out a broad definition for succession matters, encompassing the various consequences of the dissolution of the deceased's estate, whether this process occurs according to a testamentary disposition, or domestic rules on intestate succession. The delineated subject area can also be seen as wider than that set out in the 1989 Hague Convention on the law applicable to succession, which excluded transmission of assets from its scope.[482]

Further elucidation is added by Article 23(2) of the regulation, which sets out an extensive, non-exhaustive list of inclusions to the scope of the applicable law:

(a) the causes, time and place of the opening of the succession;
(b) the determination of the beneficiaries, of their respective shares and of the obligations which may be imposed on them by the deceased, and the determination of other succession rights, including the succession rights of the surviving spouse or partner;
(c) the capacity to inherit;

---

481 Whilst the other EU regulations discussed here were introduced on the basis of Article 81(3) TFEU, a special legislative procedure through which Council unanimity is required, the Succession Regulation was adopted using the ordinary legislative procedure (Article 81(2) TFEU).

482 See Waters (Chapter 2, n.107), at para.39 and Frimston (n.363 above), at p.53, paras.4–5.

(d) disinheritance and disqualification by conduct;
(e) the transfer to the heirs and, as the case may be, to the legatees of the assets, rights and obligations forming part of the estate, including the conditions and effects of the acceptance or waiver of the succession or of a legacy;
(f) the powers of the heirs, the executors of the wills and other administrators of the estate, in particular as regards the sale of property and the payment of creditors, without prejudice to the powers referred to in Article 29(2) and (3);
(g) liability for the debts under the succession;
(h) the disposable part of the estate, the reserved shares and other restrictions on the disposal of property upon death as well as claims which persons close to the deceased may have against the estate or the heirs;
(i) any obligation to restore or account for gifts, advancements or legacies when determining the shares of the different beneficiaries; and
(j) the sharing-out of the estate.

A number of points can be enumerated with regard to the established inclusions to the scope of applicable law:

1. Firstly, this list is considerably more comprehensive than that which is set out in Article 1(2) of the 1989 Hague Convention on the Law Applicable to Succession, extending its remit to cover the causes, time and place of the opening of the succession; the capacity to inherit; the transfer of rights and obligations, including the conditions and effects of the acceptance or waiver of the succession by the heirs/legatees, as well as the liability for debts under the succession; the power of those involved in the succession in matters such as the sale of property and the payment of creditors; and the sharing out of the estate. In comparing the two lists, it can be seen that the Succession Regulation goes into significantly greater detail than the Hague Convention with regard to the content and consequences of the process of succession.
2. Attention is drawn to Article 23(2)(f), which concerns the powers of those concerned with administering the estate. This provision intends to ensure, in particular, that the same applicable law applies to both the transfer of assets, rights and obligations (Article 23(2)(e)), and powers of administration. However, allowances are nevertheless made by Article 29 of the regulation for the potential situation in which jurisdiction and applicable law are split, and the applicable law does not provide sufficient powers to fulfil an administrator role that is considered mandatory by the law of the competent court. According to Article 29(2), in such an instance, the competent court may vest the administrator with residual powers in this regard in accordance with its own law, whilst maintaining regard for the impact of the applicable law upon the process of succession. Article 29(3) further provides that where the law which is applicable to the succession is that of a third state, the competent court may confer all the powers of administration available according to its own law.

3. One more subtle inclusion to the scope of the applicable law can be found in Article 25(3), which provides that the chosen law should be extended to cover the admissibility, substantive validity and binding effects between parties of agreements as to succession. Article 24(2) and (3) makes similar provision for dispositions of property other than agreements as to succession. These can be seen to parallel a similar extension to the material validity of property agreements between spouses or registered partners under Article 27(g) of both Property Regulations. However, the Succession Regulation is considerably more prescriptive than the aforementioned regulations in outlining the specific elements that pertain to substantive validity (Article 26(1)),[483] arguably increasing legal certainty by protecting the expectations as to the manner in which a particular agreement will be adjudged.

In line with the general format of EU instruments discussed here, there is also a lengthy list of exclusions, which is contained in Article 1(2):

(a) the status of natural persons, as well as family relationships and relationships deemed by the law applicable to such relationships to have comparable effects;
(b) the legal capacity of natural persons, without prejudice to point (c) of Article 23(2) and to Article 26;
(c) questions relating to the disappearance, absence or presumed death of a natural person;
(d) questions relating to matrimonial property regimes and property regimes of relationships deemed by the law applicable to such relationships to have comparable effects to marriage;
(e) maintenance obligations other than those arising by reason of death;
(f) the formal validity of dispositions of property upon death made orally;
(g) property rights, interests and assets created or transferred otherwise than by succession, for instance by way of gifts, joint ownership with a right of survivorship, pension plans, insurance contracts and arrangements of a similar nature, without prejudice to point (i) of Article 23(2);
(h) questions governed by the law of companies and other bodies, corporate or unincorporated, such as clauses in the memoranda of association and articles of association of companies and other bodies, corporate or unincorporated, which determine what will happen to the shares upon the death of the members;
(i) the dissolution, extinction and merger of companies and other bodies, corporate or unincorporated;

483 (a) the capacity of the person making the disposition of property upon death to make such a disposition; (b) the particular causes which bar the person making the disposition from disposing in favour of certain persons or which bar a person from receiving succession property from the person making the disposition; (c) the admissibility of representation for the purposes of making a disposition of property upon death; (d) the interpretation of the disposition; (e) fraud, duress, mistake and any other questions relating to the consent or intention of the person making the disposition.

(j) the creation, administration and dissolution of trusts;
(k) the nature of rights *in rem*; and
(l) any recording in a register of rights in immovable or movable property, including the legal requirements for such recording, and the effects of recording or failing to record such rights in a register.

In elaborating upon the exclusions established in the text, a number of themes emerge:

1. As is standard practice among the instruments analysed here, questions concerning the status and capacity of natural persons, and the existence of (family) relationships are excluded. One caveat to this is the limited inclusion of the determination of beneficiaries (though the establishment of family relationships[484]) and their capacity to inherit[485] as set out in Article 23(2)(b) and (c), and the considerations as to the capacity of the deceased in making a disposition under Article 26.
2. As discussed with regard to the Property Regulations, the nature of rights *in rem* to property is excluded from the scope of application of the Succession Regulation in order to avoid a situation in which a Member State has to recognise a right over a property located within its territory which in unknown in its own law.[486] For instance, usufruct should not be introduced with regard to property located in a Member State that does not recognise this right.[487] In the same manner as the aforementioned regulations, the competent Member State court may nevertheless adapt an unknown right *in rem* to the closest equivalent found in the Member State where a property is situated.[488] The transfer of rights *in rem* in the context of the Succession Regulation has been the subject of a recent CJEU ruling in which the Court clarified that the method of transfer of such rights is not excluded from the scope of the regulation by Article 1(2)(k).[489]

---

484 It will be for the courts of the Member State to determine through its own private international law the validity of a certain relationship (e.g. marriage or registered partnership). See P. Lagarde, 'Chapter III: Applicable law' in U. Bergquist et al. (eds.), *EU Regulation on Succession and Wills* (Otto Schmidt, Cologne, 2015), at pp.133–134, paras.10–11.

485 E.g. questions concerning the acceptance of an inheritance by a minor. See ibid., at pp.134–135, paras.12–14.

486 See Recital 15 of the Succession Regulation and the Explanatory Memorandum accompanying the Proposal for a Regulation of the European Parliament and of the Council on jurisdiction, applicable law, recognition and enforcement of decisions and authentic instruments in matters of succession and the creation of a European Certificate of Succession, COM(2009) 154 final, at pp.4–5, para.4.1.

487 Frimston (n.363 above), at pp.48–49, para.63.

488 See Recitals 16 and 17.

489 *Kubicka* (n.383 above), at paras.48–49. It also stated that the conditions of transfer of such rights were not to be excluded by virtue of Article 1(2)(l) of the same regulation (at para.54)

3. Building upon the exclusion of pensions which is also seen in the property regulation, any transfer of property outside of succession, such as through gifts, survivorship or insurance contracts, is also generally excluded (except where these arise as a result of an obligation to restore[490]). According to the Explanatory Report on the 1989 Hague Convention on the Law Applicable to Succession (the instrument upon which this provision was generally modelled), this exclusion is to be interpreted broadly, and applies to all non-testamentary transfers of assets, including joint bank accounts and tenancies.[491]
4. The creation, administration and dissolution of trusts are also excluded from the scope of the regulation on the basis of avoiding interference with the property law of another Member State. Notwithstanding this, Recital 13 makes it clear that where a trust is created under a will or through a statute that concerns intestate succession, the law applicable according to the regulation will apply in the devolution of the assets and the determination of the beneficiaries.
5. The realm of maintenance obligations potentially overlaps with succession. However, the Succession Regulation appears to present a high level of clarity in distinguishing between the topics.[492] Article 1(2)(e) excludes maintenance obligations that arise by reason other than death. The continuance of maintenance claims that existed prior to death is determined on the basis of the law applicable to maintenance. On the other hand, the law applicable according to the Succession Regulation may determine if a maintenance obligation arises by reason of the death concerned (if this is the case, such an obligation is treated as a claim against the estate or one of the beneficiaries).[493]
6. Another area of interplay is found between property relations and succession. Articles 1(2)(c) and (d) respectively serve to isolate succession from the dissolution of matrimonial property and property regimes of relationships deemed to have comparable effects to marriage, and maintenance obligations other than those arising by reason of death. In the former regard, Recital 12 states that the court that is responsible for a succession should take account of the winding up of the (matrimonial) property regime of the deceased in determining the division of the estate. It has been stated that this qualification is intended to urge flexibility in situations in which divergent national laws apply to the succession and the property regime upon the death of a spouse or partner.[494]

---

490 Article 23(2)(i).

491 Waters (Chapter 2, n.107), at para.46. For further discussion of this exclusion in both the Succession Regulation and Hague Convention context, see Frimston (n.363 above), at pp.45–47, paras.42–48.

492 Frimston (n.363 above), at p.44, para.33.

493 M. Weller, 'Article 1: Scope' in A Calvo Caravaca et al. (eds.), *The EU Succession Regulation: A Commentary* (Cambridge University Press, Cambridge, 2016), at p.94, para.46.

494 Ibid., at p.87, para.28.

The overlap between these two property-focused areas presents a potentially troublesome interaction with regard to differences in national approaches to characterising the rights of the surviving spouse.[495] This has been the subject of a recent CJEU judgment (*Mahnkopf*[496]), in which a German court had asked the CJEU to rule on whether a fixed allocation of accrued gains upon the death of a spouse was to fall into the succession or matrimonial property regime. Recalling the autonomous meaning of concepts in EU law, the Court found that, despite this matter being treated as relating to matrimonial property in German law,[497] since the provision in question focused primarily on determining the size of the share of the estate (rather than the allocation of assets or liquidation of the matrimonial property regime), it was to be classified as falling within the scope of the Succession Regulation.[498] Moreover, it stated that this characterisation would apply *vis à vis* the Matrimonial Property Regulation,[499] which entered into force in 2019.

4.7.2. PERSONAL SCOPE

The parties that can participate in the exercise of autonomy under the Succession Regulation can be divided into two distinct categories, namely the deceased, and the 'parties concerned' in the succession.

4.7.2.1. *Deceased*

Defining the 'deceased' for the purposes of the Succession Regulation's application is a fairly straightforward task, since this is simply the person whose succession the (future) proceedings concern. It is important to distinguish the deceased from the testator for these purposes, since the Succession Regulation also applies to intestate succession.[500]

4.7.2.2. *Parties Concerned in the Estate*

In contrast to the above discussion, the meaning of 'parties concerned' in the succession is markedly less clear. Recital 28 of the regulation provides that the identity of such parties ought to be determined on a case-by-case basis,

495 Ibid., at p.87, para.29.

496 See *Doris Margret Lisette Mahnkopf* (n.341 above).

497 Although this is also under debate on a national level – see ibid., at para.26.

498 Ibid., at para.40.

499 Ibid., at para.41.

500 Although it is likely, but not necessarily certain, that if a deceased made a choice of law, they will have also made a will.

and where only some of the parties bring an issue before the court that only concerns them, the agreement of the other potentially concerned parties does not necessarily have to be sought.[501]

This considerable breadth of discretion with regard to the participation of the concerned parties gives rise to legal uncertainty, particularly with a view to the structure of such proceedings, since the exact identity of the concerned parties might only become apparent once a court is seised and the succession is opened.[502] This can also be seen to have repercussions with regard to access to justice for subsequently recognised parties. At the same time, however, this flexibility could also be viewed as necessary to ensuring an appropriate forum of close connection for those actually involved in proceedings and avoiding the impracticalities of legal stalemates.

In searching for the identity of the parties concerned, reference can be made to the Explanatory Memorandum accompanying the Proposal for the Succession Regulation,[503] which states, in the context of a choice of court, that the interests of the 'heirs, legatees and creditors' should be taken into account.[504] According to Recital 47 of the regulation, the identity of such persons or bodies is to be determined according to the applicable law.

The first of these categories, *heirs*, are the persons who are in line to inherit based on their relationship with the deceased (e.g. relatives or persons with whom they shared a legal bond such as a spouse or a registered partner). *Legatees*, on the other hand, are other parties who have been provided for in a will (e.g. not only individuals, but also bodies such as businesses and charities). *Creditors*, in this context, are persons or bodies to whom the deceased owed a debt, whose interest arises from the necessity to recoup this from the deceased's estate.[505] There has been some resistance to the participation of the category of creditors on the grounds that this would be impractical for proceedings.[506] However, given their stated inclusion in the Explanatory Memorandum, along with the possibility to determine the appropriate participation of concerned parties on

501 F. Odersky, 'Chapter II: Jurisdiction' in U. Bergquist et al. (eds.), *EU Regulation on Succession and Wills* (Otto Schmidt, Cologne, 2015), at pp.72–74, paras.6–9.

502 F. Marongiu Buonaiuti, 'Article 7: Jurisdiction in the Event of a Choice of Law' in A. Calvo Caravaca et al. (eds.), *The EU Succession Regulation: A Commentary* (Cambridge University Press, Cambridge, 2016), at p.156, para.10. See further discussion of this with regard to the choice of court provisions in 7.4.2. and 8.3.3.

503 Explanatory Memorandum accompanying the Proposal for a Regulation of the European Parliament and of the Council on jurisdiction, applicable law, recognition and enforcement of decisions and authentic instruments in matters of succession and the creation of a European Certificate of Succession, COM(2009) 154 final.

504 Ibid., at p.5, para.4.2.

505 Depending upon the Member State legal system, this might be limited to a claim upon the estate itself, or extend to involve the transference of the debts of the deceased to his or her beneficiaries.

506 Odersky (n.501 above), at p.73, para.8.

a case-by-case basis, it is argued here that creditors may take part in a choice of court in certain circumstances.

Above and beyond this, doubt may arise as to the appropriateness of an extended number of parties participating in a choice of court where proceedings involving succession occur in tandem with the dissolution of a property regime between spouses or registered partners. This topic will be discussed in further detail in Chapter 7.[507]

4.8. SYNTHESIS

As a first step in evaluating the choice of court and choice of law rules provided with the current EU private international law framework on family matters and succession, this chapter aims to outline and evaluate the preliminary elements of agreements: namely, the general prerequisites for an issue to come within the scope of the EU's private international law rules, the subject matter over which agreements can be made, and the persons who can participate in the exercise of party autonomy in the respective areas.

This synthesis of the chapter's findings first establishes the overall delineation of the material and personal scopes of the respective instruments (4.8.1.) before moving on to consider the interaction and overlap between related subject matters in this particular context (4.8.2.) and any notable absences that have arisen through this analysis (4.8.3.).

4.8.1. OVERVIEW OF THE FINDINGS

A variety of observations regarding the findings of this chapter can be established for the purpose of this synthesis:

1. The autonomous meaning to be attached to EU provisions in the absence of specification to the contrary is a pivotal concept that runs throughout this chapter. Clarification by the CJEU in this regard brings legal certainty for international parties, who can rely on a concrete supranational definition for concepts, rather than navigating through national variations. At the same time, the EU uses autonomous concepts to stretch its remit in the face of the limitations of national law. The autonomous meaning attached by the CJEU to civil matters exemplifies this: if a topic falls within the scope of a regulation but is classed as public law, the concept of civil matters within the meaning of EU law will still encompass it.

507 See 7.4.2.

The autonomous conception of the subject matter established in this analysis leads to a generally broad conceptualisation of the material scope of the instruments (particularly exemplified in the case of parental responsibility). This embracive approach to defining the subject matter over which autonomy can be exercised can be viewed as an enhancement to free will as it was conceived in Chapter 2.

2. Turning to focus upon the third and final preliminary observation (the requisite international character), it is argued that this cross-border requirement is a more contentious matter compared to the other aspects discussed in 4.2. above, since it is undefined within the relevant instruments. In certain circumstances, this might give rise to a lack of clarity and predictability as to whether a borderline situation falls within the remit of an EU instrument.
3. With regard to the substance of the findings in this chapter, it is apparent that questions relating to status, the capacity of those involved and establishing the existence of relationships upon which the relevant proceedings are based, are universally excluded as matters that are ancillary to the primary proceedings at hand. Such delineation aims to prevent encroachment onto areas that are excluded from the scope of the subject matter by some Member States, but included by others, such as rights to pensions that have been accrued during the marriage or registered partnership in the context of the property regulations.
4. Another focal point of exception is exemplified in the exclusion of the nature of rights *in rem* rights from the Property Regulations and the Succession Regulation. This is designed in order to avoid the untenable situation in which Member States can create property clauses that apply in a territory other than their own. It should be noted that the extent of this exception has been the subject of clarification in a recent judgment from the CJEU.
5. With regard to the parties that can participate in an act of autonomy in the realms of parental responsibility and succession, it has been shown that the composition of the potentially wide number of concerned parties leads to a degree of legal uncertainty. This is exacerbated in the latter instance by the fact that the concerned parties might not become apparent until after the court has been seised for the purposes of instigating succession proceedings (thus also leading to problems relating to access to justice). This topic will be considered in greater detail in Chapter 7.[508]
6. It has been proposed here that the answer to the question of whether the relevant regulations apply to 'non-traditional' relationships such as same-sex marriage and registered partnership has become more clear in recent years with the introduction of the 'get-out clause' manifested in Article 13

508 See 7.4.2.

of the Rome III Regulation and, more recently, the express exclusion of the recognition of a marriage or registered partnership by Article 1(2)(b) of both of the Property Regulations.

This emerging approach is unsatisfactory for those in same-sex marriages or registered partnerships in the sense that they cannot be assured of recognition of their relationship in the relevant proceedings as they exercise their right to free movement around the Union, thus negatively impacting legal certainty by making it hard to predict the outcomes or protect the consequences of their relationships. However, there has recently been an indication of a shift in the CJEU's attitude towards national recognition of same-sex spouses that, if not presently influential, is at least promising for future developments.

7. Following on from the above discussion, another related concern involves the potential situation in which a Member State refuses to recognise a relationship between the holder of parental responsibility and the child that has arisen in another Member State (e.g. non-biological same-sex parentage or parenthood through surrogacy). A regard for the best interests of the child is paramount in such a scenario. However, it is unclear how this would be dealt with in the EU cross-border context. This scenario, along with the potential (non-)recognition of same-sex spouses will be further explored with regard to the enforcement of choice in Chapter 10.[509]

8. There is a perceivably high degree of inconsistency with regard to the areas in which party autonomy can be exercised in situations involving minors and vulnerable adults. Whilst prorogation of a court can be made in matters of parental responsibility under Brussels II bis, and there is a possibility to express a limited choice of law in situations involving minors under the Hague Maintenance Protocol, no parallel choice of court opportunity is permitted in such circumstances under the Maintenance Regulation. However, there nevertheless appears to be a possibility for minors or their representatives to accept jurisdiction through submission under the Maintenance Regulation.

   Another point to be highlighted is that whilst the same level of restricted party autonomy is established for both minors and vulnerable adults under the Hague Protocol, no form of protection appears to be in place for the latter group with regard to choice of court agreements under the Maintenance Regulation.

9. In comparison with the bulk of the instruments considered here, the instruments concerning maintenance obligations (particularly the Maintenance Regulation) provide considerably less elaboration as to

509 See 10.6.

the material scope that they covers, most notably due to the absence of a list of exclusions from their scope. In the case of the Maintenance Regulation it has, however, been proposed here that this was intentionally not included in order to allow for as broad an application of the instrument as possible (in order to protect the position of creditors). However, in view of the potential overlap between maintenance and matrimonial property (see discussion of this in 4.8.2. below), further delineation would be helpful in providing a greater degree of clarity.

10. Although there are certainly grey areas that can be identified with regard to the subject matter delineated in these regulations, which can be considered of greater (e.g. whether the lists of exclusions contained in the regulations are to be considered exhaustive) or lesser importance (e.g. whether the personal effects of a marriage or partnership are included under the Property Regulations), in overview of the framework in its entirety, it can be said that the relevant instruments present a fairly comprehensive and coherent picture with regard to their delineation of the subject matter over which agreements may be made.

4.8.2. INTERPLAY BETWEEN RELATED AREAS

The relevant instruments present a generally congruent approach to delineating their subject matter. This has the positive impact of improving usability of the EU instruments by allowing lawyers and internationally active parties to become accustomed to their format. Notwithstanding this, a number of points can be made with regard to the interaction between the material and personal scope of the respective instruments:

1. Firstly, divorce and legal separation, the division of matrimonial property and maintenance obligations are interlinked by the parties that may be involved in proceedings under these instruments (i.e. spouses). The first two regulations (and to a lesser extent, the third) can also be seen to meet on temporal terms, through a joint focus upon the end-point of the marriage.[510] Although it has been established that parental responsibility is not generally tied to divorce and legal separation proceedings, there is nevertheless a possibility for linkage between these areas. Furthermore, parental responsibility is seen to be tied to the maintenance proceedings that follow the dissolution of a relationship between the holders of parental responsibility.

[510] Although maintenance obligations do, of course, apply to a much wider range of relationships than marriage, and the dissolution or variation of a property regime can occur outside the dissolution or weakening of a marriage through divorce or legal separation.

2. This initial examination of the framework has also highlighted the areas in which party autonomy is not permitted and has made preliminary observations on the impact that this has upon coordination. Most notably, a choice of court is not currently permitted for matrimonial matters (divorce, legal separation and marriage annulment) under Brussels II bis. In addition, there is a very limited opportunity for proceedings concerning children (most notably concerning parental responsibility and maintenance). Opportunities for linkage between related subject areas and the above-mentioned fields are thus restricted.
3. An area of potential overlap can be seen to arise in terms of the respective subject matters dealt with by the regulations on the property relations between spouses or registered partners, and that of the Maintenance Regulation, particularly in situations involving common-law systems that lack a clear property regime in their domestic law. There have, however, been efforts to clarify the boundaries between these two areas by the CJEU. In this regard, the Court has established general guidelines, providing that where the aim[511] of the order is to help one party provide for him or herself, or if the respective needs and resources of the parties are taken into consideration, then the order would be classified as maintenance, whilst if it purely involves the division of property owned, this would be considered to involve a property regime.
4. A connection can also be made between maintenance and succession, in the sense that the latter governs maintenance obligations that occur following a death of a certain party. However, this delineation is fairly well demarcated and does not appear to give rise to problems. The above statement does not, however, hold for the relationship between succession and property relations, whereby national rules vary with regard to the area of law through which the surviving spouse or partner can pursue the allocation of assets. This has recently been subject to a degree of clarification by the CJEU, which ruled that, despite the categorisation of this matter as matrimonial property under German law, the fixed allocation of accrued gains following the death of a spouse was to be viewed as relating to succession in the autonomous EU context, since it concerned the size of the share of the estate.
5. The CJEU appears to apply a particularly wide autonomous interpretation to matters of parental responsibility, most likely due to the permeation of the best interests criterion throughout this area. This is demonstrated by the intersection of parental responsibility with several subject areas, most prominently in the recent cases concerning succession that have come before the court.

[511] The form of the order (e.g. periodic payment) is considered irrelevant.

4.8.3. GAPS TO BE ADDRESSED

In closing this chapter, it can be observed that the evaluation of the material and personal scope of the relevant instruments has revealed a number of issues that merit additional action on a legislative or judicial level:

1. As mentioned above, a choice of court in matrimonial matters (divorce, legal separation and marriage annulment) is sorely lacking, and leaves this area incomplete in comparison with the other instruments that concern proceedings arising from marriage or registered partnership. It is unfortunate that this possibility has not been included in the recent Brussels IIa (Recast) Regulation, meaning that that fragmentation in this regard will continue for the foreseeable future.
2. The introduction of the Partnership Property Regulation has had the effect of highlighting the lack of party autonomy for registered partners with regard to the dissolution of such relationships. It is clear that parties in 'non-traditional' relationships face unpredictability and an inability to protect their expectations concerning the effects of their partnership in the exercise of their free movement rights within the Union. A well-drafted opportunity to make a choice of court and applicable law with regard to the dissolution of registered partnerships would allow them ease of access to justice.
3. In overview of the comparison between the Brussels II bis Regulation, the Maintenance Regulation and the Hague Maintenance Protocol, there is a perceivably high degree of inconsistency with regard to the areas in which party autonomy can be exercised in situations involving both minors and vulnerable adults. The cultivation of a strong, nuanced stance concerning how to proceed with protecting the interests of these vulnerable groups whilst allowing enough flexibility to conduct proceedings with their best interests in mind is necessary.
4. Finally, on a more general basis, it is evident that the novel, autonomous nature of the subject matter that the relevant instruments address naturally gives rise to issues of interpretation for Member State courts. In particular, questions relating to the treatment of rights *in rem* under the Property Regulations and Succession Regulation, or the distinction between the respective subject areas (chiefly maintenance vis-à-vis property relations or succession) have been, and may continue to be, forthcoming. This can be seen as part and parcel of the piecemeal process of distinguishing the subject matter covered by the relevant instruments from national conceptions and developing an autonomous meaning that can be uniformly applied.

CHAPTER 5
FOCUS OF CHOICE

5.1. INTRODUCTION

The previous chapter has delineated the subject matter (material and personal scope) of the instruments that allow for party autonomy in the EU's private international law rules relating to family matters and succession. Before embarking upon an examination into the precise connections through which a choice can be made in those contexts, it is also necessary that the 'focus' of the choice at hand is established.

For the present purposes, this focal point is either the competent Member State court or the applicable national law that applies to a particular matter or proceeding. The parameters of these elements within the context of the EU private international law rules on family matters and succession will be established and contrasted in the following sections ('court' – 5.2. and 'applicable law' – 5.3.).

This examination will follow the format of the previous chapter in presenting this evaluation in a synthesis (5.4.), which will present the findings on the delineation of the focal points, the coordination and interaction between related subject matter in this particular context, and the gaps to be addressed.

5.2. COURT

The first of the two focal points upon which party autonomy is based is that of the 'court': the authority that applies the law and pronounces a decision on the matter at hand. This section will begin by outlining the general definition of 'court' as set out in the relevant instruments concerning property relations, maintenance, parental responsibility and succession (5.2.1.), before delving further into issues that arise from these provisions, namely: the scope permitted for the inclusion of non-judicial authorities by the respective instruments (5.2.2.); the procedural guarantees and requirements that are imposed upon the functioning of these bodies (5.2.3.); the question of whether religious or other private authorities (5.2.4.) or arbitral tribunals (5.2.5.) are to be viewed as decision-making bodies within the scope of the relevant regulations; and finally, the requirement for Member States to notify the Commission regarding the presence of non-judicial bodies in their jurisdictions (5.2.6.).

5.2.1. GENERAL DELINEATION

First and foremost, it should be emphasised that 'court' for the present purposes solely refers to an authority within a Member State, and is subject to the participation of the Member State in the relevant instrument. On this latter point, it ought to be highlighted that Denmark, the United Kingdom and the Republic of Ireland generally opt out of the relevant instruments,[512] and there is limited Member State participation in the Property Regulations as a result of the enhanced cooperation that brought about these instruments.[513]

Turning to further elucidate upon the meaning of 'court' within the settings addressed by the relevant instruments, it is seen that Article 3(2) of the Property Regulations and the Succession Regulation offer the most extensive description of this role, whilst Article 2(2) of the earlier Maintenance Regulation is slightly more limited:[514]

---

512 Denmark does not participate in any of the EU Regulations concerning judicial cooperation in civil matters in the field of family matters or succession: see Articles 1 and 2 of the Protocol on the position of Denmark annexed to the Treaty on European Union and the Treaty establishing the European Community [1997] OJ C340/101. One partial exception is Denmark's parallel agreement to implement the contents of the Maintenance Regulation in so far as it amends the Brussels I Regulation. The United Kingdom and the Republic of Ireland have the opportunity to opt into regulations in these fields if they wish, and have done so in the case of the Brussels II bis Regulation and the Maintenance Regulation (although the UK is not party to the Hague Protocol on the Law Applicable to Maintenance and therefore also the component of the regulation which relates to this): see Articles 1–4 of the Protocol (No.4) on the position of the United Kingdom and Ireland annexed to the Treaty on European Union and the Treaty establishing the European Community [1996] OJ C321E/198.

513 Although enhanced cooperation has also been used to introduce the Rome III Regulation, this instrument does not provide jurisdictional rules. As of 2019, 19 Member States have agreed to participate in the Property Regulations: Belgium, Bulgaria, Cyprus, Czech Republic, Germany, Greece, Spain, France, Croatia, Italia, Luxembourg, Malta, Netherlands, Austria, Portugal, Slovenia, Finland, Sweden and Estonia. See European Council of the European Union, *Press release: 18 EU countries agree to clarify rules on property regimes for international couples* (9 June 2016), available at: http://www.consilium.europa.eu/en/press/press-releases/2016/06/09/property-regimes-for-international-couples/, in which it was announced that Estonia intended to be the 19th participant following the adoption of the regulations.

514 The Property Regulations and the Succession Regulation are indicated on the left-hand column and the Maintenance Regulation is shown on the right.

Property Regulations/Succession Regulation	Maintenance Regulation
For the purposes of this Regulation, the term 'court' means any judicial authority and all other authorities and legal professionals with competence in matters of [matrimonial property regimes / property consequences of registered partnerships / succession] which exercise judicial functions or act by delegation of power by a judicial authority or under its control, provided that such other authorities and legal professionals offer guarantees with regard to impartiality and the right of all parties to be heard, and provided that their decisions under the law of the Member State in which they operate: (a) may be made the subject of an appeal to or review by a judicial authority; and (b) have a similar force and effect as a decision of a judicial authority on the same matter. The Member States shall notify the Commission of the other authorities and legal professionals referred to in the first subparagraph in accordance with Article 64 [Property Regulations] / Article 79 [Succession Regulation]	For the purposes of this Regulation, the term 'court' shall include administrative authorities of the Member States with competence in matters relating to maintenance obligations provided that such authorities offer guarantees with regard to impartiality and the right of all parties to be heard and provided that their decisions under the law of the Member State where they are established: (i) may be made the subject of an appeal to or review by a judicial authority; and (ii) have a similar force and effect as a decision of a judicial authority on the same matter. These administrative authorities shall be listed in Annex X. That Annex shall be established and amended in accordance with the management procedure referred to in Article 73(2) at the request of the Member State in which the administrative authority concerned is established

With regard to the format of the descriptions above, it is clear that there is a high level of consistency between the four regulations. The definition provided in the Maintenance Regulation largely mirrors that provided in the Property Regulations and Succession Regulation, particularly with regard to the obligation for non-judicial authorities to meet the same procedural guarantees and requirements as courts, and the duty placed upon the Member States to notify the Commission of such bodies.

The most notable difference seen between the Maintenance Regulation, on the one hand, and the Property Regulations and Succession Regulation on the other relates to the delineation of non-judicial authorities. Whilst the former simply refers to 'administrative authorities', the latter state that the jurisdictional rules apply to 'any judicial authority and all other authorities and legal professionals … which exercise judicial functions or act pursuant to a delegation of power by a judicial authority or act under the control of a judicial authority'. The consequences of this distinction will be explored in greater detail in the subsection immediately below (5.2.2.).

The extended, reasonably consistent description and the accompanying procedural guarantees and requirements found in the regulations concerning property relations, succession and maintenance contrasts sharply with the considerably more meagre definition of a 'court' that can be identified in the Brussels II bis Regulation with regard to matrimonial matters or matters of parental responsibility (in so far as the latter context is of relevance for the purposes of party autonomy). Article 1(1) of this instrument simply states that the regulation is applicable 'whatever the nature of the court or tribunal' and Article 2(1) deems that the term 'court' covers 'all the authorities in the Member States with jurisdiction in the matters falling within the scope of this Regulation'. Ramifications of the vast gulf seen in the definitions between Brussels II bis and the other relevant instruments will be considered in greater depth in the proceeding subsections.

5.2.2. NON-JUDICIAL AUTHORITIES

As outlined in the subsection above, the relevant instruments can be divided into three categories with regard to their treatment of non-judicial authorities. Article 3(2) of the Property Regulations and Succession Regulation establish the widest scope of application, whereby 'all other authorities and legal professionals' may be defined as a court within these instruments, provided that these bodies 'exercise judicial functions or act pursuant to a delegation of power by a judicial authority or act under the control of a judicial authority' and accord with the procedural guarantees and requirements established in the same provision.

Recital 29 of both Property Regulations and Recital 20 of the Succession Regulation also reiterate the broad definition to be attached to 'court' in this setting (in particular, to respect the different systems that exist in dealing with the subject matter in the Member States), and take the important step of stressing that non-judicial authorities do not fall within the scope when they are not exercising judicial functions (it employs the example of notaries when, 'as is usually the case, they are not exercising a judicial function').

It is also to be noted that the Proposal for a Succession Regulation[515] stressed that the definition of court in its context was to be understood 'in the broadest sense' (since 'more often than not, successions are settled out of court'). This Proposal provided further examples of the type of non-judicial body that might come within its scope, including 'other authorities where they exercise a function falling within the jurisdiction of the courts, in particular by means of delegation, including notaries and court clerks'.[516]

With regard to the Property Regulations, it is conceivable that decision-making might occur during the course of a relationship that does not necessitate judicial involvement but nevertheless falls within the scope of one of the regulations (e.g. a change of property regime[517]), it is proposed here that despite the assertions of Recital 29 (see above), the inclusion of bodies such as notaries might also be of relevance in this context.

---

[515] See Chapter 3, n.191.

[516] Ibid., at p.5, para.4.1.

[517] See the Explanatory Memorandums accompanying the Property Regulations Proposals (Chapter 2, n.179).

In view of the preceding detail, it would appear that the regulations concerning property relations and succession follow a functional approach to defining 'court' for their respective purposes, whereby a body is included not by merit of the category it falls into, but on the basis of how it operates in practice. Such instruments contrast with the earlier Maintenance Regulation, which follows a similar format, but adopts a more prescriptive approach to defining the type of authority that may be competent. It simply states in Article 2(2) that the term court shall include 'administrative authorities' (rather than the more embracive 'all other authorities and legal professionals').[518] The direct reference to administrative authorities focuses on entities such as social welfare boards which have the power to decide on matters of maintenance (particularly found in Scandinavian countries[519]), and appears to exclude persons such as notaries that would be treated as competent under the regulations on property relations and succession.

Finally, attention can be turned to Article 1(1) of Brussels II bis, in which, as outlined previously, there appears to be a considerable gap in terms of the definition of 'court' compared to the four aforementioned instruments. To recap, Article 1(1), taken in conjunction with Article 2(1), simply states that the regulation is applicable 'whatever the nature of the court or tribunal', and the term 'court' covers 'all the authorities in the Member States with jurisdiction in the matters falling within the scope of this Regulation'. It fails to follow the trend established in the other four regulations in terms of imposing procedural guarantees and requirements for non-judicial authorities, or the obligation to notify the Commission of such bodies.

A clear disadvantage of the less detailed scope of 'court' under Brussels II bis is that it may not be completely clear to the parties or their legal representation whether a particular body comes within the scope of the instrument. For instance, in a survey of legal professionals from the Member States carried out in a recent study,[520] the Reporter from Romania attributed a wide scope of interpretation (including notaries, registrars, government offices and welfare authorities[521]), whilst other national Reporters expressed doubt as to whether administrative divorce[522] or decisions by social work bodies[523] were in fact included. In the presence of more guarantees and requirements established in the legislation,

---

518 See also Recital 12 of the Maintenance Regulation, at p.8, para.5.2.

519 S. Daugule, Brochure: Jurisdiction, applicable law, recognition and enforcement of decisions and cooperation in matters relating to maintenance obligations (Riga, Latvia, 2012), at p.8, available at: https://www.tm.gov.lv/files/l1_aWVwaXJrdW1pL3Byb2pla3RpLzQwMDY1X1RNX2Jyb3N1cmFfRU4ucGRm/iepirkumi/projekti/40065_TM_brosura_EN.pdf.

520 T.M.C. Asser Institute et al. http://www.asser.nl/media/4649/m-5796-ec-justice-cross-border-proceedings-in-family-law-matters-10-publications-02-guide-for-application-chapter-1.pdf (Chapter 4, n.358).

521 Ibid., at p.25, para.3.1.

522 Ibid., at p.26, para.3.1.

523 Ibid., at p.26, para.3.1.

practitioners might be able to proceed with greater confidence as to whether the body in question falls within the scope of the relevant instrument.

Although the definition of 'court' actually appears to have been further scaled back in the text of the Brussels IIa (Recast) Regulation,[524] considerable detail is now provided in Recital 14 of this new instrument in which it is stated that 'court' ought to be understood broadly and includes 'administrative authorities, or other authorities, such as notaries, who or which exercise jurisdiction in certain matrimonial matters or matters of parental responsibility'. In a similar manner to the Property Regulations and Succession Regulation, this instrument thus appears to cover a wide range of authorities. In this present instance, the adoption of an embracive approach can be seen as permitting flexibility that is particularly important to ensuring that national differences in the structure of the child protection framework do not stand in the way of a case coming within the scope of the regulation. This being said, although the elaboration provided in the recitals of the new recast inserts a vital element of specificity that is lacking in the present instrument, it still fails to include the procedural guarantees and requirements and the obligation to notify which appears to be standard in the other four relevant instruments within the present framework (see discussion in the following subsections below).

5.2.3. PROCEDURAL GUARANTEES AND REQUIREMENTS

As has briefly been touched upon above, the Property Regulations, Maintenance Regulation and Succession Regulation all establish the same procedural guarantees and requirements for assessing whether or not a non-judicial body falls within their scope.[525] The guarantees relating to impartiality can be seen to stem from the 'right to a fair trial' (Article 47 EU Charter of Fundamental Rights (EU CFR) and Article 6 ECHR), whilst the right of all parties to be heard is reflective of the rights to good administration (Article 41 EU CFR), and equality before the law (Article 20 EU CFR and Protocol 12 ECHR), the principle of non-discrimination (Article 21 CFR and Article 14 and Protocol 12, Article 1 ECHR) and the right to equality between spouses (Protocol 7, Article 5 ECHR). These requirements form baseline standards for decision-making authorities that reflect the rights and principles that are upheld within the European Union.

On the other hand, the requirement that decisions be subject to review or appeal by a judicial authority pertains to the need for actions taken by

524 Whilst Article 2(2)(1) of Brussels IIa more or less replicates Article 2(1) of Brussels II bis, the reference to 'whatever the nature of the court or tribunal' in Article 1(1) of Brussels II bis has been removed from the revised instrument.

525 See Article 3(2) and 3(2)(b) of the Property Regulations and Succession Regulation and Article 2(2) and 2(2)(b) of the Maintenance Regulation.

non-judicial authorities to remain within the sphere of influence of the judicial authorities within the Member State.[526] The final requirement, that decisions must have a similar force and effect to a decision of a judicial authority on the same matter, simply concerns the need for the non-judicial authority to produce decisions that emulate those produced by its judicial counterpart. The above requisites can be seen as safeguarding access to justice for those who come within the competence of such non-judicial authorities.

In contrast to the above, turning to the context of parental responsibility, it can be seen that Brussels II bis lacks any reference to the guarantees and requirements as to the functioning of a (non-)judicial authority that can be identified in the Property Regulations, Maintenance Regulation and Succession Regulation.[527] In particular, the lack of additional requirements pertaining to impartiality of the decision-making body, and the right of all parties to be heard in such matters means that there is a potential for an authority to become competent that lacks these safeguards toward ensuring the right to a fair trial, equality before the law and non-discrimination as established in the EU Charter of Fundamental Rights and the ECHR.

However, it should be noted that the nature of party autonomy in the context of parental responsibility under Brussels II bis contains a number of inherent safeguards that mitigate this risk, such as the agreement of the parties involved and ascertainment of whether prorogation or transfer would be in the best interests of the child.[528] Although this does not necessarily prevent a decision-making authority from becoming competent which does not accord to the procedural guarantees and requirements established in the instruments concerning maintenance, property relations and succession, the protective effect of these additional requirements cannot be discounted.

A further mitigating point is that the CJEU[529] has recently ruled in *Sahyouni* that decisions by private or religious authorities who are not supervised by a public authority cannot come within the scope of Rome III or Brussels II bis[530] in the context of divorce (see discussion in next subsection). By applying this judgment to parental responsibility under Brussels II bis, it can be seen that the risks of the lack of procedural guarantees contained in this instrument are reduced to a very low level.

526 There is no general 'right to appeal' to be identified in Article 47 of the EU Charter of Fundamental Rights or Article 6 ECHR.

527 See Article 3(2) and 3(2)(b) of the Property Regulations and Succession Regulation and Article 2(2) and 2(2)(b) of the Maintenance Regulation.

528 See discussion of the mechanisms set out in Articles 12 and 15 of Brussels II bis at 7.2.3. and 8.2.1–8.2.2.

529 *Sahyouni* (Chapter 4, n.345).

530 The case concerned Rome III, but made use of Brussels II bis in its interpretation: see ibid., at para.40.

5.2.4. RELIGIOUS AND OTHER PRIVATE AUTHORITIES

The realms of family and succession law clearly present an intersection between state law and religious authorities, with most major religions possessing, to varying extents, parallel rules concerning the subject matters discussed here.[531] At the genesis of the unification of EU private international law on family matters and succession, the Borras Report made it clear that the Brussels II Convention would not apply to religious proceedings,[532] which was echoed in the Brussels II Regulation.[533] However, this exclusion is not expressed in the instruments that exist within the present framework or their accompanying documentation.[534]

One possible explanation for this omission is that the drafters assumed that repetition of the exclusion of proceedings conducted by religious authorities was simply not necessary given the delineation already set out in documentation concerning prior instruments. Indeed, it has been purported that the exclusion set out with regard to the Brussels II Convention and Brussels II Regulation continues in the present regulations.[535] However, it could also be the case that the express exclusion established in the early instruments was overly constricting for Member States in which the judicial system intertwined with decision-making by religious bodies.

This interaction has been exemplified in a recent survey of legal practitioners concerning the application of Brussels II bis in Member States for the purposes of the recognition and enforcement of decisions, in which a number of respondents referred to the possibility for some decisions by religious authorities to come within the scope of the regulation.[536] The mentioned instances in which this would occur were where the religious authority has recognised jurisdiction in

---

531 Most prominently, see the prescribed Catholic (Canonical), Islamic (Sharia) and Jewish (Halakha) laws concerning the dissolution of marriage. There are also examples of the participation of religious bodies in other areas of family and succession law, such as the power of the rabbinical court to make decisions concerning financial provision and inheritance of Jewish persons in Israel, and a similar role of the Sharia courts in countries such as Saudi Arabia and the United Arab Emirates. For broader insights into religion and family law, see: J. Mair and E. Örücü (eds.), *The Place of Religion in Family Law: A Comparative Search* (Intersentia, Antwerp, 2011).

532 A. Borrás, *Explanatory Report on the Convention, drawn up on the basis of Article K.3 of the Treaty on European Union, on Jurisdiction and the Recognition and Enforcement of Judgments in Matrimonial Matters, approved by the Council on 28 May 1998* [1998] OJ C 221 at paras.20 and 20(B).

533 See Recital 8 of the Brussels II Regulation.

534 As a side note, this lack of clarity can be contrasted with the series of agreements between the Holy See and Italy, Malta, Portugal and Spain that allow for the recognition and enforcement of decisions emanating from the Holy See (see Article 62 of Brussels II bis).

535 Pintens (Chapter 4, n.348), at p.55, paras.12–13.

536 T.M.C. Asser Institute et al. (Chapter 4, n.358), at p.7, para.2.1.1.3.

a Member State to pronounce a divorce[537] and where their decision-making powers have been recognised as equivalent to the judicial authority in their jurisdiction.[538] Given such exemplification, it might be concluded that the drafters of later instruments intentionally omitted reference to an express exclusion in order to permit a degree of flexibility in this context.

However, as already discussed briefly with regard to procedural guarantees (5.2.3.), the question of the inclusion of proceedings conducted by private or religious authorities within the scope of Rome III (and, by analogy, Brussels II bis) has recently been addressed by the CJEU in *Sahyouni*.[539] The Court ruled that the scope and objectives of Rome III indicate that this instrument is only intended to cover divorces pronounced by a national court or under the supervision of a public authority.[540] Given the particular propensity for the involvement of religious authorities in the realm of matrimonial matters, this ruling is especially important for the present context.

It is clear from the focused wording of the CJEU's judgment that it is intended to apply only to matrimonial matters within the meaning of Rome III and Brussels II bis. Although it is not expressly mentioned, it is proposed that a similar interpretation to that established in *Sahyouni* can be attached under Brussels II bis with regard to matters of parental responsibility.[541] It is difficult to substantiate the impact of this case in the respective contexts addressed by the remaining instruments. However, it ought to be recalled that the delineation of the (non-)judicial authorities that come within the scope of the other relevant instruments is considerably more nuanced, with the imposition of procedural guarantees and the requirement that the decisions of such authorities be subject to appeal or review by a judicial authority and have a similar force and effect to a decision by such a body.[542] It is therefore argued that the likelihood of a purely religious or private decision-making authority falling within the scope of these instruments is minimised.

---

537 The French Reporter to the aforementioned guide stated: 'if the religious authority pronouncing the divorce "has jurisdiction" in the Member State to do so, its decision will fall under the Brussels IIa recognition regime' (ibid., at p.26, para.3.1).

538 In the same guide, the Greek reporter stated: 'religious decisions or decisions of private nature are excluded from the scope of the regulation except for those that are recognised as equivalent to the decisions of judicial authorities' (ibid.).

539 *Sahyouni* (Chapter 4, n.345), at paras.35–49.

540 Ibid., at paras.45–46.

541 See ibid., at para.40 in which it is stated that the substantive scope of Rome III and Brussels II bis are to be treated as the same. The latter instrument does not differentiate its definition of 'court' in Articles 1(1) and 2(1) for the purposes of matrimonial matters and parental responsibility.

542 See Article 3(2) of the Property Regulations and the Succession Regulation and Article 2(2) of the Maintenance Regulation.

5.2.5. ARBITRAL TRIBUNALS

It has been stated that there is an open question as to whether arbitral tribunals are included within the scope of the Succession Regulation[543] (or, by extension, other relevant instruments in which arbitral tribunals are involved in the subject matter in the domestic context). In this regard, it appears that neither arbitration nor arbitration agreements are expressly excluded from the scope of any of the relevant instruments.[544] Furthermore, there is a likelihood that such tribunals may fulfil the procedural requirements and guarantees set out in Article 3(2) of the Property Regulations and Succession Regulation, and Article 2(2) of the Maintenance Regulation.[545]

Notwithstanding the above, it has been suggested that the jurisdictional rules established in instruments such as the Succession Regulation would be unsuitable in the context of arbitration, since their application would have a constraining effect upon the parties in choosing the seat of the tribunal.[546] Furthermore, in terms of fulfilling the requirement upon the Member States to notify the Commission of other authorities and legal professionals that are competent under the Property Regulations, Maintenance Regulation and Succession Regulation, it can be observed that since arbitral tribunals are temporary in nature, it is not clear how this requirement would be satisfied in this context.

Casting the net beyond the EU's instruments concerning family matters and succession, it is important to note that the Brussels I Recast does explicitly exclude the application of its rules to arbitration. At the same time, it also states that Member State courts are free to independently refer parties to arbitration, stay or dismiss their own proceedings on the basis of the existence of an arbitral agreement, or examine whether such an agreement is 'is null and void, inoperative or incapable of being performed, in accordance with their national law'.[547]

This extended elucidation of the position of arbitration within the scope of Brussels I sits in sharp contrast to the silence in the Union's instruments concerning family matters and succession. The considerable attention paid to this matter under the former raises the question of whether the drafters of the

543 M. Weller, 'Article 3: Definitions' in A. Calvo Caravaca et al. (eds.), *The EU Succession Regulation: A Commentary* (Cambridge University Press, Cambridge, 2016), pp.122–123, para.20.

544 In contrast to the situation under Council Regulation (EC) No 1215/2012 of 12 December 2012 on jurisdiction and the recognition and enforcement of judgments in civil and commercial matters (Recast) OJ L 351/1 (the Brussels I Recast): see further discussion below in this subsection.

545 See Weller (n.543 above), in the context of succession.

546 Ibid.

547 See Recital 12 and Article 1(2)(d) of the Brussels I Recast.

latter set of regulations merely ascertained that the possibility of arbitration occurring within the respective scopes of these instruments was so minimal it did not merit acknowledgment.

Moving further away from the present realm, it should be mentioned that the question of whether an arbitral tribunal could be classified as a court or tribunal 'of a Member State' for the purposes of a reference for a preliminary ruling (concerning the protection of investments) was recently addressed by the CJEU. It was ruled that since the arbitral tribunal in that case was brought about as a result of a Bilateral Investment Treaty (BIT) and was an exception to the jurisdiction of the courts of the two Member States involved in this agreement, it could not be viewed as forming part of the judicial systems of these states.[548] However, given the remoteness of this subject matter from the remit of this examination, it is difficult to draw any firm conclusions from this judgment with regard to the present context.[549]

5.2.6. NOTIFICATION OF NON-JUDICIAL AUTHORITIES

The residual uncertainty brought about through 'borderline' examples of non-judicial authorities is also mitigated by the duty imposed upon the Member States to notify the Commission of the non-judicial bodies (or in the case of maintenance, 'administrative authorities') within their jurisdiction that fall within the scope of 'court' for the purposes of the instrument under Article 3(2) of the Property Regulations and Succession Regulation, as well as Article 2(2) of the Maintenance Regulation,

This requirement is formulated slightly differently between the Property Regulations and Succession Regulation on the one hand, and the Maintenance Regulation on the other. With regard to the former three regulations, it is required that the Member States shall notify the Commission of the non-judicial authorities and legal professionals concerned in accordance with the procedure set out in Article 65 (Property Regulations) or Article 79 (Succession Regulation). Through this process, the Commission will go on to publish this information in the *Official Journal of the European Union*[550] and make it available publicly through means such as the European Judicial Network in civil and commercial matters.[551] Under the Maintenance Regulation, the appropriate non-judicial authorities are listed in Annex X of the instrument, and are

548 Case C-284/16 *Slowakische Republik v. Achmea BV.* Reference for a preliminary: Bundesgerichtshof - Germany [2018] ECLI:EU:C:2018:158, at paras.45–49.

549 Particularly since the instances of arbitration in family law and succession do not involve the use of bilateral treaties between Member States.

550 Article 65(2) of the Property Regulations and Article 79(3) of the Succession Regulation.

551 Article 65(3) of the Property Regulations and Article 79(4) of the Succession Regulation.

amended periodically in accordance with a management procedure listed in Article 73(2) of the same instrument (which in turn refers to Articles 4 and 7 of Council Decision 1999/468/EC).

It can be observed, from the lists of non-judicial authorities that have been made available in accordance with the procedures described above, that relatively few Member States have notified the Commission of their usage of such bodies. Under the Maintenance Regulation, only three Member States have made submissions of their competent administrative authorities,[552] five and three Member States have done so under the Matrimonial Property Regulation and Partnership Property Regulation respectively,[553] whilst under the Succession Regulation nine Member States have notified the Commission.[554] With regard to this final instrument, it is interesting to note that the vast majority of submissions concerned the possibility for a notary to be a decision-making body, with only Finland and Sweden diverging from this trend.

Given the heightened legal certainty that notification brings by making the identity of non-judicial authorities easily accessible, as well as facilitating the smooth running of cross-border judicial cooperation, it is unfortunate that this requirement is not included under Brussels II bis. This omission will be explored further in the concluding synthesis under 'Gaps to be addressed' (5.4.3.).

---

552 Finland: the Social Welfare Board; Sweden: the Enforcement Authority; UK: in England and Wales and Scotland, the Child Maintenance and Enforcement Commission (CMEC) and in Northern Ireland: the Department for Social Development Northern Ireland (DSDNI).

553 **Matrimonial Property**: Czech Republic: notarial entities such as court commissioner; Italy: lawyers acting under the assisted negotiation (*negoziazione assistita*) procedure and civil registrars acting under the assisted negotiation procedure; Portugal: Civil registry offices; Finland: judge-appointed laymen; Sweden: property registrars, executors, The Swedish Enforcement Authority. **Partnership Property**: Italy: lawyers acting under the assisted negotiation (*negoziazione assistita*) procedure and civil registrars acting under the assisted negotiation procedure. Finland: judge appointed layman; Sweden: property registrars, executors, The Swedish Enforcement Authority. Information provided by: European Commission, *E-Justice Portal: Matters of matrimonial property regimes*, available at: https://e-justice.europa.eu/content_matters_of_matrimonial_property_regimes-559-en.do and European Commission, *E-Justice Portal: Matters of the property consequences of registered partnerships*, available at: https://e-justice.europa.eu/content_matters_of_the_property_consequences_of_registered_partnerships-560-en.do.

554 Czech Republic, Greece, Spain, Croatia, Hungary, Portugal: Notary; Finland: 'estate distributer'; Sweden: (a) Swedish Tax Agency (*Skatteverket*); (b) estate distributor (*skiftesman*); (c) executor of the will (*testamentsexekutor*), when in the role of the estate distributor without a special appointment to that effect; (d) special estate administrator (*särskild boutredningsman*), when in the role of the estate distributor without a special appointment to that effect. Information provided by: European Commission, *The information referring to Article 79 of Regulation (EU) No. 650/2012 of the European Parliament and of the Council of 4 July 2012 on jurisdiction, applicable law, recognition and enforcement of decisions and acceptance and enforcement of authentic instruments in matters of succession and on the creation of a European Certificate of Succession*, available at: https://e-justice.europa.eu/fileDownload.do?id=92645e67-621a-486f-9907-f2b74fd6377a.

5.3. APPLICABLE LAW

Following on from the extensive examination of jurisdiction within the context of the relevant instruments above, attention is now turned to the second focal point to be examined in this chapter: 'applicable law'. It is the determinant of the rules that apply to the matter in question and resolves the substantive outcome of a proceeding. The various aspects that comprise applicable law within the EU private international law context will be established and examined in the following subsections, namely, the requirement that this is the law of a state (5.3.1.); its universal (5.3.2.) and unified nature (5.3.3.); and the exclusion of *renvoi* in this present setting (5.3.4.)

5.3.1. STATE LAW

The relevant instruments that provide for a choice of applicable law (Rome III, the Property Regulations, the Hague Maintenance Protocol and the Succession Regulation) all necessitate that a *state* law be selected. A state might well comprise multiple legal systems, whereby the applicable law is determined on the basis of territorial[555] or personal considerations (e.g. the law is determined on the basis of the party's religion).[556] In such instances, the relevant instruments generally first defer to internal conflict-of-laws rules before setting out a safety net of solutions.[557]

Parties cannot directly opt for the application of a religious or customary law in this context.[558] However, there is no express barrier to selecting a state law that is based on religious or customary law, or that refers the subject matter to the application of such a non-state law.[559] The applicability of such a law may be subject to variation on the basis that it is considered contrary to the public policy of the forum or the application of supranational mandatory rules (e.g. the fundamental right to divorce under Article 10 of the Rome III Regulation). The influence of such factors will be considered in greater detail in Chapter 10.

---

555 For example, Spain, the United Kingdom, Canada and Australia.

556 For example, the United Arab Emirates, Lebanon and Morocco.

557 See Articles 33–34 of the Property Regulations. Articles 16–17 of the Hague Maintenance Protocol, Articles 36–37 of the Succession Regulation. Articles 14–15 of the Rome III Regulation diverges from first deferring to the state's law in situations involving more than one territorial conflict-of-laws context (Article 15).

558 See discussion in the context of the Rome III Regulation in: Kruger (Chapter 1, n.60), at para.7.

559 Ibid.

5.3.2. UNIVERSAL SCOPE

All relevant instruments provide that the law of any state, including those outside the EU, may be chosen to apply to the subject matter at hand.[560] This addresses the situation of a third country national or an EU national who has ties to a third state (e.g. through dual-nationality or habitual residence) who has seised an EU Member State court for a relevant matter. In the enhanced cooperation context, it is useful to highlight that this also allows the laws of a non-participating Member State to be chosen. In the above situations, the opportunity to select a law on a universal basis places such parties on equal footing with those who only hold EU ties in designating a law with an affinity to themselves or their relationship.

The application of the law of a non-EU state conceivably opens up the possibility for the imposition of rules of a legal system that is far removed from that found amongst the Member States. However, as has been previously touched upon in this chapter, a law's applicability can be varied by the forum on the basis of public policy or mandatory rules.[561]

5.3.3. UNITY OF THE LAW

The three instruments concerning the property relations between spouses and registered partners, and succession, explicitly exclude *dépeçage* (the application of laws from different states to different issues in a single case), stating that the applicable law governs the matter as a whole.[562] This point is particularly crucial in subject areas concerning property, whereby a distinction might otherwise be made between immoveable and moveable assets for the purposes of determining the applicable law ('scission'[563]). This could result in a complicated fragmentation in subject matter that would conceivably hinder the process of decision-making

560 See Recital 12 and Article 4 of Rome III, Article 20 of the Property Regulations, Article 2 of the Hague Maintenance Protocol, and Article 20 of the Succession Regulation.

561 See also the comment regarding universality of the choice of law in the Proposal for a Council Regulation (EU) implementing enhanced cooperation in the area of the law applicable to divorce and legal separation, COM(2010) 104 final, at para.6: 'Safeguard clauses have been introduced to prevent the application of foreign laws on divorce or legal separation which are incompatible with the common values of the European Union'.

562 See Article 21 of both Property Regulations; Recital 43 of the Matrimonial Property Regulation; Recital 42 of the Partnership Property Regulation and Recital 37 of the Succession Regulation (and reference to 'succession as a whole' throughout this instrument).

563 See, for instance, the distinction that is made in English succession law whereby moveable property (e.g. money in bank accounts, possessions) is governed by the law of the domicile of the deceased, whilst immoveable property (e.g. houses) is subject to the law where it is physically located.

over the dissolution of the property regime of the parties or the succession.[564] Although, where a choice of law has been exercised, scission would not present the same concerns relating to legal certainty as it would in the context of objective conflict-of-laws rules, the practical inconvenience of applying multiple state laws during one proceeding[565] would remain the same.

Neither the Rome III Regulation nor the Hague Maintenance Protocol contains an express reference to the unity of the applicable law or the exclusion of *dépeçage*. With regard to the nature of the proceedings that take place under these instruments, there is little scope for divergent laws to apply.[566] Furthermore, given the stated critique of *dépeçage* in the instruments concerning property relations and succession, it would be inconsistent for the EU legislator to diverge from this trend.

5.3.4. EXCLUSION OF *RENVOI*

It is made clear in the relevant instruments concerning proceedings that arise from marriage or registered partnership that *renvoi* is excluded, and that the choice of law rules of the state whose law is applicable may not be applied by the forum in dealing with a case.[567] On the other hand, the Succession Regulation *does* allow for the acceptance of *renvoi* where the conflict of laws has led to the application of a law of a third state, but not in instances where a choice has been made by the deceased for the application of this law.[568] Discussion of *renvoi* is therefore outside this present context, although it can be extrapolated from the above format that even if *renvoi* were to be permitted in all relevant instruments, it is unlikely that it would be applied in the context of party autonomy.[569]

---

564 See the justification for unity of applicable law contained in Recital 43 of the Matrimonial Property Regulation; Recital 42 of the Partnership Property Regulation; and Recital 37 of the Succession Regulation.

565 For example, the possible cost of hiring separate legal representation specialised in the respective national laws and the additional temporal and monetary costs of a longer process.

566 With the exception of preliminary questions (e.g. relating to the capacity of the parties, the validity of the marriage or the existence of the relationship which gives rise to a maintenance claim). Under the Rome III Regulation, such preliminary questions are left to the conflict-of-laws rules of the forum (Recital 10). The Hague Protocol is silent on the approach to be taken in this regard.

567 See Article 11 of the Rome III Regulation, Article 32 of the Property Regulations, and Article 12 of the Hague Maintenance Protocol.

568 See Article 34 and Recital 57 of the Succession Regulation.

569 See discussion in A. Davì, 'Article 34: Renvoi' in A. Calvo Caravaca et al. (eds.), *The EU Succession Regulation: A Commentary* (Cambridge University Press, Cambridge, 2016), pp.481–482, para.13, which exemplifies such exclusions in the private international laws of Member States in fn. 18: 'Article 19.2 of the Portuguese civil code of 1966 and article 13.2(a) of the Italian act on private international law of 1995. Article 6 of the Slovenian act on private international law goes even further, excluding *renvoi* in any areas in which the said act grants the parties the faculty to choose the applicable law, regardless of whether this faculty has in practice been exercised'.

5.4. SYNTHESIS

In culmination of the foregoing examination into 'court' and 'applicable law' in the EU private international law framework on family matters and succession, this synthesis will provide an overview of the manifestations of these two focal points within the present context (5.4.1.), before considering the impact of (in) consistency in the ability to achieve coordination between both the competent court and applicable law, and between the related subject areas (5.4.2.) and, as a final step, presenting the gaps that have emerged during the course of this chapter that need to be addressed (5.2.3.).

5.4.1. OVERVIEW OF THE FINDINGS

From the discussion undertaken in the preceding sections, a number of key points regarding the conception of 'court' and 'applicable law' can be established:

1. Proceeding first with the definition of 'court' contained in the instruments that establish jurisdictional rules, a division can be made in terms of the level of detail provided. The Maintenance Regulation, Property Regulations and Succession Regulation[570] establish a well-delineated scope, providing procedural guarantees and requirements for non-judicial authorities and an obligation to notify the Commission of such bodies.

   In contrast, Brussels II bis simply states that the term 'court' applies to all authorities with competence over the subject matter in the Member State, 'whatever the nature of the court or tribunal'.[571] Although the new recast of this instrument increases the level of detail, the accompanying safeguards that are standard in the other instruments are still sorely lacking.
2. A hierarchy can be created between the relevant instruments in terms of the breadth of scope permitted for the competence of non-judicial authorities. The two Property Regulations and Succession Regulation provide the widest delineation this regard, establishing the possibility for the involvement of 'all other authorities and legal professionals', subject to the requirement that such bodies 'exercise judicial functions or act pursuant to a delegation of power by a judicial authority or act under the control of a judicial authority' and that they accord with the same procedural safeguards and guarantees set out in the same provision. By way of exception, the Maintenance Regulation only appears to extend competence to administrative authorities such as social welfare boards.

570 Article 2(2) of the Maintenance Regulation and Article 3(2) of the Property Regulations and Succession Regulation.

571 Article 2(2) in conjunction with Article 1(1) of Brussels II bis.

As discussed above, whilst little guidance is provided as to the nature of the decision-making authorities that will be considered to be competent under the current version of Brussels II bis, the change of wording in the recent recast of this instrument[572] indicates that it has a broad scope that emulates the Property Regulations and Succession Regulation.

3. The question of whether a religious or private authority could fall within the scope of 'court' for the purposes of the EU Regulations has been clarified by a recent CJEU judgment that excludes such an application for the purposes of Rome III (and Brussels II bis). It is proposed here that, in the absence of any indication to the contrary, this exclusion should apply by analogy to other relevant instruments.
4. In surveying the non-judicial authorities that have been notified to the Commission under Article 2(2) of the Maintenance Regulation and Article 3(2) of the Succession Regulation,[573] it is interesting to note that the majority of states do not provide for the operation of non-judicial authorities within the context of the instruments. Thus, whilst the differences above can be considered to be of academic interest, in practice, their relevance is limited.
5. Moving onto the delineation of 'applicable law' within the instruments that provide for a choice of law in the EU family matters and succession context, it can generally be observed that the approach is much more streamlined than in the jurisdictional setting. In summary an applicable law within the relevant instruments is to be a state law (rather than a religious or customary law) that may originate from either an EU Member State or third country.
6. For the purposes of a choice of law, *renvoi* is not permitted under any of the relevant instruments. Unity of the applicable law is expressly provided for under the instruments concerning property relations and succession through the explicit exclusion of *dépeçage*; it is proposed here that the remaining instruments (Rome III and the Maintenance Regulation) implicitly follow suit in this regard.

5.4.2. INTERPLAY BETWEEN RELATED AREAS

With regard to coordination between the relevant instruments, it can be seen that the differing delineations of non-judicial authorities between, on the one

---

572 See Article 1(1) of Brussels IIa which provides that the regulation is applicable 'whatever the nature of the court or tribunal' and Article 2(1) which states that 'court' covers 'all the authorities in the Member States with jurisdiction in the matters falling within the scope of this Regulation'.

573 The Member States have until April 2018 to notify the Commission of non-judicial authorities that are competent in the context of the Property Regulations.

hand, the Property Regulations, the Succession Regulation and the Brussels II bis Regulation,[574] and on the other, the Maintenance Regulation, theoretically increase the likelihood of divergent authorities being competent for related matters. However, it is proposed here that the impact of this is mitigated by a number of factors.

Firstly, if the courts of the same Member State were to be seised to deal with related matters, the parties would not have to undertake the inconvenience of having to travel between countries or hire additional legal expertise with competence in the law of another jurisdiction. Furthermore, provided that there existed a pathway of interaction between the various judicial and non-judicial bodies in a given Member State, the competence of different authorities for related matters in a single Member State should not be treated as posing an undue practical burden on proceedings. In addition to this, in view of the small number of notifications to the Commission of non-judicial authorities, the likelihood of this posing even a minimal inconvenience in the context of coordination is lessened even further.

Given the consistency that is demonstrated between the relevant instruments concerning applicable law, the delineation of this area should not pose a problem for coordination between related subject matter. The universal scope of the applicable law poses a clear challenge to coordination with choice of jurisdiction. If parties wish to unify the law and court that governs the same matter they are therefore limited to selecting a law of a Member State to apply to the area in question.

5.4.3. GAPS TO BE ADDRESSED

This chapter has revealed a couple of minor gaps with regard to the definition of 'court' within the present framework that would benefit from further clarification. As has been extensively discussed above, Brussels II bis lacks the procedural guarantees and requirements imposed upon a non-judicial authority that have been established in the other relevant instruments. Although the consequences are mitigated by several factors (including a recent ruling by the CJEU that appears to exclude decisions by private or religious authorities that lack supervision by a public authority) there is nevertheless a noticeable gap in the drafting of this instrument.

In addition, it is not made clear whether an arbitral tribunal is considered to be a 'court' within the meaning of the relevant instruments. Notwithstanding the fact that this question is very residual to the wider context since the involvement of such tribunals is not commonplace in cross-border family and succession matters, it would nevertheless increase clarity in the relevant instruments if this matter were elucidated by the EU legislator.

---

574 Proceeding with the expanded definition provided in Recital 14 of the recast of this instrument (Brussels IIa).

PART III
CONTENT OF CHOICE

CHAPTER 6
DIRECT CONNECTIONS

6.1. INTRODUCTION

Having established the subject matter and focus of choice of court and choice of law agreements in the EU's private international law rules relating to family matters and succession, the central point of this investigation comes to the fore: the 'connections' between parties and their choice of court or choice of law through which party autonomy can be exercised.

This chapter will represent the first stage in carrying out the presentation, examination and evaluation of the connecting factors through which a choice can be manifested in the present context by looking at the criteria available to be *directly* chosen. It is one of three chapters on the content of choice, with the other two chapters addressing choice of court or choice of law provisions that operate through coordination ('coordinating provisions') and the jurisdictional mechanisms that include a residual element of party autonomy that is subsidiary to a primary function (and 'subsidiary choice of court provisions').

The chapter will describe, examine and evaluate the direct connections that are made available in the EU's unified private international law rules concerning family matters and succession, namely: habitual residence (6.2.); nationality/domicile (6.3.); and the place where a relationship was created (6.4.).[575]

A synthesis will be presented at the end of this chapter (6.5.), which will bring together the findings in the same format as has been used in Chapters 3 and 4. As well as considering the functions of the particular connections, particular regard will be given to the breadth of choice that is observed within and between the various areas, as well as the role of the parties in selecting a particular connection.

---

575 This chapter is organised to reflect the prominence of the criteria within the wider EU private international law framework relating to family matters and succession, rather than their prevalence in the specific party autonomy context, which will be considered in the synthesis at 6.5.

6.2. HABITUAL RESIDENCE

This section begins with the most prominent connecting factor currently found within the EU private international law framework on family matters and succession: habitual residence. The following series of subsections analyse this criterion by exploring its general characteristics (6.2.1.), before examining and contrasting its manifestations in both the choice of court (6.2.2.) and choice of law (6.2.3.) provisions in the relevant instruments.

6.2.1. GENERAL DESCRIPTION

Habitual residence, the primary ground of close connection within the EU private international law instruments relating to family matters and succession, first emerged as a connecting factor within the Hague conventions around the turn of the twentieth century and rose to prominence following World War II.[576] Today, it has risen to surpass nationality as the chief determinant in jurisdictional and conflict-of-laws matters in national and supranational private international law instruments concerning this realm.[577] This ground is a flexible one, which is hard to succinctly describe. At the outset of this discussion, it should be established that habitual residence carries an autonomous meaning, understood within the EU context and in the specific instrument in which it is contained.[578]

The EU's private international law instruments concerning the various areas addressed here contain sparse guidance on the meaning to be attributed to habitual residence. The Succession Regulation provides the most elaboration,

576 The Hague Convention of 12 June 1902 on the Settlement of the Guardianship of Minors is cited as the first example of the use of this criterion in an international instrument: see R. Mańko, Library of the European Parliament Briefing: '"Habitual residence" as connecting factor in EU civil justice measures' (January 2013), at p.1, available at: http://www.europarl.europa.eu/RegData/etudes/ATAG/2013/130427/LDM_BRI(2013)130427_REV1_EN.pdf. According to Basedow, habitual residence rose to prominence in the Hague Convention instruments following World War Two: see examples of the Hague Convention of 5 October 1961 concerning the powers of authorities and the law applicable in respect of the protection of infants; the 1973 Hague Convention on the law applicable to maintenance obligations; the Hague Convention of 14 March 1978 on celebration and recognition of the validity of marriages; and 1978 Hague Convention on the law applicable to matrimonial property regimes: Basedow (Chapter 1, n.46), at pp.314–316, paras.486–488.

577 See commentary of this development in: Basedow (ibid.), at pp.311–320, at paras.482–495.

578 Case C-497/10 *Barbara Mercredi v. Richard Chaffe*. Reference for a preliminary ruling: Court of Appeal (England & Wales) (Civil Division) – United Kingdom [2010] ECR I-14309, at para.46. See also, for discussion, Shúilleabháin (Chapter 4, n.348), at p.38, para.2.08.

establishing criteria for determining habitual residence in its particular context in its preamble. It states that authorities should

> make an overall assessment of the circumstances of the life of the deceased during the years preceding his death and at the time of his death, taking account of all relevant factual elements, in particular the duration and regularity of the deceased's presence in the State concerned and the conditions and reasons for that presence. The habitual residence thus determined should reveal a close and stable connection with the State concerned taking into account the specific aims of this Regulation.[579]

Another (fleeting) reference is made in the Maintenance Regulation, which simply states in Recital 32 that this concept is to be more strictly construed than simple 'residence'.[580] In addition to this, the Explanatory Report accompanying the Hague Maintenance Protocol provides that habitual residence ought to be stable and not strictly temporary in nature.[581] It also mentions that habitual residence should be determined with a mind to a uniform concept, based on the purposes of the Protocol, not domestic criteria.[582]

Some principles on determining habitual residence can also be garnered from the interpretation of this concept by the CJEU in other contexts (e.g. the claiming of social security benefits), as well as national judgments concerning the definition of habitual residence in matrimonial cases (although these diverge quite significantly from one another in certain regards[583]). An overview of the existing jurisprudence relating to habitual residence demonstrates that assessment of this concept is primarily based upon (i) the *length of the duration of residence* (however, there is no set amount of time: persons may become habitually resident immediately upon returning to their state of origin,[584] but it may take a number of months for this to be established where a person moves to

---

579 Recital 23 of the Succession Regulation.

580 The criterion for determining a person's right to request assistance from a Central Authority should be less strict than the connecting factor of 'habitual residence' used elsewhere in this Regulation. However, the 'residence' criterion should exclude mere presence'.

581 Bonomi (Chapter 4, n.400), at paras.42 and 47.

582 Ibid., at paras.41 and 200.

583 See for discussion Shúilleabháin (Chapter 4, n.348), at pp.36–66 and Viarengo (Chapter 4, n.356), at p.557, para.5.1.

584 See, for example, EU Court of Justice judgment: Case C-90/97 *Robin Swaddling v. Adjudication Officer.* – Reference for a preliminary ruling: Social Security Commissioner – United Kingdom [1999] ECR I-01075, at para.30, and the English High Court decision concerning Article 2 of the Brussels II Regulation (and by extension Article 3 of Brussels II bis): *Marinos v. Marinos* [2007] EWHC 2047 (Fam), at para.89. This approach is, however, controversial, since it could be viewed as discrimination on grounds of nationality under Article 18 TFEU. See Shúilleabháin (Chapter 4, n.348), at p.51, para.2.11 for greater discussion of the merits of this argument.

a state with which they had no previous connection[585]), (ii) *intention to remain*[586] (although persons do not have to intend to remain in a new state indefinitely upon arrival, a lack of intention to remain will mean that the requisite duration needed for habitual residence to be established will likely be longer[587]) and (iii) *nature of abode* (particular weight has been assigned to the purchase or lease of property in a state when assessing a transfer of habitual residence,[588] but this is not an essential prerequisite to establishment[589]). Furthermore, importance is attached to the existence of employment and business ties,[590] as well as social

---

585 See, for example, House of Lords judgment in *Nessa v. Chief Adjudication Officer* [1999] 1 WLR 1937 (HL), in which a Bangladeshi migrant who intended to move to the UK permanently was found not to be able to claim income support as a habitually resident person until she had lived in the UK for 'a period'. It has been suggested that such a requisite period would amount to a number of months: see P. Rogerson, 'Habitual residence: the new domicile?' (2000) 49(1) *International and Comparative Law Quarterly* 86, at pp.93–95.

586 Although Viarengo has cited national case law from France and Spain in which intention to remain did not appear to feature as an consideration of particular importance in ascertaining habitual residence in the context of Rome III: Viarengo (Chapter 4, n.356), at para.5.1.

587 The requisite amount of time for which someone has to remain in a state before being considered habitually resident varies between national courts. Contrast the French *Cour de Cassation* case concerning the Brussels II Regulation, *Moore v. Moore* [2006] *International Litigation Procedure* 628, in which an English woman was not considered to be habitually resident in France after one year living in a family property with the intention of moving back to England after 18 months, with the English High Court case *L.K. v. K. (No.2)* [2006] EWHC 3280 (Fam) at paras.23 and 33, in which a Frenchman posted to England for work was found to be habitually resident there after two months, even though it was likely he would relocate to another country in the future. It should, however, be noted that the parties in this case had lived in the UK twice before for significant periods of time.

588 See the Opinion of Advocate General Kokott in the CJEU Case C-523/07 *A*. Reference for a preliminary ruling: Korkein hallinto-oikeus – Finland [2009] ECR I-2805, at para.44, in which it was stated that intention to settle permanently in a state and therefore acquire habitual residence, manifested by certain tangible steps such as the purchase or lease of a residence in the host Member State, may constitute an indicator of the transfer of the habitual residence. Another indicator may be constituted by lodging an application for social housing with the relevant services of that State. The Court followed the AG's Opinion. See also, for example, the English High Court case *Munro v. Munro* [2007] EWHC 3315 (Fam), at para.55, in which the Court emphasised that the fact that couple had sold their English homes and had acquired a primary matrimonial residence in Spain had an important bearing on the finding of a Spanish habitual residence.

589 For example, see the English High Court case *L.K. v. K. (No. 2)* [2006] EWHC 3280 (Fam), at paras.18 and 20, where someone who lived in a serviced apartment and subsequently a hotel in London was nevertheless found to be habitually resident in England.

590 See, for example, the opinion of the EU Court of Justice in Case T-90/92 *Pedro Magdalena Fernández v. Commission of the European Communities* [1993] ECR II-971, at para.30, in which the Court held that an expatriate employee in Belgium who retained strong links with his home country of Spain (he still had financial interests in Spain and ultimately intended to move back there), was nevertheless habitually resident in Belgium where he had been working for five years. See also the English High Court case *Marinos v. Marinos* [2007] EWHC 2047 (Fam), at paras.50–52 and 75, in which the Court, in finding that the wife was habitually resident in England immediately upon her return to the country, emphasised that the woman had been employed as a flight attendant working from Heathrow and had taken steps in an attempt to qualify as a solicitor in England and Wales.

and family links.[591] Although there are divergent views from Member State courts on the issue, it has been suggested that to perceive a party as holding two habitual residences would run counter to the objectives of the EU legislator (e.g. by increasing legal uncertainty).[592]

The balancing of the above factors (amongst others) was neatly consolidated in the *Swaddling* judgment, in which the then ECJ sought to define habitual residence for the purposes of social welfare benefits. The Court employed the following reasoning for determining where the 'habitual centre of interests' could be found:

> account should be taken in particular of the employed person's family situation; the reasons which have led him to move; the length and continuity of his residence; the fact (where this is the case) that he is in stable employment; and his intention as it appears from all the circumstances ... the length of residence in the Member State in which payment of the benefit at issue is sought cannot be regarded as an intrinsic element of the concept of residence ... In particular, when, as in the present case, an employed person, on returning to his State of origin after exercising his right to freedom of movement, has made it clear at the time of applying for income support that he intends to remain in his State of origin, where his close relatives live ... he cannot be deemed not to satisfy the condition concerning residence within the meaning of Article 10a merely because the period of residence completed in his State of origin is too short.[593]

It should be noted that, in contrast to the hotchpotch of case law that has to be relied upon in defining habitual residence for the purposes of proceedings involving adults, the CJEU has directly ruled on the hallmarks of this connection in the context of parental responsibility under Article 8 of Brussels II bis. In doing so, it stated that particular regard should be paid to 'the child's nationality, the place and conditions of attendance at school, linguistic knowledge and the family and social relationships of the child in that State'.[594] In a similar manner to adults, societal and familiar integration is important for the establishment of the habitual residence of a child, although it has been stated that the existence of family ties play an even greater role here than in the other areas discussed.[595]

---

591 See the Spanish case of Audiencia Provincial, Valladolid 12.3.2013 (95/2013) cited by Viarengo (Chapter 4, n.356), at p.557, para.5.1. in which social and family links were a paramount consideration in finding habitual residence of a couple in the context of Rome III. See also the English case of *Oundjian v. Oundjian* [1979] 1 FLR 198, in which the court's finding that the wife was habitually resident in England was partially based on her strong ties to her sister and her son who were based in England.

592 Viarengo / Villata (Chapter 3, n.268), at pp.87–88.

593 Ibid., at paras. 29–30.

594 *A.* (n.588 above), at paras.37–44; *Mercredi v. Chaffe* (n.578 above), at paras.47–52.

595 Shúilleabháin (Chapter 4, n.348), at p.52, para.2.27.

Despite the fact that these cases concerning parental responsibility form part of the framework that is presently being investigated, due to the different interests at play in evaluating the position of the child,[596] caution should be used in transposing the notion of habitual residence discussed in this paragraph to the realm of adult relationships.[597]

From the overview set out above, it can generally be stated that habitual residence offers the benefit of being a flexible, social criterion,[598] reflecting 'the life actually lived'[599] by the parties. In contrast to nationality (see 6.3.1. below), it is suited to encompassing the often transient links created through globalisation and the growth in migration. The emphasis placed on factual integration also means that the law or court of habitual residence is likely to be relevant to family relationships, since this is where the epicentre of family life is most likely to be based. As a jurisdictional connection, a party's habitual residence offers the benefit of being easily accessible, not only in terms of physical proximity, but also for obtaining information and interacting with relevant authorities. In the context of applicable law, the factual integration associated with habitual residence might allow most parties to benefit from at least a degree of knowledge of the language, as well as an appreciation for the context and content of the rules that are applied to them. Application of the law of habitual residence might also be seen to reflect the present cultural associations and expectations of the parties. However, due to the entrenched nature of culture, this can be considered a much more subjective and tenuous link.

For the specific purposes of party autonomy, the flip side of the inherent flexibility of habitual residence and its lack of a detailed definition means that it may be hard for those who have made use of their free movement rights within the EU to definitively pinpoint their own habitual residence when making an agreement. This could, however, be remedied through specific reference to the state of habitual residence at the time of the agreement. It might furthermore not be clear to parties that a particular habitual residence has been lost, or a new one gained (this is particularly important where a choice in favour of an undetermined connection has been made). In view of the potential for complexity, it is important to note that there is a present belief that a party cannot have more than one habitual residence; thus the search for this criterion is focused on one 'end point'.[600]

---

596 *Mercredi v. Chaffe* (n.578 above), at para.46.

597 Viarengo (Chapter 4, n.356), at p.556, para.5.1.

598 J. Carrascosa González, 'La ley aplicable a la separación judicial y al divorcio en defecto de elección de ley por los cónyuges. Análisis del artículo 8 del Reglamento 1259/2010 de 20 de diciembre de 2010' (2011) 4(1) *Cuadernos de Derecho Transnacional* 52, at p.69: this social criterion is preferred above the cultural criterion of nationality.

599 See the prioritisation of this in the Explanatory Memorandums accompanying the Property Regulations Proposals (Chapter 2, n.179), at p.10, para.5.3.

600 Kruger (Chapter 3, n.231), at p.357.

Additional guidance in the preambles of future instruments, as well as further elucidation by the CJEU as to the autonomous meaning of habitual residence in the various family and succession law contexts would be useful in addressing the lack of clarity described above and improving the uniformity of application. However, this has to be balanced against a need to maintain the very flexibility that makes this concept capable of meeting the needs of a transient population.[601]

6.2.2. CHOICE OF COURT: ARTICLE 4(1)(a) AND (c)(ii) OF THE MAINTENANCE REGULATION

Turning first to examine the manifestation of habitual residence as a direct choice of court connection within the relevant legislation, it can be seen that the Maintenance Regulation is the only such instrument that allows for a direct choice of court to be made, and therefore is the only one that allows for a straightforward selection of the Member State of habitual residence to govern proceedings.

Under Article 4(1)(a) of this instrument, the courts of the habitual residence of one (or both) of the parties at the time the agreement is made, or at the time the court is seised, may be agreed.[602] At the outset of this analysis, it is clear that the former option secures a much higher degree of predictability by designating the precise forum in advance compared to the indeterminate nature of the latter option (see the specific critique of habitual residence in this regard above).[603]

In terms of the substance of this choice, the opportunity set out in Article 4(1)(a) does not contribute any further value if the court that is agreed upon is also that of the habitual residence of the creditor or defendant at the time proceedings are instituted, since Article 3(a) and (b) of the Maintenance Regulation already allow for such grounds to be relied on. Additional value only really emerges if the court of the habitual residence of the creditor and/or defendant at the time that the designation is made is different from both of their habitual residences at the time the court is seised.

---

601 It has been suggested that this lack of definition is a deliberate attempt to avoid the rigidity associated with other connecting factors, such as nationality: P. Rogerson, 'Habitual Residence: The New Domicile?' (2000) 49(1) *International and Comparative Law Quarterly* 86, at p.87.

602 F.C. Villata and L. Valkova, 'Model Choice of Court and Choice of Law Clauses' in Università degli Studi di Milano et al., (eds.), *Planning the future of cross-border families: a path through coordination* (2017), at p.17, fn.18, available at: http://www.eufams.unimi.it/wp-content/uploads/2017/12/EUFAMS-Model-Clauses-v1.0.pdf.

603 See also discussion of specificity in the context of formal requirements in 9.3.1.2.

Furthermore, in view of the standing of the creditor and the difficulties in accessing justice associated with this position,[604] the utility for the creditor to freeze their habitual residence at the moment of choice is questionable, since if this location subsequently changes the practical benefits in terms of a conveniently located forum (the habitual residence of the creditor), or ease of enforcement and interaction with administrative authorities (the habitual residence of the defendant) may be lost. Nevertheless, it could be the case that selecting a past habitual residence of the creditor holds practical benefits, such as familiarity with the language and the culture of the Member State in which proceedings are to be conducted. In such an instance, the breadth of the choice offered here would offer the opportunity to secure this.[605]

In principle, nominating the courts of the present habitual residence of the debtor as the defendant holds the benefit of allowing ease of the recovery of maintenance and a clear view of the context in which the defendant finds him or herself.[606] However, as with the discussion concerning the creditor's habitual residence, under Article 4(1)(a) of the Regulation there is accordingly a risk that a past habitual residence of the defendant is found to govern proceedings (following a prior choice of court agreement). In such a situation, the crucial practical benefits will be lost. If the creditor wishes to secure the habitual residence of the defendant at the time the court is seised as a connecting factor, arguably they should in fact wait to seise this court using the first of the alternative objective grounds set out in Article 3 of the Regulation, since this would entail more predictability for achieving the aforementioned practical outcomes.

In addition to the simple choice of court option set out in Article 4(1)(a), the Maintenance Regulation also provides the opportunity under Article 4(1)(c)(ii) for (former) spouses to agree to have their proceedings take place in the court or courts of the Member State which was their last common habitual residence at the time the agreement is made or when the court is seised, provided they have lived in that country for at least one year.

Selection of the last habitual residence of the (former) spouses may provide them with the opportunity to deal with the consequences of their relationship in a jurisdiction in which it had been integrated, even if neither (former) spouse continues to be habitually resident at the relevant point in time (either at the time of agreement or when the court is seised). However, even though this criterion may be viewed as providing an additional 'common' ground for proceedings to take place, as discussed with regard to Article 4(1)(a), the actual utility of selecting a former habitual residence for purposes of claiming maintenance can

604 See discussion of the position of creditor in 2.4.2.

605 See further discussion of this temporal consideration in 9.2.1.1.

606 It is, in fact, the first objective ground under Article 3(a) of the Maintenance Regulation.

be validly questioned if neither the creditor nor the defendant continues to hold links with this Member State.

One additional question that arises is whether the two choices provided for (former) spouses by Article 4(1)(c)[607] ought to be considered *lex specialis*, and thus the only options available to be selected by (former) spouses under the Maintenance Regulation. Whilst the answer to this is not made clear by the instrument itself or the accompanying documentation, to employ such an interpretation would have the effect of depriving (former) spouses of the chance to select a court of potentially closer connection, thus further impinging upon the exercise of free will in this already constrained terrain. In view of the goal of facilitating the recovery of maintenance across borders and maximising access to justice, it is therefore argued here that Article 4(1)(c) ought rather to be considered as a broadening for (former) spouses of the choices already available.[608]

6.2.3. CHOICE OF LAW

In contrast to the meagre scope permitted for directly selecting the Member State *court* of a party's habitual residence within the present framework, the opportunity to select the *law* of the habitual residence of one or both of the parties is established in all the instruments concerning adult relationships (the Rome III Regulation, the Property Regulations and the Hague Maintenance Protocol).

6.2.3.1. Article 5(1)(a) and (b) of the Rome III Regulation

Article 5(1)(a) provides for the designation of the law of the common habitual residence of the spouses at the time the agreement was concluded, whilst Article 5(1)(b) establishes that a former common habitual residence may be selected, provided that one of the spouses still resides there at the time of agreement.

Unlike in the choice of court context, close connection to the applicable law entails a stronger emphasis on affinity rather than considerations of practicality and convenience, being reflective of cultural rather than physical proximity. Given the relative longevity of affinity-based ties, the application of a law of a past habitual residence does not pose the same risk of becoming out-dated

607 See also Article 4(1)(c)(i), which provides that (former)spouses can select the court which has jurisdiction to settle their dispute in matrimonial matters: see 7.2.2.

608 P. Reuss, 'Art 4 EuUntVO' in R. Geimer and R. Schütze (eds.), *Internationaler Rechtsverkehr in Zivil- und Handelssachen*, 43rd edn. (Beck, Munich, 2012), at para.26 and Abendroth (Chapter 4, n.337), at pp.466–467.

compared to a situation in which a past habitual residence is a determinant of jurisdiction.

The objective criteria that apply in the absence of choice under Article 8 of Rome III mirror the two grounds established above, though in a consecutive manner and with the relevant point in time being at the moment the court is seised.[609] Thus, it can firstly be said that the aforementioned choice of law provisions add value to the options available to international couples by allowing the spouses to pick between these connections and extending this opportunity backwards through time.

One marked feature of these provisions is the emphasis on a factual close connection that is shared by *both* spouses. The manifestation of this criterion is thus focused towards the marriage rather than the individuals. This approach contrasts with both the two Property Regulations and the Hague Maintenance Protocol (see the subsequent subsections), which respectively establish the opportunity to designate the law of *either* of the parties' habitual residences at the time an agreement is made according to the criteria of the instrument.[610]

Despite the inconsistency it presents with the format of the other direct connections,[611] this restriction in Rome III can be welcomed in view of the problems associated with the application of law unconnected to one of the parties (see discussion in the context of the free movement of persons[612]). It is also important to recall that legislative action in this realm is constrained by the need for a law to have a close connection to the parties and their relationship. The opportunity to select a law that is linked to only one party appears in fact to be out of step with the collective language employed in the recitals in describing the nature of this connection.[613] Whilst in one sense Article 5(1)(a) and (b) are inconsistent with the overall framework, it could also be argued that the remaining provisions are not coherent with the aim of safeguarding close connection.

609 Article 8(a) and (b) provide for: either the law of the state where the spouses are habitually resident at the time the court is seised; or, failing that, where the spouses were last habitually resident, provided that the period of residence did not end more than 1 year before the court was seised, in so far as one of the spouses still resides in that state.

610 See Article 22(1)(a) of the Property Regulations and Article 8(1)(b) of the Hague Maintenance Protocol.

611 In particular, with regard to horizontal coordination between related areas, see 6.5.2.

612 See 3.4.

613 See use of the pronoun 'they' in the recitals when describing the connection between the parties and the grounds provided: for instance, under Recital 16 of the Rome III Regulation: 'Spouses should be able to choose the law of a country with which they have a special connection'. Similar language is employed in Recital 45 of the Matrimonial Property Regulation and Recital 44 of the Partnership Property Regulation.

6.2.3.2. Article 22(1)(a) of the Property Regulations

Article 22(1)(a) of both the Matrimonial Property Regulation and Partnership Property Regulation allows for the designation of the law of the state where either party is habitually resident at the time the agreement is concluded. It can be succinctly stated that since only the first common habitual residence of the spouses/partners after marriage/creation of their partnership is a general objective ground for determining applicable law,[614] Article 22(1)(a) adds additional value by allowing the designation of the law of habitual residence of either spouse/partner during the course of the marriage up until the court is seised for the relevant proceeding.

Clear criticism can be levelled against individual connection to a law that applies to a relationship, and the potential practical implications that may arise from selecting a connection with which at least one party does not share an active link. However, it is proposed here that the risks associated with such a disconnect are lessened in the choice of law context compared with the jurisdictional setting.[615] This is so by reason of the fact that the substance of the law and a party's affinity to it and/or perception of its merits play a much greater role in this context. Parties may agree to 'capture' the law of a present habitual residence that they deem to be of close affinity to themselves or their relationship (e.g. reflective of their conservative / liberal / religious concerns). Equally, the law of habitual residence may be designated for more pragmatic reasons, such as the parties' knowledge of the law or the language it is written in, or on the basis that they perceive it to provide an efficient process.[616] The perception of 'close connection' in this context is a much more flexible and much less outwardly appreciable concept than in the choice of court context.

6.2.3.3. Article 8(1)(b) of the Hague Maintenance Protocol

Article 8(1)(b) of the Hague Maintenance Protocol also allows for the selection of the law of the state of the habitual residence of either party at the time of designation. In view of the general default imposition of the law of the habitual residence of the creditor at the time the court is seised,[617] this establishes the

---

[614] See Article 26(1)(a). By way of exception, it should be noted that according to Article 26(3) of the Matrimonial Property Regulation and Article 26(2) of the Partnership Property Regulation, the law of the last common habitual residence of the parties can be exceptionally applied upon application of one/both of the spouses/partners and subject to judicial discretion, based on the length of time the spouses/partners were habitually resident in this country and their reliance upon its law in planning/arranging their property relations.

[615] See 6.2.2.

[616] Viarengo (Chapter 4, n.356), at p.552, para.4.

[617] Article 3 of the Hague Maintenance Protocol.

additional possibility to capture the law of a past habitual residence of the creditor, as well as that of a past/present habitual residence of the debtor to apply to a matter of maintenance.

The law of the present habitual residence of the creditor offers a particular advantage in terms of entrenchment in the circumstances in which they live. Reference can be made to the Explanatory Report of the Hague Maintenance Protocol, which states its supports the general application of the law of the creditor's habitual residence on the basis that it allows for 'determination of the existence and amount of the maintenance obligation with regard to the legal and factual conditions of the social environment in the country where the creditor lives and engages in most of his or her activities'.[618] Notwithstanding this, it might be anticipated that the law of a former habitual residence, particularly one that the creditor has left recently and/or aims to return to in the near future, could still offer some of the benefits discussed above.

Despite this, however, it can generally be submitted that a former habitual residence, alongside the habitual residence of the debtor, does not support the aim described in the Explanatory Memorandum. Although it has been submitted in the subsection immediately above that the practical disadvantages associated with the governance of a 'disconnected' court of habitual residence cannot be directly transposed into the choice of law setting, the realm of maintenance entails an entirely different balance of interests, whereby the creditor is perceived to have an inbuilt disadvantage in comparison to the debtor.

Although considerations relating to affinity and suitability of the applicable law are much less temporally tied than the necessity for physical access to a court in the jurisdictional setting, it might rightly be questioned whether the option of securing a law in a moment in time before maintenance proceedings arise is appropriate given the specific sensitivities of this realm. This is a topic that will be returned to in view of the temporal considerations in Chapter 9.[619]

6.3. NATIONALITY AND DOMICILE

This examination of the party autonomy provisions continues with a connecting factor which has in recent times 'played second fiddle' to habitual residence as a criterion in the private international law rules relating to family matters and succession: nationality (and to a residual extent, domicile). This section will again start with a general description (6.3.1.), before examining the placement of this criterion in both the choice of court (6.3.2.) and choice of law (6.3.3.) contexts.

618 Bonomi (Chapter 4, n.400), at para.37.

619 See 9.2.2.3.

6.3.1. GENERAL DESCRIPTION

Nationality is lauded as being a concrete, easy-to-ascertain criterion, centring upon a fairly stable aspect of a person's status. Compared with habitual residence (or, to a lesser extent, domicile, see 6.3.2. below), it is a matter of official status, and therefore much easier for a layperson to determine.[620] Whilst the habitual residence of internationally active parties may change a considerable number of times during the course of their lives, nationality is more difficult to lose or acquire, and is much more likely to remain fixed during the course of a lifetime. Upon designating the court of their state of nationality to govern a process or relationship, parties can therefore be assured with a high degree of predictability of the particular jurisdiction that will ultimately govern proceedings or a legal process.

As a determinant of applicable law, nationality rose to prominence in national and multinational private international law instruments throughout the nineteenth and early twentieth centuries.[621] Drawing strength from the writings of Mancini and the desire to assert state sovereignty, this criterion was based on the belief that a person's legal status can be localised in a particular legal order based on their perceived 'membership' of a nation state's community.[622]

Nationality has since lost a considerable degree of favour in the face of a growth in the number of persons migrating across state borders (particularly following World War II),[623] which led states to seek to apply laws in a manner that encouraged social integration in their territory rather than merely asserting geo-political control.[624] As rules on acquiring nationality were loosened in the face of increased immigration, this criterion lost some of its appeal as a steadfast link to cultural or ethnic ties.[625]

In view of the discussion of its decline, it could be argued that nationality is no longer a guarantee of factual connectedness with a particular state[626] (e.g. in

---

620 Shúilleabháin (Chapter4, n.348), at p.73, para.2.55: the determination of nationality is usually not subject to much judicial deliberation.

621 See, for example, Article 2 of the Hague Convention of 17 July 1905 on the effects of marriage, which subjected the effects of marriage upon the property of the spouses to the law of the nationality of the husband at the time of marriage.

622 For commentary on this development, see Basedow (Chapter 1, n.46), at pp.247–248, para.402; Kruger (Chapter 3, n.231), at pp.351–352 and P. Franzina, 'The Evolving Role of Nationality in Private International Law' in A. Annoni and S. Forlati (eds.), *The Changing Role of Nationality in International Law* (Routledge, London, 2013), at pp.194–195.

623 Basedow (Chapter 1, n.46), at pp.247–250, para.402–403.

624 Franzina (n.622 above), at pp.200–202.

625 Basedow (Chapter 1, n.46), at pp.247–248, para.402–403.

626 J. Fawcett and J. Carruthers, *Cheshire, North and Fawcett: Private International Law*, 14th edn. (Oxford University Press, Oxford, 2008), at p.181 and P. McEleavy, 'The communitarization of divorce rules: what impact for English and Scottish law?' (2004) 53(3) *International and Comparative Law Quarterly* 605, at pp.619–620.

certain circumstances it could simply be inherited by an individual from their parents without ever having been present in a territory and/or they could have multiple nationalities). However, it can nevertheless be asserted that people still *tend* to have some degree of relationship with their state of nationality,[627] since this status is usually derived from a connection at birth (*jus sanguinis / jus soli*), or as a result of a process of naturalisation.

One potentially troublesome issue that arises (particularly in the face of increasing globalisation of populations) is the matter of how to deal with situations in which the parties have two or more nationalities. This status gives rise to uncertainty due to the differing Member State approaches in consideration of the role of dual nationality (in particular, in the determination of jurisdiction). Whilst some Member States employed a preference towards the nationality of the forum, others used the technique of attempting to identify the 'effective' nationality (the nationality of closest connection to the party).[628]

The Member States' treatment of dual nationality has previously been dealt with by the CJEU in the context of name law (whereby it was concluded that it was discriminatory for a Member State to simply ignore the presence of additional nationality in this context).[629] However, more crucial for this context is the fact that dual nationality has since been addressed in the context of the EU's private international law rules relating to matrimonial matters. In the *Hadadi* case,[630] the Court struck down the use of effective nationality in this setting as an imprecise determinant of connection in jurisdictional matters, which created an onerous decision-making process that would not always lead to clear results, and therefore ran counter to the objectives of the regulation.[631] Crucially, the CJEU has also embraced party autonomy in this context, establishing that parties ought to have the freedom to nominate the courts of any of their nationalities on an equal basis under this instrument.[632] In the present context, it is proposed that this means that the parties may choose between their nationalities in making a choice of law or choice of court agreement without interference from national law.[633]

---

[627] The Law Commission, *Family Law Report on Jurisdiction in Matrimonial Causes* (Law Com. No.48) (1972), at p.7, para.19.

[628] T. Kruger and J. Verhellen, 'Dual Nationality = Double Trouble?' (2011) 7(3) *Journal of Private International Law* 601, at pp.606–609.

[629] See the CJEU's judgment in *Garcia Avello* (Chapter 2, n.139), in which the Court ruled that, on the basis of non-discrimination and EU citizenship, Belgian authorities could not simply ignore the additional Spanish nationality of the applicant's children and automatically apply their own name law.

[630] Case C-168/08 *Laszlo Hadadi (Hadady) v. Csilla Marta Mesko, épouse Hadadi (Hadady)*. Reference for a preliminary ruling: Cour de cassation – France [2009] ECR I-6871.

[631] Ibid., at para. 55.

[632] See *Hadadi* (ibid.), at paras.53 and 58. For discussion, see also: Kruger / Verhellen (n.628 above), at pp.615–617 (2011) and S. Bariatti, 'Multiple Nationalities and EU Private International Law – Many Questions and DSome Tentative Answers' (2011) 13 *Yearbook of private international law* 1, at pp.8–9.

[633] See in context of multiple nationalities under Rome III: Kruger (Chapter 1, n.60), at para.2.

6.3.2. SUBSTITUTION WITH DOMICILE

For the purposes of choice of court agreements under Article 4 of the Maintenance Regulation (see 6.4.1. below), it is provided that domicile shall replace nationality as a connecting factor for maintenance obligations in those Member States that use this criterion as a connecting factor in family matters.[634] Interestingly, although the same substitution is made according to Article 9 of the Hague Maintenance Protocol (in order to address the position of Ireland), it expressly omits the application of this interchange for choices of law made under Article 8.[635]

Domicile has been appropriated by the EU's instruments on family matters[636] as a substitute for nationality in instances involving the United Kingdom and the Republic of Ireland. The intention here is to provide a substitute criterion for common law Member State jurisdictions that do not use nationality as a connecting factor in their domestic private international laws.[637] Since this exception is aimed at addressing a scenario where a Member State is not accustomed to using nationality in its legal system, it has been asserted that a civil law jurisdiction which uses both domicile and nationality in their private international law cannot employ the former as a connecting factor in this EU context.[638]

The (common law[639]) concept of domicile concentrates on identifying what would generally be described as a person's permanent home.[640] It can be understood in two principal forms: the *domicile of origin* and *domicile of choice*.[641] Whilst the former is attributed at birth (usually the domicile of the father or mother, depending on their marital status[642]), the latter can only be acquired

---

634 See Recital 18 and Article 2(3) of the Maintenance Regulation.

635 It only applies to the connection of nationality under Articles 4 and 6.

636 Namely the Brussels II bis Regulation and the Maintenance Regulation (as well as the accompanying Hague Protocol on the Law Applicable to Maintenance).

637 Bonomi (Chapter 4, n.400), at para.155.

638 Ibid.

639 There are also civil law manifestations (that are more similar to mere residence), but it is the common-law form which is relevant for these purposes: Kruger (Chapter 3, n.231), at p.358, One key point to note is that, akin to nationality (and in contrast to habitual residence), domicile is attributed the meaning employed by the Member State that uses it (i.e. the UK and Republic of Ireland): A. Borrás, 'Chapter II – Jurisdiction, Section 1 – Divorce, Legal Separation and Marriage Annulment' in U. Magnus and P. Mankowski (eds.), *Brussels IIbis Regulation* (Sellier, Munich, 2012), at p.92, para.12, fn.13.

640 L. Collins et al. (eds.), *Dicey, Morris and Collins on the Conflict of Laws*, 14th edn. (Sweet and Maxwell, London, 2006), at paras.6-004–6-005.

641 For description see: M. Harding, *Conflict of Laws*, 5th edn. (Routledge, Abingdon, 2013), at pp.17–21. There is also the domicile of dependency (see ibid. at pp.17–19) which applies to persons who lack legal capacity (e.g. minors and mentally incapacitated adults). Such persons are assigned the domicile of those legally responsible for caring for them.

642 Ibid., at p.17.

where a party has demonstrated a clear intention to live in a state permanently, or indefinitely. Like habitual residence, it takes into account physical presence in a state and the intention of the parties to remain in that state for a certain period, as well as personal and economic ties.[643] However, whilst habitual residence may be established even when a party only intends to reside in that state for the medium term, in order to acquire domicile, it has to be demonstrated that the party has the intention to remain permanently or indefinitely in the new state.[644]

From the description above, it can be seen that nationality and domicile share a certain fixity in their character. However, there remains a discernible gap between the two concepts in terms of the fact that whilst nationality is generally acquired (after birth) deliberately, and renounced on a conscious basis, domicile has to be ascertained (with this inviting a greater degree of subjectivity and flexibility). This arguably places parties who are subject to this criterion in a less stable, certain position than those who are connected through their nationality.

Uncertainty also arises as to the circumstances in which domicile will replace nationality for the purposes of a choice of court under Article 4 of the Maintenance Regulation. It is unclear from the text when exactly domicile will serve as a substitute with regard to such agreement: would this occur whenever parties who are domiciled in either the Republic of Ireland or the United Kingdom make an agreement, only when they stipulate either of these Member State jurisdictions in their agreement, and/or simply when the authorities of these Member States are called on to decide upon their competence to hear a case?

Furthermore, where the parties have chosen a court of their nationality, and their agreement comes within the remit of one of the common-law jurisdictions (by reason of one of the possible links discussed above), should their designation of nationality be automatically transformed to domicile (without further investigation as to whether the selected Member State was in fact the state of their domicile)? Or, to take a much more hard-line approach, should designations of nationality which do not align with the party's (or parties') domicile be entirely set aside? The former approach would certainly be more embracive of the will of the parties and their need for legal certainty, thereby securing two of the principal aims of introducing party autonomy onto the EU stage. However, if no distinction were to be made between the two concepts, it could be questioned why domicile would be used in the first place.

Given the marginal role that common-law jurisdictions play in this realm, these problematic instances are not likely to affect international parties on a large

643 Shúilleabháin (Chapter 4, n.348), at pp.68–69, para.2.48.

644 Ibid., at pp.69–70, para.2.49.

scale. However, regardless of this, the substitution of domicile for nationality does provide considerable food for thought. Those who fall within the remit of a common-law jurisdiction are at risk of suffering from increased legal uncertainty and being unable to secure the distinct benefits that nationality brings as a criterion. It is suggested that the aims of party autonomy would be better served by introducing domicile as an *additional* choice alongside nationality, since this would remove any distinction between parties and maximise the choice of courts available for those who are internationally active within the EU.

6.3.3. CHOICE OF COURT: ARTICLE 4(1)(b) OF THE MAINTENANCE REGULATION

As discussed above with regard to habitual residence in the choice of court context (see 6.2.2), the Maintenance Regulation is the only relevant instrument that allows parties to make a direct selection of the competent Member State courts. Akin to the construction of the habitual residence connection, they may also choose between the courts of either of their nationalities (or, as discussed immediately above, domicile(s)) either at the time the agreement is made, or when the court is seised). In terms of the benefits of this criterion, it can be asserted that the selection of the court of nationality may offer a possibility to enhance a party's access to justice through considerations such as familiarity with the legal system and the language in which the court operates.

However, as already established in the habitual residence context, securing the past or present nationality or domicile of one or both of the parties as a determinant of jurisdiction in this context clearly carries a risk that the jurisdiction will with the passage of time become physically inconvenient for the creditor to access. On top of this, if the forum is that of the nationality of the debtor as the defendant, there might be linguistic or cultural barriers that the creditor has to overcome in instigating proceedings in this jurisdiction. In this latter situation, the benefits associated with the habitual residence of the debtor (e.g. ease of enforcement of a maintenance order) clearly do not apply in the present context.

6.3.4. CHOICE OF LAW

Nationality is a connecting factor in the choice of law provisions in all relevant instruments concerning adult relationships (the Rome III Regulation, the Property Regulations and the Hague Maintenance Protocol), as well as being the sole ground through which a *professio juris* can be exercised under the Succession Regulation.

6.3.4.1. *Article 5(1)(c) of Rome III, Article 22(1)(b) of the Property Regulations and Article 8(1)(a) of the Hague Maintenance Protocol*

Turning first to examine the instruments that establish conflict-of-laws rules for adult relationships, it can be seen that the manifestation of this connecting factor is uniform between these four instruments, since all allow the nationality of either party to be selected, and the relevant point of concentration is the same, being the time at which the agreement is concluded[645] (or the time of designation[646]). This manifestation once again demonstrates the inconsistency in Rome III, requiring that the parties must both share a link to a chosen law of a (former) habitual residence (see 6.2.3.1. above).

As established at the beginning of this section, nationality is considered to be a more concrete, ingrained connection than habitual residence. Whilst it is indeed true that in certain instances a party may have no connection to nationality (particularly where they have dual nationality), the durability of this link means that a party is likely to have at least some affinity to this criterion (e.g. culture, language, family ties). As parties move between states, the longevity of this link means that the sands of time are less likely to corrode this choice than if the law of habitual residence were to be chosen. In addition to affinity itself, it is also proposed that application of the law of nationality might be seen as a means of reducing complexity and enhancing access to justice in a cross-border situation, by ensuring the application of a law of which a party comprehends the language in which it is written and/or its underlying values.

In view of the possibility to select the nationality of only one of the parties, the criticism that has been levelled at the use of individual connection to a habitual residence[647] is also applicable here. However, it might nevertheless be proposed that nationality could actually pose comparatively less of a risk in terms of disconnect where it is only held by one party, since a spouse's or partner's culture and their social context might foreseeably become part of the relationship.

6.3.4.2. *Article 22 of the Succession Regulation*

The above concerns relating to a two-party choice clearly do not apply in the case of the Succession Regulation. Under Article 22 of this instrument, the sole opportunity to deviate from the default applicability of the law of the deceased's habitual residence is offered in the form of the option to select the law of the deceased's nationality at the time of choice or at the time of his or her death.[648]

---

645 Article 5(1)(c) of the Rome III Regulation and Article 22(1)(b) of the Property Regulations.

646 Article 8(1)(a) of the Hague Maintenance Protocol.

647 See 6.2.3.

648 Article 22(1) of the Property Regulations.

In only permitting the selection of the law of the party's nationality, the Regulation demonstrates a very limited approach to the expression of free will. It allows neither selection of the law of the habitual residence of the deceased at the time of agreement,[649] nor linkage with any related subject area, such as matrimonial property.[650]

Elaborating upon its restrictive stance, the Explanatory Memorandum accompanying the Proposal for the Succession Regulation emphasises the perceived need to balance the autonomy of the deceased with the expectations of the beneficiaries of the estate. Nationality is framed as a criterion that allows a party to preserve links with their state of origin as they move around the Union (ensuring the applicability of a law with which they have a cultural tie) and plan their succession in their desired manner with a high degree of legal certainty,[651] whilst at the same time striving to safeguard expectations of the beneficiaries of the estate (particularly with regard to those entitled to a reserved share).[652] In this latter regard, the considerable stability of nationality as a connecting factor (particularly in comparison to habitual residence) reduces the likelihood that the substance of the selection changes after the choice is made,[653] or that a choice of law is employed in a contrived manner by the deceased in order to achieve a certain result in their succession.[654]

Notwithstanding the attributes of nationality as a criterion, the exclusion of the possibility for a party to nominate the law of a habitual residence at the moment of choice can be strongly critiqued. It is foreseeable that the deceased may very well hold a much stronger connection with a former habitual residence at the time of their death (particularly parties who retire overseas). Furthermore, the safeguarding of the beneficiaries' expectations in such circumstances might that way actually be optimised in circumstances in which the family of the deceased remains in their former habitual residence. Whilst the objective conflict-of-laws rule contained in Article 21(2) may address such a situation in exceptional circumstances,[655] this does not serve to provide the deceased and his or her beneficiaries with certainty regarding the law to apply.

---

649 This approach contrasts with the 1989 Hague Convention on the Law Applicable to Succession, which also allowed for the deceased to choose their habitual residence at the time of designation (Article 5(1)).

650 See the Explanatory Memorandum (Chapter 2, n.178), at p.7, para.4.3.

651 Castellanos Ruiz (Chapter 1, n.48), at p.327, para.4.

652 See Recital 38 of the Succession Regulation and the Explanatory Memorandum (Chapter 2, n.178), at p.6, para.4.3.

653 In instances where the choice of law has been designated as the nationality at the time of death.

654 Castellanos Ruiz (Chapter 1, n.48), at p.328, para.4. Of course, the decision to make a choice of law might well be made with a strategic aim in mind, but it is unlikely that nationality might be acquired and employed for the sole purposes of changing the law that applies to a succession.

655 This provision allows the court to sidestep the application of the law of the habitual residence at the time of their death: 'Where … it is clear from the circumstances of the case that, at the time of death, the deceased was manifestly more closely connected with a State other than the State whose law would be applicable under paragraph 1, the law applicable to the succession shall be the law of that other State'. See also Recital 24.

As stated above, Article 22(1) provides two options for the deceased to make their choice of law: either their nationality at the time their choice is made, or that at the time of their death. The first possibility is fairly straightforward, and allows a high degree of legal certainty for the deceased in the planning of their succession (and the probable beneficiaries, should they be aware of this choice). There does exist a possibility that the choice becomes outdated in the sense that the nationality might subsequently change, but the potential risk attached to this is less than in the case of habitual residence, both in the sense that a change is likely to occur less frequently, and that at least some entrenched link will arguably be retained with a former nationality.

Another possibility has been indicated whereby a party might make a choice in favour of a particular nationality that they *expect* to hold at the time of death.[656] Whilst this initially may sound like an unusual and uncertain construct, it might well arise if, for instance, the deceased has applied for citizenship of a certain state at the time of making the *professio juris*. The choice will, however, be invalidated if the nationality is not subsequently acquired.[657]

The second form of choice envisioned by Article 22(1) clearly presents a lower level of predictability than in the first instance, since changes in nationality during the course of a life, whilst unlikely to be frequent, cannot be ruled out. This uncertain state of affairs means that the law that is ultimately applied to the succession might not be the one that the testator had in mind when he or she was planning his or her succession, and he or she might not have been aware of the substance of its rules in making this open decision. This challenges the EU legislator's assertion that allowing a limited *professio juris* was intended to empower the deceased's interest in planning their estate.[658]

Further problems might also arise if a deceased, who had made an open-ended choice for the law of the nationality at the time of their death, ultimately had multiple nationalities at this key point in time.[659] As discussed previously, the CJEU has previously ruled that Member States' courts cannot favour one nationality above another in the context of alternative jurisdictional rules.[660] However, this reasoning is not easily transplanted into a scenario in which a party has made an indeterminate designation of their nationality to be ascertained at the time of their death and where this leads to two or more nationalities potentially being the determinants of the applicable law. Clearly at this point in time the deceased can no longer be relied upon to clarify their choice, which leads to confusion as to how to proceed.

656 Castellanos Ruiz (chapter 1, n.48), at p.334, para.8.

657 Ibid.

658 See Recital 38 of the Succession Regulation.

659 See also discussion in the context of formal requirements in 9.3.2.3.

660 *Hadadi* (n.630 above). See discussion of this case in 6.3.1. above.

Although the Succession Regulation makes no recommendation as to how to deal with this above scenario, guidance on this issue is found in the Rome III and Property Regulations.[661] These instruments state the following:

> Where this Regulation refers to nationality as a connecting factor, the question of how to consider a person having multiple nationalities is a preliminary question which falls outside the scope of this Regulation and should be left to national law, [including, where applicable, international Conventions,[662]] in full observance of the general principles of the Union. This consideration should have no effect on the validity of a choice of law made in accordance with this Regulation.

Whilst the decision on the status of multiple nationalities is delegated to national law, the recitals require that Member State courts adhere to EU general principles, including EU citizenship and non-discrimination against nationals of other Member States.[663] However, the guidance provided by the recitals does little to clarify the means by which to proceed where an indeterminate choice of law by a party leads to an uncertain outcome upon their death.

One possible solution would be to search for the 'closest connection' (effective nationality) of the deceased. This could be done by looking at factors such as where the deceased was habitually resident during their life, or tangible evidence of connection in the form of the language the deceased's will was written in or whether they made reference to specific provisions of one of the potential laws in this testament. However, the process of identifying the law of closer connection would be likely to take a significant amount of time, and form a clear impediment to the smooth running of the proceedings.[664]

However, in view of the balance that must be struck between the opportunity for the deceased to plan their estate and the interests of the beneficiaries in optimising practicality and convenience during subsequent succession proceedings, it is argued here that since the goal of party autonomy has not actually been achieved in this scenario (given the uncertain outcome of the choice of law), the interests of the beneficiaries ought to be given preference. It is submitted that the objective rule contained in Article 21 of the Succession Regulation that generally directs the law towards the last habitual residence of

661 See Recital 22 of Rome III, Recital 50 of the Matrimonial Property Regulation and Recital 49 of the Partnership Property Regulation.

662 This section in brackets is only present in the Property Regulations.

663 See also Kruger/Verhellen (n.628 above), at p.609 *et seq.*

664 This diverges from the exception contained in Article 21(2) of the Succession Regulation to the objective rule designating the law of the last habitual residence of the deceased, which is intended to cover exceptional circumstances in which the deceased clearly has much stronger ties to another Member State, e.g. where they have recently left their former habitual residence prior to their death (see guidance in Recital 25). Furthermore, such a consideration may well involve a regard for the position of the beneficiaries: see reference to 'all circumstances' in Article 21(2).

the deceased should be employed, removing the costly complexity of identifying the effective nationality of the deceased and achieving the convenience-based benefits of the union between law and forum.

6.4. THE PLACE WHERE THE LEGAL RELATIONSHIP WAS CREATED

The final direct connection that may be designated under the relevant instruments concentrates upon the place in which the legal relationship in question was created. For the present purposes, it can be found in both of the Property Regulations in the choice of court context (6.4.2.), and as an option for choice of law under the Partnership Property Regulation (6.4.3.).

6.4.1. GENERAL DESCRIPTION

The place where the relationship was created is a novel ground within the EU private international law relating to family matters and succession. However, this criterion is certainly not new to the international context, being as it is the principal means by which states ascertain the validity of a marriage celebrated in another jurisdiction.[665]

Simply denoting the state in which a marriage or registered partnership was brought into existence, the place of creation is a ground that benefits from being straightforward to ascertain, singular in nature and entirely certain from the offset (given that the creation of the relationship is a past event). In addition, it is of particular use in securing recognition in the context of 'non-traditional' relationships such as same-sex marriage or registered partnership, which entail a patchwork recognition between the Member States. The scope of usage of this criterion within the EU private international law framework is clearly limited by the fact that it focuses solely on a legalised relationship between adults, and thus will not occur outside this context.

6.4.2. CHOICE OF COURT: ARTICLE 7 OF THE PROPERTY REGULATIONS

Article 7 of the Property Regulations has introduced two new jurisdictional choices onto the EU private international law stage: the courts of the Member

665 See the historical overview provided in: Basedow (Chapter 1, n.46), at pp.306–311, paras.476–481. See also the 1978 Hague Convention on Celebration and Recognition of the Validity of Marriages.

State in which the marriage was concluded, or the courts of the Member State under whose law the registered partnership was created. Although the wording of this connection clearly differs slightly between the instruments, it is proposed here that both provisions essentially relate to the place where the legal relationship was created.

The possibility to make a choice of court provides an important opportunity for the parties to safeguard their expectations concerning the status and effects of their marriage or registered partnership[666] and to predict the outcome of future proceedings with a high degree of foreseeability. This can be seen as particularly useful in cases of same-sex marriage, or with regard to registered partnership in general, since such relationships are neither treated in the same manner, nor universally recognised, throughout the Union.

The Explanatory Memorandums[667] and the recitals[668] of the Property Regulations seem to clearly separate proceedings concerning property relations that arise upon the *dissolution* of a relationship[669] from other decision-making concerning the property regime that occurs *outside of the dissolution* of the relationship or succession, allotting the determination of the jurisdiction for the former under Article 5 of the Property Regulation, whilst appearing to state that Articles 6 and 7 are reserved for the latter.

However, in examining the interaction between these provisions, it would in fact appear that where the parties in a case linked to the dissolution of the relationship cannot reach agreement when required under Article 5,[670] Article 6 and 7 function as an alternative means of establishing jurisdiction. This is evidenced in the wording of these provisions, with Article 6 stating that it is applicable 'where no court of a Member State has jurisdiction pursuant to Article 4 or 5', and Article 7 addressing cases 'covered by Article 6'.[671] Whilst this interplay serves to facilitate access to justice for parties in such a situation, it can be questioned why this construction is so convoluted. Since agreement has to have failed under Article 5 to make use of Article 7, it would appear that parties cannot make use of this possibility in advance.[672] Furthermore, it places

666 See, with specific regard to marriage, Shúilleabháin (Chapter 4, n.348), at pp.79–80, para.2.65.

667 See the Explanatory Memorandums accompanying both Property Regulation proposals (Chapter 1, n.24), at p.8, para.5.2.

668 See Recitals 35 and 35 of both Property Regulations.

669 Through divorce, legal separation or marriage annulment (Matrimonial Property Regulation), or the dissolution or annulment of a registered partnership (Partnership Property Regulation).

670 According to the grounds of Article 5(2) of the Matrimonial Property Regulation and any linkage under Article 5 of the Partnership Property Regulation.

671 The possibility of this function is employed in: Walker (Chapter 2, n.164), at p.238 and P. Quinzá Redondo, 'The EU Regulation of 24 June 2016 in Matters of Matrimonial Property Regimes: A General Overview' in A. Corella et. al. (eds.), *Legal Challenges of the XXI Century* (Tirant lo Blanch, Valencia, 2017), 335 at p.339.

672 It is not clear whether a prior choice of court agreement for other proceedings pursuant to Article 7 would automatically apply.

spouses in an unequal position to registered partners, since the former extension is automatic where a forum is seised of jurisdiction for divorce under the first four indents of Article 3(1)(a) or Article 3(1)(b) of Brussels II bis.

It would not only be simpler and fairer, but also enhance the overall autonomy and legal certainty for those involved in property relations proceedings that accompany the dissolution of a relationship, if spouses or partners were free to link proceedings to the court of the dissolution or choose another ground according to Article 7 on an equal basis.

6.4.3. CHOICE OF LAW: ARTICLE 22(1)(c) OF THE PARTNERSHIP PROPERTY REGULATION

A significant difference between the two Property Regulations is found in the fact that only the Partnership Property Regulation permits the national law of the state where the relationship was created to be chosen to apply to the partners' property relations (Article 22(1)(c)). Such an omission appears puzzling, particularly since the option of the court of the Member State where the relationship was created is available as a jurisdictional head under both instruments.

It could be argued that this asymmetry exists due to the variation in national conceptions of registered partnership and the property consequences that are attached to this relationship,[673] meaning there is a greater need to ensure that the most appropriate law is applied to the relationship that upholds the original expectations of the parties as to the consequences of their relationship. However, since the law of the state under whose law the relationship was created applies in the absence of choice,[674] there is no risk that such original expectations will not be met.

There is an absence of a sturdy rationale concerning this comparative omission. The consequence of this omission is that the spouses cannot use their autonomy to unify the law and court of the place in which their relationship was created. This has a particularly negative impact upon those in same-sex relationships, who may find that they cannot reap the practical benefits of unifying the law and court if they wish to secure with certainty a Member State court that recognizes their relationship and its property consequences.

6.5. SYNTHESIS

This final section concludes the evaluation of the direct connections through which a choice of court and/or a choice of law can be exercised in the EU private

673 See 4.4.

674 Partnership Property Regulation, Article 26(1).

international law framework relating to family matters and succession. It aims to bring together the general findings in an overview (6.5.1.), before comparing the form and function of the connecting factors in order to identify strands of coordination between related areas and/or the law and court which governs a proceeding (6.5.2.), and highlighting the gaps within the framework that necessitate further action (6.5.3.).

6.5.1. OVERVIEW OF FINDINGS

Table 1. Direct Connections

		Habitual residence	**Nationality (Domicile)**	**Place of creation**
Matrimonial matters	Court			
	Law	x*	x	
Matrimonial property	Court			x
	Law	x	x	
Partnership property	Court			x
	Law	x	x	x
Maintenance	Court	x†	x	
	Law	x	x	
Succession	Court			
	Law		x	

* Common habitual residence or last common habitual residence in so far as one of the parties still resided there at the time the agreement was concluded.

† In the case of maintenance between ex-spouses, the additional option of the last common habitual residence for a period of at least a year is provided.

From the evaluation performed in the preceding sections and the overview of the findings provided by Table 1 above, a number of observations can be made with regard to the manifestation of the direct connecting factors within this framework:

1. It can first be observed that the opportunity to make a direct designation of a particular connection (6.2.–6.4.) is more prevalent in the choice of law context than with regard to choice of court. Whilst a direct choice of law opportunity is evident in five instruments in total (all four of the instruments concerning adult relationships and the Succession Regulation), only three of the instruments – the Maintenance Regulation and the two Property Regulations – permit a direct designation of the competent court.
2. It is also clear that the possibility to make a direct choice of law is also more broadly manifested than with regard to a direct jurisdictional choice. The

four instruments concerning adult relationships all provide for the habitual residence or nationality of either party to be designated as a determinant (with the sole exception of the need for a 'common' habitual residence under the Rome III Regulation). A choice of court is only permitted under the Maintenance and Property Regulations, with only the former allowing for both the habitual residence and nationality of either party to be a determinant, whilst the latter only permits the court of the place where the relationship was created to be seised. In the case of the Succession Regulation, there is no parallel direct choice of court to sit alongside the opportunity to make a *professio juris* in favour of a party's nationality.

3. Nationality (or domicile[675]) is the most prevalent connecting factor amongst the relevant EU instruments. The nationality of either of the parties is available as a choice of law connection in all four of the instruments concerning adult relationships, and the deceased may opt to have the law of their nationality apply under the Succession Regulation. As has been discussed, the opportunity for a direct choice of court to be made is comparatively less evident within the framework, and in line with this, the nationality of either party can only be selected as a jurisdictional ground under the Maintenance Regulation.

   Due to its entrenched nature, nationality can be seen to offer a choice with which the parties are likely to enjoy a continued affinity as they move throughout the Union (albeit, in some cases, a residual tie). In addition, in both the jurisdictional and applicable law contexts, the application of this criterion might be seen to enhance access to justice by reducing complexity in proceedings, for instance, due to a party's familiarity with the language in which the relevant legislation is written and in which the judicial system functions.

4. Habitual residence follows closely behind nationality in terms of its prevalence and the areas in which it appears. The habitual residence of *either* party may be chosen as a choice of law connection under the Property Regulations and the Hague Maintenance Protocol), whilst under the Rome III Regulation it must be in some way associated with *both* parties at the time of agreement, either as the common habitual residence of the parties, or their last common habitual residence in so far as one of them still resides there. In line with nationality / domicile, the habitual residence of either party at the time of agreement or when the court is seised can only be selected as a determinant of jurisdiction under the Maintenance Regulation.

   It can be observed that the present habitual residence of the parties can generally be viewed as the optimum setting in terms of access to justice

675 Under the Maintenance Regulation.

(e.g. since the parties will not have to travel to attend proceedings). Furthermore, as a choice of law connection, particularly in view of the position of the creditor in maintenance obligations, it holds the potential for application of a law that is reflective of the present social environment of a party, which secures both affinity- and practicality-based benefits. However, as will be discussed below in this subsection, the advantages of the application of this criterion are easily defeated by temporal or personal disconnect.

5. The third connecting factor that can be directly chosen – the place where a relationship was created – is only available as a jurisdictional choice under the Property Regulations. It is furthermore only available as an option for a choice of law under the Partnership Property Regulation. Given the potential benefits involved in its application (most prominently, recognition of the relationship by its 'home' jurisdiction) there will be discussion below of its otherwise absence from the framework and the consequences of this (see 6.5.3. – 'Gaps to be addressed').
6. It is observed that the connecting factors present various levels of legal certainty in their legislative definition, with the place of creation being the easiest concept to grasp and maintain, followed by nationality, then domicile, and finally, habitual residence. Habitual residence is inherently flexible; however, this makes it sometimes difficult to ascertain. Whilst this does not pose a great issue if habitual residence is used to make a designation at the moment of choice (which is required under the choice of law provisions in this chapter), if the selected connection is indeterminate in nature (as is permitted under the Article 4(1)(a) and (c)(ii) of the Maintenance Regulation), depending on the circumstances, it might be difficult to predict the court which will ultimately govern proceedings.
7. The matter of the temporal connectedness to the law or forum that is designated by agreement is an important consideration. All of the relevant provisions discussed in this chapter allow the choice to be frozen at the moment of designation, with a number of them also allowing the content of the choice to be ascertained at the relevant point when proceedings arise (namely, the Maintenance Regulation and Succession Regulation).

   Although this latter instance offers much less predictability, a criticism that can be levelled at freezing a connection at the moment of designation, particularly where this relates to the flexible criterion of habitual residence, is the risk that the parties lose close connection to this ground over time. This holds the potential to not only be inconvenient with regard to a choice of court (e.g. where physical proximity to the court is an important consideration), but also especially detrimental in the choice of law context for maintenance proceedings (whereby the law that determines the amount and type of maintenance reflects the social climate of the place where the creditor finds themselves). This topic will be returned to in Chapter 9.[676]

8. Concerns also arise with regard to the potential for a choice of court or law to be connected to only *one* of the parties under the relevant instruments,[677] with the exception of Article 5(1)(a) and (b) of the Rome III Regulation.[678] Whilst the essence of party autonomy is found in the exercise of free will and the opportunity for the individual to weigh up considerations relating to affinity and practicality themselves, the EU has introduced choice in the realm of family matters and succession on the basis of close connection to the parties and their relationship. In view of this established mandate, and the benefits to ensuring that both parties hold a degree of connection with the criterion in the context of family relations, it is puzzling why only Rome III employs a restrictive approach in this regard.
9. Remaining with the issue of connectedness in the specific context of maintenance obligations, it can be seen that several potential risks arise for the creditor within the present context. Firstly, there is a possibility that, through the passage of time, the court that is selected by advance agreement no longer holds a connection to either party. Although this poses significant disadvantages in terms of access to justice for both the creditor and debtor, it may be felt particularly acutely in the former instance, given the inequality in their respective bargaining positions.[679] Furthermore, as discussed in the section above, there is a possibility for a law that is unconnected to one of the parties to be chosen under the Hague Maintenance Protocol. Notwithstanding the imposition of additional safeguards,[680] the application of the law of a former habitual residence of the creditor, or the (former) habitual residence or nationality of the debtor arguably does not generally take into account the environment in which the creditor lives, which is a crucial factor in the calculation of maintenance.

6.5.2. INTERPLAY BETWEEN RELATED AREAS

The previous subsection has outlined, amongst other things, differences in distribution and scope seen between the direct choice of law and choice of court provisions that have been presented in this chapter. By referring back to Table 1 (see 6.5.1. above), coordination and cohesion between the various provisions

676 See 9.2.

677 Although this is clearly not a relevant concern under the Succession Regulation.

678 Which requires a connection of *both* parties to the criterion of habitual residence, since this must be the (last) common habitual residence of the parties.

679 See discussion in: Walker (Chapter 2, n.164), at pp.246–250.

680 See Chapters 9 and 10.

that have been outlined in the preceding subsections will now be explored in greater detail:

1. The possibility to unify the law and court – 'vertical cohesion'[681] allows for the forum to apply its own law to proceedings. By avoiding the application of foreign law, it is arguable that this possibility allows the parties to avoid the increased time and monetary costs that arise from the need for greater scrutiny of unfamiliar legislation, as well as the risk of inaccuracies in application arising at the hands of a foreign judge.[682] One point to emphasise at the outset is that the parties are clearly limited to selecting a *Member State* law (rather than the law of a third country) if they wish to achieve a union between the law and forum.

   In view of the mirroring choice of law and choice of court provisions established in Article 4 of the Maintenance Regulation and Article 8 of the Hague Maintenance Protocol, it is seen that the parties can choose to unify the law and court that govern proceedings involving maintenance obligations by opting for the same (Member State) habitual residence or nationality of either party in both contexts.

   A union of law and forum can also be secured under Article 7 (in conjunction with Article 22) of the Partnership Property Regulation, although only with regard to the place where the relationship was created. It should be noted that this possibility generally only extends to proceedings occurring outside of the dissolution of a registered partnership or succession.[683]

   Although the Member State *court* of the place where a marriage was celebrated can be designated under the Matrimonial Property Regulation, a parallel opportunity to select the *law* of this state does not exist, meaning that spouses do not enjoy the same opportunity to coordinate the law and forum. This may hold particularly negative consequences for those in same-sex marriages in terms of securing a law that recognises their relationship.
2. In view of the lack of overlap between the connecting factors available for direct designation of the competent court in the Maintenance Regulation and the Property Regulations, it is concluded that that there is no possibility for direct coordination of jurisdictional choices through this route in these (at times) related areas. Discussion of the benefits of the 'horizontal cohesion' in the jurisdictional context will thus be left to the next chapter (see discussion with regard to choice of law below).[684]

---

681 See description of both 'vertical' and 'horizontal' cohesion in 1.4.

682 See 3.5.2.2. and 3.5.2.3.

683 See also discussion at 7.4.1.

684 See 7.6.1.

3. 'Horizontal cohesion' of the laws that apply to related proceedings can be seen to combat the negative effects of 'incompatible interactions', whereby the applicable laws that are applied to related subject matters do not originate from the same legal system and might therefore not have the same compensatory interaction with one another as laws that originate from the same legal system.[685] Furthermore, it can also be proposed that the ability to unify the laws that apply to related matters avoids the costly need to hire duplicate or specialist legal representation in order to navigate the respective sets of rules.[686]

An area of clear coordination is seen between the three instruments in the context of the dissolution of a marriage by divorce or legal separation (Rome III, the Matrimonial Property Regulations and the Maintenance Regulation). These instruments permit the habitual residence or nationality of either party to be chosen, with the sole exception of the requirement under the Rome III Regulation that the law of habitual residence must be in some way connected with both parties. If the parties wish to unify the laws that apply to these related proceedings through direct choice, this difference means that individual habitual residences (e.g. those acquired after separation by the parties) cannot be selected as a determinant of the applicable law. This might pose a particular dilemma with regard to maintenance proceedings, whereby it could be important to the creditor to secure the application of the law of a present habitual residence (e.g. in order to secure a law that reflects this party's social context).

The same coordination as that discussed above can be achieved between the laws that govern property relations between registered partners and the maintenance obligations. However, a vital piece of the puzzle is missing due to the absence of unified rules on the dissolution of registered partnerships, meaning that it is not possible to unify the rules that apply to these three interlinked processes in the same manner as with regard to matrimonial matters.

With regard to horizontal coordination of the laws that apply to a succession and the dissolution of the property regime upon the death of one spouse or partner, a direct selection of the law of nationality of the party who dies is possible under both instruments. However, a major caveat to this point is that such coordination is only possible with a high level of certainty if the deceased and their spouse / partner shared a common nationality. If this is not the case, and the parties have different nationalities, it may be very difficult to coordinate by making a choice (since this would require that the parties predict which one of them will predecease the other). In the

685 See 3.5.2.3.

686 See 3.5.2.2.

event that such coordination is achieved, it should be noted that this would also achieve a vertical union between the law and forum under the Property Regulations.

It should be mentioned that a recent study has proposed a solution to the above predicament, whereby the spouses insert a clause into their choice of law agreement providing that the dissolution of their property regime upon one of their deaths will be governed by the law of the nationality of the party who predeceases the other.[687]

6.5.3. GAPS TO BE ADDRESSED

In concluding this synthesis concerning the direct connections through which a choice of court or law can be exercised within the EU's private international law rules relating to family matters and succession, a number of areas that merit improvement can be identified:

1. As has been previously established in 6.5.1., habitual residence as a concept is comparatively less easy to grasp than the place of celebration of a marriage/partnership, nationality, and to a lesser extent, domicile. This has an impact upon the legal certainty that parties experience in using this criterion, particularly when an indeterminate choice is made. Whilst the inherent flexibility of this concept is what makes it suitable for the transient context, further refinement by the CJEU would enhance the uniformity in its usage and provide a framework for parties and practitioners to predict the consequences of a designation of an as yet undetermined connection.
2. A tangible discrepancy emerges from the impossibility to select the habitual residence as a *professio juris* in advance under the Succession Regulation. A person cannot, during their lifetime, expressly opt to designate the law of their habitual residence to govern their future succession. This is a somewhat troubling exclusion given that a person might well have much stronger ties to a past habitual residence than that in which they ultimately die (e.g. they may have simply retired to their final habitual residence).

   This omission could have a number of foreseeable negative consequences: for instance, the bulk of the beneficiaries of the estate might still live in the state in which the deceased spent most of his or her life, and may have their expectations concerning the outcome of the succession frustrated by the imposition of an unfamiliar law. Alternatively, where the deceased owns property in a past habitual residence, the competent court may have to carry out the inconvenient task of adapting rights *in rem*. In view of such

687 Villata / Valkova (n.602 above), at pp.86–89, 95–99 and 124–128.

examples, it asserted here that habitual residence at the time of designation is sorely missing as a choice of law within the present framework.

3. A further gap is evident when comparing the Property Regulations alongside one another. Although spouses can select the Member State where their marriage was concluded as a determinant of the competent *court*, in contrast to the situation under the Partnership Property Regulation, spouses cannot make a parallel choice of the *law* in favour of the state where their relationship was created. This inability to unify the law and forum particularly affects same-sex spouses, who could have otherwise used this route to ensure recognition of their relationship by the applicable law.
4. Taking a step back to look at the wider framework, and in view of the aforementioned benefits of the place of creation as a connecting factor (i.e. recognition of a relationship), it would also be useful if this criterion were to be provided in the context of Rome III (and, to step momentarily outside the remit of party autonomy, Brussels II bis in the matrimonial matters context), as well as in the Maintenance Regulation and Hague Maintenance Protocol. This would go some way to safeguard against the possibility of limping, 'non-traditional' relationships arising in interactions within the relevant framework.
5. On a final note, it is clear from the overview provided in Table 1 that there are patent legislative gaps in the realm of the dissolution of relationships in EU private international law. Within the context of this chapter, it is moreover obvious that the current lack of an opportunity to make a choice of court in the context of divorce, legal separation and marriage annulment presents a major obstacle to forward planning for international couples and means that jurisdictional coordination with related areas concerning adult relationships is not possible. There is also a tangible need for EU unification of the private international law rules concerning the dissolution of registered partnerships. However, this need is explored and exemplified in greater detail in the following chapter that concerns linking provisions within the relevant instruments.

CHAPTER 7
COORDINATING PROVISIONS

7.1. INTRODUCTION

The previous chapter presented the first step in examining the content of the choice of court and choice of law within the EU private international law framework on family matters and succession by outlining the direct connections through which party autonomy can be exercised in this setting. We now turn to evaluate the second type of provision found within this present framework: choice of court and choice of law provisions that allow related areas to be linked together ('coordinating provisions').

Chapter 3 has outlined the potential problems concerning access to justice that arise from a lack of coordination and cohesion between the law and court, or between related subject areas in the cross-border context. Such related areas can be divided into two groupings of proceedings that often occur in conjunction with one another: (i) those that are connected with the dissolution of a marriage by divorce or legal separation or the dissolution of a registered partnership (proceedings dissolving the relationship, in conjunction with the dissolution of the property regime, maintenance and/or parental responsibility), and (ii) and those that arise upon the death of a spouse or registered partner (succession proceedings in conjunction with the dissolution of a matrimonial property regime or the division of the property of the registered partners).[688] To summarise once more for the purposes of the present chapter, a lack of coordination in this regard may result in tangible problems such as having to travel between Member State jurisdictions to attend closely related proceedings within a short amount of time,[689] and increased costs and complexity from the need to apply foreign law,[690] as well as more subjective issues such as laws that are not compatible being applied to interlinked processes.[691] Although such problems can be tackled to an extent by manually coordinating particular direct connections (as outlined in section 6.5.3. of the previous chapter), the

688 See description of related areas in 1.4.
689 See 3.5.2.1.
690 See 3.5.2.2.
691 See 3.5.2.3.

EU legislator has also created provisions with the sole function of achieving coordination.

The following four sections will deal with these respective opportunities for coordination through choice, namely looking at provisions that allow for connection of the jurisdictions (7.2.) or the applicable laws that govern related subject areas (7.3.), those that permit the designation of the Member State court whose law is applicable (7.4.), and the choice to apply the law of the Member State forum – the *lex fori* (7.5.). In the same manner as the previous chapter, these provisions will be evaluated in light of the values established in the first two chapters. A concluding synthesis will also be presented (7.6.) that builds on that set out in the previous chapter, outlining the manifestation and level of coordination exemplified through these linking provisions, the additional value added to the established breadth of choice, and the gaps within the framework that have been identified during this part of the evaluation that need to be addressed.

7.2. JURISDICTIONS THAT DECIDE ON RELATED MATTERS

The majority of the relevant instruments (the Property Regulations, the Maintenance Regulation and the Brussels II bis Regulation in the context of parental responsibility) offer the opportunity for parties to agree to link jurisdiction in situations where a matter is considered to be auxiliary to a principal proceeding concerning the dissolution of a marriage or registered partnership.

Such mechanisms primarily focus on furthering so-called 'procedural economy'[692] by allowing for the same Member State court to be selected to decide on related matters that readily occur in tandem. This follows from the reasoning that parties can maximise convenience by using this opportunity for linkage to avoid the additional time and expense involved in travelling between respective jurisdictions to participate in interrelated cases, and obviate the need, in most instances, to hire duplicate legal representation.

7.2.1. ARTICLE 5 OF THE PROPERTY REGULATIONS

Under Article 5(2) of the Matrimonial Property Regulation and Article 5(1) of the Partnership Property Regulation an opportunity is established to link

[692] See usage of this term in the context of parental responsibility in: Pataut (Chapter 4, n.467), at p.148, para.8.

jurisdiction to that which is competent to dissolve the marriage or registered partnership. The regulation on matrimonial property relations provides for the linkage of the jurisdiction with that which is competent to decide on an application for divorce, legal separation or marriage annulment under the Brussels II bis Regulation. The construction of this choice is fairly limited, with jurisdiction automatically being linked in cases involving divorce, legal separation or marriage annulment,[693] bar a number of specific grounds upon which it is required that there is spousal agreement.[694]

In this regard, the agreement of the parties is necessary: if a Member State court is seised under the fifth or sixth indent of Article 3(1) of the Brussels II bis Regulation (whereby the applicant has either been habitually resident in that Member State for at least one year prior to the application, or has resided there for at least six months prior to the application and is a national of that Member State);[695] in cases where a Member State court has been seised under Article 5 of Brussels II bis[696] in order to convert a legal separation to divorce; or where residual jurisdiction has been determined according to Article 7 of Brussels II bis.[697] Although no official explanation has been given as to why these grounds have been selected for additional agreement, it can be suggested that this is due to the focus on the applicant's position under the fifth and sixth indents of Article 3(1) of the Brussels II bis,[698] or the anomalous nature of jurisdiction determined according to Article 5 and 7.

The exceptional character of party autonomy under this provision in the face of otherwise default linkage is more indicative of a confirmatory function rather than an active expression of free will. From the wording of Article 5(3), it can in fact be inferred that extension remains automatic in the same manner if a court were to be seised for matrimonial matters according to the first to fourth indents of Article 3 of Brussels II bis, but continuing with proceedings is made subject to agreement of the parties.[699] Taken in this way, the autonomy established by Article 5 can primarily be seen to serve as a safeguard in instances where the jurisdiction for divorce, legal separation or marriage annulment has been seised unilaterally and only holds a link with one party, or where the parties' link to the determined jurisdiction is otherwise tenuous.

---

693 Matrimonial Property Regulation, Article 5(1).

694 Article 5(2).

695 Article 5(2)(a) and (b).

696 Article 5(2)(c).

697 Article 5(2)(d).

698 Quinzá Redondo (Chapter 6, n.671), at p.339.

699 Matrimonial Property Regulation, Article 5(3): 'If the agreement referred to in paragraph 2 of this Article is concluded before the court is seised to rule on matters of matrimonial property regimes, the agreement shall comply with Article 7(2)'. It should, however, be noted that the wording of Article 5(3) is not altogether clear in this regard, a point which will be returned to in the context of the timing of choice in Chapter 9 (see 9.2.1.3.).

Although future agreement to link jurisdiction appears to be a possibility under Article 5(2),[700] given that no choice of court for matrimonial matters is currently permitted under Brussels II bis, and in view of the limited number of grounds that require the parties' agreement, such a choice would be inherently uncertain in nature until a court is seised for the purposes of dissolving the relationship.[701]

Article 5(1) of the Partnership Property Regulation differs from the parallel provision found in the Matrimonial Property Regulation by simply allowing the partners to opt to link the court which is competent to deal with the property consequences of their partnership with that which is to be / has been seised of jurisdiction for the purposes of dissolving or annulling their relationship. The opportunity for party autonomy here appears, at least on the surface, to be a lot less convoluted than the parallel provision discussed above (although its construction indicates that the same, primarily safeguarding purposes apply here as under Article 5 of the Matrimonial Property Regulation).

One major point to be highlighted in the context of the Partnership Property Regulation is that although the same benefits of coordination between the jurisdictions that govern related matters apply in this context, in the absence of unified EU legislation providing jurisdictional rules concerning the dissolution of registered partnerships, and in light of the patchwork recognition of such relationships between Member States, it will be hard to predict in advance which jurisdiction will be competent for the purposes of dissolving the relationship. This equates to a comparatively greater level of uncertainty if an agreement precedes the court being seised for the purposes of dissolving a registered partnership.

As has been discussed in the previous chapter[702] with regard to the situation in which the parties do not agree under Article 5(2) of the Matrimonial Property Regulation or Article 5(1) of the Partnership Property Regulation, it would appear that jurisdiction can be founded through the objective jurisdictional grounds in Article 6 or a choice of court under Article 7. This construction has, however, been criticised not only because of its ambiguous nature, but also on the basis of why the jurisdictional opportunities set out in Articles 6 and 7 could not be offered to the parties on an equal basis to the linking provision contained in Article 5. This would permit a broader choice for parties within the confines of close connection, whilst giving them the opportunity to enter into an agreement under Article 7 that entails a much higher level of legal certainty (particularly in view of the legislative and participatory gaps that currently exist[703]).

---

700 Since Article 5(3) makes reference to the possibility for prior agreement, see ibid.

701 See further discussion in the context of formal requirements at 9.3.1.1.

702 See 6.4.2.

703 See discussion of the context of enhanced cooperation in Chapter 10, particularly 10.7. and 10.8.

7.2.2. ARTICLE 4(1)(c)(i) OF THE MAINTENANCE REGULATION

In addition to the linkage to the court of dissolution seen in the context of the Property Regulations, Article 4(1)(c)(i) of the Maintenance Regulation also offers the opportunity for spouses or former spouses to agree to link the jurisdiction that decides on a maintenance dispute to that which is competent over matrimonial matters at the time the agreement is concluded, or at the time the court is seised.

It should be noted that unlike the Matrimonial Property Regulation, this regulation does not actually define 'matrimonial matters' for its purposes: it has been suggested that this category includes not only divorce, legal separation and marriage annulment, but also extends to matrimonial property.[704] However, given the matching terminology employed in the Brussels II bis Regulation, it is argued here that in order to promote certainty through streamlined interpretation and consistency between instruments, it ought to be assumed that Article 4(1)(c)(i) only links jurisdiction to matters of divorce, legal separation and annulment as defined in this aforementioned regulation.[705]

In comparing the choice of court options offered by the Maintenance Regulation and the jurisdictional grounds of Brussels II bis side by side, it would appear that linkage does not generally offer any *additional* grounds to the parties. The Maintenance Regulation already permits designation of the Member State court of the habitual residence or nationality of either party at the time of agreement or when the court is seised, and the more limited grounds set out in Article 3 of Brussels II bis fall within these parameters. Of course, additional grounds might be added where a court is seised for matrimonial matters under the provisions relating to conversion of a legal separation to a divorce under Article 5 or residual jurisdiction according to Article 7. Notwithstanding this, however, the primary benefit of making use of Article 4(1)(i) remains the predictability of securing linkage in advance of proceedings involving the dissolution of the marriage occurring.

7.2.3. ARTICLE 12(1) OF THE BRUSSELS II BIS REGULATION

A very distinct form of jurisdictional linkage exists in the context of cross-border parental responsibility. This can be found in Article 12(1) of the

[704] S. Verburgt, 'Bevoegdheid, Erkenning en Tenuitvoerlegging onder Alimentatieverordening 4/2009' (2012) 7 *Tijdschrift voor Relatierecht en Praktijk* 296, at pp.300–301.

[705] I. Curry-Sumner, 'Reactie op artikel Alimentatieverordening 4/2009' (2013) 4(2) *Tijdschrift voor Relatierecht en Praktijk* 69, at pp.69–70.

Brussels II bis Regulation, which provides an opportunity for prorogation whereby jurisdiction can be assumed by the courts of the Member State whose court is seised of jurisdiction to decide on a divorce, legal separation or marriage annulment under Article 3 of this same instrument, in cases where the matter of parental responsibility is considered auxiliary to the proceedings concerning the dissolution of the marriage.[706] In comparison to the provisions in the Property Regulations and Maintenance Regulation above, the jurisdiction to which the court of parental responsibility is linked is restricted to only the grounds of general jurisdiction contained in Brussels II bis Article 3 (as opposed to also Articles 5 and 7).

Although the prorogation mechanism provided by Article 12(1) comes into play in conjunction with divorce, legal separation or marriage annulment proceedings that have been instigated by the parties, the tone of Article 12(1)(b) clearly assigns a passive role to the agreement of the spouses to link jurisdictions. Their acceptance is enumerated as a prerequisite to jurisdiction being assumed, rather than the catalyst behind the extension of jurisdiction.

In addition to necessitating the acceptance by the spouses involved in the principal proceedings (of which at least one must be a holder of parental responsibility[707]), Article 12(1) also requires the accord of any other holders of parental responsibility. This is a necessary inclusion, given that the spouses are not necessarily *both* holders of parental responsibility, nor are they always the *sole* holders of parental responsibility. Additional holders of parental responsibility could include ex-partners of one of the spouses, grandparents, or even local authorities.[708] The agreement of these other interested parties ensures that the jurisdiction is also regarded as convenient by them, and that their access to justice is not impeded through the spouses' choice of court.

In line with the mechanisms established in Article 12(3) and Article 15 of Brussels II bis,[709] the assent of the parties to the proceedings is also subject to the requisite judicial assessment of whether the assumption of jurisdiction by

---

706 Under Article 12(2), this competence is strictly limited to the two linked proceedings, whereby it will come to an end once a final decision has been made either regarding the divorce, legal separation or marriage annulment in question, or the related matter of parental responsibility (whichever comes last). Furthermore, under Article 12(2)(c), competence will also end if either of the aforementioned proceedings comes to an end for another reason.

707 In accordance with Article 12(1)(a). Previously, under Article 3(1) of the Brussels II Regulation, both spouses were required to be holders of parental responsibility. Brussels II bis changed this to only requiring one of the spouses to be a holder of parental responsibility, thus opening the way for jurisdiction to be assumed under this mechanism even where one of the spouses is a stepparent of the child concerned (and thus bringing it into line with contemporary family trends in the EU). For further discussion see: McEleavy (Chapter 1, n.56), at p.507, fn.27.

708 Under Brussels II bis, Article 2(7), a holder of parental responsibility can be a natural or legal person. See also *EC Practice Guide* (Chapter 4, n.329), at p.19, para.3.1.1.2.

709 See 8.2.1. and 8.2.2.

the court that dissolves the marriage would be in the best interests of the child (Article 12(1)(c)). As discussed in Chapter 2,[710] this reflects the international human rights standard by which in decisions involving children their best interests ought to be of primary concern[711] and is a guiding principle for consideration of parental responsibility under Brussels II bis Regulation.[712]

In this context, the best interests criterion can be seen as a necessary safeguard against the whims of pragmatism. Assessment of whether assuming jurisdiction would be in the best interests of the child allows the potential court to ascertain whether it is indeed in the position to access information on relevant aspects of the child's life and wellbeing. Although it is for the decision-making authority to consider this question, it has been suggested that the parties to the proceedings might also aid the process by submitting their own reasons for believing that prorogation is in the best interests of the child.[713]

Illustrating the typical situation which falls within the scope of Article 12(1) is relatively straightforward, for instance the scenario in which the spouses and their children live together in Member State A, after which the marriage breaks down, and one of the spouses moves with the children to Member State B. If dissolution proceedings were to be instigated in Member State A, a strong argument could be made that proroguing the parental responsibility proceedings to State A would be favourable for the children, since this is where their former (family) life was concentrated.

It has been stated that to accept jurisdiction under Article 12(1) on the basis of the best interests of the child would be unusual if the other conditions set out in Article 12(1) were to be fulfilled.[714] Reference can also be made to a recent Advocate General's Opinion on the interpretation of best interests under Article 12(3): in typical cases where the other requisite criteria involved in the mechanism have been fulfilled, best interests are to be treated as part and parcel to the prorogation process (rather than a separate test).[715] It was opined that this requirement is to be treated as an additional check through which the judge can sidestep the transference of jurisdiction if the circumstances lead him or her to believe that this extension is not in the best interests of the child.[716]

---

[710] See 2.4.2.

[711] Article 3(1) of the UN Convention on the Rights of the Child (1989) and Article 24(2) of the EU Charter of Fundamental Rights.

[712] See Recitals 12, 13 and 33 of Brussels II bis. See also Case C-195/08 PPU *Inga Rinau*. Reference for a preliminary ruling: Lietuvos Aukščiausiasis Teismas – Lithuania [2008] ECR I-5271, at para.51.

[713] Villata / Valcova (Chapter 6, n.602), at p.12.

[714] Pataut (Chapter 4, n.467), at pp.152–153, para.37.

[715] See Opinion of AG Tanchev in Case C-565/16 *Alessandro Saponaro and Kalliopi-Chloi Xylina*. Request for a preliminary ruling from the Eirinodikeio Lerou Leros – Greece [2018] ECLI:EU:C:2017:942, at para.67.

[716] Ibid., at para.70.

It has also been suggested that wider familial considerations related to the benefits of procedural economy might play a part in the assessment of best interests,[717] since the interests of the child cannot be taken in isolation from those of the adults involved in the main proceedings. For instance, increasing convenience for the spouses and allowing them to make amicable agreements has a beneficial impact on the life of the entire family. Whilst consideration of the child's interests as an individual necessarily plays a mediating role in the process of prorogation (and identifying atypical situations which need further investigation), the best interests can be adjudged within the wider context in which the child finds him-/herself.

In essence, the situation of the child of whom one or both parents are involved in divorce, legal separation or annulment proceedings under Article 3 of Brussels II bis cannot be taken entirely in insolation. Given the restrictive rules of this instrument, the court is likely to be a proximate one to the child. Refusal might only occur in quite extreme circumstances, for example, where the authorities of the minor's habitual residence clearly have a monopoly over information on the situation of the child, or where there is no real past or present factual link between the child and the requested jurisdiction.[718] It should be noted that a differently weighted decision-making process is undertaken in cases that fall within the scope of Article 12(4), which involve situations whereby a child is habitually resident in a third state that is not a contracting party to the 1996 Hague Convention on Child Protection.[719]

A further comment to be made with regard to the assessment of the child's best interests in this setting, and one that applies equally to Article 12(3) and Article 15,[720] is that discrepancies will inevitably arise with regard to the interpretation of this requirement. Whilst the CJEU can provide examples of the type of considerations that ought to guide the national courts, the subjectivity inherent in this assessment means that it is not possible to create a unified approach between Member State courts.[721]

As an afterword to the above analysis, it is important to note that the Brussels IIa (Recast) Regulation has merged the separate provisions contained in Article 12(1) and 12(3) to create a single, comprehensive choice of court

---

717 *Bush v. Bush* [2008] EWCA Civ. 865, at para.44.

718 See, e.g., the facts of case of *Bush v. Bush* (ibid.), in particular, see the conclusion of Lord Justice Thorpe at para.48.

719 See discussion in the context of Brussels II bis, Article 12(3) in 8.2.1.

720 See 8.2.1. and 8.2.2.

721 See elaboration of national case law on Article 12 in: also T.M.C. Asser Institute et al., *Regulation Brussels II bis Guide for Application: Chapter 3* (July 2018), at pp.98–100, para.7.4.2., available at: http://www.asser.nl/media/4651/m-5796-ec-justice-cross-border-proceedings-in-family-law-matters-10-publications-02-guide-for-application-chapter-3.pdf.

mechanism.[722] Thus, whilst linkage with the court that is competent for matrimonial matters is still a primary goal of this new construction,[723] there is no longer a provision specifically aimed at this purpose.[724]

7.3. LAWS THAT APPLY TO RELATED MATTERS

In contrast to the significant presence of jurisdictional linkage between subject areas in the relevant EU instruments, coordination between the *laws* that apply to related subject areas is not a common feature in this setting. It is only possible under Articles 8(1)(c) and (d) of the Hague Maintenance Protocol.

Although coordinating the laws that apply to related matters may not appear to present the clear convenience-based benefits identified with regard to the jurisdictional linkage, there is an argument that related issues (such as the example here of maintenance obligations, the dissolution of a marriage and decisions on property relationships) are optimally treated collectively in the same framework of rules.[725] For instance, parties may benefit in terms of costs from being able to employ the same legal representation during both proceedings. Furthermore, there is a belief[726] that laws originating from the same state are drafted with one another in mind (sharing a common legal, historical and cultural context), meaning that they will fit better together and promote more coordinated outcomes.[727]

Turning to examine the Hague Maintenance Protocol more specifically, it can be seen that Articles 8(1)(c) and (d) respectively establish that the law applicable to maintenance obligations may be linked to that which is designated, or in fact applied, to either the parties' property regime,[728] or their divorce or legal separation. To put this in clearer terms, extension can be made under these provisions to (i) a particular law which has been chosen by the parties to apply

722 See Article 10 of the Brussels IIa (Recast) Regulation.

723 See Recital 23 of Brussels IIa (Recast) Regulation.

724 Referring only to a Member State court of substantial connection (Article 10(1)(a)), the agreement of the parties (Article 10(1)(b)) and that the assumption of jurisdiction is in the best interests of the child (Article 10(1)(c)).

725 Župan (Chapter 4, n.397), at p.323.

726 To the author's knowledge, there has not been any in-depth research on this point.

727 Gray/Quinzá Redondo (Chapter 3, n.320), at para.4.2.2.2.

728 The Explanatory Report to the Protocol describes the property regime under Article 8(1)(c) as existing between spouses; however, it is proposed here that a relationship analogous to marriage (e.g. certain forms of registered partnership) may also be included if a state is willing to recognise this institution in this manner. This emulates the approach endorsed by the Explanatory Report with regard to Article 5 of the Hague Protocol: see Bonomi (Chapter 4, n.400), at para.92.

to the related matter, or (ii) the law which has been applied in fact in the instance that a court is already seised for the related proceeding.

In the Explanatory Report accompanying the Protocol, Bonomi appears to exclude an indeterminate designation, whereby the parties agree to link the applicable law to a future choice of law or applied law with regard to the related subject matter.[729] On the one hand, this exclusion of a choice in favour of an undetermined connection raises the level of legal certainty by making the ultimate law to be applied easy to predict. However, the fragmented Member State participation in both the Property Regulations and the Rome III Regulation means that there is a risk that a designated choice could be declared void by a forum state, thereby also negating the connected choice of maintenance law.[730] In the absence of a completely unified system of choice of law rules on divorce and property relations, it would also appear that this extension mechanism may involve interaction with national conflict-of-laws rules and thus creates only a 'semblance of uniformity'.[731] In view of these circumstances, it can be opined that there are foreseeable obstacles to predictability which hamper the functioning of the linking mechanisms contained in Article 8(1)(c) and (d).[732]

7.4. DETERMINING JURISDICTION ON THE BASIS OF APPLICABLE LAW

The possibility to link the ascertainment of the competent Member State court with the law that applies to the same subject matter is provided for by three of the relevant instruments, namely, Article 7 of the two Property Regulations (see 7.4.1.), and the Articles 5, 6(b) and 7(b) and (c) of the Succession Regulation (see 7.4.2.).

Although this linkage is not essential for ensuring the proper application of the law, this opportunity may be seen to enhance convenience for those involved in proceedings. Since the accurate application of foreign law will likely require increased judicial scrutiny in order to decipher and characterise

729 Ibid., at paras.138–143.

730 See for discussion of this prior to the Rome III and the Property Regulations emerging: Bonomi, ibid. at para.135 and A. Bonomi, 'Hague Protocol of 23 November 2007 on the Law Applicable to Maintenance Obligations' (2008) 10 *Yearbook of Private International Law* 333, at pp.354–355.

731 Bonomi (Chapter 4, n.400), at para.135 and Bonomi (n.730 above), at p.354. See also Župan (Chapter 4, n.397), at p.322.

732 See discussion of specificity in the context of formal requirements in: 9.3.2.2.

foreign legislation or legal concepts,[733] as well as possible (costly) reliance upon additional legal expertise and translation services, opting for a court to apply its own national law could be seen as a choice that optimises efficiency.

7.4.1. ARTICLE 7 OF THE PROPERTY REGULATIONS

Under Article 7 of both Property Regulations (which applies to the organisation of property outside of succession or dissolution of a relationship), the parties can select the competent Member State court whose law is applicable on the basis of objective grounds (Article 26(1)), or a result of a choice of law (Article 22).

Linkage with a prior choice of law clearly affords the parties a high level of legal certainty as to the court that will ultimately decide on their future, offering the opportunity to designate the court of either party's habitual residence or nationality at the time the agreement was concluded.[734] Where a choice of court is made in favour of an objectively applicable law, the legal certainty is clearly lower for the parties involved. However, this is mitigated by the fact that under Article 26(1) the possible connections are either successive or singular, and concentrated at the time the relationship in question was created: in the context of matrimonial property relations, first common habitual residence, then common nationality at the time of marriage[735] or state of closest connection at the time of marriage; with regard to property relations between registered partners, the state under whose law the relationship was created (which duplicates a jurisdictional ground already present in Article 7(1)).

The process by which the competent court would be determined without first establishing the applicable law (a task for the competent court) is not altogether clear. Presumably, the parties or their legal counsel would be able to gauge with a high degree of certainty which court would be competent by consulting the objective rules set out in Article 26(1). However, in the matrimonial property context, where the successive rules could lead to application of the law of the state where the spouses jointly had the 'closest connection at the time of the conclusion of the marriage, taking into account all the circumstances',[736] it is unclear how the parties would proceed with designating a court.

---

733 See, for instance, the difficulty in characterisation highlighted by the preliminary question referred to the Court of Justice in *Van den Boogaard* (Chapter 3, n.314), in which the Dutch national court asked whether the English law concept of ancillary relief would relate to maintenance or matrimonial property.

734 Article 22(1)(a) and (b) of both Property Regulations.

735 Article 26(1)(b) cannot be used where the couple has more than one common nationality (Article 26(2)).

736 Article 26(1)(c).

7.4.2. ARTICLES 5, 6(b) AND 7(b) AND (c) OF THE SUCCESSION REGULATION

Turning now to the Succession Regulation, this instrument demonstrates a particularly strong stance in favour of seeking unity between the applicable law and competent court, with the only opportunity for party autonomy in jurisdictional matters under this instrument being directed towards this aim. It essentially presents three separate possibilities for prorogation of the courts of the previously chosen [Member State] law of the deceased's nationality, which are rather complexly intertwined in Articles 5, 6, 7 and 9 of the regulation. It should be noted that since the transfer mechanism set out across Articles 6(a) and 7(a), along with the opportunity to accept jurisdiction by entering an appearance in line with Article 9, are to be examined in the next chapter,[737] such provisions will not be subject to extended discussion below.

Starting this examination with Article 5 of Succession Regulation, it can be seen that this provision extends jurisdiction to the Member State of the law that has been chosen by the deceased to govern their succession, upon the basis of agreement between all of the parties concerned (i.e. the heirs, legatees and creditors). If the requirements in this situation are fulfilled, the Member State courts which have competence under Article 4 (the deceased's last habitual residence) or Article 10 (subsidiary jurisdiction) shall decline jurisdiction according to Article 6(b), and the courts of the Member State from which the applicable law originates shall assume jurisdiction under Article 7(b).

In contrast to the straightforward functioning of Article 5, the purposes of Article 7(c) of the Succession Regulation – which establishes that jurisdiction may be assumed by the courts of the Member State of the chosen law where this action has been expressly accepted by the parties to the proceedings – are somewhat more obscure. Given the possibility for remaining parties to tacitly accept jurisdiction by entering an appearance before the relevant court in accordance with Article 9,[738] its very existence might well be questioned. However, in contrast to the aforementioned provision, the wording of Article 7(c) appears to exclude the existence of a prior agreement between (some of the parties) concerned, instead concentrating on the narrow circumstances in which the court of the *professio juris* has somehow been seised without such an agreement having been reached.[739] It is also clear that agreement ought to be express (rather than by submission as it is under Article 9).[740]

---

737 See 8.3.3 and 8.2.2.

738 See 8.3.3.

739 Van Calster (Chapter 2, n.167), at p.332, para.6.2.3.2.2.

740 Marongiu Buonaiuti (Chapter 4, n.502), at p.176, para.9. See also discussion of formal requirements in 9.3.1.4. and 9.3.1.6.

It has been suggested that use of this provision would arise in two principal circumstances, namely where (i) only one of several parties has applied to the court whose law is applicable, in which case, instead of refusing its competence immediately, the court should ask the remaining parties concerned whether they accept jurisdiction;[741] or (ii) only one person is party to the proceedings, in which case his or her application can be directly accepted under Article 7(c), since arguably one party cannot come to an 'agreement' within the meaning of Article 5.[742]

Whilst the latter situation appears to involve a more convoluted interpretation, the former instance may well occur in view of the fact that not all the parties to the succession may be known before proceedings are instigated.[743] Thus, notwithstanding its exceptional character, Article 7(c) can be seen as an additional aid (alongside Article 9) in the unification between law and court when circumstances move the situation outside the scope of Article 5.

One final matter to consider in the context of the various jurisdictional mechanisms set out in the Succession Regulation relates to the indefinite composition of the 'parties concerned'. In this regard, it is questionable whether the participation of an extended number of parties in a choice of court is appropriate where proceedings involving succession occur in tandem with the dissolution of a property regime between spouses or registered partners.[744] Under the Property Regulations extension of the jurisdiction that decides upon succession is automatic in situations where proceedings occur upon the death of one of the spouses / partners.[745]

In light of this default approach, it could be argued that where such an extension is employed, only the remaining spouse or registered partner ought to be involved in a choice of court. This limitation would allow spouses or registered partners to protect their own convenience-based considerations. However, this would come at the cost of the interests of other beneficiaries, as well as any legatees or creditors. It is argued here that it is more the automatic extension brought about by Article 4 of the Property Regulations

---

741 See Odersky (Chapter 4, n.501), at p.82, para.8.

742 Ibid., at p.82, para.8 and p.77, para.3 and Marongiu Buonaiuti (Chapter 4, n.502), at pp.175–176, paras.8–9.

743 Particularly legatees who are not necessarily obvious beneficiaries from the outset but nevertheless are named in the will: Marongiu Buonaiuti, (ibid.), at p.176, paras.9.

744 Particularly where a choice of court has been performed on the basis of Article 6(a) of the Succession Regulation, whereby just one of the parties concerned can request that the court of habitual residence decline jurisdiction in favour of the court of the chosen law of the deceased. This means that a choice of court might have been made without the agreement of the spouse or partner. For further discussion of this mechanism, see 8.2.3.

745 See Article 4 of both Property Regulations.

that can be critiqued,[746] rather than the participation of a wider group of interested parties.

7.5. DESIGNATING THE APPLICATION OF THE *LEX FORI*

The opportunity for the parties to select the *lex fori* allows a Member State court to apply its own national law to the proceedings over which it exercises competence. It arises under two instruments within the present framework, namely Article 5(1)(d) of Rome III and Article 7 of the Hague Maintenance Protocol.

The *lex fori* as a connecting factor originated in the common law countries, stemming from the notion that jurisdiction in proceedings concerning family matters was often conducted in the courts of the parties' domicile and thus the *lex fori* was nothing more than an extension of this close connection.[747] With increased globalisation the potency of domicile lessened; however, the application of *lex fori* still finds legitimacy as a pragmatic approach in the conflict-of-laws context.[748] As discussed in the section above, this unification between the law and the forum may be seen to optimise efficiency, since to otherwise apply foreign law may require increased scrutiny of unfamiliar legislation and, in some cases, reliance on additional legal expertise and translation services.[749]

7.5.1. ARTICLE 5(1)(d) OF ROME III

Parties may opt to select the law of the forum that governs their divorce or legal separation under Article 5(1)(d) of the Rome III Regulation. This interlinks with the law as determined by the jurisdictional rules contained in Brussels II bis.

---

746 It can be suggested that autonomy to accept or reject such an extension should have been inserted into Article 4 in order to give the spouse or registered partner flexibility in determining the jurisdiction that will make decisions on the dissolution of the property regime. See suggestion in this regard in: Gray/Quinzá Redondo (Chapter 3, n.320), at para.3.1.2.

747 Basedow (Chapter 1, n.46), at pp.233–234, at para.382 and V. Gaertner, 'European Choice of Law Rules in Divorce (Rome III): An Examination of the Possible Connecting Factors in Divorce Matters Against the Background of Private International Law Developments' (2006) 2(1) *Journal of Private International Law* 99, at pp.106–107.

748 Gaertner (n.747 above), p.104.

749 See discussion of benefits of the application of the *lex fori* in: Kruger (Chapter 1, n.60), at para.2(d).

There is an element of uncertainty as to whether this provision is intended to apply to indeterminate proceedings that are not yet pending[750] – a choice in favour of a yet to be ascertained forum. The English, French, Italian, Portuguese and Spanish language texts appear to be open to this possibility,[751] whilst it has been stated that the German and Dutch versions seem to limit choice to a court which is already seised.[752] It is hard to propose a concrete answer to this quandary. It can, however, be recalled that the rules contained in Article 5 of Rome III originally formed part of a revision of Brussels II bis that also included a parallel choice of court.[753] In this context, an ability to pre-emptively link the law and court makes perfect sense.

Moving beyond this point, proceeding with the broader interpretation of the temporal scope of Article 5(1)(d) of Rome III, it can nevertheless be observed that parties could use this indeterminate linkage to create a semblance of predictability with regard to the connecting factor through which the law will be determined for the purposes of future divorce or legal separation. However, the legal certainty reaped in these circumstances is clearly lower than if there were an opportunity to make a parallel choice of court in the divorce or legal separation context. Unfortunately, with the exclusion of this possibility in the final text for the new Brussels IIa (Recast) Regulation, it would appear that the limitations of the *status quo* are here to stay for the foreseeable future.[754]

7.5.2. ARTICLE 7 OF THE HAGUE MAINTENANCE PROTOCOL

In contrast to the discussion above, it is clear that under Article 7(1) of the Hague Maintenance Protocol, the *lex fori* can only be selected for the purposes of a specific proceeding that is taking place or pending. If this does not go ahead, the choice of law is no longer applicable. Furthermore, the linkage does not automatically extend to an appeal of a decision in this original case.[755] The scope of this provision is substantially narrower than that contained in Article 5(1)(d) of Rome III, focusing on offering the opportunity for the creditor in a particular

750 Basedow (Chapter 1, n.46), at p.255, at para.409.

751 Basedow (ibid.), at fn.816. The English-language version simply refers to 'the law of the forum'.

752 Ibid., translated from the German text as 'the court addressed'.

753 Proposal for a Council Regulation amending Regulation (EC) No 2201/2003 as regards jurisdiction and introducing rules concerning applicable law in matrimonial matters, COM(2006) 399 final. See also Kruger (Chapter 1, n.60), at para.1.

754 Particularly in view of the delicate nature of the legislative process in this sensitive realm and the desire to avoid further fragmentation through enhanced cooperation (see 10.7.).

755 Bonomi (Chapter 4, n.400), at paras.115–116 and Župan (Chapter 4, n.397), at p.321.

proceeding to reap the convenience-based outcomes associated with the court applying its own law.

One additional point to note here is that Article 7 provides the only instance seen amongst the instruments considered here for a law to be *selected* to apply to a proceeding involving a minor. The provision of choice in this instance with regard to cases involving children might be explained through reference to the specific merits of applying the *lex fori* in situations involving children (e.g. the enhancement of simplicity by avoiding the complexities involved in the application of foreign law by administrative authorities),[756] along with the low risk of abuse in view of its highly specific remit. Furthermore, given that the *lex fori* will usually be secured in the objective rules that usually apply to situations involving minors,[757] it is submitted here that the opportunity contained in Article 7 would only really have added value in exceptional circumstances, such as where jurisdiction has been accepted by submission according to Article 5 of the Maintenance Regulation.[758]

7.6. SYNTHESIS

In closing this chapter, the following synthesis presents an overview of the findings concerning the coordinating provisions set out in this chapter (7.6.1.), before establishing the additional value brought by these provisions to the framework that has already been established in Chapter 6 (7.6.2.) and highlighting the gaps that have emerged during the preceding examination (7.6.3).[759]

7.6.1. OVERVIEW OF FINDINGS

756 Bonomi (Chapter 4, n.400), at para.69 and 114 and Bonomi (n.730 above), at p.352.

757 See, for example, Article 3(b) of the Maintenance Regulation in conjunction with Article 3(1) of the Hague Maintenance Protocol; Article 3(a) of the Maintenance Regulation in conjunction with Article 4(3) of the Hague Maintenance Protocol. See also Walker (Chapter 4, n.401), at p.73.

758 Bonomi (Chapter 4, n.400), at para.114. See also discussion of this provision in 8.3.2.

759 The format of the synthesis differs here for two reasons: firstly, due to the focus of this chapter, there is no need to have a separate section on coordination, and secondly, it is useful to point out how the coordinating provisions add value to the framework which has been established in Chapter 6.

Table 2. Coordinating Provisions

		Matrimonial matters		Matrimonial property		Partnership property		Maintenance		Parental responsibility		Succession		Place of dissolution	
		Court	Law	Court	Law	Court	Law	Court	Law	Court	Law	Court	Law	Court	Law
Matrimonial matters	Court														
	Law	x													
Matrimonial property	Court	x			x										
	Law														
Partnership property	Court						x							x	
	Law														
Maintenance	Court	x													
	Law		x		x		x	x							
Parental responsibility	Court	x													
	Law														
Succession	Court												x		
	Law														

On the basis of the evaluation of the coordinating provisions established in this chapter, as well as in overview of the provisions outlined in Table 2, a number of principal findings can be proposed:

1. An opening remark that can be made at the start of this overview is that whereas choice of court provisions have been shown to be markedly less prominent as a direct connection (see Chapter 6), the rules examined here demonstrate a much greater scope for party autonomy with regard to jurisdictional matters.
2. The benefits of 'vertical cohesion' between the court and applicable law, and 'horizontal cohesion' between applicable laws that govern related areas have already been outlined in the previous chapter.[760] Turning now to 'horizontal cohesion' in the jurisdictional context, it is proposed that the ability to select the same Member State court to govern proceedings serves to remove obstacles that hinder access to justice, such as removing the need to travel between different jurisdictions to attend the respective proceedings[761] and the need to hire separate legal representation in these divergent jurisdictions.[762]

   Despite no choice of court being permitted under Brussels II bis, this instrument sits as the focal point around which related proceedings concerning matrimonial property, maintenance and parental responsibility can be organised. Whilst the Matrimonial Property Regulation[763] and the Maintenance Regulation[764] allow for extension to all jurisdictional grounds within Brussels II bis, prorogation under Article 12(1) of the Brussels II bis Regulation only involves the grounds for allocation of jurisdiction under Article 3 of this instrument. This accordingly has (an admittedly limited) impact on the ability to link the three of these jurisdictional choices together.

   Another point of comparison to note is that agreement of the parties is only required under Article 5(2) of the Matrimonial Property Regulation where the court is seised by virtue of the fifth and sixth indents of Article 3(1)(a), and Article 5 and 7 of Brussels II bis. Thus, it can be stated that the breadth of choice is comparatively constrained compared to the mechanisms established in Article 4(1)(c)(i) of the Maintenance Regulation and Article 12(1) of the Brussels II bis Regulation.

760 See 6.5.2.
761 See 3.5.2.1.
762 See 3.5.2.2.
763 See Article 5 of the Matrimonial Property Regulation.
764 See Article 4(1)(c)(i) of the Maintenance Regulation.

Above and beyond this, given the lack of a parallel opportunity to make a choice of court in matrimonial matters under Brussels II bis, the level of predictability and legal certainty through this extension under the Matrimonial Property Regulation and the Maintenance Regulation is accordingly low (and vulnerable to the so-called 'rush to court' when made in advance).

3. Jurisdictional linkage based around the dissolution of a registered partnership is even more limited than the situation discussed above. Although Article 5 of the Partnership Property Regulation permits the parties to agree to extend the jurisdiction that dissolves the registered partnership to also govern the dissolution of the property regime that accompanies this, there is a complete lack of unified private international law rules concerning the dissolution of this form of relationship, meaning that it might be even harder to predict as the connecting factor that will determine the ultimate jurisdiction in this regard. As a result, coordination of the connecting factors that are available under the Maintenance Regulation could be very difficult. In view of the aforementioned legislative gap, there is also clearly no opportunity for linkage with the jurisdiction for parental responsibility in the same manner as Article 12(1) of Brussels II bis.
4. In contrast to the extensive framework established for *jurisdictional* linkage discussed above, only the Hague Maintenance Protocol presents an opportunity to coordinate the *laws* that apply to related matters, providing in Article 8(1)(c) and (d) that the law that applies to maintenance obligations can be linked with that which has been designated as applicable, or in fact applied to a couple's property regime, or divorce or legal separation. However, a major mitigating factor here is the high level of coordination between the direct connections that determine the applicable law in the four instruments around which adult relationships can be organised (see Chapter 6). The affinity-based nature of a choice of law, compared with the practical considerations predominant in a choice of court context, means that the former realm is more suited to direct connections rather than direct linking provisions.

One further point to stress with regard to coordination of laws through Article 8(1)(c) and (d) of the Hague Maintenance Protocol, is that although coordination through these provisions may well coincide with the unified rules set out in the Property Regulations or Rome III, in the presence of enhanced cooperation in these fields, there is a real possibility that national rules on these areas will nevertheless apply.[765] Although this means that

765 See discussion of enhanced cooperation with regard to the enforcement of choice in 10.7.

there is potentially a wide variety of potential laws available to be chosen, one mitigating factor in the face of legal uncertainty is the opinion expressed in the Explanatory Report accompanying the Protocol, that an indeterminate choice is not permitted under these provisions.

5. This chapter has presented a continuance of the strong preference that is demonstrated in all the relevant instruments towards securing the practical outcomes associated with unifying the law and forum.[766] However, such unification holds varying outcomes in terms of legal certainty. For instance, under the Succession Regulation and the Hague Maintenance Protocol linkage is made in the present moment (and, under the former, there is only one choice to be made); thus levels of certainty as to the competent court or applicable law are very high. In contrast, since the provision allowing for the selection of the *lex fori* under Rome III can be interpreted as allowing a choice to be made in view of future proceedings and involves interaction with the alternative jurisdictional rules contained in Brussels II bis, predictability as to the ultimate jurisdiction is fairly low (see discussion of this gap in the framework in 7.6.3. below).

There is a varying picture with regard to the determination of jurisdiction on the basis of the applicable law under Article 7 of the Property Regulations. Linkage can be made with a law that has been chosen under Article 22, which clearly secures a high level of legal certainty. However, on the other hand, there is also the possibility that the parties will opt to coordinate with a law that is to be determined according to the objective rules in Article 26. In this regard, the successive grounds set out in the Matrimonial Property Regulation clearly present a lower level of predictability[767] than coordination with the sole determinant of applicable law (the place of where the partnership was registered) found in Article 26(1) of the Partnership Property Regulation.

Article 7 of the Property Regulations does not generally govern proceedings that occur in conjunction with the dissolution of the relationship or a succession. The problems with vertical coordination in the context of decisions concerning property relations in conjunction with a succession have been discussed in the previous chapter.[768] With regard to vertical cohesion between the court and applicable law in proceedings concerning a property regime

766 See discussion of 'vertical cohesion' in the previous chapter at 6.5.2.

767 Although, it has to be said that the first objective connection of the 'first common habitual residence after the conclusion of the marriage' lends itself to the majority of married couples.

768 See 6.5.2.

that occurs upon the dissolution of a marriage or registered partnership, it would not usually be possible to unify the law and court with a high degree of certainty before linkage is made or agreed upon according to Article 5 of the Property Regulations. Whilst Article 7 can act as an alternative manner of determining jurisdiction where agreement cannot be reached to link jurisdiction to the Member State court of dissolution according to Article 5, it would appear that this does not offer any clear benefit in terms of vertical cohesion, since it does not seem that this provision can be used in advance in this context.[769]

6. Turning now to examine the more distinct forms of party autonomy established in this chapter, the collaborative agreement required for a choice of court to take place under the Succession Regulation is firstly highlighted, whereby the 'parties concerned' in the succession (e.g. heirs, legatees and creditors) can agree to link jurisdiction with the deceased's choice for the law of their nationality. This unique interplay between the deceased and parties concerned in his or her succession reflects a desire to allow the former the opportunity to choose a law that gives effect to the substance of his or her estate planning, whilst allowing the latter the freedom to adjudge which court (either the habitual residence or nationality of the deceased) would be the most convenient for them as participants in proceedings.
7. Furthermore, Article 12(1) of Brussels II bis Regulation exemplifies another particular form of autonomy in this setting. Passive in nature, this provision requires that parties accept rather than agree, and the entire process is subject to the additional 'check and balance' that the act of prorogation is in the best interests of the child.[770] In this latter regard, it can be stated that the inherent subjectivity of the best interests assessment means that there is a low level of predictability in provisions for which it is a requirement (see also Article 12(3) – at 8.2.1. and Article 15 of Brussels II bis – at 8.2.2.)

7.6.2. VALUE ADDED TO THE FRAMEWORK

[769] This convoluted construction will be discussed further under 'gaps to be addressed' (7.6.3.).

[770] Although it has been argued that this is rather a formality in most instances under Article 12 Brussels II bis.

Table 3. Coordinating Provisions: Value Added

		Habitual residence	Nationality (Domicile)	Place of creation	Court of matrimonial matters	Court of dissolution	Court of maintenance	Law of matrimonial matters	Law of property relations
Matrimonial matters	Court								
	Law	x*	x		o				
Matrimonial property	Court	o	o	x	o				o
	Law	x	x						
Partnership property	Court	o	o	x		o			o
	Law	x	x	x					
Maintenance	Court	x†	x		o				
	Law	x	x				o	o	o
Parental responsibility	Court				o				
	Law								
Succession	Court		o						
	Law		x						

x = Already established; o = Additional choice.
* Common habitual residence or last common habitual residence in so far as one of the parties still resided there at the time the agreement was concluded.
† In the case of maintenance between ex-spouses, the additional option of the last common habitual residence for a period of at least a year is provided.

In observing the content of the current chapter in conjunction with that of Chapter 6, a number of conclusions can be proposed regarding the value added by the coordinating provisions discussed in this setting. Illustration of these findings is outlined in Table 3 above. It should be noted that whilst the table specifically identifies the additional grounds that can be secured through coordination with other party autonomy provisions, linkage with objectively determined connections is simply indicated by reference to a general category.[771]

1. Starting with jurisdiction, it can be seen that as the result of coordination undertaken through Articles 5, 6(b) and 7(b) and (c) of the Succession Regulation, the court of the deceased's nationality can now be designated as a result of proroguing the court of the *professio juris*.
2. Under the Property Regulations, the Member State court of the applicable law can be selected under Article 7, which additionally allows the jurisdiction of the court of the habitual residence or nationality of either party at the time of designation (in line with Article 22) to be seised. Furthermore, in the event of the application of objective rules under Article 26(1), spouses under the Matrimonial Property Regulation can link jurisdiction to a number of grounds relating to their circumstances at the time of marriage (their first common habitual residence, their common nationality at the time of marriage, or closest connection at the time of marriage).[772]
3. Although the lack of a choice of court in matrimonial matters under Brussels II bis means that jurisdictional coordination with this instrument[773] cannot be performed with a high degree of predictability or forward planning, it nevertheless offers additional grounds on which jurisdiction can be selected. Under the Matrimonial Property Regulation, such additional grounds are the Member State court of the habitual residence or nationality of the applicant,[774] the Member State court that converts the legal separation

[771] For instance, with regard to the Matrimonial Property Regulation, the table demonstrates the additional grounds by which jurisdiction can be secured by Article 7(1) in conjunction with a choice of law under Article 22(1) (i.e. the habitual residence or nationality of either party), but it does not list all the grounds through which jurisdiction might be determined under Article 26(1). This approach has been taken in order to provide the reader with a clear overview of the strategic, concrete choices that can be made by parties in organising their legal relations.

[772] For registered partners, in the absence of choice, the law of the place of creation applies, and the courts of this place are already available to be chosen under Article 7 of the Partnership Property Regulation.

[773] See jurisdictional coordination brought forth by the Article 5(2) of the Matrimonial Property Regulation, Article 4(1)(c)(i) of the Maintenance Regulation and Article 12(1) of Brussels II bis.

[774] According to the residence conditions laid out in Article 3(1)(a) fifth and sixth indents of the Matrimonial Property Regulation.

to a divorce and the court of residual jurisdiction under Article 7. Parties who coordinate with Brussels II bis under the Maintenance regulation can benefit from the availability of the latter two grounds.

In the context of parental responsibility, prorogation under Article 12(1) of the Brussels II bis Regulation brings the potential for added value in terms of any ground listed in Article 3 of the same instrument that does not coincide with the habitual residence of the child.

4. In terms of applicable law, Articles 8(1)(c) and (d) of the Hague Maintenance Protocol permit the law that applies to (ex-)spouses' property regimes or matrimonial matters to be designated. This brings the potential application of one of the laws that apply in the absence of choice under Article 26(1) of the Matrimonial Property Regulation or the law of the forum under Article 5(1)(d) of Rome III. However, in this latter regard, it should be pointed out that connection can only be made with Brussels II bis, in which the objective grounds contained in Article 3 provide no additional value to the framework. Only Article 5 (the Member State court that pronounced a legal separation) and Article 7 (residual jurisdiction) are supplementary in the limited instances in which they may apply.
5. The final point here poses a question: *What value is to be attached to the unknown?* The fragmentation of this present framework (enhanced cooperation in the law that applies to matrimonial matters and property relations, as well as a lack of legislative action on the dissolution of registered partnerships) means that some linking provisions[775] discussed here ultimately coordinate with national rules. Whilst such provisions do indeed establish additional grounds, forward planning under these rules is either not possible,[776] or leads down a road of legal uncertainty.[777]

7.6.3. GAPS TO BE ADDRESSED

The preceding analysis of the form and function of coordinating provisions contained in the EU's private international law rules relating to family matters and succession has revealed a number of legislative gaps in the framework that require addressing:

1. Firstly, one major problem area that needs to be addressed relates to the impact of legislative gaps upon the predictability of linking choices.

---

775 See Article 5(2) of the Partnership Property Regulation, as well as the opportunity to select the law applicable to matrimonial property relations or matrimonial matters under Articles 8(1)(c) and (d) of the Hague Maintenance Protocol.

776 Since it is not possible to select an undetermined law under Articles 8(1)(c) and (d) of the Hague Maintenance Protocol.

777 See discussion of enhanced cooperation in the context of the enforcement of choice – 10.8.

The first of these concerns matrimonial matters (divorce, legal separation and marriage annulment), whereby there is no provision for choice of court under the current version of Brussels II bis. This means that parties who choose to make use of the multitude of provisions[778] that link to the jurisdiction determined by Brussels II bis cannot be sure of the content of the choice that they have made until a court is seised under this instrument, consequently making forward planning difficult in the contexts of these coordinating provisions. Unfortunately, as mentioned previously, the drafters of the recent Brussels IIa (Recast) Regulation opted to omit a possibility for a choice of court in matrimonial matters in this renewed instrument, thus extinguishing (for the time being) a clear opportunity to enhance legal certainty in this setting.

2. Another gap along this same theme involves the complete lack of EU unification of the rules on the dissolution of registered partnership. The absence of any standardised rules, along with the patchwork approach to registered partnership throughout the Union, mean that linkage of jurisdiction under Article 5 of the Partnership Property Regulation lends very low levels of predictability to those who make use of this provision for the purposes of forward planning. Again, there is no known legislative initiative to change this situation on an EU level.
3. Finally, as has been discussed in this chapter and the one preceding this,[779] it would appear that Article 7 of the Property Regulations (along with Article 6) may be used where parties cannot reach an agreement to link jurisdiction to the court of dissolution under Article 5 of these same instruments. However, the stated aims and construction of the regulations make this purpose far from clear, and parties who ultimately make use of Article 7 in this context do not reap the high level of legal certainty that an advanced choice of court offers. Allowing spouses or partners to make use of the more extensive and flexible choice of court rules on an equal basis to parties in proceedings outside of the dissolution of a relationship would enhance the expression of free will (within the confines of close connection) and tackle the legal uncertainty that arises for situations under Article 5, particularly in view of the legislative gaps that currently exist.[780]

---

[778] See, in the choice of court context: Article 4(1)(c)(i) of the Maintenance Regulation, Article 5(2) of the Property Regulations and Article 12(1) of the Brussels II bis Regulation, and in the choice of law context: Article 5(1)(d) of Rome III.

[779] See also 6.4.2. and 6.5.1.

[780] See discussion in points 1 and 2 of this subsection.

CHAPTER 8
SUBSIDIARY FORMS OF PARTY AUTONOMY

8.1. INTRODUCTION

This book has now reached third and final chapter concerning the content of choice within the EU private international law framework relating to family matters and succession. As discussed in the Introduction,[781] this evaluation of party autonomy extends to the outer reaches of party autonomy as conceived within the current setting, whereby the free will of the parties serves a residual and specific role.

Two groupings of subsidiary party autonomy provisions will be examined and evaluated in this chapter, both of which concern the determination of jurisdiction: party autonomy and judicial discretion in the transfer and/or assumption of jurisdiction (8.2.) and the acceptance of jurisdiction by a party through entering an appearance in a court which has been seised of jurisdiction by another party (8.3.) The concluding synthesis (8.4.) will also emulate what has come before, providing an overview of the findings, before highlighting the added value of these provisions and the gaps that have been identified to be further addressed.

8.2. PARTY AUTONOMY AND JUDICIAL DISCRETION

The first of the two types of provisions to be discussed in this chapter concerns party participation in jurisdictional mechanisms, based on an interplay between party autonomy and judicial discretion. These provisions have been established for the purposes of proceedings involving parental responsibility in Brussels II bis, under Article 12(3) (8.2.1.) and Article 15 (8.2.2.), as well as Articles 6(a) and 7(a) of the Succession Regulation (8.2.3.). Whilst the first provision involves a prorogation by the parties in conjunction with a high degree

---

781 See 1.2.

of judicial involvement, the two latter mechanisms are primarily governed by judicial discretion, with the will of the parties serving a very subsidiary role in this setting (*forum non conveniens* provisions).

8.2.1. ARTICLE 12(3) OF BRUSSELS II BIS

Alongside the linkage of jurisdiction in matters of parental responsibility arising in conjunction with a divorce or legal separation under Article 12(1), Article 12(3) of the Brussels II bis Regulation provides a separate, distinct opportunity for prorogation of a court in the context of autonomous parental responsibility proceedings. The mechanism set out here allows the courts of any Member State with which the child has a 'substantial connection' to assume jurisdiction in isolated cases of parental responsibility, subject to the acceptance of all parties to the proceedings at hand.

Article 12(3) is a novel inclusion within the EU private international law framework, with no earlier provisions upon which it appears to base its form.[782] Clear similarities can nevertheless be drawn between the two separate provisions contained in Article 12 of Brussels II bis.[783] Firstly, the essential tone of party autonomy in both provisions is the same, with the use of the passive term 'acceptance' in place of agreement. Furthermore, both provisions require a balance between the acceptance of the parties concerned in the case of parental responsibility and judicial consideration of whether prorogation of a Member State court other than that in which the child is habitually resident would be in their best interests.

Article 12(3) encompasses a number of key characteristics that distinguish it from the first paragraph of this article. Its focus is much wider,[784] freestanding from other related proceedings,[785] and accordingly the range of parties whose acceptance it elicits is much broader than under Article 12(1), requiring the acceptance of 'all the parties to the proceedings'.[786] Furthermore, an additional aspect of judicial scrutiny is introduced in Article 12(3) by the requirement that the child has a 'substantial connection' with the Member State in question.

---

782 In contrast to Article 12(1), which draws its roots from Article 3(2) of the Brussels II Regulation and Article 10 of the Hague Convention on Child Protection.

783 See discussion of Article 12(1) in 7.2.3.

784 Whilst Article 12(1) is clearly limited to linkage with proceedings involving the dissolution of a marriage, Article 12(3) embraces all proceedings concerning parental responsibility that come within the scope of Brussels II bis.

785 Case C-656/13 *L. v. M.* Request for a preliminary ruling from the Nejvyšší soud – Czech Republic [2014] ECLI:EU:C:2014:2364, at paras.36–52.

786 See 4.6.2.3.

The presence of a substantial connection is to be ascertained on a case-by-case basis in conjunction with the requisite 'best interests' assessment.[787] In this sense, the best interests assessment is to be considered as more complex in comparison to Article 12(1). It particularly focuses on the proximity of the child to the jurisdiction in question,[788] which is usually taken to mean the present habitual residence of the child,[789] but can also refer to their nationality,[790] a past habitual residence,[791] and/or other circumstances that make the jurisdiction a proximate one (e.g. historical contact with the national authorities[792] or a connection to the particular subject matter at hand[793]). In light of the connection to succession matters in the recent case of *Sapanaro*,[794] wider considerations, including the location of the deceased's assets and their place of residence at the time of death, were also considered to be relevant in establishing connection.[795]

The accompanying Opinion of the Advocate General in the above-mentioned case provided particular insight on the best interests requirement in this setting. The AG stated that the consideration of the best interests of the child generally ought not to be treated as a separate decision, but as part and parcel, along with other elements, of the process of prorogation. In the presence of a jurisdiction that is proximate to the child and which has been accepted by the parties involved, the interests of the child will be generally regarded as protected.[796]

Furthermore, the AG stated that this criterion only really comes into play where the facts of the case are atypical, upon which the judge can use this provision to sidestep the usual process of prorogation.[797] Considering this view in conjunction with other national case law, refusal of jurisdiction on this ground might arise where the child has lost all present proximity to the requested state, a rationale which was exemplified in one Spanish judgment in which none of the involved parties held Spanish nationality or was currently resident in Spain,[798] and in a Dutch judgment in which a Dutch child held no actual links

---

787 See, for instance, the manner in which these two elements were intertwined in the CJEU's recent judgment in the context of Article 12(3) in *Saponaro* (Chapter 4, n.463), in particular at paras.36 and 39.

788 See Recital 12 of Brussels II bis.

789 Ibid.

790 *Saponaro* (Chapter 4, n.463), at para.36 and Opinion of AG Tanchev in *Saponaro* (Chapter 7, n.715), at paras.26 and 67.

791 See the facts of the case in *I. (A child)* [2009] UKSC 10.

792 E.g. Rb. Zutphen, 07-12-2005, nr. 74327 FA RK 05 2206.

793 For instance, a request for a passport: Rb. Den Haag, 11-07-2013, nr. C/09/443928 FA RK 13-4125.

794 *Saponaro* (Chapter 4, n.463).

795 Ibid., at para.36.

796 AG Tanchev in *Saponaro* (Chapter 7, n.715), at para.67.

797 Ibid., at para.70.

798 Audiencia Provincial de La Rioja (Sección 1ª) Auto num. 25/2012 de 9 marzo JUR/2012/163092.

with the state apart from her nationality (i.e. she had left the country at the age of four, and had not lived there for six years).[799]

One point which remains to be clarified with regard to the application of Article 12(3) is whether a court can assume jurisdiction of its own motion or has to wait to be seised by one or more of the parties. If the former situation is possible, it is arguable that this would rob the more restrictive Article 15 of the additional protections that it offers.[800] Given the coexistence of these two provisions, logic would dictate that this question is to be answered in the negative. Above and beyond this, in view of the more assertive tone and emphasis on the existence of an agreement between the parties in Article 10 of the new Brussels IIa (Recast) Regulation,[801] it would appear that the potential for overlap in this regard has been extinguished.

In overview of the two provisions enumerated in Article 12 of Brussels II bis, regard should also be had for the additional rule established in Article 12(4), which provides that if a child is habitually resident in a third state that is not a contracting party of the 1996 Hague Convention on Child Protection, a presumption arises that holding proceedings in the requested EU Member State jurisdiction will be deemed to be in the 'interest' (or, to use the standardised term, 'best interests') of the child, 'in particular if it is found impossible to hold proceedings in the third State in question'.

The interpretation of this provision remains rather obscure[802] (particularly where holding proceedings in such a state would not be strictly 'impossible'[803]), but it essentially reflects the stance that judicial cooperation with non-Hague Convention countries creates a (rebuttable) presumption that holding proceedings in the requested EU Member State would be in the child's best interests.[804] Although it is not impossible that Article 12(4) comes into play in

799 Rb. Alkmaar, 16-04-2008, nr. 101069/FA RK 08-239.

800 Pataut (Chapter 4, n.467), at p.156, paras.49–50. See discussion of this provision in the subsection immediately below.

801 The replacement provision for Article 12 of Brussels II bis. See previous discussion in 7.2.3.

802 For instance, in the UK High Court case *AP v. TD* [2010] EWHC 2040, although the judgment acknowledged the presence of a non-contracting state, it did not dwell on the impact of this upon the best interests consideration.

803 For example, in contrast to obvious instances such as where there is no stable legal system or there is a war going on in the country (see F. Ibili, '3.4.1 "onmogelijk" bij: Verordening (EG) Nr. 2201/2003 betreffende de bevoegdheid en de erkenning en tenuitvoerlegging van beslissingen in huwelijkszaken en inzake de ouderlijke verantwoordelijkheid, en tot intrekking van Verordening (EG) nr. 1347/2000, Artikel 12', *Groene Serie Personen- en familierecht* (Wolters-Kluwer, 2017)) would it also extend to cover instances where the third country legal system would carry out a drastically different type of procedure to that in the requested Member State (e.g. apply religious law), or does not allow equal access to justice for the parties?

804 See the opinion of Lady Hale in the UK Supreme Court judgment: *I. (A child)* (n.791 above), at para.37. See also discussion of this provision in T.M.C. Asser Institute et al. (Chapter 7, n.721), at pp.90–91, para.7.

situations involving linkage of jurisdiction under Article 12(1), the flexibility of Article 12(3) is more open to the circumstances in which Article 12(4) might come into use. It is important to note that Article 12(4) has not been maintained in the recast of Brussels II bis,[805] which can be seen as a positive step towards simplification in this new mechanism.[806]

8.2.2. ARTICLE 15 OF BRUSSELS II BIS

Having discussed the form and function of Article 12(3) of Brussels II bis, another novel introduction into the EU private international law framework by this same instrument can be presented: Article 15.[807] Although this provision is entitled 'Transfer to a court better placed to hear the case', it has been framed as a *forum non conveniens* mechanism which provides a framework of rules through which jurisdiction can be transferred from one Member State to another in certain circumstances.[808]

Article 15 provides a detailed framework through which the court that is competent for matters of parental responsibility according to the general jurisdictional rules of the regulation may, in exceptional circumstances, transfer jurisdiction to the court of another Member State with which the child has a 'particular connection',[809] namely a Member State that (a) has become the habitual residence of the child after the court has been seised; (b) was formerly the habitual residence of the child; (c) is the place of nationality of the child; (d) is the habitual residence of a holder of parental responsibility; or (e) is the place in which property of the child is located.[810] This list is exhaustive in nature,[811] which is a point of contrast with the open-ended character of Article 12(3) of Brussels II bis.

Article 15 comes within the scope of this present analysis by reason of the rule that at least one party must participate by either instigating the process of transfer, or accepting the transfer that was started by either the competent Member State court, or the court with which the child has a purported

805 See the Brussels IIa (Recast) Regulation.

806 Since the judge can, in any case, take into account the fact that a child is located in a non-Hague Convention state in the best interests assessment.

807 Although a prior base for this mechanism can be seen in Articles 8 and 9 of the Hague Convention on Child Protection. See also Pataut (Chapter 4, n.467), at p.165, para.2.

808 Ibid., at p.165, para.1 et seq. and T.M.C. Asser Institute et al. (Chapter 7, n.721), at p.114, para.10.

809 Article 15(2) of Brussels II bis.

810 Where the case concerns measures for the protection of the child relating to the administration, conservation or disposal of this property, see Article 1(2)(e) of Brussels II bis.

811 Pataut (Chapter 4, n.467), at p.170, para.25.

'particular connection' (Article 15(2)). The requirement that only one party has to instigate or accept transfer distinguishes this provision as one that is chiefly guided by judicial discretion;[812] the action of this party serves to provide an additional check and balance in a larger process of cooperation between courts. Although refusal by the party concerned will effectively end the process of transfer, in comparison to Article 12(3), there is an absence of regard for the collective autonomy of all parties concerned.[813]

In line with the international human rights standard in measures involving children, there is a requisite best interests consideration in both the decision to transfer jurisdiction by the competent court,[814] and the acceptance of jurisdiction by the court with which the child has a particular connection.[815] In this regard, the detailed Opinion issued by the Advocate General in *Saponaro* can once again be drawn upon, in which it was stated that in contrast to Article 12(3), whereby the best interests requirement is intertwined with other considerations within the process of prorogation, the exceptional nature of transferring jurisdiction under Article 15[816] calls for a distinct, comparative examination of the respective merits of hearing the case in the respective Member State jurisdictions by both of the courts involved.[817]

The AG in *Saponaro* drew upon the comparative manner in which the best interests of the child had been addressed by the CJEU in an earlier judgment concerning Article 15 (*CAFA v. J.D.*).[818] Further elaboration was provided by Advocate General Wathelet in his Opinion on this latter case,[819] where he stated that there is a strong presumption in favour of the state of habitual residence maintaining its own jurisdiction;[820] regard must be had for the importance of the child's habitual residence as the environment in which the child develops and the impact of transferring jurisdiction upon the child's wellbeing.[821] In order for this strong presumption to be rebutted, factors such as the language of the proceedings, the availability of evidence (e.g. concerning the ability of the parents to provide education or maintenance) and the availability

---

812 In contrast to the mechanisms contained in Article 12 of Brussels II bis, which are based on party autonomy with the moderation of judicial discretion.

813 Pataut (Chapter 4, n.467), at p.167, para.9.

814 Article 15(1).

815 Article 15(5).

816 Article 15(1) begins with: 'By way of exception …'.

817 AG Tanchev in *Saponaro* (Chapter 7, n.715), at para.68.

818 *CAFA v. J.D.* (Chapter 4, n.450).

819 Opinion of AG Wathelet on Case C-428/15 *Child and Family Agency (CAFA) v. J.D.* Request for a preliminary ruling from the Supreme Court (Ireland) [2016] ECLI:EU:C:2016:458.

820 Ibid., at para.90. Recalled by the court in *CAFA* (Chapter 4, n.450), at para.49.

821 AG Wathelet on *CAFA* (n.819 above), at para.96.

of medical or social reports have to be considered in order to evaluate the ability of the court to make a judgment on the child's interests.[822]

It is interesting to consider the existence of Article 15 in light of the CJEU ruling in the context of the Brussels I Regulation in which the Court refused to allow national courts to use *forum non conveniens* on the basis that this would put legal certainty at risk.[823] However, it should be noted that the critique issued by the CJEU would not be as potent in this present setting,[824] since as will be discussed, legal certainty is not a primary concern in the parental responsibility context.[825] In contrast to the undefined circumstances of the *Owusu* case, the *forum non conveniens* mechanism in this context is prescriptively manifested in the conditions set out in Article 15, meaning that there is a relatively higher degree of predictability for situations that fall within this present context.[826]

On a closing note, as discussed previously,[827] the recent Brussels IIa (Recast) Regulation has brought forth significant structural changes to the provisions that concern parental responsibility. This is particularly evident with regard to the present *forum non conveniens* mechanism, whereby under the renewed provision acceptance by at least one party to the proceedings would no longer be required in instances where the court has instigated this mechanism of its own motion or another Member State court has requested that a case be transferred to its jurisdiction.[828] There are still prescribed circumstances in which parties to the proceedings may play a role within this mechanism; namely, the possibility for a party themselves to instigate the *forum non conveniens* mechanism or for one or more parties to be invited by the Member State court with jurisdiction to introduce an application before another Member State court.[829] However, it is clear that there has been a fundamental shift in the nature of this mechanism, and party assent no longer serves as a principal 'check and balance' alongside consideration of the best interests of the child.

---

822 Ibid., at para.95.

823 Case C-281/02 *Andrew Owusu v. N.B. Jackson, trading as 'Villa Holidays Bal-Inn Villas' and Others*. Reference for a preliminary ruling: Court of Appeal (England and Wales), Civil Division - United Kingdom [2005] ECR I-1445.

824 Ibid., at paras.38–41.

825 As evidenced by the immediate construction of party autonomy provisions, see discussion here and with regard to Article 12(1) (7.2.3.).

826 Particularly relating to the exhaustive grounds of 'particular connection'. See discussion of this contrasting point in the context of *Owusu* in: Pataut (Chapter 4, n.467), at pp.164–166, paras.1–5.

827 See 8.2.1.

828 See Articles 12 and 13 of Brussels IIa (Recast) Regulation.

829 See Article 12(1) and (1)(a) of this new instrument.

8.2.3. ARTICLES 6(a) AND 7(a) OF THE SUCCESSION REGULATION

Moving away from the realm of parental responsibility, another *forum non conveniens* mechanism can be identified amongst the jurisdictional rules established in the Succession Regulation.[830] The relevant mechanism is divided between Articles 6(a) and 7(a), with the former providing that upon the request of one of the parties to the proceedings, the Member State court which has competence according to Article 4 or 10 will decline jurisdiction

> if it considers that the courts of the Member State of the chosen law are better placed to rule on the succession, taking into account the practical circumstances of the succession, such as the habitual residence of the parties and the location of the assets.

The corresponding provision contained in Article 7(a) simply serves to confirm that the Member State court of the chosen law will have jurisdiction upon the previously seised Member State declining jurisdiction.

In contrast to the more open outlook of the provisions concerning parental responsibility that were discussed in the previous subsections, the present mechanism is solely focused on connection with the court of the *professio juris*. In declining jurisdiction under Article 6(a), it should be noted that abstract perceptions concerning the benefits of unifying the law and court that govern succession proceedings ought not to be the sole determinants that guide the court.[831] Delving deeper into the potential influences upon this decision, in addition to the residence of the concerned parties and the location of the assets, the existence of special procedures for the settlement of the succession in the Member State of nationality may be a factor that carries weight in this consideration.[832] In addition, where rights *in rem* are at stake in a succession, unity between the law and forum can be seen to be particularly important.[833] On the other hand, it has also been suggested that if a deceased made a *professio juris* without having a genuine link with the state of their nationality (e.g. with the intent to deprive the heirs of a certain benefit to be

---

830 See Articles 5, 6, 7 and 9 of the Succession Regulation.

831 See Odersky (Chapter 4, n.501), at p.78, para.8.

832 F. Marongiu Buonaiuti, 'Article 6: Declining of Jurisdiction in the Event of a Choice of Law' in A. Calvo Caravaca et al. (eds.), *The EU Succession Regulation: A Commentary* (Cambridge University Press, Cambridge, 2016), pp.168–169, para.10.

833 Ibid., at p.170, para.13.

reaped under the law of habitual residence), it might be considered inappropriate to place proceedings in the courts of the Member State of the deceased's nationality.[834]

The process set out across Articles 6(a) and 7(a) represents a balance whereby the discretion of the courts to consider the convenience of unifying the law and forum in the particular circumstances is triggered by an exercise of autonomy by one of the parties concerned. A key difference between the *forum non conveniens* mechanism contained in Articles 6(a) and 7(a) and that established in Article 15 of Brussels II bis is that the court cannot instigate proceedings of its own motion. Furthermore, there is no necessity for the receiving court to consider its suitability to govern the proceedings in question as in the case with Article 15.[835] The mechanism established in Article 6(a) and 7(a) is thus guided by judicial discretion, but not judicial cooperation.

Although unified in their primary aim of identifying and securing a more appropriate forum to hear a case, the three mechanisms discussed in this section are clearly distinct from one another in terms of their form and function, and the level of party autonomy that is permitted. Article 12(3) of Brussels II bis affords the greatest regard for the autonomy of all parties concerned (albeit still of the passive variety), whilst as discussed above, Article 15 of Brussels II bis and Articles 6(a) and 7(a) of the Succession Regulation only require the participation of one of the parties. Article 12(3) also offers the most flexibility with regard to the potential Member State court that might be seised, whilst Article 15 is restrained by the closed list of 'particular' connections to the child that guide the transfer of jurisdiction, and the mechanism set out in Articles 6(a) and 7(a) is solely focused on the narrow achievement of the union between law and forum.

8.3. ENTERING AN APPEARANCE BEFORE A COURT

The final type of provision that will be discussed in this book lies at the outer reaches of what this author would define as party autonomy within the European private international law framework: entering an appearance before a court that has been seised of jurisdiction by another party to the proceedings. A party's submission to the court can be seen as an act of free will that confirms a jurisdictional choice.

834 Ibid., at pp.169–170, paras.11–12.
835 Ibid., at p.167, para.7.

The opportunity to accept jurisdiction by entering an appearance has been established on a general basis in CJEU case law;[836] however, it has been left to individual EU instruments to further delineate this process. Within the context of the EU private international law relating to family matters and succession, the opportunity to demonstrate 'tacit' acceptance[837] of a particular jurisdiction arises under all the EU instruments that allow for a choice of court in adult relationships (the Property Regulations and the Maintenance Regulation), as well as the Succession Regulation.

8.3.1. ARTICLE 8 OF THE PROPERTY REGULATIONS

Article 8 of both Property Regulations establishes that where a Member State court whose law is applicable pursuant to Article 22 or point (a) or (b) of Article 26(1) has been seised of jurisdiction by one of the parties concerned in a matter relating to the property relationship (a spouse/partner or third party), the defendant can tacitly accept this jurisdiction by entering an appearance before this court, provided that the purpose of the appearance was not to contest this jurisdiction. This provision is seen to be focused upon the practical aim of unifying the law and the court that govern a particular case.

In addition to the standard exclusion of situations in which the defendant has only entered an appearance to contest jurisdiction, it is also qualified in Article 8(2) of both regulations that this opportunity does not apply to situations that are connected with a succession under Article 4. Furthermore, with regard to the Matrimonial Property Regulation, the defendant cannot accept another jurisdiction by entering an appearance in situations that come within the scope of Article 5(1) of the same regulation. This exclusion is designed to protect the automatic linkage which occurs according to this provision. However, in cases falling within the scope of Article 5(2), as well as in all instances encompassed by Article 5 of the Partnership Property Regulation, the defendant can accept the Member State court of the applicable law by entering an appearance. Arguably, this opportunity could be used intentionally

---

836 Case C-48/84 *Hannelore Spitzley v. Sommer Exploitation SA*. Reference for a preliminary ruling: Oberlandesgericht Koblenz – Germany [1985] ECR 787, at para.13 and Case C-111-09 *Česká podnikatelská pojišťovna a.s., Vienna Insurance Group v. Michal Bilas*. Reference for a preliminary ruling: Okresní soud v Chebu – Czech Republic [2010] ECR I-4545, at paras.30–33.

837 Described as tacit choice by S. Verburgt, 'Bevoegdheid, Erkenning en Tenuitvoerlegging onder Alimentatieverordening 4/2009' (2012) 7 *Tijdschrift voor Relatierecht en Praktijk* 296, at p.299 and implicit choice by F. Ferrand, 'The Council Regulation (EC) No 4/2009 of 18 December 2008' in B. Campuzano Díaz et al. (eds.), *Latest Developments in EU Private International Law* (Intersentia, Antwerp, 2011), at p.93.

by the parties to usurp the limitations imposed by the coordinating rules contained in Article 5 of the regulations.

8.3.2. ARTICLE 5 OF THE MAINTENANCE REGULATION

Article 5 of the Maintenance Regulation offers a much broader scope with regard to acceptance by submission, establishing that the court of *any* Member State can become competent if it is subsequently accepted by the defendant through entering an appearance (notwithstanding the exception of entering an appearance to contest jurisdiction).

Subject to the tacit acceptance of the defendant, this effectively gives an applicant '*carte blanche*' in selecting a particular Member State jurisdiction. The breadth of this scope reflects the EU legislator's desire to allow the creditor ease of access to justice and prevent delays in proceedings.[838] By comparison, in the context of property relations, parties are generally on much more of an equal footing, and arguably this open provision would allow the parties to agree to bypass the general jurisdictional rules and cherry-pick amongst the Member State jurisdictions.

As briefly touched upon briefly in Chapter 4,[839] Article 5 does not appear to exclude usage in proceedings involving minors. Since the defendant does not necessarily have to be the debtor (e.g. the creditor will be the defendant in proceedings in which the debtor applies to vary a maintenance order), there might therefore conceivably arise a situation in which a minor creditor (or the party acting on their behalf) accepts jurisdiction through submission according to Article 5.

Given the inability for party autonomy to be exercised with regard to proceedings involving children under the choice of court rules in Article 4 of the Maintenance Regulation, it is firstly observed that the possibility contained in Article 5 appears out of step with the (arguably overly stringent) general approach of this instrument. This inconsistency is exacerbated by the fact that the extent of choice is in theory extremely broad compared with the limits of close connection imposed for jurisdictional choice under Article 4.

On the one hand, it can be proposed that Article 5 might nevertheless serve as a safety net in view of the general absence of an opportunity for parties to choose the forum for maintenance proceedings involving minors. This could be used, for instance, in order for the parties to avoid the harmful

---

838 Walker (Chapter 4, n.401), at p.66.

839 See 4.5.2.2.

practical impact of a split between the jurisdiction that is competent to decide on maintenance obligations between the (ex-)spouses or partners and that which has competence for maintenance proceedings concerning the couple's child(ren).

At the same time, however, by its nature this provision exists outside of regard for proximity or formal requirements, and furthermore there is no duty placed upon the court to warn the defendant of the consequences of entering an appearance (see further discussion of material requisites in 9.4.1.).[840] Thus, the opportunity for children or their representatives to accept jurisdiction in this manner is considerably more risky than partaking in the general choice of court provision under Article 4 of the Maintenance Regulation (under which obligations concerning children are excluded).[841]

8.3.3. ARTICLE 9 OF THE SUCCESSION REGULATION

The final provision to be discussed here is Article 9 of the Succession Regulation, which permits the parties to succession proceedings who were not participants in a prior choice of court agreement under Article 7 to subsequently accept jurisdiction of the court seised by entering an appearance (other than solely for the purpose of contesting the court's jurisdiction). It can thus be seen as yet another avenue contained in the Succession Regulation through which the union of the law and forum can be secured.

This is designed to address the specific situation in which an agreement was made between parties involved in the succession to prorogue the Member State court in line with the deceased's choice for the law of his or her national law, but where it later transpires that there is another party (or multiple parties) that hold an interest in the succession but who have not been included in the original exercise of autonomy. As has been discussed in Chapters 4 and 7,[842] this is not an unlikely problem in the context of a succession, whereby the identity of all the beneficiaries might not be apparent until the case is opened.[843]

Given the narrow purpose of this provision, along with the sole option to choose the jurisdiction of the deceased's *professio juris* under the Succession Regulation, the parameters of Article 9 are accordingly very limited in comparison to the provisions discussed in the previous two subsections.

---

840 In contrast to Article 8(2) of the Property Regulations.

841 See critique in Walker (Chapter 2, n.164), at pp.232–233.

842 See 4.7.2.2. and 7.4.2.

843 Marongiu Buonaiuti (n.832 above), at pp.156–157, para.10.

8.4. SYNTHESIS

In the same manner as the two chapters that have preceded this one, the present synthesis will provide an overview of findings of this evaluation concerning subsidiary forms of party autonomy (8.4.1.), before establishing the additional value brought to the overall framework by the mechanisms (8.4.2.), and then highlighting the suggestions for improvement that can be proposed on the basis of the foregoing analysis (8.4.3.).

8.4.1. OVERVIEW OF FINDINGS

The choice of court mechanisms set out in this chapter represent the outer limits of what is deemed to equate to party autonomy for the present purposes. The respective jurisdictions that can be secured through these subsidiary party autonomy provisions are mapped out in Table 4 below:

Table 4. Subsidiary Party Autonomy: Jurisdictional Connections

	Nationality	Law of property relations	Substantial connection	Particular connection	Court of appearance
Matrimonial property		x			
Partnership property		x			
Maintenance					x
Parental responsibility			x	x	
Succession	x				

1. First to be examined here were the three mechanisms that involve a combination of party autonomy and judicial discretion in the process of prorogation or transfer of jurisdiction. These provisions are grouped together by reason of the fact that each one permits a degree of judicial discretion in shifting the jurisdiction away from that which would otherwise be competent. The level of collective party autonomy varies between the respective instruments in this context: Article 12(3) of Brussels II bis requires that *all* holders of parental responsibility accept the prorogation, whilst Article 15 of Brussels II bis and Articles 6(a) and 7(a) of the Succession Regulation only necessitate that one party consent to the transfer of jurisdiction. The former provision is principally guided by the will of the parties, subject to the moderation of judicial discretion, whilst in the latter instances the process is inverted.

2. With regard to this first grouping of instruments, it can also be seen that the breadth and purpose of choice varies. Articles 6(a) and 7(a) of the Succession Regulation is solely focused on providing another route through which to secure a union between the court and applicable law, whilst Article 15 of Brussels II bis is designed to direct the proceedings concerning parental responsibility to a better placed court within the closed confines of 'particular connection' and upon the approval by both the seised and receiving courts. In contrast, Article 12(3) of Brussels II bis establishes a flexible, open approach to determining the jurisdiction with which the child has a 'substantial connection' in the view of the prorogued court.
3. The child's best interests are of primary importance under both Article 12(3) and 15, although this requisite is approached in a different manner in the respective provisions. Whilst the former provision considers this element in combination with the ascertainment of 'substantial connection', the search for the better-placed court requires a comparative analysis of the respective merits of hearing the matter of parental responsibility in the seised and receiving jurisdictions. It is helpful that the CJEU has considerably increased clarity with regard to the interpretation of these provisions in recent judgments.
4. In its second part, the chapter ventured into the outermost limits of party autonomy as conceived within the present framework: the opportunity for one party to accept a jurisdiction that has already been seised by entering an appearance. In a similar manner to the first section, the three types of provisions discussed here clearly also vary in terms the breadth of party autonomy permitted, with Article 5 of the Maintenance Regulation at the forefront in view of the open choice of jurisdictions that it permits, and Article 8 of the Property Regulations and Article 9 of the Succession Regulation narrowly aimed at the specific purpose of unifying the court with the applicable law.
5. Article 5 of the Maintenance Regulation is distinguished by the apparent opportunity it offers for minors (or their representatives) to participate under this mechanism. This sits in sharp contrast to the general exclusion of party autonomy for maintenance obligations involving minors under this instrument, an inconsistency which is particularly highlighted in view of the theoretically broad jurisdictional scope that this provision permits. This possibility might be seen as a means of remedying an impractical jurisdictional split between maintenance proceedings involving (ex-)spouses or partners and those concerning the couple's child(ren). However, this inclusion is arguably troubling in view of the fact that the mechanism is entirely lacking in material safeguards by which

the full and informed consent of parties might be ensured (see further discussion at 9.4.1.).

6. A fact that unites all the provisions discussed in this chapter is that, in theory, there is minimal opportunity for forward planning on the part of the parties. These mechanisms are directed towards other considerations, such as maximising practicality and convenience by unifying the court and applicable law, ensuring access to justice (particularly for parties under Article 5 of the Maintenance Regulation and 9 of the Succession Regulation) and establishing a suitable jurisdiction in view of the child's best interests under Articles 12(3) and 15 of the Brussels II bis Regulation. Notwithstanding the above assertion, the provisions that permit a jurisdiction to be accepted by submission are open to manipulation by the parties, particularly in the context of Article 8 of the Property Regulations in situations in which the choice of court would otherwise be restricted (i.e. upon the dissolution of a relationship).
7. The recent Brussels IIa (Recast) Regulation demonstrates a shift in the stance and scope attributed to party autonomy in matters of parental responsibility. Whilst a more assertive role is assigned to the parties under the new choice of court mechanism that replaces Article 12, the significance of party assent has been considerably reduced in the renewed *forum non conveniens* mechanism established in this instrument.[844] A further innovation to note is the express establishment of the possibility for the parties to accept jurisdiction by entering an appearance under the new choice of court provision, which can be seen to reflect recent case law on Article 12(3).[845]

8.4.2. VALUE ADDED TO THE FRAMEWORK

[844] See Articles 10, 12 and 13 of the Brussels IIa (Recast) Regulation.

[845] *Saponaro* (Chapter 4, n.463), at para.32.

Table 5. Overview of Connections Within the Framework

		Habitual residence	Nationality (Domicile)	Place of creation	Court of matrimonial matters	Court of dissolution	Court of maintenance	Substantial connection	Particular connection	Court of appearance	Law of matrimonial matters	Law of property relations
Matrimonial matters	Court											
	Law	x*	x		x							
Matrimonial property	Court	x	x	x	x							x
	Law	x	x									
Partnership property	Court	x	x	x		x						x
	Law	x	x	x								
Maintenance	Court	x†	x		x					o		
	Law	x	x				x				x	x
Parental responsibility	Court				x			o	o			
	Law											
Succession	Court		x									
	Law		x									

x = Already established; o = Additional connection.
* Common habitual residence or last common habitual residence in so far as one of the parties still resided there at the time the agreement was concluded.
† In the case of maintenance between ex-spouses, the option of the last common habitual residence for a period of at least a year is provided.

The cumulative overview of the party autonomy provisions within the present framework set out by Table 5 above demonstrates the considerable additional value in terms of the grounds that might be available to the parties through the use of these jurisdictional mechanisms:

1. Participating in the prorogation or transfer of jurisdiction in matters of parental responsibility opens up considerable additional scope for the parties in terms of jurisdictional grounds. Firstly, prorogation under Article 12(3) of Brussels II bis is limited only by the requirement that the child should have a 'substantial connection' to the jurisdiction in question. In this latter regard, although connections such as the Member State of the child's nationality or the Member State where one of the holders of parental responsibility is habitually resident are explicitly listed under Article 12(3)(a), it is conceivable that other connections relating to the specific situation of the child could come into play through this provision.
2. The *forum non conveniens* mechanism established in Article 15 of Brussels II bis offers additional value in terms of the prescriptive grounds of 'particular connection' in Article 15(3)(a)–(e): namely, the habitual residence of the child after the court has been seised; the former habitual residence of the child, the place of nationality of the child, the habitual residence of a holder of parental responsibility, or the place in which property of the child is located.
3. Flexibility also characterises Article 5 of the Maintenance Regulation, whereby the defendant can accept conceivably *any* Member State court that has been seised of jurisdiction by the creditor. As discussed, entering an appearance lies at the extreme limit of what would be classed as party autonomy within our present context, and no forward planning is invited on the part of the parties. It is an extremely open provision that is designed to serve the specific purpose of ensuring broad access to justice for the creditor (for instance, as discussed in the subsection above, it permits parties to address a jurisdictional split between maintenance proceedings involving (ex-)spouses or partners and those that concerning the couple's children).
4. Entering an appearance under Article 8 of the Property Regulations, which allows the parties to determine the court on the basis of the applicable law, has the same consequence as a choice of court under Article 7 of the same instruments. It thus does not add value as such, but provides the parties with another route through which a union between the court and applicable law can be achieved at the time when proceedings are pending.
5. In rounding off this overview of the additional value offered by the present provisions, it should be stated that due to the immediate nature of their usage, planned coordination with the wider framework is unlikely to be possible using these mechanisms.

8.4.3. GAPS TO BE ADDRESSED

The preceding evaluation of the subsidiary party autonomy provisions in the present framework has demonstrated that there are a number of areas that require further clarification by the CJEU and / or the EU legislator:

1. Article 12(3) is a novel introduction within the EU private international law relating to family matters and succession, and the exact delineation of the manner of its usage is not entirely established. Although there has been recent clarification by the CJEU regarding several aspects of this provision, it remains unclear as to whether a court could instigate the process of prorogation of its own motion under this rule. However, in view of the clear shift towards a traditional choice of court format adopted in Article 10 of the new Brussels IIa (Recast) Regulation, the answer to this question would at least appear to be answered firmly in the negative under this new instrument.
2. The apparent possibility for minors or their representatives to accept jurisdiction by entering an appearance under Article 5 of the Maintenance Regulation is inconsistent with the generally (perhaps overly) protective stance towards party autonomy in instances involving minors under this instrument. It is suggested that on the one hand the EU legislator ought to give consideration to the suitability of this distinct mechanism in the context of proceedings involving minors, whilst at the same time reflecting upon the possibility of enhancing party autonomy with regard to such matters.
3. In view of the entirety of the complex framework of opportunities to link the competent jurisdiction with the *professio juris* of the deceased's nationality (four provisions intertwined in Articles 5, 6, 7 and 9) under the Succession Regulation, it is unsurprising that a potential for overlap arises. In particular, despite the presence of Article 9 of the regulation that allows for the remaining parties to accept a jurisdiction that has already been agreed upon through entering an appearance, Article 7(c) also appears to provide a parallel opportunity for a court that has already been seised to be accepted by the other parties. It would be helpful if the purpose and interaction of the various jurisdictional provisions were to be clarified in order for parties and their representation to easily access and make use of the options available.

PART IV

VARIABLES OF CHOICE

CHAPTER 9
TEMPORAL, FORMAL AND MATERIAL REQUIREMENTS

9.1. INTRODUCTION

This final section of the examination carried out by this book aims to evaluate the choice of court and choice of law provisions contained in the EU private international law rules relating to family matters and succession in the context of the variables that further restrict the formation or enforcement of an exercise of party autonomy. The present chapter, the first of two, considers the impact of the temporal, formal and material (or substantive) requirements that are imposed upon choice.

As such, the chapter will begin by examining the beginning and end points within which party autonomy can be employed in the relevant provisions (9.2.). Following on from this, the formal validity requirements for choice of court and choice of law agreements will be discussed (9.3.). For the present purposes, a wide interpretation of this topic will be employed, extending beyond the form of written agreements in order to cover acceptance of jurisdiction through the parties' conduct. Finally the matter of material (or substantive) validity will be considered (9.4.), which will address measures designed to safeguard the fullness of the parties' consent. In the same manner as the other main chapters, there will be a concluding synthesis (9.5.) that brings together the findings of this chapter, whilst also evaluating the cohesion between the requirements imposed in related areas and presenting the gaps that have emerged during the course of this evaluation that require addressing.

9.2. TEMPORAL LIMITS OF CHOICE

The first topic to be considered in this chapter involves the delineation of the temporal limits for exercising a choice of court or choice of law in the EU private international law rules relating to family matters and succession. This will examine the point at which a choice can be manifested in relation to the proceeding that it concerns, as well as the end point of its exercise in relation to the court being seised of proceedings or the question of whether the designation can continue indefinitely. The following subsections will examine these issues in the choice of court (9.2.1.) and choice of law contexts (9.2.2.).

9.2.1. CHOICE OF COURT

This delineation of the temporal limits amongst the choice of court provisions will begin by considering the similar remits of Article 7 of the Property Regulations and Article 4 of the Maintenance Regulation (9.2.1.1.), before continuing on with examining the other remaining jurisdictional rules: Article 5 of the Property Regulations (9.3.1.2.), Articles 5, 6(b) and 7(b) and 7(c) of the Succession Regulation (9.3.1.3.), Article 12 of Brussels II bis (9.3.1.4.), the remaining *forum non conveniens* mechanisms (9.3.1.5.), and the opportunities to accept jurisdiction by entering an appearance (9.3.1.6.).

9.2.1.1. Article 7 of the Property Regulations and Article 4 of the Maintenance Regulation

As has been discussed in Chapters 6 and 7 with regard to the connecting factors established in Article 4 of the Maintenance Regulation and Article 7 of both the Property Regulations, a choice of a particular Member State court can be selected in advance of proceedings taking place.[846]

It can be inferred from the wording of Article 4(1) that a choice of court made according to this provision can be exercised at any time until the court is seised. In this regard, it is stated that 'the conditions referred to in points (a), (b) or (c) have to be met at the time the choice of court agreement is *concluded* or at the time the court is *seised*' (emphasis added). In contrast, Article 7 of the Property Regulations does not stipulate any time frame for making a choice of court for decisions concerning property relations outside of the dissolution of a relationship or succession. However, in view of the similar nature of this straightforward form of choice to that discussed above, as well as the absence of any stipulation to the contrary, it is proposed here that such a choice can also be exercised during the course of the relationship up until the court is seised of proceedings. Notwithstanding subsequent alteration by the parties, a choice of court made according to Article 4 of the Maintenance Regulation or Article 7 of the Property Regulations applies in perpetuity for all proceedings that arise from the scope of the respective provisions.

The possibility to make a choice of court well in advance of proceedings and for this designation to remain in force for subsequent processes has given rise

---

846 Article 4 of the Maintenance Regulation: see 6.2.2., 6.3.3. and 7.2.2.; Article 7 of the Property Regulations: see 6.4.2. and 7.4.1.

to concerns regarding the weakening of connection through a time lapse. This problem is particularly exacerbated with regard to maintenance obligations, whereby the creditor may face practical obstacles to accessing justice as a result of losing meaningful connection with a jurisdiction (e.g. a former habitual residence). Furthermore, it can be questioned whether the fullness of consent can persist over a long period of time, when a decision has been made at the start of a relationship on the basis of information that concerned a very different set of circumstances to those which exist at the time a choice materialises into a competent court.[847] In view of such problems, it has been suggested that a choice of court in family relationships should be limited to the time the jurisdiction is seised.[848]

9.2.1.2. Article 5 of the Property Regulations

Article 5(3) of the Matrimonial Property Regulation and Article 5(2) of the Partnership Property Regulation stipulate that

> If the agreement referred to in paragraph 1 / paragraph 2 of this Article is concluded before the court is seised to rule on matters of matrimonial property regimes / the property consequences of the registered partnership, the agreement shall comply with Article 7(2) / Article 7(1).[849]

It can be inferred from this wording that for the purposes of proceedings involving the dissolution of a property regime in conjunction with the dissolution of a relationship, agreement to the extension of jurisdiction is possible both before and after a court has been seised for such matters.

On first impressions, this provision raises the question as to how a court can be legitimately seised in the absence of consensus between the parties. Such a possibility might be evidenced from the fact that Article 5(2) of the Matrimonial Property Regulation attributes jurisdiction to the Member State court of dissolution of the marriage, *subject to* the agreement of the parties (as opposed to *through* the agreement of the parties).[850] It can, however, be remarked that this construction is nevertheless not altogether clear, and may cause confusion for those who make use of these provisions.

---

847 Walker (Chapter 2, n.164), at pp.249–250.

848 Ibid. at p.251.

849 Synthesis between Article 5(3) of the Matrimonial Property Regulation and Article 5(2) of the Partnership Property Regulation: 'If the agreement referred to in paragraph 1 [/ paragraph 2] of this Article is concluded before the court is seised to rule on matters of matrimonial property regimes [/ the property consequences of the registered partnership], the agreement shall comply with Article 7(2) [/ Article 7(1)]'.

850 However, the wording of Article 5(1) of the Partnership Property Regulation is less strong in this regard, with jurisdiction only being linked 'where the partners so agree'.

It is also uncertain whether parties can make an agreement linking the jurisdictions prior to proceedings concerning the dissolution of the relationship being instigated. Whilst it can be argued that the wording of the provisions contained in the respective regulations does not exclude this possibility, the utility of a prior agreement could be strongly called into question given the lack of certainty as to the ultimate forum (in view of the lack of parallel, unified choice of court rules for the dissolution of a marriage or registered partnership) and the absence of an opportunity for the parties to reflect on the desirability of the precise jurisdiction to which they are opting to be linked.[851]

The regulations neglect to establish the end point of jurisdiction determined according to Article 5. However, it would appear logical to employ an analogous approach to that enunciated by Article 12(2) of Brussels II bis with regard to linkage between the court of the dissolution of a marriage and that which decides on a related matter of parental responsibility – whereby jurisdiction concludes when a final decision is pronounced on either the dissolution of the relationship or the related matter (whichever occurs later), or jurisdiction ends during either proceeding for another reason.[852] Notwithstanding this, it would be helpful if the Property Regulations presented a similar level of clarity to that demonstrated in Article 12(2) of Brussels II bis.

9.2.1.3. *Articles 5, 6(b) and 7(b) and 7(c) of the Succession Regulation*

This section turns now to examine the two possibilities to link jurisdiction with the applicable law contained in Article 5, 6(b) and 7(b), and Article 7(c) of the Succession Regulation. When considering the starting point for these processes, at the risk of stating the obvious, it should be emphasised that this form of autonomy can only take place after the death of the person whose succession they concern.

The use of the future tense in Article 5(1)[853] would appear to confirm that this first choice of court possibility may only be used before a court has been seised of jurisdiction for succession proceedings. In contrast, in line with its generally obscure nature, the timing involved in the usage of Article 7(c) is harder to identify with a high degree of certainty. However, given the purposes proposed for this mechanism in Chapter 7,[854] it is proposed here that autonomy can be exercised in its context before and after the court of the chosen law is seised.

---

851 See further discussion of this in 9.3.1.1.

852 See 9.2.1.4. below.

853 See the use of future tense in Article 5(1): 'Where the law chosen by the deceased to govern his succession pursuant to Article 22 is the law of a Member State, the parties concerned may agree that a court or the courts of that Member State *are to have* exclusive jurisdiction to rule on any succession matter' (emphasis added).

854 See, at 7.4.2. the suggestion that Article 7(c) may come into play in two chief instances: (i) where only one of several parties has applied to the national court instead of refusing its competence immediately, the court should ask the remaining parties concerned whether

No indication is provided in the text with regard to the point at which the temporal competence ends under the respective choice of court provisions. It might arguably appear most practical for the jurisdiction seised through such processes to retain competence for the entirety of the succession until it is finalised. However, Recital 28 of the Succession Regulation appears to open the way for choice of court agreements to be formed with regard to different matters that arise from a succession. It can thus be proposed that a choice of court can only be made with regard to a particular proceeding (which might well equate to the succession in its entirety), with competence ending upon resolution of the matter(s) at stake. Although this adds considerable complexity, it can be seen to allow flexibility for situations in which the parties only view a particular matter as requiring ascertainment in the Member State courts of the deceased's nationality.[855]

9.2.1.4. *Article 12 of Brussels II Bis*

Firstly, it can be stated with confidence that the tone and nature of prorogation under Article 12 indicates that prior agreement is not relevant in this context;[856] the passive notion of acceptance that distinguishes these mechanisms does not invite forward planning on the part of those involved.[857] Agreement to jurisdiction under both Article 12(1) and (3) is required to be demonstrated 'at the time the court is seised'.[858] This would equate to the point in time determined by Article 16 of Brussels II bis: when the document instituting the proceedings or an equivalent document is lodged with the court.[859] However, a more

---

they accept jurisdiction according to this provision; and (ii) if only one person is party to the proceedings, his or her application can be directly accepted under Article 7(c), since arguably one party cannot come to an 'agreement' within the meaning of Article 5.

855 See discussion of 'partial choice-of-court agreements' in F. Marongiu Buonaiuti, 'Article 5: Choice-of-Court Agreement' in A. Calvo Caravaca et al. (eds.), *The EU Succession Regulation: A Commentary* (Cambridge University Press, Cambridge, 2016), p.161, para.19.

856 R. Geimer, 'EG-VO Ehesachen, Verfahren betr elterl Verantwortung' in R. Zöller (ed.), *Zöller Zivilprozessordnung*, 29th edn. (Dr. Otto Schmidt, Köln, 2012), at p.3147, para.9. It has been suggested, with regard to instances that fall within the scope of Article 12(1), that spouses can make prorogation of the court which is competent for decisions on parental responsibility part and parcel of a wider agreement that coordinates jurisdiction for proceedings that may arise from the dissolution of their marriage. However, such an agreement would clearly not be binding in nature: See Villata / Valkova (Chapter 6, n.602), at p.42.

857 F. Ibili, '3.1 Tijdstip en wijze van aanvaarding bij: Verordening (EG) Nr. 2201/2003 betreffende de bevoegdheid en de erkenning en tenuitvoerlegging van beslissingen in huwelijkszaken en inzake de ouderlijke verantwoordelijkheid, en tot intrekking van Verordening (EG) nr. 1347/2000, Artikel 12', *Groene Serie Personen- en familierecht* (Wolters Kluwer, 2017). See also Rb. Maastricht, 07-09-2012, nr. 167777 / FA RK 11-1688, at para.3.7, in which the court rejected the notion that a forum choice for future parental responsibility proceedings could be inserted into a divorce agreement or parenting plan.

858 See Article 12(1)(b) and (3)(b).

859 *Saponaro* (Chapter 4, n.463), at para.30; Case C-436/13 *E. v. B.* Request for a preliminary ruling from the Court of Appeal (England and Wales) [2014] ECLI:EU:C:2014:2246, at para.38; and *L. v. M.* (Chapter 8, n.785), at para.55.

contentious issue arises with regard to whether acceptance can validly be given *after* a court has been seised.

With regard to Article 12(1), it has been argued that to require prorogation to take place at the moment the court is seised of proceedings concerning the dissolution of the marriage would often be unworkable, since parties to such proceedings may not think about matters of parental responsibility at the time the court is seised for this first process. It is proposed that a more liberal approach be taken, allowing for acceptance to be given after the court has been seised of the divorce proceedings, when the case is pending.[860]

The setting of a strict deadline for prorogation has been critiqued with regard to applications under Article 12(3). In the UK Supreme Court case of *I. (A Child)*, a deadline tied to the moment at which the court is seised was said to be limiting[861] since, given the manner of litigation, it is more likely that one party will petition the court, and the other(s) will respond, rather than all parties coming together to seise the court with a joint acceptance of jurisdiction.

This matter has been recently addressed in a general manner by the CJEU in upholding a subsequent refusal of a party that occurred after the court had been seised of jurisdiction by the main applicants under Article 12(3).[862] Advocate General Tanchev's Opinion on this case addressed this question more directly, stating that acceptance should be clarified during the initial stages of proceedings:

> i.e. as soon as the parties on whom a copy of the document instituting the proceedings is served have either taken the first steps open to them or can be considered to have failed to do so on the expiry of the period within which they are required to take such steps.[863]

This pragmatic, flexible approach has been documented in Member State practice.[864] Furthermore, and more perhaps importantly, this gap appears to

860 T. Rauscher, 'Parental responsibility cases under the new Council Regulation "Brussels IIa"' (2005) 1 *The European Legal Forum* 37, at p.40.

861 *I. (A child)* (Chapter 8, n.791), at para.28.

862 *Saponaro* (Chapter 4, n.463), at paras.31–32.

863 Opinion of AG Tanchev in *Saponaro* (Chapter 7, n.715), at para.59.

864 See Dutch cases of Rb. Arnhem, 17-11-2008, nr. 157203 / FA RK 07-11485; Rb. Den Haag, 14-02-2013, nr. C/09/422710 FA RK 12-5002, in which a father, upon giving his verbal submission, was requested to provide his assent to competence; Rb. Den Haag, 11-07-2013, nr. C/09/443928 FA RK 13-4125, in which the court also ackowledged that this was an analogous approach to that strictly prescribed in Article 12(3). See also information in T.M.C. Asser Institute et al. (Chapter 7, n.721), at p.101, para.7.4.3: The Czech courts hold the view that since the non-applicant party should be given the opportunity to react to the request at hand, parties do not always have to consent at the very start of proceedings. In contrast, the Romanian courts appear to adopt a strict approach to agreement, in which the parties must consent before the court is seised.

have been addressed in the Brussels IIa (Recast) Regulation, which establishes a broader temporal frame with regard to the new mechanism that encompasses both Article 12(1) and 12(3). In this respect, it is stated that parties and any other holders of parental responsibility must have '(i) agreed freely upon the jurisdiction, at the latest at the time the court is seised; or (ii) expressly accepted the jurisdiction in the course of the proceedings'.[865]

Concerning the outer temporal limits, Article 12(2) provides that jurisdiction determined under Article 12(1) ceases upon conclusion of (i) the decision on the matter of divorce, legal separation or marriage annulment,[866] or (ii) the related matter of parental responsibility (whichever occurs later),[867] or when either of these proceedings end for another reason.[868] In contrast, no explicit end point is provided for Article 12(3) in the text. However, this matter has been clarified by the CJEU in *E. v. B.*,[869] in which the Court stated that the best interests of the child could only be safeguarded if jurisdiction is determined under Article 12(3) on a case-by-case basis.[870]

The recent Brussels IIa (Recast) Regulation again brings change to both the beginning and end points of competence under the single choice of court mechanism that it establishes. Firstly, it elaborates upon the possibility included in the 2016 draft recast for the parties to accept jurisdiction during proceedings where the law of the Member State provides for this, establishing that agreement can be demonstrated during proceedings by entering an appearance without contest.[871] Secondly, the recast not only provides a clear delineation of the points at which proceedings under this proposed mechanism would come to an end, but also suggests that competence can continue if the parties so agree.[872] With regard to this latter point, it is, however, somewhat unfortunate that the circumstances in which competence could continue are not further elaborated upon in the text or the recitals (e.g. it is not clear whether this would require a new assessment of the child's best interests).

865 See Article 10(1)(b) of the Brussels IIa (Recast) Regulation. With regard to the latter possibility it is furthermore stated in Recital 23: 'The acceptance of jurisdiction in the course of the proceedings should be recorded by the court in accordance with national law and procedure'.

866 Article 12(2)(a).

867 Article 12(2)(b).

868 Article 12(2)(c).

869 *E. v. B.* (n.859 above).

870 Ibid., at paras.44–50.

871 See Recital 23 and Article 10(1)(b)(ii) and (2) of the Brussels IIa (Recast) Regulation: in the last-mentioned instance, it is stated: 'Persons who become parties to the proceedings after the court was seised may express their agreement after the court was seised. In the absence of their opposition, their agreement shall be regarded as implicit'.

872 See Article 10(3) of this new instrument.

9.2.1.5. *Forum Non Conveniens Mechanisms*

In view of the nature of the *forum non conveniens* mechanisms established for matters of parental responsibility under Article 15 of Brussels II bis and in Articles 6(a) and 7(a) of the Succession Regulation, it is clear that the requisite initiative or consent of the party involved cannot be exercised until after the transferring court has been seised.

Furthermore, since there is a possibility according to Article 15(1) of Brussels II bis for just part of the case to be transferred, it can be inferred that the exercise of initiative or consent by a party may occur during the course of proceedings coming within the scope of this instrument. The same possibility does not appear for the *forum non conveniens* mechanism set out in the Succession Regulation.

With regard to the end point of competence, it would appear that Article 15 of Brussels II bis is only intended to determine a single matter of parental responsibility. Although this is not explicitly mentioned in Article 15, in view of the approach endorsed by the CJEU for Article 12(3),[873] the only solution that serves the best interests of the child appears to be assessment on a case-by-case basis. With regard to the mechanism set out in Articles 6(a) and 7(a) of the Succession Regulation, in the absence of qualification to the contrary, the same discussion with regard to the end point of competence is applied here as established for choice of court agreements under Articles 5, 6(b), 7(b) and 7(c).[874]

9.2.1.6. *Acceptance of Jurisdiction by Entering an Appearance*

This temporal delineation has finally reached the outer limits of party autonomy within the present context: the acceptance of jurisdiction by entering an appearance according to Article 5 of the Maintenance Regulation, Article 8 of the Property Regulations and Article 9 of the Succession Regulation. At the outset, it is clear that by its very nature, this subsidiary form of party autonomy invites no forward planning, with the defendant (or remaining party or parties[875]) accepting jurisdiction at the time the court has already been seised by the applicant(s).

The temporal limits of accepting jurisdiction are not defined in the above provisions. This is an area that could benefit from clarification, particularly in light of the possibility to make a choice of court that extends indefinitely under other provisions included in the Property Regulations and the Maintenance Regulation.[876] However, it is proposed here that due to the immediate nature of

---

873 *E. v. B.* (n.859 above) at paras.44–50.

874 See 9.2.1.3.

875 Under Article 9 of the Succession Regulation.

876 See Article 7 of the Property Regulations and Article 4 of the Maintenance Regulation under 9.2.1.1. It is not clear whether competence extends indefinitely for proceedings arising from a party's succession under the Succession Regulations: see 9.2.1.3.

submission by appearance, the jurisdiction that is accepted in this manner will only relate to the case that is already pending.

9.2.2. CHOICE OF LAW

Turning now to the rules that provide for the designation of the applicable law, the following subsections will discuss the temporal limits of the choice of law rules contained in Article 5 of Rome III (9.2.2.1), Article 22 of the Property Regulations (9.2.2.2.), and Articles 8 and 7 of the Hague Maintenance Protocol (9.2.2.3.–9.2.2.4.).

9.2.2.1. Article 5 of Rome III

According to Article 5(2), an agreement on the law to apply to a divorce or legal separation under the Rome III Regulation can generally be concluded at any time during a marriage. However, unlike the Property Regulations (see subsection 9.2.2.2. below), there is nothing in Rome III to indicate that future spouses have the possibility to make a choice of law. This lack of opportunity to make a choice of law to govern the dissolution of the marriage prior to its creation is out of step with the possibility to make other prenuptial arrangements in substantive law.[877]

The latest point for a choice of law to be made is generally the time at which the court is seised of the proceedings concerning divorce or legal separation.[878] By exception to this, it is provided in Article 5(3) that if the law of the forum so provides, a choice of law may also be exercised during the course of proceedings.[879] In such an instance, the formal requirements would be governed by the law of the forum.[880] A choice of law agreement is indefinite in nature, in the sense that the same choice of law could conceivably apply to a couple's legal separation and a subsequent conversion to a divorce.[881]

Although there are clear benefits to be reaped from a choice of law that is made in advance of proceedings taking place (namely, legal certainty and the ability to capture a legal system of close affinity), particularly in view of the long-term nature of family relationships, it can be remarked that this has to be balanced with the disadvantage that a choice might become outdated with

---

877 Viarengo (Chapter 4, n.356), at p.554, para.4.1.: 'it seems reasonable that the parties can agree on the law applicable to their divorce in a prenuptial agreement'.

878 Article 5(2) of Rome III.

879 See the example of Belgian law mentioned in Kruger (Chapter 1, n.60), at para.3, whereby the spouses have until their first appearance in court to make a choice of law.

880 See further discussion of formal requirements in the choice of law context in 9.3.2. below.

881 Subject to the existence of this possibility under the applicable law: see Article 9(2) of Rome III.

the passage of time and no longer equate to an 'informed' choice in light of new circumstances.[882]

9.2.2.2. *Article 22 of the Property Regulations*

As mentioned in the preceding subsection, in contrast to Rome III, the reference to 'future spouses' or 'future partners' in Article 22 the Property Regulations makes it clear that the parties can make a choice of law both before and during the marriage or registered partnership. This allows parties to make a choice of law alongside prenuptial property arrangements concerning substantive law. It has been stated that this inconsistency between Rome III and the Matrimonial Property Regulation has particular consequences in terms of coordination between these two instruments (see 9.5.2.).[883]

In contrast to Rome III, the Property Regulations do not provide any express stipulation in the text regarding the latest point at which a choice of law can be made. In examining this latter subject area, it would appear logical that a choice of law is made at the beginning of the relationship rather than the start of proceedings, since according to Article 22(2), a choice of law is generally prospective in nature. However, it would still be useful for the parties to have the flexibility to make a choice of law around the time that proceedings are pending or have been instigated (especially since the opportunity exists for a choice with retrospective effect to be made[884]). Whilst the recitals[885] do establish that a choice may be made 'at any moment', 'during the course' of the marriage or registered partnership, the extent to which this can be interpreted is not altogether clear.[886] It is suggested here that greater delineation of the temporal end point in the same prescriptive manner as Article 5(2) and (3) of Rome III would improve the clarity and usability of these instruments.

9.2.2.3. *Article 8 of the Hague Maintenance Protocol*

In contrast to the format of Article 5 of Rome III, the Hague Maintenance Protocol states that a choice of law agreement can be made 'at any time'. Although

---

[882] Boele-Woelki (Chapter 1, n.1), at pp.30–31 and Walker (Chapter 2, n.164), at pp.249–250.

[883] See criticism of the lack of a parallel opportunity by Viarengo, in: I. Viarengo, 'Choice of Law Agreements in Property Regimes, Divorce, and Succession: Stress-testing the New EU Regulations' (2016) 17(4) *ERA Forum* 543, at pp.549–550, para.3.1.1. and Viarengo (Chapter 4, n.356), at pp.553–554.

[884] See the Property Regulations, Article 22(2); subject to protection of third parties in Article 22(3).

[885] Recital 45 of the Matrimonial Property Regulation and Recital 44 of the Partnership Property Regulation.

[886] Although it is suggested by Viarengo that, in view of this recital, a choice can be made during proceedings: see Viarengo (n.883 above), at p.550, para.3.1.1.

this stipulation is not elaborated upon in the Protocol itself, the Explanatory Report makes it clear that a choice of law can be made under this provision both before, and during proceedings concerning maintenance obligations.[887] In this latter regard, it ought to be pointed out that the Protocol does not require that a choice exercised during proceedings be recorded according to the law of the forum (as is the case with Rome III, see 9.2.2.1. above)[888]

In the same manner as the Property Regulations (and, notwithstanding the limitations of the subject matter, Rome III[889]), a choice made under Article 8 of the Hague Maintenance Protocol continues indefinitely, applying to future proceedings that emerge with regard to maintenance obligations arising from the relationship between the parties.[890] The point made at the start of this section[891] with regard to the effect of the passage of time upon a concrete choice is particularly relevant in the realm of maintenance obligations, where an outdated law holds the potential to become particularly harmful to the ability of the creditor to reap maintenance in line with their present social and economic circumstances. Notwithstanding this, it can be argued that an unconnected law does not pose the same immediate barriers to accessing justice as a jurisdiction that has become disconnected through time.

9.2.2.4. *Article 7 of the Hague Maintenance Protocol*

In contrast to Article 8 of the Protocol, it is made clear that a choice in favour of the law of the forum made according to Article 7 is intended to only apply to a 'particular proceeding', with jurisdiction thus ending once the proceeding is concluded.[892] The Explanatory Report elaborates upon this, stating that this choice can be made when the creditor 'has already brought, or is about to bring, a maintenance claim before a specific authority'.[893] Notwithstanding the need for a choice to be directed towards a particular law,[894] it is possible parties can make a choice according to Article 7 in advance of proceedings (there is no time limit in this regard). The timing and form required for a choice which is made during proceedings are regulated by the law of the forum.[895]

---

887 Bonomi (Chapter 4, n.400), at para.117, where it is made clear from the discussion of the interaction between Article 7 and Article 8.

888 It is instead recorded according to the formal requirements of the chosen law: see 9.3.2. below.

889 Since divorce and legal separation are concentrated on a definite end point.

890 Walker (Chapter 2, n.164), at p.236.

891 See 9.2.2.1. in the context of Article 5 of Rome III.

892 Bonomi (Chapter 4, n.400), at paras.115–117.

893 Ibid., at para.115.

894 Ibid., at paras.120–121.

895 In other words, the chosen law. See ibid., at para.122.

9.2.2.5. *Article 22 of the Succession Regulation*

In consideration of the temporal limits of a *professio juris* exercised according to Article 22 of the Succession Regulation, it is clear that the situation in this setting is very straightforward. The law itself can be left to the time of death to be determined (although it can also be secured in advance),[896] but the choice can clearly only be exercised up until the party's death.

The regulation establishes 'Transitional Provisions' in Article 83 that address the situation in which a party has made a choice of law prior to the instrument coming into force on the 17 August 2015 but has died after this date. Subject to the conditions set out therein (see 9.3.2.3.), an apparent *professio juris* may be upheld.

9.3. FORMAL VALIDITY

The fulfilment of the formal requirements established for a choice or agreement is understood to be the primary indicator of the consent of the parties.[897] Given the wide variances in the expression of free will within the realm of the EU's private international law rules relating to family matters and succession, formal validity in this present setting is to be analysed broadly, taking into account not only the written format of choice (where applicable), but also the other prescribed ways in which the consent of the parties can be expressed. The choice of court provisions will be examined first (9.3.1.), before turning to the choice of law rules (9.3.2.).

9.3.1. CHOICE OF COURT

The formal requirements in the relevant instruments for jurisdictional choice to be expressed are established under Article 7(2) of the Property Regulations (9.3.1.1.), Article 4(2) of the Maintenance Regulation (9.3.1.2.), and Article 5(2) of the Succession Regulation (9.3.1.3.). In addition, requirements of acceptance can be identified in Article 7(c) of the Succession Regulation (9.3.1.4.), Article 12 of Brussels II bis (9.3.1.5.) and in the other subsidiary party autonomy provisions (9.3.1.6.).

---

896 See 6.3.4.2.

897 Abendroth (Chapter 4, n.337), at p.464. See CJEU case law cited in support of this by the aforementioned author: Case C-159/97 *Trasporti Castelletti Spedizioni Internazionali SpA v. Hugo Trumpy SpA*. Reference for a preliminary ruling: Corte suprema di cassazione – Italy [1999] ECR I-1597, at para.20 and Case C-106/95 *Mainschiffahrts-Genossenschaft eG (MSG) v. Les Gravières Rhénanes SARL*. Reference for a preliminary ruling: Bundesgerichtshof – Germany [1997] ECR I-911, at para.19.

9.3.1.1. *Article 7(2) of the Property Regulations*

The requisites for formal validity for a choice of court under Article 7 of the Property Regulations are well defined: an agreement has to be in writing or expressed electronically in a durable fashion, as well as dated and signed by both parties to the agreement. Although the latter two requirements might appear to simply be further hoops to jump through, these additional steps can also be seen as means of drawing the parties' attention to what they are consenting to and to provide greater evidence of consensus.[898] On a more general note, it has been proposed that an exercise of autonomy between parties under the relevant instruments can be executed in counterpart agreements[899]

The same formal requirements that are provided in Article 7(2) apply to agreements to link jurisdiction with the court which dissolves the marriage or partnership according to Article 5(2) of the Matrimonial Property Regulation and 5(1) of the Partnership Property Regulation. However, according to Article 5(3) of the former and 5(2) of the latter, these requirements do not apply when the court has already been seised of jurisdiction for the related question of property relations. In such an instance, it is not made clear in what manner consensus would be expressed by the parties. As previously discussed, the construction of Article 5 of the Property Regulations is puzzling,[900] and the lack of elaboration as to the form by which the parties are to 'approve' the jurisdiction that has already been seised only adds to this confusion.

The level of specificity required by the Property Regulations with regard to designating the connecting factor for a choice of court is not made entirely clear. This is not an issue where the place of creation of the relationship is chosen under Article 7 of the Property Regulations, since this is clearly predetermined for the duration of the relationship. Likewise, given that there is a possibility for a choice of law to be made under the regulations,[901] and the conflict-of-laws rules that apply in the absence of choice[902] are generally focused upon circumstances at the time the relationship was created, there would be little tangible benefit in terms of the flexibility that an undetermined choice might offer, since the applicable law is unlikely to shift with the passage of time.

---

898 A. Bonomi (Chapter 4, n.400), at paras.144–145 and Bonomi (Chapter 7, n.730), at pp.355–356. See also discussion in the context of material validity in 9.4.1 below.

899 See Villata / Valcova (Chapter 6, n.602), at pp.13 (fn.11), pp.14, 20, 22 (fn.29), p.25 (fn.32), pp.26, 29 (fn.38), pp.30, 45 (fn.57). This assertion holds true for choice of court and choice of law agreements concerning adult relations (property relations, maintenance and divorce or legal separation), subject to the law applicable to formal validity.

900 See 9.2.1.2.

901 Article 22(1). It should also be mentioned that all grounds for selection connect to the time the agreement is concluded.

902 Article 26(1).

As discussed above, any linkage through Article 5 of the Property Regulations prior to a court being seised for the purposes of the dissolution of a marriage or registered partnership is essentially tentative. Although a specific jurisdiction or connecting factor might be selected in advance in view of the jurisdictional rules that may determine the court that is responsible for the dissolution of the relationship,[903] the level of legal certainty with regard to the success of such an agreement is low. Furthermore, if the parties were to designate a particular connecting factor under these conditions, there is a risk that they are held to a choice that they do not ultimately view as desirable once proceedings are instigated in the court of dissolution.

9.3.1.2. Article 4(2) of the Maintenance Regulation

Article 4(2) of the Maintenance Regulation stipulates that agreements on jurisdiction ought to be in writing, or expressed by analogous electronic means that provide a durable record of the agreement. In contrast to Article 7(2) of the Property Regulations, there is no requirement for an agreement to be signed or dated, which arguably would have secured a higher standard of formal and material validity, further drawing the party's (particularly the creditor's) attention to the consequences of their choice.

It can, however, be observed that the requirements established for a choice of court under Article 4(2) of the Maintenance Regulation are more stringent that those used for maintenance obligations under Article 23 of the Brussels I Regulation, which employed the more flexible option of alternative formal requirements for agreements – for the purposes of maintenance, these being either in written (or electronic) format,[904] or 'in a form which accords with practices which the parties have established between themselves'.[905]

From the wording of Article 4(1), it would appear that an agreement does not have to refer to the connecting factor directly; it is enough to identify a court that aligns or will align with one of the established connecting factors at the time the court is seised.[906] More controversially, it can also be deduced, on the basis of the possibility for the conditions of the connecting factor to be met at the time the court is seised, that an indeterminate choice can be made in favour of a connection rather than a specific court (although the text is not altogether

---

903 Either in view of Brussels II bis or the Member States' own private international law rules on jurisdiction for the dissolution of registered partnership.

904 Article 23(1)(a).

905 Article 23(1)(b).

906 See Article 4(1): 'The conditions referred to in points (a), (b) or (c) have to be met at the time the choice of court agreement is concluded or at the time the court is seised'. See also Abendroth (Chapter 4, n.337), at p.467.

clear in this regard). Indeed, in the absence of the opportunity to make a choice of court under Brussels II bis, in order to link in advance the jurisdiction that decides upon maintenance proceedings with that which decides on matrimonial matters (Article 4(1)(c)(i)), parties would have to instead refer to the connection to this ground in their agreement.[907] It is highly questionable whether this possibility is appropriate in the realm of maintenance obligations, whereby legal certainty is important for ensuring that the parties (particularly the creditor) are adequately informed regarding the content of their choice.

9.3.1.3. *Article 5(2) of the Succession Regulation*

For a choice of court exercised according to Articles 5, 6(b) and 7(b) of the Succession Regulation, Article 5(2) imposes the same formal requirements as those set out in Article 7(2) of the Property Regulations (see subsection 9.3.1.2. above), with these conditions required to be fulfilled by all the 'parties concerned' in the succession.[908] Given the present nature of a choice of court exercised under the Succession Regulation, concerns relating to specificity do not apply directly to this mechanism.[909]

9.3.1.4. *Article 7(c) of the Succession Regulation*

In contrast to the prescribed form established by Article 5(2) for a choice of court made according in Article 5, 6(b) and 7(b), Article 7(c) simply states that the parties to the proceedings should have 'expressly accepted the jurisdiction of the court seised'. No further guidance is provided in the text as to the manner in which such express acceptance can be demonstrated; it has been suggested in literature that this would equate to written agreement (or agreement recorded electronically in a durable fashion), as well as oral submissions by the parties (subject to the procedural rules of the law of the forum).[910]

Given the exceptional nature of the circumstances in which Article 7(c) would be employed, a more flexible approach to demonstrating acceptance might be seen as appropriate in these circumstances. Nevertheless, it would have increased the usability of the regulation for both practitioners and concerned parties to have the meaning of 'expressly accepted' further defined in the text or its accompanying documentation.

907 The exact Member State court would remain, in principal, uncertain until matrimonial proceedings were pending or had been instigated; until this time, this is essentially a choice for a connecting factor, and not the Member State court itself.
908 Article 5(2): 'expressed in writing, dated and signed by the parties concerned'.
909 See discussion with regard to the *professio juris* under Article 22(2) in 9.3.2.3.
910 Marongiu Buonaiuti, (n.855 above), at pp.175–176, para.8.

9.3.1.5. *Article 12 of Brussels II Bis*

The parties' acceptance of jurisdiction pursuant to Article 12 is required to be express or otherwise demonstrated in an unequivocal manner.[911] An express agreement does not, however, have to be written; similarly to Article 7(c) of the Succession Regulation (see preceding subsection), in view of the existence of the possibility to demonstrate acceptance through conduct, it would appear that express acceptance can also take the form of oral declarations during the proceedings.

Leading on from this, it is not entirely resolved what form of conduct by the parties may be taken as indicative of 'unequivocal acceptance'.[912] Although actively litigating in a particular forum has been exemplified as constituting unequivocal acceptance,[913] according to the English Court of Appeal, this is 'not to be lightly inferred'.[914] It has also been suggested that acceptance cannot merely be tacit; neither entering an appearance in a purported jurisdiction,[915] nor seemingly posing no objection to instigation or continuance of proceedings in the court,[916] is said to be sufficient in this regard.

The differences in Member States' approaches to interpreting 'unequivocal acceptance' under Article 12 were highlighted in a recent guide on the Brussels II bis Regulation.[917] Contrary to the assertions highlighted in the preceding paragraph, it can be remarked that several Member States in fact appear to treat this requirement rather superficially. For instance, the French national reporter highlighted that divorce by mutual consent has been taken as a desire of the parties to extend jurisdiction according to Article 12(1),[918] and the Belgian reporter stated that there were instances whereby entering an appearance before a court without challenge was framed as indicative of the required acceptance.[919] In addition, there is also evidence of divergences in approach within national legal systems.[920]

The extent of 'unequivocal acceptance' of jurisdiction by the parties under Article 12(3) has been the subject of recent preliminary rulings by the CJEU. In one case, making a joint application to a court was recognised as

---

911 Article 12(1)(b) and (3)(b).

912 *I. (A child)* (Chapter 8, n.791), at para.28.

913 See facts of the case in *C. v. C.* [2006] EWHC 3247 (Fam) and the opinion of Hedley J in that case at para.17.

914 *Bush v. Bush* (Chapter 7, n.717), at para.53.

915 Geimer (n.856 above), at p.3147, para. 9.

916 Ibili (n.857 above).

917 T.M.C. Asser Institute (Chapter 7, n.721), at pp.94–97, para.7.4.

918 Ibid., at p.94, para.7.4.

919 Ibid.

920 For example, Spain: some courts have employed barely any reasoning to find agreement, whilst others have been thorough. See ibid., p.94, para.7.4.

demonstrating unequivocal acceptance on the part of the parties.[921] With a view to another specific set of circumstances, it was found that even if a defendant brings a second set of proceedings in the same Member State court as that in which the applicant has already instigated proceedings, this cannot be taken as unequivocal acceptance if the defendant nevertheless refuses to accept the jurisdiction in the first proceedings.[922] In this regard, acceptance of jurisdiction can only be understood on a case-by-case basis.[923] Notwithstanding the degree of clarification provided by the above cases, it is clear that the judgments represent a piecemeal approach to comprehending a complicated requirement.

The recent Brussels IIa (Recast) Regulation has given rise to a significant overhaul in terms of the formal requirements for agreements, by the single comprehensive mechanism that replaces the two separate provisions currently contained in Article 12.[924] The drafters have removed reference to 'unequivocal acceptance' entirely from the text, and considerably elaborated upon the formal manner through which agreement can be established: the parties must demonstrate their agreement

> in writing, dated and signed by the parties concerned or included in the court record in accordance with national law and procedure. Any communication by electronic means which provides a durable record of the agreement shall be equivalent to 'writing'.

The parties also have the prescribed possibility to accept jurisdiction during proceedings by entering an appearance, in which case an absence of opposition will be taken to indicate implicit agreement.[925]

It is proposed here that although the written requirement is arguably not necessary given the immediate nature of proceedings in this realm, it would appear that the drafters wished to place a particular emphasis on informed consent.[926] This can be seen as part and parcel of the aim of bringing the parties' attention to the consequences of their agreement and heightening clarity in the usage of this instrument.

9.3.1.6. Other Subsidiary Party Autonomy Provisions

The remaining subsidiary party autonomy provisions (with the exception of Article 12(3), see above) that have been outlined in Chapter 8 will now be

---

921 *Saponaro* (Chapter 4, n.463), at para.25.
922 *L. v. M.* (Chapter 8, n.785), at paras.53–59.
923 Ibid., at para.58.
924 Article 10 of the new Brussels IIa Regulation. See further discussion in 7.2.3.
925 See the requirements in Article 10(1)(b) and (2) of the Brussels IIa Regulation.
926 See further discussion in 9.4.1.

collectively discussed in the context of formal requirements (or, as the case may be, the absence thereof). The aforementioned chapter identifies two types of provisions for which party autonomy plays a marginal role, and it is useful to allude to the characteristics of these categories in examining this absence of formal requirements.

Firstly, there are the two remaining provisions that involve an interaction between party autonomy and judicial discretion (Article 15 of Brussels II bis and Articles 6(a) and 7(a) of the Succession Regulation). These two transfer provisions represent *forum non conveniens* mechanisms, whereby the court first seised of proceedings under the rules of the respective instrument might decline jurisdiction on the basis that there is another, more appropriate court available to decide on the case. In both instances, only one concerned party is required to instigate (or, also under Article 15 of Brussels II bis, accept), the transfer of jurisdiction. This contrasts with Article 12(3) (9.3.1.5. above), where all parties to proceedings are required to unequivocally accept the assumption of jurisdiction by a certain Member State court. No further delineation of the level of acceptance required is provided by Article 15; in the absence of further elaboration it can be presumed that the bar established to find consent is not set high.[927]

The principal role attributed to judicial discretion in this present context arguably means that the imposition of additional formal requirements would detract from the marginal role attributed to autonomy in this context. Indeed, as discussed in 9.3.1.5., the flexible but present requirements of Article 12(3) have given rise to confusion as to the requisite level of demonstrated agreement. However, the omission to impose any baseline delineation of acceptance clearly presents the risk that parties are taken to tacitly accept the transfer of jurisdiction without intending to do (e.g. by failing to expressly disagree with this process). This has repercussions in terms of ensuring full consent, as well as safeguarding predictability during proceedings.

The second type of subsidiary party autonomy provision set out in Chapter 8 – accepting jurisdiction by entering an appearance – presents a clearer case for the absence of formal requirements. This opportunity is provided in Article 8 of the Property Regulations, Article 5 of the Maintenance Regulation and Article 9 of the Succession Regulation, and permits the defendant (or in the case of succession, the remaining party or parties) to tacitly accept the competence of a court which would not be competent under the objective jurisdictional rules of the relevant instrument by entering an appearance in the court which has been

927 An incidence of acceptance being refused on the basis of its form was documented in the recent Asser guide on Brussels II bis: however, this was only due to the fact that acceptance was expressed *after* the transferring court had already made its decision to transfer jurisdiction: see T.M.C. Asser Institute et al (Chapter 7, n.721), at p.118, para.10.3.

seised (except where the party has done so to contest jurisdiction). The present nature of this mechanism does not appear to leave room for the imposition of additional formal requirements. Nevertheless, as will be discussed below (see material or substantive validity – 9.4.1.), it can be remarked that where a party tacitly accepts jurisdiction in such a manner, the duty of the court to ensure they are appropriately informed becomes particularly pertinent.

9.3.2. CHOICE OF LAW

The formal requirements for a choice of law to be expressed within the relevant framework are established in Article 7 of Rome III and Article 23 of the Property Regulations (9.3.2.1.), Article 7(2) and 8(2) of the Hague Maintenance Protocol (9.3.2.2.) and Article 22(2) of the Succession Regulation (9.3.2.3.).

9.3.2.1. Article 7 of Rome III and Article 23 of the Property Regulations

With respect to agreements designating a choice of law made pursuant to Article 5 of Rome III and Article 22 of the Property Regulations, identical formal requirements are established in Article 7 of the former instrument and Article 23 of the latter. The principal paragraphs of both provisions provide that an agreement is to be expressed in writing (or by durable electronic means), dated and signed by both spouses. This mirrors the highest standard in formal requirements for choice of court within this framework (see Article 7(2) of the Property Regulations (9.3.1.1.) and Articles 5(2) of the Succession Regulation (9.3.1.3.) above).

Additionally, both provisions establish a framework of guidance concerning the imposition of additional formal requirements:[928] firstly, if the law of the participating Member State in which the parties have their habitual residence at the time the agreement is concluded lays down additional formal requirements, such requirements shall apply.[929] Secondly, if the parties are habitually resident in different Member States at the time the agreement is concluded and the laws of these states provide for different formal requirements, the agreement will be valid if it fulfils the requirements of either of these laws.[930] Thirdly and finally, if only one of the parties is habitually resident in a participating Member State at the time the agreement is concluded and that state lays down additional formal requirements for this type of agreement, those requirements shall apply.[931]

928 See examples of additional guarantees of authenticity cited by Viarengo, such as a notarial act that is required in Germany: Viarengo (2014) (Chapter 4, n.356), at p.554, para.4.1.

929 Article 7(2) of Rome III and 23(2) of the Property Regulations.

930 Article 7(3) of Rome III and Article 23(3) of the Property Regulations.

931 Article 7(4) of Rome III and Article 23(4) of the Property Regulations.

These respective sets of prescribed rules are tailored towards the recognition of differences in evidential requirements between Member States. Although these frameworks add complexity, such rules are aimed at ensuring a high level of clarity and predictability as to the requirements of formal admissibility of a choice of law made according to these instruments.

Returning to the exception contained in Article 5(3) of Rome III,[932] it can be seen that a choice of law can be made after the court has been seised of proceedings if the law of the forum so provides. It is also stated that, in this scenario, the choice would also be recorded in line with the law of the forum. This point is not further elaborated upon, but it can be strongly speculated that the formal requirements established under Article 7 do not necessarily apply here.[933] For example, it is conceivable that it might be appropriate, given the present nature of proceedings, for an oral submission to be made to the court in such an instance. This open-ended approach clearly removes the baseline level of formal safeguards that are applicable to a choice made *prior* to the court being seised. However, a choice expressed during proceedings concerning divorce or legal separation is arguably much less likely to be subject to compromised consent than one made during the course of the relationship.[934]

In contrast to the situation under certain choice of court provisions,[935] it is largely made clear from the nature of the grounds for a choice of law under Article 5(1) of Rome III and Article 22(1) of the Property Regulations that the designation must be ascertained at the moment of choice.[936] The only exception to this is the possibility to select the *lex fori* under Article 5(1)(d) of Rome III. It is not made clear whether this ground can be selected in advance (and thus specified in an indeterminate manner) or only when a court has been seised under Brussels II bis.[937] Although the former approach would not offer the parties the legal certainty that comes with the possibility to pinpoint the specific law that will apply, there would be residual predictability in being able to secure the union of the law and forum in advance. However, one point to consider with regard to an indeterminate choice of law is the requirement that parties are informed regarding their choice; where the choice is not ascertained at the moment of designation,[938] it is questionable whether the parties will be adequately aware of the content of the law that will ultimately apply.

932 See also 9.1.1.2.

933 Kruger (Chapter 1, n.60), at para.3.

934 For instance, since the parties are no longer in a relationship, there will not be the same opportunity for manipulation by one party upon another. Choice made during proceedings might be seen as taking place in a more controlled environment.

935 See discussion in the context of the Maintenance Regulation at 9.3.1.2. and the Property Regulations at 9.3.1.1. above.

936 In view of the phrase 'at the time the agreement is concluded'.

937 See further discussion on this question in 7.5.1.

938 See Recital 18 of Rome III and further discussion in 9.4.2.1.

It has previously been proposed that inserting alternative choice of law options into an agreement concerning the law that applies to the dissolution of a property regime upon the death of one of the parties is a way of ensuring linkage with the law that applies to the deceased's succession in the event that the parties do not share a nationality (see 6.5.2.).[939] In the context of this subsection, two further remarks can be made: firstly, even though there is nothing stated in the Property Regulations concerning the usage of an alternative choice of law construction, given the potential for Member States to impose their own additional formal requirements according to Article 23, it is possible that this option is not permissible in certain instances. Furthermore, given that the choice of law is to be applied to the couple's property relations as a whole, in the event that proceedings are instigated prior to the death of one of the parties (e.g. in conjunction with divorce), the specificity of this designation would render the choice ineffective.[940]

9.3.2.2. *Articles 7(2) and 8(2) of the Hague Maintenance Protocol*

For choices made before proceedings are instituted under Article 7 of the Hague Maintenance Protocol,[941] and for all choices made under Article 8(1), the parties are required to submit their selection in writing or recorded in any medium that can subsequently be referred back to (e.g. electronic documents), and signed by both persons involved (this can include electronic signature).[942] This approach largely emulates the form established by Rome III and the Property Regulations, but lacks the framework for the imposition of additional requirements set out in these instruments.

A choice expressed under Article 7(1) after proceedings have been instituted need not accord with the Protocol's formal requirements; the desired linkage can be declared directly to the court. Although the evidential requirements of written (or equivalent) consent are clearly not necessary in this context, the complete absence of any requirements for agreements during proceedings arguably robs the parties (particularly the creditor) of the opportunity to reflect upon their choice. Presumably, it is assumed that the consequences of a choice of law are highlighted during the proceedings themselves, although this is by no means a given certainty.

---

939 The designation of the law of the nationality of either of the parties at the time of agreement, depending on which one predeceases the other: Villata / Valkova (Chapter 6, n.602), at pp.86–89, 95–99 and 124–128.

940 Ibid., at p.86.

941 See requirements in Article 7(2) of the Hague Maintenance Protocol.

942 Article 7(2) and Article 8(2) respectively. See Bonomi (Chapter 4, n.400), at paras.144–145 and Bonomi (Chapter 7, n.730), at pp.355–356.

With regard to the level of specificity required for a choice of law under Articles 7 and 8 of the Hague Maintenance Protocol, it is made clear that the indeterminate choice is not permitted under this instrument. Whilst the first two grounds established in Article 8(1) explicitly refer to nationality or habitual residence 'at the time of designation', it is clarified in the Explanatory Report that any reference to the *lex fori* under Article 7(1), or the law applicable to the property regime or the divorce or legal separation of the parties under Article 8(1)(c) or (d), must indicate a particular law.[943] This necessity to identify the applicable law at the time of agreement ensures a high level of legal certainty, which is particularly important given the sensitivities of the field of maintenance obligations and the need for the creditor to be adequately informed regarding the content and consequences of their choice.

9.3.2.3. Article 22(2) of the Succession Regulation

A *professio juris* made according to Article 22 of the Succession Regulation may be established either 'expressly in a declaration in the form of a disposition of property upon death' or as 'demonstrated by the terms of such a disposition' (Article 22(2)). Article 3(1)(d) of the Succession Regulation clearly establishes that a disposition of property upon death means 'a will, a joint will[944] or an agreement as to succession'.[945] This first option is relatively uncomplicated, whereby express reference to a choice of law is included in one of the aforementioned formats, or otherwise meets the formal requirements established for such instruments.[946] An important exclusion from the regulation are oral dispositions of property upon death; it can thus be construed that a declaration must be in writing.[947]

Concerning the formal validity of the disposition of property itself, as well as any subsequent modification or revocation,[948] Article 27 of the Succession Regulation establishes a list of alternative conflict-of-laws rules. It is sufficient that the disposition adheres to the formal validity requirements of one of the states determined by this provision. The delegation of formal validity to the law of a certain state without establishing baseline standards within the text diverges from the trend in the other relevant instruments that permit advanced

---

943 Bonomi (Chapter 4, n.400), at paras.115–116, 138–143.

944 See Article 3(1)(c): '"joint will" means a will drawn up in one instrument by two or more persons'.

945 See Article 3(1)(b): '"agreement as to succession" means an agreement, including an agreement resulting from mutual wills, which, with or without consideration, creates, modifies or terminates rights to the future estate or estates of one or more persons party to the agreement'.

946 Castellanos Ruiz (Chapter 1, n.48), at p.345, para.23.

947 Lagarde (Chapter 4, n.484), at p.129, para.10.

948 See Articles 22(4) and 27(2).

choice. This approach reflects the intertwining between a choice of law and dispositions of property upon death, whereby the regulation seeks to respect variation between Member State laws in the formal validity of such dispositions. By way of exception to the general course of Article 27, in the 16 Member States that are party to the Hague Convention of 5 October 1961 on the Conflicts of Laws Relating to the Form of Testamentary Dispositions, the rules set out in this instrument are to be used to establish the law applicable to the formal validity of a will or a joint will.[949]

With regard to the level of specificity required for express choice, it is made clear that a party can secure the law of their nationality at the moment of designation, or stipulate that this is to be determined at the time of their death.[950] By making use of this latter option, the party can opt for greater flexibility; however, due to the indeterminate nature of this designation, as discussed in the other subject areas where this form of choice appears to be possible,[951] there may be concerns as to whether they were adequately informed regarding the content of their choice.[952] Furthermore, a shift in nationality might arguably defeat the stable purpose of this limited choice of law, particularly in light of the stated necessity for legal certainty and a desire to protect the expectations of the beneficiaries to an estate.[953]

Furthermore, in the event of dual nationality upon death, it is unclear how the connecting factor would be ascertained in this indeterminate scenario. It is possible that a party stipulates the nationality that they believe they will have at the time of their death, although this clearly invites uncertainty unless the party already has concrete plans in place to acquire this nationality (failing which the agreement will not be valid).[954] Above all, it appears to be a requirement under Article 22(1) that the party stipulates whether their choice refers to the law of their nationality at the time of making the choice or at the time of death.[955] If the nature of the choice is not specified and the nationality of the deceased has changed since the moment of designation, identification of the intentions of the deceased would be very difficult, and the *professio juris* would have to be invalidated.[956]

---

949 See Article 75(1) of the Succession Regulation. See also Lagarde (Chapter 4, n.484), at p.155, para.1.

950 See extended discussion of this topic in 6.3.4.2.

951 See Articles 5 and 7 of the Property Regulations – 9.3.1.1.; Article 4 of the Maintenance Regulation – 9.3.1.2.; and Article 5 of the Rome III Regulation – 9.3.2.1.

952 Castellanos Ruiz (Chapter 1, n.48), at p.335, para.8.

953 See Recital 38 of the Succession Regulation and the Explanatory Memorandum (Chapter 2, n.178), at p.6, para.4.3. See also 6.3.4.2.

954 Castellanos Ruiz (Chapter 1, n.48), at p.334, para.8.

955 Ibid. at p.335, para.8.

956 Ibid.

The second possibility provided for in Article 22(1) involves a situation in which the deceased did not explicitly refer to a choice of law in their disposition, but a choice can nevertheless be construed from evidence in the document. This option accommodates the scenario where a person lacks 'choice consciousness',[957] for instance, where they believed that the objectively applicable law was that of their nationality, or where they made a disposition with a view to a purely domestic situation, only to subsequently move away from the state of their nationality.[958] The acceptance of this approach can be seen as a means of empowering the expectations of the deceased and facilitating the smooth running of their succession by recognising the law that the deceased had in mind when organising his or her estate.

Regarding the level of evidence required for an implicit choice to be accepted in this context, it has been suggested that, for example, mentioning legal concepts that are particular to the law of the deceased's nationality but absent from the law of the deceased's habitual residence would be a clear indicator in this regard.[959] In contrast, the mere use of the language of the state of which the deceased was a national would not, in itself, be sufficient to indicate a choice of its law.[960] Above all, it should be emphasised that indication ought to be patent to those that observe it.[961]

Whilst it is clear that there is a high degree of uncertainty with regard to the limits at which an implicit choice will be treated as sufficiently 'demonstrated' for the purposes of formal validity, the alternative, to only allow for an express reference to a chosen law, would ignore the authentic intentions of many who pass away in the cross-border context. The open construction of Article 22(1) accommodates the essential fact that, unlike the other areas that are being dealt with here, the deceased is clearly not present to clarify their choice once succession proceedings begin. The flexibility permitted by this provision can be seen to empower the judiciary to identify the authentic will of the deceased. Notwithstanding the above assertion, the provision of guidance concerning the outer limits of demonstrable choice for the purposes of Article 22(1) would be a useful tool that would serve to aid and streamline the interpretation of dispositions.[962]

---

957 Ibid., at p.348, para.24. See also the debate as to whether 'choice consciousness' is required, at pp.345–348, para.24; it appears that the position of the EU legislator is to allow flexibility in this regard.

958 Ibid., at p.347, para.24.

959 Ibid., at p.348, para.24. See also Recital 39 of the Succession Regulation: 'reference to a particular law of the deceased's nationality or specific provisions thereof'.

960 Ibid., at p.349, para.24.

961 Lagarde (Chapter 4, n.484), at pp.129–130, para.11.

962 In particular, the treatment of external factors (e.g. the place where the disposition was granted or the nationality of the notary) as evidence of demonstrable choice. See Viarengo / Marchetti (Chapter 3, n.313), at pp.63–64.

The Succession Regulation contains specific transitional rules in Article 83 that address the validity of a *professio juris* that has been made prior to this instrument entering into force (17 August 2015). In situations in which the person who has made the choice of law dies after the regulation entered into force, the designation may be found to be valid if it meets either the conditions established in Chapter III of the regulation (rules concerning applicable law) or those that were in place in the state which the deceased was habitually resident in, or held the nationality of, at the time the choice was made (Article 83(2)). Article 83(3) establishes a similar rule that applies to the formal and substantive validity of a disposition of property upon death that has been made prior to the regulation entering into force.[963]

Turning back to Article 83(2), it is observed that whilst this provision serves to protect the expectations of the deceased and his or her beneficiaries where a person has made a *professio juris* in respect of the law applicable to their situation at the time of designation,[964] this construction may also have the effect of giving credence to ill-founded or unreasonable beliefs concerning the legal conditions prior to 17 August 2015.[965] Indeed, Article 83(2) can be seen to permit choice on the basis of a fictitious set of circumstances by providing for the validity of a designation made according to the rules of the Succession Regulation prior to this instrument entering into force.[966]

Article 84(4) represents a step further in terms of legislative creativity in addressing the transitional period: where a disposition upon death has been made according to the rules of the law that the deceased could have chosen under the regulation (i.e. the law of his or her nationality), a presumption arises that this law will apply to the succession as a whole. This provision does not appear to focus upon giving force to an apparent choice of law (as is the case under Article 83(2)), but rather is a pragmatic solution that aims to reconcile the employment of nationality as the principal connecting factor in the private international law codes in a number of Member States with the application of habitual residence as a the default criterion in the absence of choice under Article 21 of the Succession Regulation.[967]

---

963 With the additional opportunity to align with the conditions 'in the Member State of the authority dealing with the succession'.

964 P. Franzina, 'Article 83: Transitional Provisions' in A. Calvo Caravaca et al. (eds.), *The EU Succession Regulation: A Commentary* (Cambridge University Press, Cambridge, 2016), at pp.857–858, para.10.

965 Viarengo / Marchetti (Chapter 3, n.313), at pp.60–61.

966 B. Reinhartz, 'Chapter VII: General and Final Provisions' in U. Bergquist et al. (eds.), *EU Regulation on Succession and Wills* (Otto Schmidt, Cologne, 2015), at p.306, para.4.

967 Thus aiming to cater for the expectations of the deceased and his or her beneficiaries with a view to estate planning and applying the law best suited to implementing the wishes of the deceased in this regard. See Franzina (n.964 above), at p.861, para.17 and Viarengo / Marchetti (Chapter 3, n.313), at pp.60–61.

9.4. MATERIAL OR SUBSTANTIVE VALIDITY

Having examined the formal validity requirements established for choice of court and choice of law agreements in the respective instruments, attention is now turned to the second variable upon enforcement to be discussed in this chapter: material validity (known in the Succession Regulation as 'substantive validity'). As has been previously stated, the fulfilment of formal requirements is the first step to signifying consensus between parties (or, in the case of succession, a reflection of the party's free will). This section delves further into the provisions that are designed to facilitate the fullness of the parties' consent, particularly examining the presence of safeguards relating to informed choice, and designed to combat elements such as coercion or fraud.[968] In line with the other sections in this chapter, this will begin with the choice of law context (9.4.1.), before proceeding on to consider the choice of law rules (9.4.2.).

9.4.1. CHOICE OF COURT

Linking back to the discussion of formal requirements in 9.3.1., it can be seen that the Property Regulations,[969] along with the Succession Regulation,[970] impose a duty for a choice of court agreement to be dated and signed by the parties. This, although it might seem like an insignificant requirement, arguably has the effect of drawing a party's attention to what they are consenting to. However, moving beyond this, in overview of the choice of court provisions established in the relevant instruments, it is apparent that only Article 8(2) of the Property Regulations imposes express material validity requirements, whereby the court has a duty to 'ensure that the defendant is informed of his right to contest the jurisdiction and of the consequences of entering or not entering an appearance.'

A few reasons can be proposed for the general dearth of regard for material validity in the choice of court provisions in the relevant EU instruments. Firstly, particularly in the presence of a parallel choice of law (evident in all subject areas that permit party autonomy in the jurisdictional context, bar parental responsibility), the impact of a choice of court upon the substantive outcome of a case is limited. Secondly, whilst it is crucial for parties to be informed as to the substantive content of their choice of law (discussed below), the objective of a choice of court is usually concrete[971] and self-explanatory.

---

968 See the requisite elements of free will discussed in 2.2.1.

969 9.3.1.2.

970 9.3.1.3.

971 With the exception of indeterminate choice exercised under Article 4 of the Maintenance Regulation.

In addition, with regard to a choice of court made in the contexts of succession and parental responsibility (as well as most instances that fall within the scope of Article 5 of the Property Regulations), a choice of court is made when a case is imminent and with an destination and function in mind (e.g. to unify the court with the applicable law, closely related subject matter or to a court which is has been identified as better placed to rule in the circumstances). The nature of such immediate and limited choices means that there is a much lower likelihood of coercion or other tactics being used by another party to elicit a certain outcome.

It ought to be emphasised that the failure to establish material requirements in the relevant instruments does not indicate a complete absence of material requirements. The Property Regulations[972] and the Succession Regulation[973] make it clear that, in general, issues of legal capacity are excluded from the scope of the instruments, and thus delegated to the Member States to determine. It has also been suggested that matters such as representation and the avoidance of an agreement might also be regulated on a national level.[974] Although the relevant instruments are silent on the manner in which the law that governs these aspects ought to be ascertained, it has been proposed that such matters ought to be governed by the law of the Member State whose court has been seised.[975] However, there is little guidance in the texts of the relevant instruments concerning Member State competence to deal with these elements relating to material validity; in order to cultivate clarity and a streamlined approach to such issues, it is suggested that further delineation is necessary.

Notwithstanding the above discussion, particular criticism can be levelled at the lack of additional material requirements or specification referred to in the Maintenance Regulation. This instrument not only concerns a relationship (creditor-debtor) which has a inbuilt imbalance of power, but Article 4 of this instrument also appears to allow a choice of court to be made prior to proceedings being anticipated. Reference to a specific need to be informed as to the nature of a choice,[976] or at least for an agreement to be additionally dated and signed in order to bring the parties' attention to the consequences of what they are consenting to would be particularly useful in this context.

---

972 See Article 1(2)(a) of the Property Regulations and Recital 20: 'Accordingly, this Regulation should not apply to questions of general legal capacity of the spouses [partners]; however, this exclusion should not cover the specific powers and rights of either or both spouses [partners] with regard to property, either as between themselves or as regards third parties, as these powers and rights should fall under the scope of this Regulation'.

973 See the exclusion in Article 1(2)(b) of the Succession Regulation: 'the legal capacity of natural persons, without prejudice to point (c) of Article 23(2) and to Article 26'.

974 See in the context of the Maintenance Regulation: Abendroth (Chapter 4, n.337), at p.464.

975 Ibid.

976 For instance, the consequences of making an indeterminate choice versus securing a specific connecting factor at the time of the choice of court agreement.

Furthermore, in view of the single instance of material requirements being imposed in a jurisdictional context, namely Article 8(2) of the Property Regulations, as well as a similar provision aimed at weaker parties under Brussels I,[977] it is particularly surprising that the opportunity to accept jurisdiction by entering an appearance according to Article 5 of the Maintenance Regulation does not include a similar safeguard. Furthermore exacerbating the concerns that arise from this omission is the fact that it appears that minors (or their representatives) are permitted to make use of this provision.[978] With a view to this context, it is arguable that as the formal requirements decrease, scrutiny of material validity ought to be raised.

On a closing note, it is important to highlight that the new Brussels IIa (Recast) Regulation[979] demonstrates a significant emphasis on ensuring that the agreement of the parties to a choice of court in matters of parental responsibility is an informed one. In addition to introducing more stringent formal requirements that draw the parties' attention to what they are agreeing to,[980] the renewed provision stresses the importance of free and informed choice, and mandates that the court ensures that parties who enter an appearance are informed of their right not to accept jurisdiction.[981] If this emphasis is maintained in the final draft of the new instrument, it would signify a shift in stance for jurisdictional matters that would hopefully set a higher legislative bar in this regard.

9.4.2. CHOICE OF LAW

In contrast to the discussion in the above subsection, the framework of material requirements established for a choice of law in this present setting is considerably more developed. In contrast to the rationale discussed for the lack of elaboration of material requirements in the jurisdictional context, it can be proposed that a choice of law requires a more in-depth understanding of the respective advantages and disadvantages of a particular designation. The outcome of a choice of law has a decisive influence on the case, meaning the negative effects of a lack of information or coercion would be particularly potent. Furthermore, the general possibility for a law to be selected in advance of proceedings taking place also perpetuates the need to be informed. The following subsections will scrutinise the framework of material (or substantive) validity conditions

977 See Article 26(2) of the Brussels I Regulation (Recast). See also discussion of the existence of this possibility in the context of Article 5 of the Maintenance Regulation in: Walker (Chapter 4, n.401), at p.67.

978 Walker (Chapter 2, n.164), at p.233.

979 See Article 10 of the Brussels IIa Regulation.

980 See 9.3.1.5. above.

981 See Recital 23 and Article 10(1)(b)(i) and (ii) of the Brussels IIa Regulation.

established in the context of the Rome III Regulations (9.4.2.1.), the Property Regulations (9.4.2.2.), the Hague Maintenance Protocol (9.4.2.3.) and the Succession Regulation (9.4.2.4.).

9.4.2.1. *The Rome III Regulation*

Beginning with the Rome III Regulation, which provides for a choice of law to be made in the realms of divorce and legal separation, the drafters expressly emphasise in Recitals 18 and 19 that judges ought to remain aware of the importance of 'informed consent' of both parties in exercising party autonomy, particularly with regard to the social and legal implications of this choice and ensuring the equal rights of the parties. This advice is laudable, particularly in view of the power (im)balances that might foreseeably exist within a marriage. However, the strength of the guidance contained in the recitals can be questioned, given that it does not offer concrete direction with regard to the manner in which judges should proceed with ensuring the established standards are ensured.[982]

With regard to the law that should govern the existence and material validity of an agreement on choice of law, Article 6 provides that this ought to be the law which would apply if the agreement or term were valid,[983] unless reliance is not deemed reasonable for the purposes of determining whether one of the parties did not consent, in which instance he or she may rely on the law of his or her habitual residence at the time the court was seised.[984] This provision emulates Rome I,[985] with the additional safeguarding exception designed to protect parties who may have been pressured into making a choice for a law whose foreign content they were not familiar with, or who may have exercised their consent on the basis of inadequate legal advice.[986]

9.4.2.2. *The Property Regulations*

In a similar manner to Rome III, the Property Regulations also impart an emphasis on informed consent in Recital 46 (Partnership Property Regulation) and Recital 47 (Matrimonial Property Regulation), although with less elaboration on its purpose compared to the preceding instrument. The general imposition of the chosen law as a determinant of material validity (alongside a safeguarding exception) is constructed in the same way as Article 6 of Rome III, under Article 24 of the Property Regulations.

---

982 Kruger (Chapter 1, n.60), at para.4.
983 Article 6(1).
984 Article 6(2).
985 See Article 10 of the Rome I Regulation.
986 Kruger (Chapter 1, n.60), at para.4.

9.4.2.3. *The Hague Maintenance Protocol*

The text of the Hague Maintenance Protocol is silent on the law that governs the material validity of a choice of law. However, the Explanatory Report states that, in line with other private international law instruments (including the relevant instruments discussed here),[987] this aspect will also be determined by the law designated by the parties.[988]

It should be noted that the Protocol does not include the safeguarding exception contained in Article 6(2) of Rome III and Article 24(2) of the Property Regulations, which permit additional flexibility in protecting weaker parties in the cross-border context. However, it instead imposes a much more extensive safety net in the form of Article 8(5). This provision establishes that, unless the parties were fully informed and aware of the consequences of their choice at the time of designation, the law shall not apply where its application would lead to manifestly unfair or unreasonable consequences for any of the parties. Although this provision is comparatively paternalistic, it appears appropriate for safeguarding the interests of the parties (particularly the creditor) in the face of particularly detrimental consequences as a result of an uninformed choice.[989]

In order to illustrate the instances in which Article 8(5) may be used, *Bonomi* employs the example in which the parties, at the time of designation, had a very weak link with the applicable law or one of the parties (especially the creditor) was not sufficiently informed concerning the consequences of the choice.[990] It is questionable, however, particularly with regard to the latter example, whether such instances would in themselves be classed as unfair or unreasonable in terms of *consequences*.[991] Beyond extremely meagre or absent provision of maintenance by the applicable law,[992] the situations in which Article 8(5) would be employed do indeed appear obscure, making it hard for parties to predict when an authority will use this criterion, and how it will be interpreted.

987 E.g. Article 10 of the 1978 Hague Convention on the Law Applicable to Matrimonial Property Regimes; Article 10(1) of the Hague Convention of 22 December 1986 on the Law Applicable to Contracts for the International Sale of Goods; Article 5(2) of the 1989 Hague Convention on the Law Applicable to Succession; Articles 3(4) and 8(1) of the Rome Convention of 19 June 1980 on the Law Applicable to Contractual Obligations; and Articles 3(5) and 10(1) of the Rome I Regulation. This approach also aligns with the general stance taken in Article 6(1) of Rome III and Article 24(1) of the Property Regulations.

988 Bonomi (Chapter 4, n.400), at para.151.

989 Župan (Chapter 4, n.397), at p.324.

990 Bonomi (Chapter 4, n.400), at p.357.

991 Failure to be sufficiently informed could rather be seen as an obstacle to consent, rather than necessarily indicative of an unfair outcome.

992 Unlikely to include the possibility of renunciation in the applicable law, since it is determined according to the law of the law of the habitual residence of the creditor at the time the agreement was made: see delineation of this matter in 4.5.1.

9.4.2.4. *The Succession Regulation*

The treatment of material validity (or, in this instance, 'substantive validity') of a *professio juris* is brief under the Succession Regulation, which states in Article 22(3) that, in line with the trend of the other relevant instruments, the governing law ought to be the chosen law. No additional guidance or safeguards are provided. This might arguably seem logical, since at the time the court is seised the person who chose the law is no longer around to contest their consent. It would, however, have been useful for the regulation to provide further elucidation for concerned parties (e.g. beneficiaries) with regard to disputing the authenticity of the deceased's autonomy.[993]

The rules concerning the law applicable to the admissibility and substantive validity of dispositions of property upon death are principally contained in Articles 24 and 25 of the Succession Regulation.[994] Parties can choose the law that applies to admissibility and substantive validity of such dispositions in accordance with the same conditions established in Article 22 of the regulation.[995] Article 26 clarifies the particular matters that shall pertain to substantive validity for the purposes of these aforementioned provisions; it can be assumed that this delineation also applies to the meaning of the substantive validity of a choice of law under Article 22(3).

A few observations can be made regarding the relationship between a *professio juris* expressed through Article 22, and the choice of the law that governs the substantive validity of dispositions according to Article 24(2) or 25(3) of the Succession Regulation. Firstly, whilst it is possible for a designation of applicable law to govern only the substantive validity of the disposition of property upon death rather than the succession as a whole, in the event that this is not specified in the choice of law clause contained in the disposition, it should be presumed that the designation applies to the entire succession.[996] Secondly, the validity of a choice of law clause in a disposition is to be treated as independent of the

993 Especially in light of the particular risk of coercion of elderly or vulnerable persons in organising their estates in the context of succession.

994 Article 25 governs 'Agreements as to succession' whilst Article 24 concerns 'Dispositions of property upon death other than agreements as to succession'. Whilst the former is defined as 'an agreement, including an agreement resulting from mutual wills, which, with or without consideration, creates, modifies or terminates rights to the future estate or estates of one or more persons party to the agreement' (see Article 3(1)(b)), the latter category addresses wills and joint wills (see Article 3(1)(d)). See also Article 83(3) of the Succession Regulation for the transitional provisions that apply to dispositions of property upon death made prior to the regulation entering into force on 17 August 2015 (see further discussion in 9.3.2.3.).

995 See Article 24(2) and Article 25(3) of the Succession Regulation.

996 See the assertion of this point in the context of dispositions that fall within the scope of Article 24: J. Rodrigo Rodríguez, 'Article 24: Dispositions of Property upon Death Other than Agreements as to Succession' in A. Calvo Caravaca et al. (eds.), *The EU Succession Regulation: A Commentary* (Cambridge University Press, Cambridge, 2016), at p.377, para.18.

validity of the document in which it is contained. Thus, for example, even if a will is adjudged to be void, the choice of law might nevertheless be viewed as valid.[997] Thirdly, where a couple have made mutual wills, the law of either of their nationalities can be chosen to govern the substantive validity according to Article 25(3). If the couple does not share a nationality, this construct might foreseeably lead to an inconvenient split between the law that governs the substantive validity of the disposition and that which applies to the rest of the succession.[998]

A brief comment to conclude with relates to the topic of evasion of the law through a *professio juris*. Recital 26 provides that that nothing in the regulation prevents Member State courts from applying mechanisms designed to tackle such practices. However, it has been argued that this guidance should be employed sparingly in order to safeguard the goals of predictability and stability with regard to the deceased's choice of law. The examples of acts that might merit a Member State taking action in the manner anticipated by Recital 26 are thus rare; for instance, a party who intentionally creates an artificial connection with another state in order to acquire nationality.[999]

9.5. SYNTHESIS

The preceding subsections have outlined the temporal, formal and material requirements that restrict a choice of court or choice of law within the EU private international law framework relating to family matters and succession. In line with this book's format, this synthesis considers the established elements in general (9.5.1.) and in conjunction with one another (9.5.2.), as well as gaps that have become apparent during this evaluation that require addressing (9.5.3.).

9.5.1. OVERVIEW OF THE FINDINGS

The following observations can be made in view of the evaluation that has been carried out in this chapter concerning the temporal, formal and material requirements for choice of court and choice of law designations:

1. The widest temporal limits, whereby a choice can be made in advance and apply indefinitely to forthcoming proceedings, are seen in the jurisdictional context under Article 4 of the Maintenance Regulation and Article 7 of the

997 Ibid., at p.376, para.16 and 'Article 25: Agreements as to succession', in Caravaca, ibid., at p.387, para.9.

998 Villata / Valcova (Chapter 6, n.602), at p.40.

999 Castellanos Ruiz (Chapter 1, n.48), at p.330, para.6.

Property Regulations, and under all the instruments that concern applicable law with the exception of Article 7 of the Hague Maintenance Protocol. Whilst this arguably allows parties to heighten legal certainty through forward planning, a number of caveats apply to this (see subsequent points).

2. Although designating a concrete choice of court that continues indefinitely permits a high degree of predictability regarding the forum that will govern proceedings, the possibility has come under criticism in this chapter. Most prominently, there is a tangible risk that the forum that ultimately decides on proceedings becomes unsuitable over time. Moreover, it is arguable that the parties cannot make a fully informed choice due to the propensity for circumstances to shift.

   This argumentation is particularly potent in view of Article 4 of the Maintenance Regulation: this is an area in which access to justice is particularly crucial, and the potential problems discussed above might be particularly detrimental to a creditor. Drawing on the opinion of Walker,[1000] it can be proposed that at least in the area of maintenance, the temporal limits should be brought forward to the time at which the proceedings are pending in order to safeguard the suitability of the connection (in a similar manner to prorogation under Article 12).

3. The remaining (primarily jurisdictional) provisions focus upon particular proceedings, and are thus tied to the point at which this relevant event occurs. The one exception to this is found under Article 5 of the Property Regulations, whereby it would appear that an agreement to link jurisdiction might be made prior to proceedings concerning the dissolution of the marriage or partnership being instigated. However, the utility of such an agreement would be extremely limited in view of its lack of legal certainty and opportunity to consider the merits of the forum to the particular proceedings.

4. Turning to the choice of law context, as mentioned above, the temporal limits are generally wide, which gives parties the ability to capture a law of close affinity that they can employ in proceedings as they move around the Union. Although similar criticism to that discussed above with regard to jurisdictional choice can be levelled in the present scenario, this has to be balanced against the tangible benefits in terms of legal certainty of capturing an applicable law at a particular moment in time. It is only in the realm of maintenance obligations that the disadvantages of advanced choice appear to outweigh its purported advantages.

5. The possibility for an indeterminate choice in favour of an unsubstantiated connecting factor appears to be possible (or at least is not expressly excluded[1001]) under Article 5(1)(d) of Rome III, Article 4 of the Maintenance

1000 Walker (Chapter 2, n.164), at p.250.

1001 It is not made altogether clear whether this possibility is permitted under Rome III, the Maintenance Regulation and the Property Regulations: see 9.5.3. 'Gaps to be addressed'.

Regulation, Articles 5 and 7 of the Property Regulations and Article 22 of the Succession Regulation. Although this might invite a greater opportunity for forward planning (and thus an ability to secure a residual element of predictability), this possibility gives rise to similar concerns to those discussed with regard to wide temporal limits, whereby the designation of the law or forum is not made on the basis of adequate information regarding the content of the specific choice, and might ultimately prove to be unsuitable for the parties.

6. The highest standards in formal requirements, whereby a choice of court or choice of law must be made in writing (or otherwise expressed electronically), dated and signed by the parties involved in the exercise of autonomy, are demonstrated under Article 7 of Rome III, Articles 7(2) and 23 of the Property Regulations and Article 5(2) of the Succession Regulation.[1002] Although such requirements might seem like simply another hoop for parties to jump through, the additional requirement to date and sign a designation arguably brings a party's attention to what they are consenting to, which also represents evidence of material validity.

   It can furthermore be highlighted that Article 7 of Rome III and Article 23 of the Property Regulations set out a framework of prescribed rules concerning the recognition of differences in evidential requirements between Member States, and ensure a higher level of clarity and predictability as to the requirements of formal admissibility of a choice of law made according to these instruments.

   In view of the discussed benefits of adhering to a high standard of formal validity, it is disappointing that the Maintenance Regulation only requires that an agreement is in writing or expressed electronically in an equivalent form. Especially in view of the power imbalances that are inherent in this area, such additional safeguards are sorely lacking.

7. Certain subject areas, such as the transfer of jurisdiction through judicial discretion or the acceptance of jurisdiction by entering an appearance, clearly, by their immediate nature, do not invite the imposition of stringent formal requirements. It can also be seen that no baseline standard is provided for a choice of law under Article 22 of the Succession Regulation.[1003] Formal validity is delegated to national rules through Article 27, which can be viewed as reflective of the intertwining of the *professio juris* and dispositions of property upon death, and the need to respect national rules on the formal validity of such dispositions.

1002 Agreements under Articles 7(2) and 8 of the Hague Maintenance Protocol have to be signed but not dated.

1003 Although from the exclusion of oral declarations in Article 1(2)(f) of the Succession Regulation, it would appear that a choice of law must at least be made in written form.

8. A vast gulf emerges between choice of court and choice of law agreements in terms of the material (or substantive) requirements that apply to the respective rules. Whilst the regulations generally (with the exception of Article 8(2) of the Property Regulations and the improvements brought about in Article 10 of the new Brussels IIa (Recast) Regulation) impose no such requirements upon party autonomy in the jurisdictional context, there is considerable regard for material validity under the choice of law provisions.

   Although it might be stated that a choice of court does not present the same risk in terms of the negative substantive consequences that flow from an uninformed or coerced choice, it can be argued that the present dearth of material requirements does not adequately serve, in particular, the sensitive realm of maintenance obligations. This is particularly exemplified under Article 5 of the Maintenance Regulation in which the court currently has no duty to inform the defendant of the right to contest jurisdiction, or of the consequences of submission. The critique levelled against this dearth in material requisites is all the more potent in view of the possibility for minors or their representatives to accept jurisdiction by using this mechanism.

9. It has been highlighted at the start of this book (Chapter 2) that the need for parties to be sufficiently informed regarding the content and consequences of their choices is a prerequisite for the full expression of free will. It was argued that the intricacies of this subject area mean that parties ought to consult (preferably specialist) independent legal advice concerning their choice of court or choice of law. Whilst there is degree of rhetoric within the relevant instruments on the importance of informed choice, as well as certain provisions aimed at tackling situations in which this element may have been compromised, it is striking that there is no established requirement within the relevant instruments for the parties to seek impartial advice before making an agreement or designation. In view of the general propensity for a power imbalance to arise in close personal relationships, as well as the specifically disadvantaged position of parties such as the maintenance creditor, it is argued that the establishment of an EU standard in this regard is imperative.

10. In overview of the relevant provisions in the present context, it can be observed that there are crucial areas in which the EU legislator has failed to express its intentions in sufficiently clear terms, thus impacting upon legal certainty. This topic will be revisited in greater detail in the following subsection that considers 'Gaps to be addressed' (9.5.3.); however, it can be stated that this lack of clarity is particularly patent with regard to the temporal end point at which a choice terminates and the lack of guidance as to the manner in which the Member State courts are to fulfil certain objectives (e.g. ensuring informed consent).

On the other hand, it ought also to be highlighted that the CJEU has improved the clarity of Article 12 of Brussels II bis in recent judgments, establishing its purpose as a mechanism that should only be used on a case-by-case basis, and that acceptance by the parties may be expressed after the court has been seised, in the initial stages of the proceedings. Furthermore, the Court has contributed (albeit in a specific, piecemeal manner) to the developing meaning of 'unequivocal acceptance' in the context of Article 12.

9.5.2. INTERPLAY BETWEEN RELATED AREAS

The overview of cohesion and the opportunity for coordination within the framework of temporal, formal and material restrictions provides significant scope for consideration within the context of this evaluation:

1. Starting with the temporal limits of choice with a view to securing 'vertical cohesion', it can be seen that the Property Regulations present cohesion with regard to temporal requirements, since a choice of law can be made in advance under Article 22 of the instruments, and this can be secured as a determinant of jurisdiction for forthcoming proceedings under Article 7. In the context of the Partnership Property Regulation, the parties can additionally designate in advance the Member State where their partnership was created as the choice of court and applicable law. In a similar manner to the realm of maintenance obligations, such choice continues in perpetuity. Since this scenario sees the court being linked to a determined applicable law or the place of creation (an event that has already occurred), the issue of an indeterminate choice of court does not arise in this instance. A caveat that must be mentioned with regard to the Property Regulations is that, due to the unsubstantiated nature of linkage under Article 5, vertical coordination is not possible in advance for situations that fall within the scope of this provision.
2. It is also apparent that cohesion is achieved between the respective connecting factors in Article 4 of the Maintenance Regulation and Article 8 of the Hague Maintenance Protocol, due to the fact that the law and court can be chosen in advance and coordinated where these factors coincide (habitual residence and nationality of the parties, and the law and court which govern the spouses' divorce or legal separation). Choice of court and choice of law agreements made according to these provisions continue in perpetuity for future proceedings.

   The strength of this cohesion in the above scenario is moderated by the fact that an undetermined choice of law is expressly not permitted under the Hague Maintenance Protocol, but might be a possibility under the Maintenance Regulation. In order to ensure coordination, the parties would have to opt for a definitive choice under both instruments. As discussed in the previous subsection[1004] this would, in any case, be the situation in which the interests of the parties are best served in this realm.

3. The remaining subject areas do not, by their nature, elicit a possibility for coordination in this regard. For instance, under the Succession Regulation, a choice of court is undertaken by the parties concerned only after the death of the person who made the *professio juris*. Furthermore, the immediate nature of subsidiary party autonomy provisions means that temporal coordination is not a possibility within and between subject areas.
4. There is an opportunity for temporal cohesion to be achieved between the jurisdictional party autonomy rules contained in Article 7 of the Property Regulations and Article 4 of the Maintenance Regulation. A union between the competent courts can be secured if the parties opt to link jurisdiction under the former instrument with the law designated according to Article 22 of the same instrument. Through this, the court of either of the parties' habitual residence or nationality can be harnessed and coordinated with the same choice selected under the Maintenance Regulation.[1005] This coordination can be secured indefinitely.
5. Temporal coordination can also be secured in the choice of law setting for related proceedings arising from the dissolution of a marriage. Under Article 5 of Rome III, Article 22 of the Matrimonial Property Regulation and Article 8 of the Hague Maintenance Protocol, an advance designation can be made in favour of the law of the common habitual residence of the parties, their last common habitual residence, or one of their nationalities. In addition, under the Hague Maintenance Protocol, the law can be directly linked to a choice of law under the Property Regulations or Rome III.[1006] The possibilities for linkage discussed above can continue in perpetuity.

One point to note is that where a choice of law has been made by future spouses under Article 22 of the Matrimonial Property Regulation, and the connection subsequently changes after marriage (e.g. the couple moves to another state), this agreement will have to be amended to achieve coordination with Rome III and the Hague Maintenance Protocol.[1007] Although the Hague Maintenance Protocol has a wider personal scope, it is not stated whether the relationship between future spouses falls within the scope of this instrument for the purposes of making a choice of law.

1004 See 9.5.1.

1005 With the caveat that it arguably does not appear that a choice of court can be selected by future spouses or partners under the Maintenance Regulation, whilst a choice of law *can* be made prior to the marriage or registered partnership under Article 22 of the Property Regulations.

1006 Thus providing another route to linking choice of law agreements: see Article 8(1)(c) and (d) of the Hague Maintenance Protocol.

1007 Viarengo (n.883 above), at pp.549–550, para.3.1.1.

The reference to 'creditor' and 'debtor' would indicate that a prenuptial designation would, in any case, appear to be inappropriate.

Where only the Property Regulations and Hague Maintenance Protocol are coordinated (as would be the case for registered partnership), the habitual residence or nationality of either party can be secured in advance of proceedings taking place and continue indefinitely. As discussed above, Article 8(1)(c) of the Hague Maintenance Protocol can also be used to link directly to a choice of law agreement made under Article 22 of the Property Regulations.

6. The law that applies under Article 22 of the Property Regulations can be coordinated temporally with a *professio juris* under Article 22 of the Succession Regulation if the party designates the law of their nationality at the time of agreement. The same level of legal certainty cannot be secured if, under Article 22 of the Succession Regulation, the party stipulates that the law will be that of their nationality at the time of death. However, this is mitigated by the fact that this criterion is not one that is readily altered during the course of time.
7. With regard to the cohesion of formal requirements within subject areas, it can be seen that the Property Regulations impose the same high standard for choices made according to Articles 7(2) and 22, whereby the agreement must be in writing, signed and dated by the parties. In contrast, Article 4(2) of the Maintenance Regulation and Articles 7(2) and 8(2) of the Hague Maintenance Protocol do not align: the former only requires that the agreement be writing, whilst the latter adheres to the same standards as the Property Regulations (with the exception that the document does not have to be dated). However, the consequences of coordination or the lack thereof do not appear to be considerable: in the latter scenario, if the parties wished to include the choice of court and choice of law in the same document, they would simply have to remember to adhere to the higher formal standard set out in the Protocol, which appears to be a relatively minor step.
8. Turning to examine the formal requirements that exist between related subject areas, it is observed in the choice of law context that Article 7 of Rome III and Article 23 of the Matrimonial Property Regulation adhere to the same prescribed approach with regard to formal requirements alongside a framework for the imposition of additional requirements. This arguably enhances convenience by allowing a joint choice to be made in the same marriage contract.[1008]

   There are inconsistencies in the formal requirements imposed for a choice of court under Article 7(2) of the Property Regulations and Article 4(2)

[1008] See criticism of inconsistency in this regard between the 2011 Proposal for the Matrimonial Property Regulation and Rome III in: Gray / Quinzá Redondo (Chapter 3, n.320), at para.4.2.3.

of the Maintenance Regulation and, and to a lesser extent, Article 7(2) and 8(2) of the Hague Maintenance Protocol. However, it is hard to substantiate the impact of such differences beyond simplicity for legal practitioners in the drafting process, since parties do not necessarily benefit from these choices being made under the same document.

Subsidiary party autonomy provisions are again distinguished by their immediate nature, with the respective formal requirements being distinct, minimal or non-existent depending on the mechanism in question. Coordination within and between the formal requirements that apply to the various subject areas is thus not relevant in this context.

9. It is difficult to ascertain the impact of differing material (or substantive) requirements between and within subject areas. The biggest divergence is demonstrated between choice of court and choice of law provisions, for instance Article 7(2) and Article 22 of the Property Regulations. This might simply equate to the circumstances surrounding a choice of law being placed under increased scrutiny in comparison with the choice of court. It can, however, be speculated that coordination between a court and an applicable law might be frustrated in certain situations in which a choice of law is side-stepped on the basis of more stringent material requirements.[1009]

9.5.3. GAPS TO BE ADDRESSED

The final step in this chapter highlights the points for improvement that are proposed in view of the evaluation of the temporal, formal and material requirements that apply to a choice of court or a choice of law within the present setting:

1. This evaluation has demonstrated that there is a striking lack of clarity in the delineation of the aforementioned requirements within the relevant instruments. Firstly, this has been exemplified prominently with regard to the temporal end point of jurisdiction, whereby it is not made clear whether competence extends beyond the original proceedings of which a court was seised under the jurisdictional rules in Succession Regulation or the mechanisms that permit acceptance of jurisdiction by entering an appearance.[1010]
2. Another matter that requires resolution relates to whether a choice can be made in favour of an undetermined connecting factor under Article 5

1009 E.g. under Article 8(5) of the Hague Maintenance Protocol.

1010 See Article 5 of the Maintenance Regulation, Article 8 of the Property Regulations and Article 9 of the Succession Regulation.

of the Property Regulations, Article 4 of the Maintenance Regulation or Article 5(1)(d) of Rome III.[1011] Although the aforementioned instruments do not appear to exclude this application, it is suggested here that to allow such an interpretation impacts significantly on the fullness of the parties' consent, since they may not be able to easily ascertain in advance the ground for selection of law to which they are agreeing.

3. The CJEU has begun to clarify the obscure meaning of 'unequivocal acceptance' that is required under Article 12 of Brussels II bis. However, its rulings have so far only given piecemeal definition to this term; it would be helpful to ensuring uniformity of interpretation by Member State courts if a more comprehensive definition were to be provided. Notwithstanding this, it can be observed that the most recent version of the revision of Brussels II bis removes reference to this standard and instead focuses on formal requirements.
4. Although the accommodation of an implicit choice of law is seen as a necessary inclusion in view of the specific nature of the subject area covered by the Succession Regulation, it is suggested that further guidance be provided on the outer limits of demonstrable choice in order to aid in the interpretation of dispositions.[1012]
5. In addition to clarification, it is also suggested that the baseline standards for formal requirements should be streamlined, necessitating that choice of court and choice of law designations within the relevant framework should generally require that consent be expressed in writing (or in a durable electronic form), dated and signed. This requisite serves to draw the parties' attention to what they are agreeing to, which in turn contributes to material validity.

   By way of exception, such formal requirements are not necessarily appropriate with regard to the specific nature of prorogation under Article 12 of Brussels II,[1013] as well as the other *forum non conveniens* mechanisms and provisions that permit acceptance to be demonstrated by entering an appearance.
6. In view of the comparative lack of material or substantive requirements imposed upon choice of court agreements within the present framework, it is proposed that the EU legislator should reconsider its position, particularly in the context of the Maintenance Regulation. It has been suggested that the drafters might take Article 25(1) of the Brussels I Recast or Article 10 of the new Brussels IIa (Recast) Regulation as an example of a regard for material requirements in the jurisdictional context.[1014]

1011 In favour of the *lex fori*.

1012 Viarengo / Marchetti (Chapter 3, n.313), at pp.63–64.

1013 Although the new Brussels IIa Regulation nevertheless sets out a more prescribed level of formality for choice of court agreement in matters of parental responsibility: see Article 10(2) of this instrument.

1014 Viarengo / Marchetti (Chapter 3, n.313), at p.31, fn.61.

7. In comparison to the other choice of law provisions within the present framework, there is a comparative absence of regard for material validity in the context of a *professio juris* under Article 22 of the Succession Regulation. Although the choice of law is admittedly limited, there might arise circumstances in which a party is coerced into choosing a law to the advantage of a beneficiary to the will. In light of this, it is suggested that further emphasis or guidance is provided in the text concerning a situation in which the autonomy of the deceased appears to have been compromised.
8. It has been highlighted during the course of this evaluation that constructions of party autonomy rules do not appear to impose sufficient safeguards in the realm of maintenance obligations. In contrast to Article 8 of the Property Regulations, Article 5 does not contain any duty upon the court to inform the defendant of their rights upon entering an appearance to accept jurisdiction, or of the consequences that flow from this. In order to protect weaker parties (in particular, children[1015]), it is argued that similar safeguards are put in place in order to facilitate the fullness of their consent.
9. Despite the rhetoric contained in the Rome III Regulation and the Property Regulations that places a strong emphasis on the need to ensure that spouses or partners demonstrate informed consent, the manner in which this is to be ensured is not elaborated upon in the respective texts. The establishment of an EU-level standard that explicitly requires parties to consult with an independent legal professional before making a designation would be an appropriate safeguard in view of the general and specific power imbalances that may foreseeably arise in the interpersonal nature of this realm.
10. As a closing remark, it is useful to mention the soon-to-be-published EU-funded project that is focused upon producing model choice of court and choice of law agreements for those in cross-border family relationships (e.g. married couples and registered partners) in the European Union. The templates, which are primarily intended for usage by legal professionals, represent a high standard in formal requirements and are aimed at allowing parties to coordinate the laws and/or courts that govern related proceedings. The agreements also contain a detailed checklist for practitioners that aims to address the need for parties to be sufficiently informed regarding the content and consequences of their choices.[1016] The dissemination of these model agreements for usage on a Member State level would go some way in tackling a number of the problem areas relating to formal and material requirements that have been highlighted in this synthesis.

[1015] See further discussion on the inclusion of these parties at 4.5.2.2. and 8.3.2.

[1016] See for instance: Utrecht University / University of Vienna (Chapter 3, n.323).

CHAPTER 10
ENFORCEMENT OF CHOICE

10.1. INTRODUCTION

At the ultimate stage of this evaluation into the EU's private international law rules on family matters and succession, this final substantive chapter seeks to address the factors that influence the enforcement of choice: the diverse range of variables that affect a choice of court and/or choice of law made according to the relevant instruments.

The influences that will be discussed in this chapter fall into a broad range of categories: the variables that impact upon the success of a designation of a competent court (exclusivity of jurisdiction and the *lis pendens* rule – 10.2.); the variance of the applicable law through overriding mandatory provisions (10.3.), public policy (10.4.), and the application of substantive provisions from the relevant instruments (10.5); and finally, the impact of fragmentation upon the recognition of agreements, both in terms of the Member States' approach towards the growing number of parties in 'non-traditional' relationships (10.6.) and the patchwork participation of Member States in certain of the instruments in this present framework (10.7). In the same manner as the preceding chapters in this evaluation, there will be a concluding synthesis (10.8) that establishes an overview of the findings identified in the respective sections, an examination of the interplay between the respective provisions within this context and a presentation of the author's suggested improvements that have emerged as a result of this evaluation.

10.2. EXCLUSIVITY OF JURISDICTION AND *LIS PENDENS*

The first topic to be dealt with in this exploration of the variables that impact upon the enforcement of choice in the EU private international law framework relating to family matters and succession centres on jurisdictional context. This section firstly examines the exclusive nature of jurisdiction (and the exceptions thereof) established by the choice of court provisions in the relevant instruments (10.2.1.), before considering the impact of the *lis pendens* rule on this present context (10.2.2.)

10.2.1. EXCLUSIVITY OF JURISDICTION

Both the Property Regulations and the Succession Regulation stipulate that a choice of court is to be considered exclusive in nature.[1017] The matter of exclusive jurisdiction is not mentioned with regard to a choice of court for matters of parental responsibility under Article 12 of Brussels II bis, but this omission is of less relevance, given the immediate nature of the prorogation under these mechanisms.[1018]

The exception to this trend towards exclusivity is found in the Maintenance Regulation, which states in Article 4(1) that the selected jurisdiction shall be considered to be exclusive unless agreed otherwise. Provided the wording of an agreement is sufficiently clear in this regard,[1019] parties may choose to designate the court(s) of multiple Member States,[1020] create an asymmetrical jurisdictional agreement,[1021] exclude certain courts(s),[1022] or indicate that a particular choice of court is simply non-exclusive (thus meaning another Member State court may also be seised under Article 3).[1023] In addition, agreements may be used to designate local or international jurisdiction.[1024]

The reason for this increased level of flexibility (at the inevitable expense of predictability) can be found in the acute need for access to justice experienced by the creditor in maintenance proceedings. For instance, by making a non-exclusive choice of court agreement in advance, that stipulates the court that has jurisdiction to pronounce a divorce,[1025] the creditor spouse can benefit

---

1017 See Article 7(1) of the Property Regulations. Agreements under Article 5 of these instruments (linking jurisdiction in cases of the dissolution of the relationship) must comply with the same conditions as Article 7 if made in advance of dissolution proceedings taking place; thus it is presumed that a choice of court will also be exclusive in such an instance. See also Article 5(1) of the Succession Regulation.

1018 Nevertheless, Article 10(4) of the new Brussels IIa Regulation has inserted a stipulation that jurisdiction for matters of parental responsibility determined according to Article 10(1)(b)(ii) – namely that which is accepted during the course of proceedings – is to be considered exclusive in nature.

1019 P. Vlas, '4. Exclusieve bevoegdheid bij: Verordening (EG) nr. 4/2009 betreffende de bevoegdheid, het toepasselijke recht, de erkenning en de tenuitvoerlegging van beslissingen, en de samenwerking op het gebied van onderhoudsverplichtingen, Artikel 4 Forumkeuze', *Groene Serie Burgerlijke Rechtsvordering* (Wolters Kluwer, 2011).

1020 For example, an agreement could state that the courts of the Member State of either the habitual residence of the creditor or that of the defendant are competent. Alternatively, it could simply not be specified in whose habitual residence competence lies with: S. Verburgt, 'Bevoegdheid, Erkenning en Tenuitvoerlegging onder Alimentatieverordening 4/2009' (2012) 7 *Tijdschrift voor Relatierecht en Praktijk* 296, at p.300.

1021 Whereby one party is limited to an exclusive designation whilst the other party (presumably the one in the financially weaker position) is permitted to choose from a wider range of fori. See Villata / Valcova (Chapter 6, n.602), at p.18.

1022 Abendroth (Chapter 4, n.337), at p.469.

1023 Vlas (n.1019 above).

1024 Abendroth (Chapter 4, n.337), at p.469.

1025 See Article 4(1)(c)(i) of the Maintenance Regulation.

from an additional potential head of jurisdiction to choose from. Moreover, it can be employed in order to mitigate the effects of a choice of court that becomes inconvenient with the passage of time. Furthermore, bearing in mind that proceedings concerning maintenance often centre on a unilateral claim to obtain maintenance by the creditor against the debtor, the potential availability of additional jurisdictions is unlikely to give rise to a 'rush to court' in the same manner as it would in the other areas of law surveyed here.

10.2.2. *LIS PENDENS*

Emerging in order to address situations in which proceedings involving the same cause of action and the same parties are brought before courts of different Member States, the *lis pendens* rule denotes that any court other than the court first seised should stay its proceedings until such time as the jurisdiction of the court first seised has been established. The objective of this rule is to prevent contending proceedings taking place and to avert the concomitant possibility of irreconcilable judgments being pronounced on the same issue.[1026] This principle is to be found in all the relevant EU instruments,[1027] and applies even where an exclusive choice of court agreement has been made.[1028]

In the context of cross-border patent litigation in the EU, an infamous form of abuse of the *lis pendens* rule has emerged, known as a 'torpedo actions', whereby the apparent infringer pre-emptively seises the courts of a certain jurisdiction (usually Italian) in order to deliberately cause harmful delays in hearing the case whilst the court first seised determines its jurisdiction.[1029] Use of this technique foreseeably causes negative outcomes to parties by impeding access to justice and frustrating their expectations. The recast of the Brussels I Regulation has sought to address the detrimental impact of this tactic in situations where a prior choice of court agreement has been made. As an exception to the general *lis pendens* rule, Article 31(2) states that any Member State court other than that which has exclusive jurisdiction according to a choice of court agreement shall

1026 Recital 42 of the Matrimonial Property Regulation, Recital 41 of the Partnership Property Regulation and Recitals 33–34 of the Succession Regulation. See also Recital 21 of the Brussels I Recast.

1027 See Article 19 of the Brussels II bis Regulation, Article 12 of the Maintenance Regulation, Article 17 of the Property Regulations and Article 17 of the Succession Regulation.

1028 See Case C-116/02 *Erich Gasser GmbH v. MISAT Srl.* Reference for a preliminary ruling: Oberlandesgericht Innsbruck – Austria [2003] ECR 1-14693 (which concerned *lis pendens* where a choice of court clause had been agreed under Article 17 of the Brussels Convention) at paras.41–54.

1029 Van Calster (Chapter 2, n.167), at p.8, para.1.5: 'justice delayed is justice denied' and p.50, para.2.2.2.10. and Carruthers (Chapter 2, n.168), at p.910.

stay proceedings until the court seised on the basis of this agreement declares that it has no jurisdiction under the agreement.

Until recently, no analogous provision was included in the relevant family and succession law instruments. Such inclusion might arguably seem unnecessary, since even though torpedo actions could theoretically be used by a debtor in order to sink or hinder maintenance claims, the low-key, interpersonal nature of this area makes such orchestrated abuse of this rule unlikely.[1030] In the other areas of addressed in this chapter, use of this tactic is even less likely, given that the parties have a more equal interest in proceedings being heard, meaning that the delays brought about through this tactic would also harm the perpetrator.

On the other hand, it is conceivable that the *lis pendens* rule might well come into play where a non-exclusive agreement has been concluded between parties pursuant to Article 4(1) of the Maintenance Regulation. More generally, it is conceivable that the *lis pendens* rule might be invoked in situations in which a party who no longer wishes to be bound by a prior choice of court agreement seises a court other than that which is designated in it. In the event that this agreement provided for exclusive jurisdiction, a similar provision to Article 31(2) of the Brussels I Recast would be useful in preventing costly and inconvenient delays whilst the court first seised ascertains its competence.

On a closing note, it should be mentioned that the situation in this realm changed last year (2019) with Article 20(4) and (5) of the new Brussels IIa (Recast) Regulation introducing the assignment of priority to an exclusive jurisdiction designated by a choice of court, in a similar format to that demonstrated in Article 31(2) of the Brussels I Regulation. It should, however, be noted that this does not appear to apply to choice of court agreements entered into before the court is seised of proceedings, since such agreements are seemingly not considered to be exclusive according to Article 10(1)(b)(ii).

10.3. OVERRIDING MANDATORY PROVISIONS

Moving away from jurisdictional matters to consider applicable law, this section begins with the observation that the application of foreign law has the propensity to give rise to a confrontation between state sovereignty and the parties' interest in the application of a law with which they have an affinity. In this regard, it should be recalled that party autonomy is not absolute; although it is guided by the free will of individuals, Member States are permitted to protect their national interests where necessary.[1031]

1030 According to Abendroth (Chapter 4, n.337), at pp.469–470, the torpedo action is generally unknown in maintenance disputes.

1031 Carruthers (Chapter 2, n.168), at p.908.

The first category of safeguards[1032] involves the possibility to apply 'overriding mandatory provisions' (or *lois de police*) over the chosen law. By their imperative nature (designed to protect political, social or economic interests in the state in question[1033]), such rules take precedence over the applicable law with regard to the subject matter that comes within its scope. Overriding mandatory rules apply *irrespective* of the law that applies, thus distinguishing such provisions from internal mandatory rules which can be contracted out of through making a choice in favour of another applicable law.[1034] In contrast to public policy (see 10.4. below), overriding mandatory provisions are active in their imposition, applying directly to any situation falling within the scope of an instrument's subject matter.[1035]

In terms of the framework, it can be seen that the presence of overriding mandatory provisions is limited to instruments that involve the distribution of property, namely the Property Regulations (10.3.1.) and the Succession Regulation (10.3.2).

10.3.1. ARTICLE 30 OF THE PROPERTY REGULATIONS

The Property Regulations are the only relevant instruments that include a general provision permitting the use of overriding mandatory provisions by the forum. Article 30 of the Property Regulations emulates Article 9(1) and (2) of the Rome I Regulation[1036] by firstly establishing the precedence of overriding provisions over the rules of the regulation ('Nothing in this Regulation shall restrict the application of the overriding mandatory provisions of the law of the forum'), before defining these rules as those that are considered 'crucial by a Member State for safeguarding its public interests, such as its political, social or economic organisation'.

1032 The second category being 'public policy': see 10.4.

1033 See definition provided in Cases C-369/96 *Criminal proceedings against Jean-Claude Arblade and Arblade & Fils SARL* and C-376/96 *Bernard Leloup, Serge Leloup and Sofrage SARL*. References for a preliminary ruling: Tribunal correctionnel de Huy – Belgium [1999] ECR I-8453, at para.30. That definition provided a model for Article 9(1) of the Rome I Regulation. See also Proposal for a regulation on the law applicable to contractual obligations (Rome I), COM(2005) 650 final, at pp.8–9.

1034 M. Pauknerová, 'Mandatory Rules and Public Policy in International Contract Law' (2010) 11(1) *ERA Forum* 30, at pp.30–31, para.1.2. and W. Grajdura, 'Mandatory Rules and Public Policy', *ERA Conference on Rome I & Rome II Applicable Law in International Contracts and Torts* (Krakow, Poland, 3–4 November 2016), at pp.2–3. See also the extended definition of overriding mandatory provisions in the context of the Rome I Regulation by A. Bonomi, 'Overriding Mandatory Provisions in the Rome I Regulation on the Law Applicable to Contracts' (2008) 10 *Yearbook of Private International Law* 285, at pp.287–295, para.2.

1035 Grajdura (n.1034 above), at pp.3–4.

1036 Providing the same content, albeit in an inverted format. There is a similar, but much less elaborate provision in Article 16 of the Rome II Regulation.

In the context of property relations, the recitals of both regulations identify provisions concerning the protection of the family home as a principal example of an overriding mandatory provision in this setting.[1037] In an Interinstitutional File submitted to the Council of the European Union during the drafting of the Property Regulations,[1038] the Swedish delegation identified several overriding mandatory provisions in its national law which fell within the regulations' scope: namely, limitation on a spouse's ability to control his or her own property;[1039] the right to take over property in the event of its division;[1040] the adjustment of the division of property;[1041] and a minimum amount of inheritance for a surviving spouse.[1042] From the second and third examples listed above, it can be observed that there might also be a regard for the social purpose of meeting the needs of the less financially-secure spouse or partner in this context.

In line with the CJEU's judgment in *Arblade*[1043] and the stance of the Rome I Regulation,[1044] it is emphasised in the recitals of the Property Regulation that the usage of overriding mandatory rules as an exception to the generally applicable law is to be *strictly interpreted* in order to secure the objectives of the

---

1037 See Recital 52 of the Partnership Property Regulation and Recital 53 of the Matrimonial Property Regulation.

1038 Council of the European Union, Interinstitutional File of the 18 January 2013: *Proposal for a Council Regulation on jurisdiction, applicable law and the recognition and enforcement of decisions in matters of matrimonial property regimes. Proposal for a Council Regulation on jurisdiction, applicable law and the recognition and enforcement of decisions regarding the property consequences of registered partnerships – Comments from the Swedish delegation on overriding mandatory provisions*, 16188/12 JUSTCIV 333.

1039 Ibid., at p.3, para.1: 'One spouse may not, without the consent of the other spouse, sell, give away, mortgage or rent out the spouses' joint dwelling and household goods, even if the first-mentioned spouse is the sole owner of the property'.

1040 Ibid., at pp.3–4, para.2: (subject to certain caveats) 'In the event of a division of property, the spouses' joint dwelling and household goods should be allocated to the spouse who has the greatest need of the property, provided this is deemed reasonable having regard to the circumstances generally'.

1041 Ibid, at p.4, para.3: 'In the event of a division of property, the spouses' joint dwelling and household goods should be allocated to the spouse who has the greatest need of the property, provided this is deemed reasonable having regard to the circumstances generally'; 'If the division of property is conducted as a result of the death of one of the spouses, the surviving spouse may decide that the division of property should be conducted so that each party retains her or his own property'; and 'a general provision of the Swedish Marriage Code states that an unreasonable condition in a marital property agreement may be adjusted or not considered'.

1042 Ibid., at p.5, para.4: by the base amount rule, 'after the division of marital property and the distribution of the estate, [the surviving spouse] should always receive at least four base amounts (176 000 SEK in 2012)'.

1043 See emphasis on the exceptional nature of overriding mandatory provisions and the need to protect the exercise of community freedoms in this context in *Arblade* and *Sofrage* (n.1033 above), at para.31.

1044 See also the requirement in Recital 37 of the Rome I Regulation that overriding mandatory provisions are only to be applied in 'exceptional circumstances'.

regulation.[1045] States are thus urged to consider the aims behind facilitating the free movement of persons (most notably legal certainty[1046]) in making use of Article 30. This threat to legal certainty is particularly pertinent in the choice of law context, whereby the parties have sought to secure a certain set of rules that will apply to proceedings concerning their property relations.

10.3.2. ARTICLE 30 OF THE SUCCESSION REGULATION

The Succession Regulation establishes a narrower opportunity for Member States to impose overriding mandatory provisions under Article 30. It should be noted that this provision is not titled as concerning overriding mandatory provisions, but it nevertheless functions as such.[1047] This provision permits an exception to the principle of the unity of the succession by allowing the law where certain assets (immovable property, certain enterprises or other special categories of asset) are located to apply special rules – irrespective of the applicable law – which affect the transferability of assets upon death. Such rules are defined by Article 30 as those 'which, for economic, family or social considerations, impose restrictions concerning or affecting the succession in respect of those assets'.

In contrast to the forum-centric nature of Article 30 of the Property Regulations, Article 30 of the Succession Regulation is designed to allow for the application of foreign overriding mandatory rules that emanate from the place where the *particular assets* are located. This can foreseeably extend to rules that originate from a non-EU state. On this point, it can be emphasised that without regard being given to the overriding mandatory rules of a non-EU state where the particular assets are located, it might be very difficult to fully enforce judgments in such countries.[1048]

A principal example of the type of overriding mandatory rules that the EU legislator had in mind by including Article 30 in the Succession Regulation are those aimed at protecting agricultural enterprises during the course of succession by ensuring that such an asset passes to persons or groups who have a link with it or will carry it on.[1049] Such special rules might also be those which are intended to guide the transfer of an asset (or assets) to a single heir (e.g. a

1045 Recital 52 of the Partnership Property Regulation and Recital 53 of the Matrimonial Property Regulation.

1046 Predictability as to the content of the applicable law and expectations held concerning its impact.

1047 G. Contaldi, 'Article 30: Special Rules Imposing Restrictions Concerning or Affecting the Succession in Respect of Certain Assets' in A. Calvo Caravaca et al. (eds.), *The EU Succession Regulation: A Commentary* (Cambridge University Press, Cambridge, 2016), at p.430, para.1.

1048 Since the Succession Regulation excludes the application of the *lex rei sitae*. See Contaldi, ibid., at p.431, para.2.

1049 See example provided by Contaldi, ibid., at p.432, para.7.

spouse or descendent who works in the business concerned) by allowing this party to acquire the asset(s) from other heirs in exchange for compensation.[1050] With regard to special regimes with a social purpose, this category includes those rules designed to keep valuable collections (e.g. artworks, books or historical archives) together.[1051] Finally, such rules might reflect family considerations by, for instance, ensuring that a spouse or cohabitee of the deceased can maintain a lease of their shared home.[1052]

In line with the stance of the Property Regulations[1053] and Rome I Regulation[1054] in this regard, as well as the aforementioned judgment in *Arblade*,[1055] Recital 54 of the Succession Regulation requires that Article 30 be interpreted strictly in order that its application remain compatible with the objectives of the regulation.

10.4. PUBLIC POLICY (*ORDRE PUBLIC*)

In contrast to the scant regard for overriding mandatory provisions within the current framework, all relevant instruments that provide for a choice of law[1056] establish the opportunity for the forum to set aside provisions of the applicable law through a reservation based on public policy (*ordre public*).[1057] The reservation of public policy is designed to counter the 'value-neutral' approach of private international law.[1058] By using this provision to protect its own public interests (e.g. fundamental social, economic or moral considerations[1059]), the state retains a degree of sovereignty in safeguarding the enforcement of its fundamental values in matters coming within its jurisdiction.

As briefly mentioned in the preceding section (10.3.), public policy can be distinguished from overriding mandatory rules by the passive, flexible nature of its usage.[1060] Whilst overriding mandatory provisions take precedence over

---

1050 Found under French, Austrian, Belgian, Finnish, German, Luxembourgish, Norwegian, Polish and Swiss law: Contaldi, ibid., at p.433, para.8.

1051 Ibid., at pp.434–435, paras.9–10.

1052 Ibid, at p.435, para.11. See extended commentary of these described purposes in: ibid., at pp.432–437, paras.5–15 and Lagarde (Chapter 4, n.484), at p.165, paras.1–5.

1053 Recital 52 of the Partnership Property Regulation and 53 of the Matrimonial Property Regulation.

1054 See Recital 37 of the Rome I Regulation.

1055 *Arblade* and *Sofrage* (n.1033 above), at para.31.

1056 See Article 12 of the Rome III Regulation, Article 31 of the Property Regulations, Article 13 of the Hague Maintenance Protocol and Article 35 of the Succession Regulation.

1057 A reservation based on public policy can also be made in the context of the enforcement of a judgment, but this is outside the scope of this present examination.

1058 S. Gössl, 'The Public Policy Exception in the European Civil Justice System' (2016) 4(16) *The European Legal Forum* 85, at p.86, para.2 and Carruthers (Chapter 2, n.168), at p.907.

1059 The remit of public policy is not explicitly defined in any of the EU regulations.

1060 Grajdura (n.1034 above), at pp.3–4.

the applicable law in any area coming within their scope,[1061] public policy only comes into play if a provision of the applicable law is found to be contrary to the fundamental values of the forum (therefore revealing a positive-negative dichotomy between these two concepts).[1062] It follows that whilst overriding mandatory rules can be imposed from the onset of proceedings, public policy can only be used once the applicable law has been determined.[1063]

10.4.1. ARTICLE 12 OF THE ROME III REGULATION, ARTICLE 31 OF THE PROPERTY REGULATIONS AND ARTICLE 35 OF THE SUCCESSION REGULATION

The public policy provisions contained in the EU's rules on the law applicable to divorce and legal separation, property relations and succession follow a uniform format. The latter three regulations state: 'the application of a provision of the law of any State specified by this Regulation may be refused only if such application is manifestly incompatible with the public policy (*ordre public*) of the forum'. The Rome III Regulation diverges slightly (but not substantively) in terms of wording.[1064]

The first aspect to be considered here involves the mandated restrictive approach to the application of the public policy provision. In a similar line of reasoning to that discussed with regard to overriding mandatory provisions above,[1065] the impact of this provision upon the exercise of the EU's fundamental freedoms (most prominently, a negative effect upon legal certainty[1066]) means that its usage should be limited to exceptional circumstances,[1067] whereby a rule is considered to be *manifestly* incompatible with the forum's public policy.[1068]

This restriction aligns with CJEU case law on the use of the public policy reservation by Member States, whereby it has been firmly established that this

---

1061 Notwithstanding the EU legislator's stipulation that their identification as overriding mandatory provisions must be strictly interpreted: see Recital 52 of the Partnership Property Regulation and Article 53 of the Matrimonial Property Regulation.

1062 Grajdura (n.1034 above), at pp.3–4.

1063 Ibid.

1064 'Application of a provision of the law designated by virtue of this Regulation may be refused only if such application is manifestly incompatible with the public policy of the forum'.

1065 See 10.3.

1066 In terms of the predictability of the content and effects of the applicable law, and the expectations that accompany this.

1067 See Recital 54 of the Matrimonial Property Regulation, Recital 53 of the Partnership Property Regulation and Recital 58 of the Succession Regulation. See also Recital 37 of the Rome I Regulation and Recital 32 of the Rome II Regulation.

1068 The same mandate is also established in Article 21 of the Rome I Regulation and Article 26 of Rome II Regulation.

may only be employed in exceptional instances.[1069] More specifically, it was stated in the *Krombach* case that the recognition and enforcement of a judgment (the issue at stake in this instance) 'would have to constitute a manifest breach of a rule of law regarded as essential in the legal order of the State in which enforcement is sought or of a right recognised as being fundamental within that legal order' for the rule of public policy to prevail.[1070] In a similar manner to its treatment of overriding mandatory provisions,[1071] the Court emphasised in the aforementioned case that whilst it was left to a Member State to determine the content of its own public policy, it is ultimately up to the CJEU to determine the limits of the exercise of this exception.[1072]

A striking point of comparison to the standardised approach to public policy of the relevant EU instruments on divorce and legal separation, property relations and succession can be found in the 2005 Proposal for the Maintenance Regulation.[1073] This draft instrument also addressed applicable law,[1074] and provided that the public policy exception could not be used by the forum *vis-à-vis* the law of another Member State. This two-tier system was clearly never replicated in any of the relevant EU instruments that unify the rules on applicable law; it would seem that this was a step too far in terms of mutual trust between Member States.

Turning to scrutinise the usage of the public policy exception, this has been observed to involve a consideration of not only the interests of the parties to the proceedings, but also the dignity of the court and the safeguarding of the values of society.[1075] It is not made clear in the relevant public policy provisions whether this evaluation ought to take place on an abstract or concrete basis. Under the former approach, a choice of law rule can be excluded because its content is seen to contravene the public policy of the forum, whilst under the latter, a rule can

---

1069 See Case 145/86 *Horst Ludwig Martin Hoffmann v. Adelheid Krieg.* Reference for a preliminary ruling: Hoge Raad – Netherland [1988] ECR 645, at para.21; Case C-78/95 *Bernardus Hendrikman and Maria Feyen v. Magenta Druck & Verlag GmbH.* Reference for a preliminary ruling: Hoge Raad – Netherlands [1996] ECR I-4943, at para.23; Case C-7/98 *Dieter Krombach v André Bamberski.* Reference for a preliminary ruling: Bundesgerichtshof – Germany [2000] ECR I-1935, at para.21; and Case C-38/98 *Régie nationale des usines Renault SA v. Maxicar SpA and Orazio Formento.* Reference for a preliminary ruling: Corte d'appello di Torino – Italy [2000] ECR I-2973, at para.26.

1070 Case C-7/98 *Krombach v. Bamberski* (ibid.), at para.37.

1071 See *Arblade* and *Sofrage* (n.1033 above), at para.31.

1072 *Krombach* (n.1069 above), at paras.22–23. See also *Renault v. Maxicar* (n.1069 above), at paras.26–33.

1073 See Article 20 of the Proposal for a Council Regulation on jurisdiction, applicable law, recognition and enforcement of decisions and cooperation in matters relating to maintenance obligations, COM(2005) 649 final.

1074 Delegated to the Hague Maintenance Protocol in the final regulation.

1075 See description in M. Bodgan, 'Private International Law as Component of the Law of the Forum. General Course on Private International Law' in *Collected Courses of the Hague Academy of International Law, Volume 348* (Brill Nijhoff, Leiden, 2011), at p.216.

only be set aside if its *effects* are viewed as such (e.g. a provision being excluded because it is discriminatory vs. due to its discriminatory results).[1076]

The abstract method allows courts to present a strong stance on protecting fundamental rights within their jurisdictions (e.g. the equal rights of men and women in succession). However, employment of public policy in this manner arguably frames it as a 'blunt instrument', particularly in view of the existence of differences in the recognition of certain types of relationships between Member States. Under this abstract approach, a rule could be set aside merely on the basis that it is connected to a relationship that is not recognised by the forum.[1077] In contrast, a concrete approach would involve a more specific consideration of the impact of the law upon the parties, and appears to align more with the restrictive stance emphasised by the EU legislator and the CJEU towards the use of this exception. Notwithstanding the above discussion, support for usage of public policy in an abstract manner has recently been given by the Advocate General on the *Sahyouni* case,[1078] although this case concerned Article 10 of Rome III, which has a distinct mandatory character (see 10.5.1. below).

The precise content of the public policy exception clearly varies between Member States and between subject areas. Across all the subject areas addressed here, discriminatory rules present a clear instance in which a forum might invoke public policy to prevent the application of a provision.[1079] In this setting, it might foreseeably equate to discrimination on grounds of gender (in all the legal processes discussed here)[1080] or on the basis of illegitimacy (in the context of succession). Protection from discrimination has been safeguarded in Article 21 of the EU Charter of Fundamental Rights and Article 14 of the European Convention on Human Rights,[1081] as well as being specifically established in mandatory form in Article 10 of Rome III, which requires that laws that

---

1076 Gössl (n.1058 above), at pp.91–92, para.3.

1077 See discussion of this in the context of Article 13 of the Hague Maintenance Protocol at 10.4.2 and the (non-)recognition of relationships at 10.6.

1078 Opinion of Advocate General Saugmandsgaard Øe, delivered on 14 September 2017 on Case C-372/16 *Soha Sahyouni v. Raja Mamisch*. Reference for a preliminary ruling: Oberlandesgericht München – Germany [2017] ECLI:EU:C:2017:686, at paras 94–103.

1079 E. Pataut, European Parliament Note: *The public-policy exception and the Proposal for a Regulation of the European Parliament and of the Council on jurisdiction, applicable law, recognition and enforcement of decisions and authentic instruments in matters of succession and the creation of a European Certificate of Succession* (COM(2009)154) (November 2010), PE 432.741, at pp.15–16, para.3.2.1.

1080 See further discussion, in particular in the context of the application of Islamic law to divorce in EU Member States in: Viarengo / Villata (Chapter 3, n.268), at pp.201–304.

1081 See, for instance, in the context of inheritance rights: *Mazurek v. France*, Application no. 34406/97, ECtHR (1 February 2000), in which the ECtHR found that inequality in treatment of children born from adultery in French inheritance law in succession was contrary to Article 1, Protocol 1 (right to enjoyment of possessions) in conjunction with Article 14 (protection from discrimination) ECHR.

discriminate between sexes in the context of divorce and legal separation are to be set aside (see 10.5.1.). Linking back to the discussion of the manner of applying public policy, the protection from discrimination, due to its entrenchment in fundamental rights, represents an area in which an abstract approach might be favoured by the Member States.[1082]

The CJEU has stated that a mere difference between Member State laws is not sufficient to warrant making use of this exception.[1083] However, there are nevertheless grey areas in which the absence of certain features in an applicable law might be seen by the forum to run counter to its public policy. The existence of reserved shares and forced heirship in the succession laws of many civil law systems presents a particular problem in this regard. Where the applicable law does not provide for a reserved share, an attempt might be made to invoke the public policy of the forum in order to protect the position of children or the spouse of the deceased.[1084] However, given that the matter of reserved shares and forced heirship is essentially a variation between Member State succession laws, it could be argued that to enact a public policy exception on such grounds would run counter to the aims of the Succession Regulation.[1085] Furthermore, such an approach could involve an element of discrimination, since it would be likely to offend public policy if the deceased or the interested parties had strong ties to the forum (e.g. nationality).[1086]

The Proposal for the Succession Regulation included a provision stating that

> the application of a rule of the law determined by this Regulation may not be considered to be contrary to the public policy of the forum on the sole ground that its clauses regarding the reserved portion of an estate differ from those in force in the forum.[1087]

This specification was ultimately left out of the regulation, and it has been argued that this omission can be taken to indicate a degree of flexibility for Member States in the use of public policy on this matter.[1088] The lack of clarity that arises

---

1082 Gössl (n.1058 above), at p.91, para.3. See also the abstract nature of the substantive rule against discrimination on grounds of sex contained in Article 10 of Rome III.

1083 See *Krombach* (n.1069 above), at para.36 and *Maxicar* (n.1069), at para.29.

1084 Lagarde (Chapter 4, n.484), at pp.176–177, para.6 and G. Contaldi and C. Grieco, 'Article 35: Public Policy (ordre public)' in A. Calvo Caravaca et al. (eds.), *The EU Succession Regulation: A Commentary* (Cambridge University Press, Cambridge, 2016), p.512, para.14.

1085 Lagarde (ibid.), at pp.176–177, para.6.

1086 Ibid., at pp.176–177, para.6. It is suggested by Lagarde that a compromise solution would be to allow Member States to apply the public policy exception in certain cases where the applicable law is that of a third state and where the application of this law would have a particularly negative impact on particular parties (e.g. minor children) – see ibid, at p.177, para.7.

1087 See Article 27(2) of the Succession Regulation Proposal (Chapter 2, n.178).

1088 Contaldi and Grieco (n.1084 above), at p.511, para.11.

from the deletion of this stance in the regulation is, however, mitigated by the fact that few Member States actually consider reserved shares to be an issue against which they would invoke public policy.[1089]

A final point to be discussed in this subsection involves the uniform caveat imposed upon the use of the public policy exception by the respective recitals of the relevant EU instruments, according to which a court or other competent authority is not permitted to set aside the law of another state 'when doing so would be contrary to the Charter of Fundamental Rights of the European Union, and in particular Article 21 thereof, which prohibits all forms of discrimination'.[1090]

The above statement has been criticised as unclear with regard to its purpose.[1091] Whilst the finding that a law violates a fundamental right is a clear example of an instance in which the public policy exception might come into play, this is not the scenario that appears to be alluded to here. Instead, this segment of the recitals seems to state that the forum cannot make use of public policy when the result of doing so would *in itself* be discriminatory (e.g. using the public policy exception in a different manner on the basis of the nationality of the parties). Whilst there may be a limited usage of the public policy exception in this regard, the wording and inclusion of this statement is confusing.[1092] It is submitted here that it would have been considerably more useful to have referenced contravention of the EU Charter of Fundamental Rights as exemplification of the use of the public policy exception.

10.4.2. ARTICLE 13 OF THE HAGUE MAINTENANCE PROTOCOL

Article 13 of the Hague Maintenance Protocol diverges from the public policy provisions contained in Rome III, the Property Regulations and the Succession Regulation, by instead beginning 'the application of *the law* determined under

1089 See Pataut (n.1079 above), at p.14, para.3.1. It is stated here that a lack of adherence to reserved shares is explicitly considered *not* to contravene public policy in Germany, Greece and Portugal, and that the French Court of Cassation has also never found contravention in this regard.

1090 The example used here is from Recital 58 of the Succession Regulation; there are slight differences in wording between the instruments. See also Recital 25 of the Rome III Regulation, Recital 54 of the Matrimonial Property Regulation and Recital 53 of the Partnership Property Regulation.

1091 See Pataut (n.1079 above), at pp.18–20, para.3.2.1.

1092 See, for instance, the citing of the reference to Article 21 of the EU Charter of Fundamental Rights contained in Recital 58 of the Succession Regulation as an example of the usage of the public policy exception: Contaldi and Grieco (n.1084 above), at pp.512–513, para.15.

the Protocol …' (emphasis added).[1093] In the absence of specification to the contrary in the Explanatory Report accompanying the Protocol,[1094] the omission of the qualification 'provision' before 'the law' could be taken to indicate that, even if only a single provision of the maintenance law in question has the effect of offending the public policy of the forum, the entire law will be set aside.

It could, however, be argued that this absence is merely a terminological difference. In support of this, reference can be made to the emphasis that Article 13 of the Hague Maintenance Protocol (along with the parallel public policy provisions contained in the regulations on property relations and succession) ought to be interpreted very restrictively.[1095] Surely, to bluntly refuse an entire applicable law in all situations (including those where to do so would not be strictly necessary in order to safeguard a national imperative) would run counter to this mandate? Secondly, on a more general basis, it is emphasised in the Report accompanying the Protocol that the substance of Article 13 corresponds with many other instruments of private international law (although it does not expressly refer to the EU framework).[1096] If the stance that this difference is merely terminological were to be pursued, it can be asserted that the *status quo* is a cause for confusion and ought to be remedied.[1097]

A second point of distinction of Article 13 of the Hague Maintenance Protocol is the explicit stipulation that regard should only be had for the *effects* of a law in adjudging whether it is manifestly contrary to the public policy of the forum. The express reference to an *in concreto* approach provides greater clarity concerning the assessment of public policy by the forum, and secures a minimal level of encroachment upon the exercise of the EU's fundamental freedoms.

It can also be seen to set a higher bar for public policy in situations in which a maintenance claim may be made on the basis of a relationship that is not recognised by the forum state (e.g. same-sex marriage, registered partnership or, less commonly, polygamous marriage or a marriage involving transgender persons). It is not enough that the relationship in question is adjudged to offend the public policy; it must be ascertained whether the act of granting

---

1093 In full: 'The application of the law determined under the Protocol may be refused only to the extent that its effects would be manifestly contrary to the public policy of the forum'. Note that although there is also a slight difference with the reference to 'manifestly contrary' rather than 'manifestly incompatible', it is proposed here that this difference is purely terminological.

1094 The Report would, in fact, appear to reiterate the apparent stance of Article 13: 'This article provides an option to exclude the applicable law where its effects are manifestly contrary to the public policy of the forum'. See Bonomi (Chapter 4, n.400), at para.175.

1095 See Bonomi, ibid., at para.176.

1096 Ibid., at para.175.

1097 See suggestion of N. Natov, 'Applicable Law in Matters Relating to Maintenance Obligations – The 2007 Hague Protocol', *EJTN seminar on Maintenance obligations in Europe* (Sofia, Bulgaria, 5–6 December 2013), at pp.13–14.

maintenance on the basis of this relationship manifestly contravenes the forum's public policy.[1098] This distinction is particularly important in the context of maintenance obligations, since a forum's blanket refusal to get involved in a claim involving a relationship that it views as controversial could have a highly detrimental effect on the ability of a vulnerable party to exercise their free movement rights.

10.5. SUBSTANTIVE PROVISIONS

The third and final type of measure that holds the potential to restrict a choice of law are the substantive provisions that are imposed directly by the relevant instruments discussed here. These provisions can be distinguished from overriding mandatory rules and public policy by the source of their authority within the EU instruments themselves and their prescribed nature therein. Substantive provisions can be identified amongst relevant instruments in Article 10 of the Rome III (10.5.1.), Articles 22(3) and 28 of the Property Regulations (10.5.2.) and Articles 8(5) and 14 of the Hague Maintenance Protocol (10.5.3. and 10.5.4.).

10.5.1. ARTICLE 10 OF THE ROME III REGULATION

The fundamental right to divorce is safeguarded through Article 10 of Rome III, which requires that where the applicable law makes no provision for divorce, or where it does not grant one of the spouses equal access to divorce or legal separation on account of their sex, the law of the forum will apply. Although this provision can be viewed as a specific public policy exception, it is to be distinguished from the general public policy provisions contained in the rules of the relevant instruments concerning applicable law (see 10.4.) in view of the mandatory nature of its application by participating Member States.[1099]

With regard to the first focus of this provision – the potential non-provision for divorce by an applicable law – its usage is likely to be minimal, since most legal systems permit divorce to some extent.[1100] Moreover, for these present purposes, it seems unlikely that the parties would expressly choose to select a law that would prevent them from getting divorced. The first requirement

---

1098 Bonomi (Chapter 4, n.400), at para.177.

1099 Opinion of AG on *Sahyouni* (n.1078 above), at paras.94–103.

1100 Malta, the one EU Member State that did not allow for divorce, introduced it following a referendum in 2011. The only remaining states in the world where divorce is not permitted are the Philippines and the Vatican City.

contained in Article 10 may, nevertheless, come into play where a particular legal system uses internal connecting factors to refer to canon law (which would render divorce impossible for the parties).[1101]

The second part of Article 10, which addresses the situation in which the applicable law places the spouses on an unequal footing in their access to divorce or legal separation on account of their sex, provides considerably greater scope for usage. Given the universal application of Rome III, it is foreseeable that a chosen law might be based on, or lead to, the application of a religious law that does not permit women equal rights in obtaining a divorce. Sharia law, which is applicable to divorces in many predominantly Muslim countries (e.g. Saudi Arabia, the United Arab Emirates and Qatar) prescribes different processes for men and women in obtaining a divorce (with the latter having to apply to a religious court for consideration in this regard).[1102] Jewish law, which is applicable to couples that have married religiously in Israel, makes divorce dependent on the consent of the husband.[1103]

It is important to note that the law that is set aside on the basis of Article 10 must make *no* provision for equal access to divorce. For instance, although Moroccan law traditionally only provided for divorce according to sharia law (*talaq*), there is now a new form of divorce which permits the application for divorce by either spouse on an equal basis. The mere existence of the possibility for *talaq* in Moroccan law would not be sufficient in order to set the applicable law aside according to Article 10.[1104] It is not entirely clear how pluralistic legal systems that differentiate between those who have been married religiously and secularly in order to determine the form of divorce (e.g. Israel) would be considered in this regard. Would the forum disregard the religious status of the parties' marriage and apply the secular law that ensures equal access to divorce? This would technically equate to an erroneous application of foreign law that would defeat the purpose of allowing party autonomy in this setting.

10.5.2. ARTICLES 22(3) AND 28 OF THE PROPERTY REGULATIONS

Although the relationship between spouses or registered partners lies at the heart of the Property Regulations, this subject area also involves the interaction of the

---

1101 Kruger (Chapter 1, n.60), at para.6(a).

1102 A. Black, 'Window into Shariah Family Law: Part 2 – Aspects of divorce' (2010) 16 *Family Relationships Quarterly* 2–4 (Newsletter of the Australian Family Relationships Clearinghouse).

1103 Mair / Örücü (Chapter 5, n.531), at p.207 *et seq*.

1104 Kruger (Chapter 1, n.60), at para.6(a).

spouses or partners and third parties.[1105] As discussed in Chapter 2,[1106] an inherent vulnerability arises for such third parties due to the fact that although they are not directly involved in the primary relationship in this field, they are nonetheless affected by changes that occur within it. More specifically, if the spouses or partners make changes to their property regime, third parties such as creditors might face frustration of expectations that they based on the previous *status quo*.

In order to protect these expectations, the Property Regulations set out a framework of rules designed to protect such parties in the event of a change of applicable law. Firstly, Article 22(3) establishes that the retroactive change in the applicable law brought about by express agreement between the spouses or partners cannot adversely affect the interests of third parties.[1107] It would appear that this provision necessitates identification and reinstatement of the rights of third parties vis-à-vis the spouses or partners that have been lost in the change of law. It is unclear whether this would involve application of the formerly applicable law to the issue that the right concerns, or recognition of such rights as 'vested' (to avoid the co-existence of more than one applicable law).[1108]

In addition, Article 28 encompasses a more general provision that protects third parties from the application of a law to a dispute with the spouses or partners, unless they knew (or in the exercise of due diligence, should have known) that this law applied to the property regime.[1109] A typical example of such a situation would be that in which the spouses have made a choice of law for a state other than their present habitual residence.[1110] Instead of relying on a subjective ascertainment of actual knowledge, Article 28(2) proceeds to establish a number of prescribed scenarios in which the third party will be adjudged to have known of the applicable law.[1111] By adopting this latter approach, this provision ensures

---

1105 See Article 27(f) of both Regulations. See also the Explanatory Memorandums accompanying the Property Regulations Proposals (Chapter 2, n.179), at p.4, para.3.1.

1106 See 2.4.2.

1107 This provision emulates Article 8 of the 1978 Hague Convention on the Law Applicable to Matrimonial Property Regimes and Article 3(2) of the Rome I Regulation.

1108 L. Rademacher, 'Changing the Past: Retroactive Choice of Law and the Protection of Third Parties in the European Regulations on Patrimonial Consequences of Marriages and Registered Partnerships' (2018) 10(1) *Cuadernos de Derecho Transnacional* 7, at pp.16–17, paras.26–28 (2018).

1109 This is a more developed version of Article 9 of the 1978 Hague Convention on the Law Applicable to Matrimonial Property Regimes.

1110 Rademacher (n.1108 above), at pp.17–18, paras.29–30.

1111 Either 'if (a) that law is the law of: (i) the State whose law is applicable to the transaction between a spouse and the third party; (ii) the State where the contracting spouse and the third party have their habitual residence; or, (iii) in cases involving immoveable property, the State in which the property is situated; or (b) either spouse had complied with the applicable requirements for disclosure or registration of the matrimonial property regime specified by the law of: (i) the State whose law is applicable to the transaction between a spouse and the third party; (ii) the State where the contracting spouse and the third party have their habitual residence; or (iii) in cases involving immoveable property, the State in which the property is situated.'

predictability for the parties involved and clarity of interpretation for Member State courts. Where the applicable law cannot be invoked against the third parties on the basis of the aforementioned assessment, Article 28(3) establishes the grounds for determining the law that will apply to the effects of the property regime regarding the third party.[1112]

10.5.3. ARTICLE 6 OF THE HAGUE MAINTENANCE PROTOCOL

Article 6 of the Hague Maintenance Protocol establishes an 'escape-clause' rule, designed to be invoked by the debtor in maintenance cases whereby the creditor has raised a claim on the basis of an obligation which is not found in the law of the state of the habitual residence of the debtor and the law of the state of the common nationality of the parties (if this exists).[1113] Although this rule is primarily designed to balance the effects of the creditor-centric objective conflict-of-laws rule contained in Article 3 of the Protocol,[1114] its application to the choice of law provisions contained in Articles 7 and 8 does not appear to be excluded.[1115]

It is, however, highly questionable whether this provision is appropriate to be applied in this setting, considering a choice of law agreement is a positive action that (presumably) has been entered into with the informed consent of both parties.[1116] Furthermore, it is striking that there is not a parallel escape-clause that can be invoked in a situation in which a chosen law is disconnected from the creditor.

10.5.4. ARTICLE 14 OF THE HAGUE MAINTENANCE PROTOCOL

The second Hague Maintenance Protocol provision to be discussed here, Article 14, establishes that even if the applicable law provides otherwise, the

---

1112 '(a) by the law of the State whose law is applicable to the transaction between a spouse and the third party; or (b) in cases involving immoveable property or registered assets or rights, by the law of the State in which the property is situated or in which the assets or rights are registered.'

1113 It does not apply to parent-child relationships and relationships covered by Article 5 of the Protocol.

1114 See extensive discussion of Article 6 in Bonomi (Chapter 4, n.400), at paras.95–108.

1115 See, in particular, the phrase 'Notwithstanding Articles 3 to 6' at the beginning of Articles 7(1) and 8(1).

1116 Particularly in light of the fact that a choice of law has to be ascertained at the moment of choice under the Hague Maintenance Protocol, thus meaning that the debtor cannot plead ignorance regarding the content of an indefinite choice: see 9.3.2.2.

needs of the creditor and the resources of the debtor should be taken into account in the determination of maintenance, as well as any compensation which the creditor was awarded in place of periodical maintenance payments. Unlike the other provisions examined in this section, the positive nature of Article 14 means that it applies equally, whether the applicable law is foreign, or that of the forum.[1117] Furthermore, it is distinguished by the *manner* in which it is to be applied, whereby it is intended to guide the manner in which maintenance is calculated according to the applicable law.[1118]

One important caveat to be mentioned is that compensation other than periodic payments (e.g. a lump-sum settlement) can be taken into account for the purposes of applying Article 14. This flexibility acknowledges the diversity between domestic laws, catering for systems that aim to provide a 'clean break' for the parties involved, and avoiding the potential for unfair consequences of ignoring the aim of such settlements.[1119]

It might be argued that Article 14 could also come into use where the applicable law does not *adequately* take into account the needs of the creditor and the resources of the debtor. However, to permit the forum court this opportunity would lend a significant degree of discretion that, in the party autonomy context, would impinge upon the free will of the parties and the benefits that this brings to free movement by allowing a sizeable opportunity for the content of the applicable law to be varied. It is therefore proposed here that Article 14 applies in a binary fashion: either the needs and resources of the parties have been taken into account, or they have not.

10.6. (NON-)RECOGNITION OF A RELATIONSHIP

Earlier in this chapter (10.4.2.), Member States' treatment of certain types of 'non-traditional' relationships was touched upon in the context of the use of the public policy exception. The variances in recognising 'non-traditional' relationships (chiefly in this context same-sex marriage and registered partnership, but also cohabiting couples, polygamous marriage and marriage involving transgender persons) requires further elaboration due to the fragmented approach to recognition within the Union.[1120]

1117 Bonomi (Chapter 4, n.400), at para.181.

1118 Ibid., at para.182: It should be noted that this duty does not have to be performed by the authority responsible for the case at hand; it can also be performed by administrative authorities, who may use more abstract methods (e.g. tables) to calculate maintenance, whilst still acknowledging the creditor's needs and debtor's resources.

1119 Ibid., at para.183.

1120 For instance, this was the reason why Poland did not participate in Rome III: Boele-Woelki (Chapter 1, n.1), at p.27.

This section will begin by considering the general approach towards recognition of such relationships within the EU and by individual Member States, and the possibilities offered within the relevant instruments in this regard (10.6.1.). Following this, the impact of specific substantive provisions contained in Article 13 of Rome III (10.6.2.) and Article 9 of the Property Regulations (10.6.3.) will be considered.

10.6.1. GENERAL APPROACH

The Member States vary between one another with regard to their approaches towards relationships that fall outside of traditional male-female marriage and the family relationships that accompany this. This variance is particularly infamous in the context of same-sex marriage and registered partnership, but also extends to defining the holders of parental responsibility and the family relationships that give rise to maintenance obligations.

For the purposes of the discussion below, non-recognition in the *jurisdictional* context will be the centre point of analysis, since this holds the greatest potential to frustrate the expectations of the parties and hinder their access to justice. However, it should also be acknowledged that limping relationships might also emerge where there is no *law* available that recognises the form of relationship in question.

The topic of same-sex spouses has been briefly examined in Chapter 4 in the context of subject matter and parties concerned in an exercise of autonomy,[1121] and it is useful to reiterate here that the Member States' attitude towards same-sex marriage is an evolving one. Whilst this institution did not exist in any Member State 16 years ago, as can be seen in Table 6 below, it is now present in 14 out of these 28 countries.[1122] However, with this development, there has also emerged a distinct divide between those states that permit and generate same-sex marriages, and those that refuse to acknowledge their legal existence (particularly newer Member States, such as Poland, Lithuania and Romania). This polarisation, in combination with the increasing number of same-sex spouses in Europe, presents a growing risk of the frustration of the expectations of such couples and for limping relationships to emerge.

[1121] See 4.3.2.

[1122] At least, soon to be 14 Member States, with the predicted introduction of same-sex marriage in Austria in 2019.

Table 6. Fragmentation: 'Non-Traditional' Relationships

Member States	Same-Sex Marriage	Registered Partnership
Austria	x	x
Belgium	x	x
Bulgaria		
Croatia		x
Cyprus		x
Czech Republic		x
Denmark	x	x
Estonia		x
Finland	x	x
France	x	x
Germany	x	x
Greece		x
Hungary		x
Ireland	x	x
Italy		x
Latvia		
Lithuania		
Luxembourg	x	x
Malta	x	x
Netherlands	x	x
Poland		
Portugal	x	
Romania		
Slovakia		
Slovenia		x
Spain	x	x
Sweden	x	x
United Kingdom	x	x
	14	21

Registered partnership is also an area of significant divergence between the Member States. As also discussed in Chapter 4,[1123] this type of legal relationship varies both in terms of its existence in the Member States (see Table 6 above),[1124]

1123 See elaborated discussion at 4.4.2.

1124 Currently 21 Member States provide for some form of registered partnership in their legislation.

as well as its form and function.[1125] Whilst the respective approaches to recognising registered partnership vary from Member State to Member State, the EU has stated that this type of relationship is not provided for in Bulgaria, Latvia, Lithuania, Poland, Romania and Slovakia.[1126] Furthermore, given the aforementioned differences in form and function of the status between Member States that do provide for registered partnership, there is also a risk that the parties' expectations as to the effects of their relationship face a risk of frustration in the event of the application of a foreign law.

Although the values of gender-neutrality[1127] and non-discrimination[1128] are generally emphasised in the relevant instruments, it would appear that it is ultimately left to the Member State jurisdictions to decide whether or not to recognise the existence of a particular relationship. This is evidenced by the express exclusion of decisions on the existence, validity or recognition of the relevant relationships from the scope of the majority of the EU instruments[1129] and the manifestation of this position in Article 13 of Rome III (see 10.6.2.) and Article 9 of the Property Regulations.[1130] When faced with a relationship form which does not exist in its own legal system, a Member State court thus effectively has three options: (i) to refuse to hear the case on the basis of non-recognition; (ii) to characterise the relationship as another type of institution which exists within its legal system; or (iii) to nevertheless give partial or full recognition to the relationship and its effects.

It can be seen that, at least in the first two approaches described above, there is a particular risk to legal certainty for internationally active parties who are in 'non-traditional' relationships. Such parties face difficulty in predicting the effects of their relationships and protecting the expectations that arise from these ties. The opportunity to make a choice of court clearly offers a remedy in

---

1125 Whilst it is sometimes used as a substitute for marriage for same-sex couples in jurisdictions which do not provide for this (e.g. Slovenia) in other countries it is designed to be a form of marriage 'light' that is open to both same-sex and opposite-sex couples (e.g. Belgium).

1126 European Union, *Civil unions and registered partnerships* (30 April 2018), available at: https://europa.eu/youreurope/citizens/family/couple/registered-partners/index_en.htm.

1127 See reference to 'spouses' rather than husband and wife in the regulations concerning married couples. Although there is nevertheless a reference to 'husband' and 'wife' in Annex I of Brussels II bis, this terminology has been replaced by 'spouses' in the recent recast of this instrument (see Annexes II and VIII of the Brussels IIa (Recast) Regulation).

1128 See reference to the EU Charter of Fundamental Rights (in particular, Article 21) in: Recital 30 of the Rome III Regulation, Recital 73 of the Matrimonial Property Regulation, Recital 71 of the Partnership Property Regulation, Recital 81 of the Succession Regulation and Recital 33 of the Brussels II bis Regulation.

1129 Article 1(2)(b) of Rome III and the Property Regulations, Article 1(2)(a) of the Succession Regulation and Article 1(3)(a) of the Brussels II bis Regulation. See also Recitals 17, 21, 38 and 64 of the Matrimonial Property Regulation and Recitals 17, 21, 36 and 63 of the Partnership Property Regulation.

1130 See commentary in sources such as: Kruger (Chapter 1, n.60), at para.6(b); Hess / Spancken (Chapter 4, n.401), at p.333; and Bonomi (Chapter 7, n.730), at pp.339–340 (2008).

the sense that the parties have the chance to try and direct a relationship towards a jurisdiction in which it is characterised and/or recognised in an anticipated manner. This is, however, dependent upon whether a suitable jurisdiction is available to be chosen under the relevant instruments. Furthermore, it can be commented that prioritising recognition of a couple's relationship might come at the cost of other considerations relating to access to justice, as well as connection with a law of actual affinity to the parties.

The Property Regulations allow for the selection of the court of the Member State where the relationship was created,[1131] as well the possibility to choose the law of the place of creation under Article 22(1) of the Partnership Property Regulation, which can both be seen as routes by which parties can opt to safeguard the effects of their relations in subsequent movements around the Union. The position of registered partners is comparatively enhanced in view of the joint opportunity to choose the court and the law of the place of creation; through this choice such parties can safeguard their expectations upon the basis of a very high probability that their relationship will be recognised.

In the context of maintenance obligations, a setting in which non-recognition of a relationship might ultimately equate to financial hardship for the creditor, no attempt is made to attach a formal definition to 'family relationship' in either the Maintenance Regulation or the Hague Maintenance Protocol. The scope of the instruments is thus considered broad,[1132] with Member States not forced to attempt to characterise a particular relationship within the confines of the definition of a certain relationship found in its own legal system.[1133] This situation benefits not only formalised 'non-traditional' bonds, but also informal relationships such as cohabitation. However, it must be emphasised that the general approach described above still stands, and it is left to states themselves to establish the existence of a relationship that falls within the definitions provided.[1134]

Although the Succession Regulation is primarily directed towards an individual, the (non-)recognition of family relationships may have an impact upon the wider process of succession, particularly with regard to the concerned parties who may participate in a choice of court according to Articles 5, 6, 7 and 9, or the identification of beneficiaries of the will according to the law that applies to an intestate succession. In this regard, this follows the trend in the other EU instruments by delegating the determination of a family relationship to the Member State level.[1135]

1131 See Article 7(1) of both Property Regulations.

1132 Hess / Spancken (Chapter 4, n.401), at p.333.

1133 See reference in Article 1(1) of both the Maintenance Regulation and the Hague Maintenance Protocol to a maintenance obligation arising from 'a family relationship, parentage, marriage or affinity'.

1134 Bonomi (Chapter 4, n.400), at para.31.

1135 See Article 1(2)(a) of the Regulation. See also discussion in: Frimston (Chapter 4, n.363), at pp.41–42, paras.15–18.

The treatment of 'non-traditional' relationships is an ever-evolving matter. Case law from the CJEU[1136] indicates a growing tendency towards paralleling same-sex relationships with marriage for the purposes of achieving equal treatment in other fields (e.g. staff employment benefits). Parallel reference can also be made to the ECHR context in which it has been ruled that a Contracting State's refusal to attribute any form of legal recognition to a same-sex marriage is in violation of Article 8 of the Convention.[1137]

The recent case of *Coman and others*[1138] has been lauded as a milestone judgment by the CJEU in this present regard. The Court ruled that, in the context of the right to free movement (Article 21 TFEU and with analogy to Directive 2004/38 – the Citizens' Rights Directive/Free Movement Directive) and family reunification, the term 'spouse' is to be treated as gender-neutral.[1139] It stated that a Member State (in this instance, Romania) could not rely on national legislation to justify its refusal to recognise a same-sex marriage that has been concluded in another state,[1140] since to do so would impede the right to free movement of the EU citizen who was married to the third country national.[1141]

However, notwithstanding the importance of the Court's stance in this judgment, the actual impact of this case ought not to be prematurely overstated. It cannot be interpreted to impose a general requirement upon Member States to recognise foreign same-sex marriages.[1142] The judgment actually only definitively provides an autonomous interpretation of 'spouse' in the context of Directive 2004/38. For these purposes, Member States must replace their own domestic definition of 'spouse' with one that is gender-neutral and does not discriminate against same-sex couples.

It can also be observed that the judgment in *Coman* employed restrictive language that focused on the enjoyment of the EU citizen's right to a family life in conjunction with the exercise of their right to free movement. In contrast to the CJEU's reasoning in the cases concerning name law and incorporation (see 2.3.2.), regard for the fact that the marriage represented a pre-existing status did not feature prominently in this judgment. This makes it difficult to form a meaningful linkage with the vested rights theory and the accompanying discussion that this could bring to the party autonomy context.

1136 See *Maruko v. Versorgungsanstalt der deutschen Bühnen* (Chapter 4, n.404) and *Hay v. Credit agricole* (Chapter 4, n.404).

1137 See *Orlandi v. Italy* (Chapter 4, n.371); *E and Others v. Italy* (Chapter 4, n.404); and *Pajić v. Croatia* (Chapter 4, n.404).

1138 *Coman v. Romania* (Chapter 2, n.156).

1139 Ibid., at para.35.

1140 Ibid., at para.36.

1141 Ibid., at paras.39–40.

1142 See B. Rudevska, 'The "Coman" Case (C-673/16): Some reflections from the point of view of private international law', *Conflict of Laws* (2 July 2018), available at: http://conflictoflaws.net/2018/the-coman-case-c-673-16-some-reflections-from-the-point-of-view-of-private-international-law.

As discussed in Chapter 4,[1143] there is also the potential for a situation to emerge in which one, or even both, of the parents of a child are not recognised as being a holder of parental responsibility upon exercising their right to free movement. This might obviously arise in the case of a non-biological same-sex parent,[1144] but could also be an issue with parents who have acquired their status through surrogacy. Non-recognition has the potential to impact on the opportunity to participate in Article 12 of the Brussels II bis Regulation, whereby a holder of parental rights must be asked for their consent for prorogation in such a scenario,[1145] as well as potentially extending to the question of whether a maintenance obligation is considered to arise from a parent-child relationship for the purposes of the Maintenance Regulation or Hague Maintenance Protocol.[1146]

The ECtHR's judgment in *Wagner*[1147] drew heavily upon the child's best interests in finding that one state's refusal to recognise a legal status (the parent-child relationship), created in another state, ignored a social reality[1148] and gave rise to obstacles (e.g. an absence of full legal protection for the child) that contravened Article 8 ECHR.[1149] Although the recognition of the parent-child relationships across borders has not always been upheld by the ECtHR,[1150] it has been established that states have a narrower margin of appreciation in matters that concern the parent-child relationship,[1151] and it is clear that the best interests of the child are required to weigh heavily in decision-making involving minors.[1152] Given the strength attributed to this norm, the manner in which Member States ought to proceed with their treatment of 'non-traditional' forms of parenthood is markedly less clear than in the case of adult relations.

1143 See 4.6.2.2.

1144 See highlighting of this point in the context of adopted children of same-sex spouses in: C. Chateau, European Parliament Briefing: *Adoption: Cross-border legal issues and gaps in the European Union* (December 2015), PE 536.480 at p.4, para.3.1.3.

1145 This is less of an issue for instances falling within the scope of Article 15 of Brussels II bis, whereby only one concerned party may instigate or accept jurisdiction.

1146 Although the impact of this, for these purposes, is lessened by the fact that only very limited possibilities are permitted for party autonomy in light of the parent-child relationship under the Hague Maintenance Protocol (Article 7) and, to a more questionable extent, the Maintenance Regulation (Article 5).

1147 *Wagner v. Luxembourg* (Chapter 2, n.123), at paras.133–134.

1148 Ibid., at para.132.

1149 Ibid., at paras.133 and 136.

1150 See *Paradiso* (Chapter 4, n.471), at para.215.

1151 *Mennesson v. France* (Chapter 4, n.471), at paras.77–80 and *Labassee v. France* (Chapter 4, n.471), at paras.56–59.

1152 Framed as a primary consideration in Article 3(1) of the UN Convention on the Rights of the Child (1989) and Article 24(2) of the EU Charter of Fundamental Rights, and a paramount or primary norm in the context of ECtHR cases concerning adoption/surrogacy in the context of Article 8 ECHR. See *Wagner* (Chapter 2, n.123), at paras.133–134, *Mennesson* (Chapter 4, n.471), at paras.81 and 84, *Labassee* (Chapter 4, n.471), at para.60; and *Paradiso* (Chapter 4, n.471), at paras.127 and 208. See also L. Bracken, 'Assessing the Best Interests of the Child in Cases of Cross-border Surrogacy: Inconsistency in the Strasbourg Approach?'

10.6.2. ARTICLE 13 OF ROME III

As discussed in the previous subsection, there has been a huge shift in recent years in terms of the occurrence and legal recognition of intimate bonds between adults. This is primarily evident when observing the evolving approach to same-sex marriage in the Member States and in CJEU case law. As discussed above, the EU legislator has been reluctant to cement an approach in its instruments with regard to recognising such relationships in this present context. An exception in this regard is found in Article 13 of Rome III, which provides that nothing in the regulation will oblige a participating Member State to pronounce a divorce where its law does not consider the marriage in question to be valid for the purposes of divorce proceedings.

This provision primarily functions to confirm the view that the recognition of a relationship is a matter that is ultimately left to the Member States. It has, however, been argued that Article 13 is in fact a superfluous inclusion (merely a token gesture to encourage participation in Rome III by more conservative Member States[1153]), since Article 1 of the same instrument already provides that the determination of the validity of a marriage falls outside its scope.[1154]

Regardless of the value added by Article 13 of Rome III, it is clear that a couple whose union is not recognised by a Member State is at risk of suffering from a 'limping relationship'. In view of this, it is disappointing that the Brussels IIa (Recast) Regulation makes no provision for a choice of court in matrimonial matters (which could be used by couples to direct their proceedings towards a forum that will apply their chosen law under Rome III). In addition to this, a much-needed *forum necessitatis* or a provision similar to that of Article 9 of the Property Regulations (see 10.7.3. below) – which would provide a crucial safety net where a forum has refused to hear proceedings – is missing from both the Brussels II bis and Brussels IIa (Recast) Regulations.[1155]

On a final note, it should be pointed out that whilst the other relevant instruments do include a *forum necessitatis*,[1156] the wording of such provisions

(2017) 39(3) *Journal of Social Welfare and Family Law* 368–379 and R. Blauwhoff and L. Frohn, 'International Commercial Surrogacy Arrangements: The Interests of the Child as a Concern of Both Human Rights and Private International Law' in C. Paulussen et al. (eds.), *Fundamental Rights in International and European Law* (T.M.C. Asser Press, the Hague, 2016), at pp.219–227, para.10.3.

1153 Boele-Woelki (Chapter 1, n.1), at p.37.

1154 Kruger (Chapter 1, n.60), at para.6(b).

1155 See discussion of the absence of a choice of court and a *forum necessatis* provision in Brussels II bis in conjunction with Rome III in: Boele-Woelki (Chapter 1, n.1), at pp.37–38.

1156 Article 11 of the Property Regulations, Article 7 of the Maintenance Regulation and Article 11 of the Succession Regulation.

indicates that their primary purpose is to address situations in which a case is unable to be heard in a third state to which it is closely connected (e.g. due to civil war).[1157] It is not clear whether such provisions may be used in an intra-EU context.

10.6.3. ARTICLE 9 OF THE PROPERTY REGULATIONS

The Property Regulations establish a jurisdictional escape-clause for Member States that do not recognise the form of marriage or registered partnership that comes within their competence to hear a case pursuant to Article 4, 6, 7 or 8 of the Regulations. In contrast to the functioning of Article 13 of Rome III, this provision has the effect of facilitating access to justice by directing the case to another jurisdiction in accordance with Article 9(2).[1158] For these purposes, an alternative jurisdiction might be found in the Member State courts of the place where the relationship was created, on the grounds listed in Article 6.

In order to avoid an inconsistent interpretation with regard to the treatment of the marriage or registered partnership within a single jurisdiction, Article 9 serves to prevent a Member State from making use of its exception if this state would nevertheless recognise the parties' divorce, legal separation, marriage annulment or dissolution of the registered partnership (Article 9(3)).

10.7. THE IMPACT OF ENHANCED COOPERATION

A final barrier to the enforcement of a choice of law and/or court in this present context can be identified in the patchwork participation of the Member States in the current legislative framework. The failure of Member States to unanimously approve[1159] the most recent EU instruments in this field within a reasonable period of time has led to 'enhanced cooperation' (a legislative procedure involving agreement between a smaller number of Member States) being used to

---

1157 Recital 41 of the Matrimonial Property Regulation, Recital 40 of the Partnership Property Regulation, Recital 16 of the Maintenance Regulation and Recital 31 of the Succession Regulation.

1158 Quinzá Redondo (Chapter 6, n.671), at p.340. See also the stated intentions of EU legislator in Recital 38 of the Matrimonial Property Regulation and Recital 36 of the Partnership Property Regulation.

1159 The legislative process is more demanding (requiring Council unanimity) for the adoption of measures concerning family matters (maintenance, matrimonial matters, parental responsibility and property relations) under Article 81(3). Failure to adopt the regulations was based on form and function of the proposed rules and/or political reasons: see discussion in the context of Rome III in Boele-Woelki (Chapter 1, n.1), at pp.25–28.

introduce the Rome III Regulation and the Property Regulations. Although the United Kingdom, Republic of Ireland and Denmark generally do not participate in any of the relevant instruments,[1160] enhanced cooperation presents a much larger-scale and fragmented issue.

Table 7. Fragmentation: Enhanced Cooperation

Member States	Rome III	Property Regulations
Austria	x	x
Belgium	x	x
Bulgaria	x	x
Croatia		x
Cyprus		x
Czech Republic		x
Denmark		
Estonia	x	x
Finland		x
France	x	x
Germany	x	x
Greece	x	x
Hungary	x	
Ireland		
Italy	x	x
Latvia	x	
Lithuania	x	
Luxembourg	x	x
Malta	x	x
Netherlands		x
Poland		
Portugal	x	x
Romania	x	
Slovakia		
Slovenia	x	x
Spain	x	x
Sweden		x
United Kingdom		
	17	19

1160 See Chapter 5, n.526.

As can be seen from Table 7 above, 17 of the 28 Member States participate in the Rome III Regulation,[1161] whilst 19 Member States have signed up to join the Property Regulations once these instruments come into force in 2019.[1162] Whilst there is a core group of 13 Member States that participate in all three regulations (Austria, Belgium, Bulgaria, Estonia, Italy, France, Germany, Greece, Luxembourg, Malta, Portugal, Slovenia and Spain), there is nevertheless a small but significant variation demonstrated in the remaining participants in the respective regulations (Rome III: 4 of the 17 Member States;[1163] Property Regulations: 6 of the 19 Member States[1164]).

The principal consequence of this patchwork participation is clear; agreements formed pursuant to one of these instruments are not universally acceptable around the European Union. As a result, the benefits that party autonomy brings to those that exercise their right to free movement cannot be enjoyed in situations that fall outside of the enhanced cooperation. The more specific outcomes of fragmentation for those who exercise party autonomy according to Rome III (10.7.1.) and the Property Regulations (10.7.2.) will be explored in the subsections below.

10.7.1. THE ROME III REGULATION

In view of the participatory fragmentation under the Rome III Regulation discussed above, it can be observed that the absence of a parallel choice of court in matrimonial matters within the current EU framework means that parties have no means of directing their proceedings towards a jurisdiction that will recognise their choice of law agreement.[1165] International couples cannot be assured with a high degree of certainty that they will ultimately reap the benefits that party autonomy brings in the choice of law setting.

Of course, the reality of this assertion will vary depending on how 'internationally active' a couple is. For instance, a German couple who have moved to Spain for retirement can make a choice of law agreement under Rome III with a high degree of legal certainty as to its enforcement and the benefits this will bring, whilst a couple whose jobs necessitate movement throughout the Union cannot be assured to the same degree.

1161 Austria, Belgium, Bulgaria, Estonia, France, Germany, Greece, Hungary, Italy, Latvia, Lithuania, Luxembourg, Malta, Portugal, Romania, Slovenia and Spain. See Chapter 1, n.62.

1162 Belgium, Bulgaria, Cyprus, Czech Republic, Germany, Greece, Spain, France, Croatia, Italia, Luxembourg, Malta, the Netherlands, Austria, Portugal, Slovenia, Finland, Sweden and Estonia. See Chapter 1, n.65.

1163 Hungary, Latvia, Lithuania and Romania.

1164 Cyprus, Czech Republic, Finland, Sweden, the Netherlands and Croatia.

1165 Since it is the participation of the competent Member State in the relevant instrument that is the deciding factor in the success of an agreement in this regard.

The potential for the frustration of a couple's expectations after making a choice of law agreement according to Rome III is also particularly potent. Although the importance of informed choice is stressed in Recitals 18 and 19 of this instrument, there is clearly a risk that a couple will be unaware of the specific participants in the enhanced cooperation as they exercise their right to free movement around the Union.

10.7.2. THE PROPERTY REGULATIONS

The inclusion of an opportunity for a choice of court under both Property Regulations goes some way in mitigating the problems discussed in the subsection above. Under Article 7 of both instruments, parties can opt for either the courts of the Member State where their relationship was created, or those of the applicable law under this instrument. Through a strategic choice in favour of a participating jurisdiction, the parties can direct their choice of law agreement towards a Member State court that will enforce it; although it ought to be commented that this might come at the cost of other considerations relating to access to justice, or affinity with the applicable law through which the choice of court is made.

A number of caveats exist with regard to the above assertion. Firstly, there might not be a connection through which a couple can make a choice of court under one of these instruments. It is perfectly possible that the neither the place of creation, nor one of the spouses' habitual residences or nationalities align with a participating Member State at a moment in time. However, it should in that case at least be clear to the parties when examining the rules in pursuit of finding a connection that their present situation falls outside the remits of the enhanced cooperation (thus removing the risk of the frustration of expectations).

Furthermore, a choice of court under Article 7 cannot generally be made with regard to property proceedings that occur upon the dissolution of a relationship[1166] or in conjunction with a succession.[1167] Thus, generally speaking, the same negative outcomes for a choice of law that have been highlighted on the basis of the lack of a parallel choice of court for divorce or legal separation in the Rome III context also apply here.

[1166] According to Article 5, jurisdiction is generally linked to the court of dissolution upon the agreement of the parties (and automatically linked for spouses if a court for dissolution of the marriage is seised under the first four indents of Article 3(1)(a) or under Article 3(1)(b) of Brussels II bis). A choice of court can only be made where agreement cannot be reached according to Article 5.

[1167] See automatic linkage with the court seised under the Succession Regulation according to Article 4.

10.8. SYNTHESIS

The preceding subsections have outlined the variables that emerge from different quarters to impact upon the enforcement of a choice of court or choice of law within the EU private international framework relating to family matters and succession. In line with this book's format, the following synthesis will establish an overview of the evaluation that has taken place (10.8.1.), before examining these considerations in light of the interplay between related areas (10.8.2.), and the gaps that necessitate further action (10.8.3.).

10.8.1. OVERVIEW OF THE FINDINGS

In view of the evaluation regarding the variables affecting enforcement discussed in this chapter, the following observations can be made:

1. This chapter began with an examination of the variables that apply specifically in the jurisdictional context. Choice of court agreements generally benefit from a high degree of predictability with regard to their enforcement, since the majority of the relevant instruments provide that an agreement should be exclusive in nature. The exception to this is found in the flexibility permitted in Article 4 of the Maintenance Regulation, whereby the parties can contract out of the default exclusivity of jurisdiction. Although this lowers legal certainty, it increases the number of jurisdictional possibilities for the parties, which can be viewed as particularly important in facilitating access to justice for the creditor (especially given the risks involved in an outdated choice of court agreement).
2. Given the interpersonal nature of the family and succession law setting, the risk of the orchestrated abuse of the *lis pendens* rule (i.e. so-called 'torpedo actions') that would give rise to considerable delays and the frustration of other parties' expectations is low. However, in view of the residual possibility for a party who no longer wishes to be bound by a prior choice of court agreement to use the *lis pendens* rule to hamper proceedings taking place, the insertion of provisions that give priority to party autonomy in Article 20(4) and (5) of the new Brussels IIa (Recast) Regulation can be seen as a progressive step.
3. The variables that may potentially be imposed upon a choice of law are comparatively more extensive than those discussed for jurisdiction. These restrictions come in three forms: overriding mandatory provisions, public policy and the substantive rules prescribed by the instruments within the framework. Whilst the first two categories are principally for the Member State court to ascertain and to impose, the final group of rules emanate from relevant instruments and bind the Member State courts to act accordingly.

Overriding mandatory provisions and public policy can be furthermore distinguished from one another in terms of the respective active and passive natures of their imposition.

4. With regard to both overriding mandatory provisions and public policy, it is clear that the EU legislator intends that these restrictions are identified or employed sparingly, only in order to protect imperative national interests (overriding mandatory provisions) or fundamental values (public policy). This strict interpretation is required in order to safeguard the objectives behind the EU's introduction of unified private international law rules, most prominently the need for legal certainty in the enforcement of an agreement. Whilst overriding mandatory provisions are concentrated in the instruments that concern property, rules permitting the use of public policy are present in every instrument that addresses the choice of law context.

5. The delineation of public policy within the present framework is unclear in a couple of regards. Firstly, in contrast Article 13 of the Hague Maintenance Protocol, the EU Regulations do not establish whether an examination of public policy has to be performed on an abstract or concrete basis (i.e. whether an exclusion is made on the basis of the law itself, or its actual effects).

   Secondly, it is argued here that the inclusion of the guidance provided in the recitals of the respective EU Regulations, which states that a provision of the law cannot be set aside when to do so would be contrary to the EU Charter of Fundamental Rights (in particular, Article 21), is confusing and disproportionate. Whilst the presence of discrimination is one of the principal grounds for which public policy would be invoked, the recitals are instead referring to the more obscure situation in which to apply a public policy exception would in itself be discriminatory.

   Finally, in view of the wording of the Hague Maintenance Protocol, it is not clear whether the drafters intended that an entire applicable law should be set aside in the event that a provision of this law contravenes the public policy of the forum. Although there is nothing in the Protocol or in the accompanying Explanatory Report to indicate to the contrary, this approach would be entirely out of step with the relevant EU instruments and the requirement that this provision be interpreted very restrictively.

6. The substantive provisions prescribed in the relevant instruments serve a variety of protective purposes that help to establish an autonomous EU standard for an applicable law, namely ensuring (equal) access to divorce or legal separation, protecting third parties with regard to a change in the law that applies to a couple's property regime, and ensuring the needs of both the creditor and the debtor are taken into account for in the calculation of maintenance.

   Notwithstanding the generally positive light in which the above substantive provisions are viewed, the inclusion of the escape-clause which can be invoked if the applicable law is not sufficiently connected to the debtor, in accordance with Article 6 of the Hague Maintenance Protocol, is highly questionable, considering that the choice of law agreement is a positive action that has (presumably) been entered into with the informed consent of both parties, and that there is no parallel provision to apply to a chosen law that is judged to be disconnected from the creditor.

7. The recognition of 'non-traditional' relationships, most prominently same-sex marriage, is an evolving area of law within the European Union (see Table 6 at 10.6.1. for comparison of the occurrence of same-sex marriage and registered partnership in Member States' national laws). Whilst it appears that Member States are still free to refuse to recognise such relationships for the purposes of conducting proceedings, the increasing inclusion of same-sex marriage in national laws and the case law emanating from the CJEU indicate that the tide is turning in favour of Union-level recognition. For now, those in 'non-traditional' relationships will have to contend with legal uncertainty, and make use of the avenues for safeguarding their expectations where these exist within the framework (prioritising recognition of their relationship above other considerations that influence choice).[1168]

   Notwithstanding the above *status quo*, it is considerably less clear how Member States ought to deal with a 'non-traditional' parent-child relationship, in view of the additional need to factor in the primary or paramount consideration of the best interests of the child.

8. Participatory fragmentation brought about through enhanced cooperation in Rome III and the Property Regulations results in much lower levels of legal certainty for international couples in these subject areas. As evidenced in Table 7 (see 10.7.), agreements can only be enforced in 17 (Rome III) and 19 Member States (Property Regulations). Where a choice of court is not possible[1169] and the jurisdictional grounds direct the relationship towards a jurisdiction that is not a participant in the relevant regulations, there is a significant risk that parties who have made a choice of law according to its rules will have their expectations frustrated. Furthermore, it can be stated that since priority will have to be given to *jurisdictions* that participate in the enhanced cooperation above other considerations relating to access to justice and affinity with the applicable *law*,[1170] this will have a constraining

[1168] For instance, the option to direct a relationship to the courts of the Member State in which the relationship was created, under Article 7 of the Property Regulations.

[1169] As is the case for the determination of jurisdiction for divorce or legal separation under Brussels II bis, as well as for all cases concerning succession (Article 4) and most cases involving the dissolution of the relationship (Article 5) under the Property Regulations.

[1170] Since jurisdiction can be determined on the basis of a choice of law through Article 7 of the Property Regulations.

effect upon the breadth of choice under the Property Regulations. The topic of enhanced cooperation will be considered further in the next subsection with regard to the interplay between related areas (10.8.2.).

10.8.2. INTERPLAY BETWEEN RELATED AREAS

The circumstantial nature of many of the variables affecting enforcement discussed in this chapter does not facilitate in-depth examination of the interplay between related areas. Notwithstanding this, conclusions can be proposed in view of the general interplay between jurisdiction and applicable law, as well as on the basis of the limitations brought about through non-recognition of 'non-traditional' relationships and enhanced cooperation in Rome III and the Property Regulations.

1. A choice of court that fulfils the temporal, formal and material requirements set out in the previous chapter encounters few additional variables to the enforcement of choice. In contrast, it has been demonstrated that a choice of court might be restricted through variables imposed by the Member States and the EU instruments. It can thus be generally remarked that where jurisdiction and applicable law are coordinated through choice, the latter is more susceptible to variation that may form an obstacle to cohesion.
2. The non-recognition of a relationship (most prominently, same-sex marriage and registered partnership) has the potential to impact upon coordination. Firstly, it can be observed that for a choice of law to be successful for parties in 'non-traditional' relationships, it is necessary that a choice of court be made in favour of a jurisdiction that is likely to recognise this form of relationship (chiefly, but not exclusively, one that provides for this relationship in its national law – see Table 6 at 10.6.1.). However, this might not always be possible, either because a jurisdiction that recognises the relationship is not available under the grounds of close connection or due to the lack of an opportunity to make a choice of court under Brussels II bis.

   It is also important to consider the intersection of the potential non-recognition of certain relationship forms with the limited Member State participation in enhanced cooperation. In order to illustrate this, Table 6 (Recognition of same-sex marriage and registered partnership – 10.6.1.) and Table 7 (Participation in enhanced cooperation – 10.7.) have been combined in Table 8 below.

Table 8. Fragmentation: Enhanced Cooperation and 'Non-Traditional' Relationships

Member States	Rome III	Property Regulations	Same Sex Marriage	Registered Partnership
Austria	x	x	x	x
Belgium	x	x	x	x
Bulgaria	x	x		
Croatia		x		x
Cyprus		x		x
Czech Republic		x		x
Denmark			x	x
Estonia	x	x		x
Finland		x	x	x
France	x	x	x	x
Germany	x	x	x	x
Greece	x	x		x
Hungary	x			x
Ireland			x	x
Italy	x	x		x
Latvia	x			
Lithuania	x			
Luxembourg	x	x	x	x
Malta	x	x	x	x
Netherlands		x	x	x
Poland				
Portugal	x	x	x	
Romania	x			
Slovakia				
Slovenia	x	x		x
Spain	x	x	x	x
Sweden		x	x	x
United Kingdom			x	x
	17	19	14	21

With regard to property relations it can be seen that parties are further hindered by the fact that a choice of law must be enforced in a participating Member State, which limits the possibility for recognition of their relationship even further. For instance, in the context of registered partnership, whilst the court of the Member State of creation[1171] or dissolution of the registered

[1171] Article 7 of the Partnership Property Regulation.

partnership[1172] will be one that recognises its effects, it does not necessarily follow that this will be a participating Member State that will apply the choice of law agreement (see further discussion of the impact of enhanced cooperation below).[1173] The situation is further exacerbated under the Rome III Regulation: since there is no parallel choice of court under Brussels II bis, the parties are not even given the opportunity to strategically select in advance a forum that will recognise both their relationship and a choice of law made under the aforementioned instrument.

3. As has been discussed in the previous section, agreements made according to the Regulations that have been adopted through enhanced cooperation clearly elicit a lower level of legal certainty compared with those made under other instruments within the framework. In order to ensure the enforcement of agreements, parties must secure the courts of a Member State that participates in the relevant instruments; however, due to the previously discussed legislative gaps, this is not always possible. This legal uncertainty impacts upon the opportunity to achieve both vertical and horizontal cohesion.

Firstly, under the Rome III and Property Regulations, a choice of law that unifies the law and forum can only be achieved if the jurisdiction that is seised is that of a participating Member State. Due to the limitations discussed in 10.8.1., depending on the circumstances, this might be difficult to achieve.

With regard to horizontal cohesion in jurisdictional matters, due to the default linkage under the Property Regulations to the court of the dissolution of the relationship (Article 5) or that which is competent to decide upon succession (Article 4), cohesion between such jurisdictions is assured with a high level of predictability (subject to the agreement of the parties where necessitated under Article 5). However, if the court that is determined for the purposes of dissolution of the relationship or succession is not that of a Member State that participates in the Property Regulations, this automatic linkage will not be achieved and jurisdiction for property relations in conjunction with these proceedings will be determined by the Member States' own rules.

Where parties wish to achieve horizontal cohesion by selecting the same law to apply to a couple's divorce, dissolution of the matrimonial property regime and decisions concerning maintenance between the parties (e.g. the designated law of their (last) common habitual residence

1172 Article 5 of the Partnership Property Regulation.

1173 The court of the applicable law could also be seised according to Article 7; however, this also depends on whether these connections lead to a court of a Member State that both participates in the Regulation and recognises the relationship.

or nationality[1174]), it is essential that a Member State which participates in both Rome III and the Matrimonial Property Regulation[1175] is seised for the proceedings concerning the divorce and the resulting dissolution of the matrimonial property regime in order to ensure the enforceability of this agreement (refer to Table 7 in 10.7 for comparison). Predictability regarding the success of horizontal cohesion in this setting will in principle be low. Although advanced agreement on linking jurisdictions appears possible under Article 5 of the Property Regulations, this choice is indeterminate since there is currently no possibility for a choice of court for matrimonial matters under Brussels II bis.

Attempts to achieve horizontal cohesion between the law that applies to decisions concerning a couple's property regime and that which governs maintenance obligations in the context of the dissolution of a relationship under the Partnership Property Regulation[1176] entail even less legal certainty.[1177] Since the private international law rules on the dissolution of registered partnerships are not unified, it may be very difficult to predict the Member State court that will be competent for the dissolution of the relationship, and therefore the jurisdiction that will be linked to it in accordance with Article 5 of the Partnership Property Regulation. The question of whether this will be a jurisdiction that participates in the Property Regulations will thus be difficult to answer in advance.

With regard to the above scenarios, the parties could attempt to work together to nominate a jurisdiction for the dissolution of the relationship that participates in the required instruments.[1178] Alternatively, parties could open up a broader range of fora by intentionally refusing to form an agreement under Article 5 and opting to make a choice of court under Article 7 of the Property Regulations. However, the construction of these instruments would appear to indicate that this possibility is not available

---

1174 See Article 5(1)(a), (b) and (c) of the Rome III Regulation, Article 22(1)(a) and (b) of the Matrimonial Property Regulation and Article 8(1)(a) and (b) of the Hague Maintenance Protocol. Alternatively, under the Protocol, the law that is designated as applicable to either the property regime (Article 8(1)(c)) or their divorce or legal separation (Article 8(1)(d)) can be selected.

1175 Austria, Belgium, Bulgaria, Estonia, Italy, France, Germany, Greece, Luxembourg, Malta, Portugal, Slovenia and Spain. See mapping out of participation in 10.7. above.

1176 See Article 22(1)(a) and (b) of the Partnership Property Regulation and Article 8(1)(a), (b) and (c) of the Hague Maintenance Protocol.

1177 Due to a legislative gap in this subject area, a choice of law agreement cannot be made for the dissolution of a registered partnership itself.

1178 In matrimonial matters, by seising the court of a Member State under Brussels II bis that participates in Rome III and the Matrimonial Property Regulation; with regard to registered partnership, the parties could seise a jurisdiction that, according to national private international law rules, participates in the Partnership Property Regulation.

to spouses or partners prior to proceedings being instigated for the dissolution of their relationship.

Furthermore, it can also be recalled that Article 8(1)(c) and (d) of the Hague Maintenance Protocol may be used to secure horizontal cohesion between the law applicable to maintenance and that which applies to a couple's divorce or legal separation or their property regime, even where the applicable law is determined on the basis of national rules (outside of enhanced cooperation). However, in the scenario that the court (or courts) seised for matrimonial matters and the resulting dissolution of the matrimonial property regime is that of a Member State that does not participate in either Rome III or the Property Regulations, there is a chance that divergent laws will apply to these proceedings, and thus parties will have to make the choice to coordinate with just one of these related areas under the Protocol's rules.

Where a couple wishes to coordinate the laws that apply to their respective successions and the dissolution of the property regime that arises from this, given the automatic jurisdictional linkage under Article 4 of the Property Regulations,[1179] recognition of the choice of law under these Regulations would be dependent on whether the court of the deceased's last habitual residence or nationality aligns with a participating Member State. It is suggested that the parties concerned might keep this in mind as a deciding factor in their agreement to a choice of court under the mechanisms established in Articles 5, 6, 7 and 9 of the Succession Regulation.

10.8.3. GAPS TO BE ADDRESSED

A number of notable areas to be addressed have arisen as a result of the evaluation that has been carried out in the present chapter:

1. Although the risk of co-called 'torpedo actions' is low in the interpersonal fields of family matters and succession, it is suggested here that out of respect for the autonomy of the parties and in order to tackle any

[1179] This is done by either selecting the law of the common habitual residence of the parties or of their common nationality under Article 22(1). It would be necessary to select a connection shared by the parties, since in most circumstances it will not be clear which spouse will pass away first. Linkage with habitual residence would clearly entail less predictability in achieving coordination between the laws that apply to the succession and the property consequences that arise therefrom, since connection to the law of the habitual residence at the time of death is the default rule under Article 21(1) of the Succession Regulation, and unless a designation is made under Article 22(1) of the Property Regulations very close to the point of death of one of the spouses, there is a risk that this criterion will shift over time.

inconvenient delays that might arise from the *lis pendens* rule where there is a pre-existing choice of court, the instruments that establish party autonomy in the jurisdictional context should include a provision similar to that contained in Article 31(2) of the Brussels I Regulation. In this regard, the recent insertion of such a rule in the new Brussels IIa (Recast) Regulation (Article 20(4) and (5)) represents a sign of progress.

2. In order to encourage a restrictive interpretation of public policy in line with the aims of the EU legislator (most notably with a view to safeguarding legal certainty), the EU Regulations and/or the documentation that accompanies these instruments should emulate the approach established in the Explanatory Report of the Hague Maintenance Protocol by specifying that the use of this exception should be performed on the basis of a concrete analysis.
3. The terminology employed by Article 13 of the Hague Maintenance Protocol does not make it clear whether an entire applicable law ought to be set aside upon the finding that a provision of this is contrary to the public policy of the forum. It is suggested here that this approach is not in line with the intention stated in the Explanatory Report that public policy is to be interpreted restrictively, and therefore the provision should be clarified by instead referring to 'the application of *a provision* of the law …' in Article 13.
4. Given the positive impact of Article 10 of Rome III in establishing an autonomous EU standard for the applicable law that is imposed through this instrument, it would be beneficial if a similar approach were to be extended to other related instruments, such as the Property Regulations (e.g. ensuring that the applicable law does not discriminate between men and women in terms of the division of matrimonial property or succession).
5. Remaining with the topic of substantive standards established in the EU regulations, it seems appropriate to point out that the recent recast of Brussels II bis includes a separate provision that mandates a court to give a child the opportunity to express his or her views with regard to matters that fall within the scope of parental responsibility according to this instrument.[1180] It is not entirely clear whether this obligation also extends to allow minors to express their views regarding a possible choice of court in conjunction with a consideration of the child's best interests.[1181] If this were to be the case, the inclusion of this requirement would equate to a significant shift in the adjudication of this criterion.
6. It would appear that the CJEU is slowly working its way towards cultivating an embracive right to recognition for those in non-traditional relationships,

1180 See Recital 39 and Article 21 of the Brussels IIa Regulation.

1181 Rather than simply an obligation to give an opportunity to the child to express their views with regard to the focus of the proceedings of which the court has been seised.

in particular same-sex marriage. In the meantime, access to justice for those in such relationships could be better delineated in the relevant instruments by emulating the prescribed approach to identifying an alternative jurisdiction that is set out in Article 9 of the Property Regulations, or by including a *forum necessitatis* provision that is designed to tackle such circumstances.[1182]

Furthermore, a greater and more expansive opportunity for a choice of court, particularly upon the dissolution of the relationship and with regard to property relations, would allow parties in a 'non-traditional' relationship to direct their proceedings towards a jurisdiction that will recognise it. In view of the points of critique established in the two preceding subsections, it can be proposed that a choice of court possibility under Brussels II bis, a set of unified jurisdictional rules (including an opportunity for a choice of court) for registered partners, and a general possibility for parties to make use of the choice of court opportunity under Article 7 of the Property Regulations upon dissolution of their relationship, would greatly enhance the scope for the parties to overcome obstacles to justice through exercising autonomy.

7. It is clear that the expectations of international parties are jeopardised by the fragmentation brought forth by enhanced cooperation within the current EU private international law framework. Whilst it is not entirely clear how the EU legislator would go about providing a safeguard for protecting the expectations attached to a choice of law agreement made according to the rules of the Rome III or the Property Regulations, it would appear appropriate to establish a provision that directs proceedings towards a participating jurisdiction in situations in which it is clear that the parties were acting under the law as determined by one of these instruments.
8. On a final note, in view of the discussion in this chapter and the preceding one, it is striking that there is no provision within the present framework to address a situation in which a chosen jurisdiction or applicable law has become disconnected from one or both of the parties through the passage of time. As discussed in the previous chapter,[1183] the possibility to make a choice of court or law in advance of proceedings taking place and/or in favour of an undetermined connection raises problems relating to the continuation of informed consent (particularly in the context of maintenance obligations, and especially under the Maintenance Regulation).[1184]

1182 As opposed to the present manifestation of the *forum necessitatis* provisions in the Property Regulations, Maintenance Regulation and Succession Regulation, which appear to be aimed at circumstances involving obstacles to justice in a third country.

1183 See, in particular, 9.2. and 9.3.

1184 Walker (Chapter 2, n.164), at pp.249–250 and Boele-Woelki (Chapter 1, n.1), at pp.30–31.

It has been suggested that a discretionary approach similar to that set out in Article 12 of Brussels II bis would be appropriate in the realm of family matters, whereby jurisdiction is determined at the time of proceedings on the basis of close connection, and the parties can choose the law of the forum.[1185] This stance would indeed tackle the matter of a problematic time lapse, as well as the propensity for a compromise in consent to arise as a result of parties in family relationships not dealing with one another 'at arm's length'. Whilst this approach could be framed as an appropriate means of dealing with the specific deficits in the realm of maintenance obligations, it is argued here that such temporal constraints and the general involvement of judicial discretion would be overly paternalistic for agreements between adults in other areas of cross-border family law.

Less intrusive means of addressing the problems associated with a temporal lapse could include a more moderate discretionary provision that allows a judge to set aside a choice of court or law where one party no longer wishes to be bound by it and there has been an appreciable shift in circumstances since the point at which the choice was made. Another possibility would be to mandate that parties periodically reaffirm their consent to an agreement (e.g. every five years) in order to ensure the continuance of its validity. Although this requirement would be more burdensome on the parties and legal professionals, it would have the effect of moving the parties' consent with the passage of time.

1185 In the absence of agreement, objective conflict of laws rules would determine the applicable law. See proposal of this approach in Walker (Chapter 2, n.164), at pp.251–253, 255–257.

PART V
CONCLUSION

CHAPTER 11
CONCLUDING SYNTHESIS

11.1. INTRODUCTION

This examination has arrived at the end point of its journey through the various aspects involved in exercising a choice of court or choice of law within the present EU private international law framework relating to family matters and succession. By employing a simultaneous approach, the provisions that allow for party autonomy within the relevant instruments have been evaluated in successive stages: (i) the preliminary elements of choice; (ii) the content of choice; and (iii) the variables affecting choice. This final step involves a reconsideration of the established manifestation of party autonomy with a view to establishing coherence with the parameters attached to this concept in the Union context.

This concluding synthesis brings together the strands of this investigation by integrating the findings back into the context of the values through which this evaluation has been conducted. In the interests of clarity, the synthesis will invert the order of the two introductory chapters that established these principles, presenting the impact of the relevant provisions in view of the EU legislator's objectives in unifying Member States' private international law rules (11.2.–11.4.), before taking the final step of (re-)considering the manifestation of free will in the EU's private international law rules relating to family matters and succession in light of the findings that have been established (11.5.).

The following sections follow the pattern established in the main chapters by examining (i) the general findings; (ii) the interplay between related areas; and (iii) the gaps to be addressed. The final considerations, set out in 11.6., will propose a number of closing suggestions in view of the key findings of this book.

11.2. LEGAL CERTAINTY

Turning attention first to the impact of party autonomy upon the specific obstacles that the unification of the EU's private international law rules on family matters and succession seeks to address (see Chapter 3), this synthesis begins by recapping on the aspects of legal uncertainty that international parties face in exercising their right to free movement in the European Union. Legal certainty is a difficult principle to succinctly describe, and its definition is not comprehensively examined in the relevant instruments or accompanying documentation. However, it is nevertheless proposed that legal certainty emerges from the rule of law, and for these present purposes, is seen to be composed of two principal elements:[1186] predictability and the protection of the parties' legitimate expectations. Whilst the former relates to an ability to plan future actions based on rules that are 'clear, stable and understandable',[1187] the latter extends backwards to protect expectations that have arisen as a result of a certain judicial or administrative decision, or through the attribution of a particular right or status.

Four layers of potential legal uncertainty have been identified with specific regard to the organisation of family and succession matters of internationally-active parties within the European Union. Firstly, there is the legal uncertainty that emerges from framework's sheer complexity, which makes it hard for parties to predict in advance the law that will apply to the processes that may arise as they move around the Union. This situation is perpetuated by the generally indeterminate nature of private international law rules (e.g. the availability of multiple fora to be seised or the ascertainment of a connection at the moment of choice). Moving on to a more abstract perspective, legal uncertainty also arises from the frustration of expectations that have been created in a previously applicable legal system (e.g. where a change in applicable law changes the consequences of a relationship) or entrenched expectations regarding the recognition of a relationship (e.g. the refusal to recognise same-sex marriage).

11.2.1. GENERAL FINDINGS

The essential premise of party autonomy – the ability to organise the legal conditions to which a person's relationships are exposed – inherently invites a regard for legal certainty. Through this possibility, the outcomes of proceedings can be predicted and the expectations that parties cultivate on the basis of such agreements can be safeguarded. However, this examination is focused upon the actual *manifestation* of party autonomy within the EU private international law relating to family matters and succession, and thus involves a much more

[1186] Given the obscure nature of legal certainty, there might arise situations in which other related components (e.g. non-retroactivity) are brought to the forefront: Kruger (Chapter 3, n.231), at p.297.

[1187] Paunio (Chapter 3, n.241) at p.1469.

in-depth examination of the multiple aspects that comprise the formation, content and enforcement of choice within this context:

1. In view of the delineation of the subject matter over which an agreement might be made, it is observed that the framework of inclusions and exceptions established in the majority of the instruments contributes towards a generally high level of clarity. It is also noted that where no reference is made to the national law of the Member States with regard to concepts in EU legislation, a uniform and autonomous meaning is attached to the matter at hand. This contributes to legal certainty through the development of a common meaning on a supranational level, independent of the variations in national rules.

   However, there are nevertheless a number of caveats to this general assertion, most prominently the unresolved question of what constitutes a cross-border situation for the purposes of the present context, as well as certain residual grey areas such as whether the list of exclusions contained in the EU Regulations is considered to be exhaustive in nature. Furthermore, it can be highlighted that the instruments concerning maintenance obligations (particularly the Maintenance Regulation) present comparatively less delineation of their subject matter than the other relevant instruments. However, it is proposed here that this omission might foreseeably be intentional in order to allow a particularly broad scope of application that facilitates access to justice.
2. It is also concluded here that the delineation of the focus of choice – the Member State court or applicable law – is generally well defined and unproblematic. Whilst the definition of 'court' for the purposes of the EU's jurisdictional rules is the more convoluted of the two concepts, a well-prescribed framework of rules is nevertheless presented. Furthermore, additional clarification has been added in this regard through recent CJEU rulings,[1188] most notably the apparent exclusion of a religious or private authority from the definition of a 'court' for the purposes of Rome III and Brussels II bis.[1189]
3. With regard to the main content of this investigation – the connections through which a choice of court or choice of law can be exercised – it can be seen that direct connections invite a sliding scale of legal certainty during the course of a relationship to the point of proceedings, with the place of creation most easy to ascertain and maintain, followed by nationality, then domicile, and finally habitual residence.

1188 *Saponaro* (Chapter 4, n.463); *CAFA v. J.D.* (Chapter 4, n.450); and *L. v. M.* (Chapter 8, n.785).

1189 It is asserted here that, in the absence of indication to the contrary, religious or private authorities also fall outside the definition of court for the other relevant instruments: see *Sahyouni* (Chapter 4, n.345).

The flexible nature of habitual residence makes it suitable for transient parties; however, particularly in view of the possibility to employ it in an indeterminate manner as a jurisdictional choice under the Maintenance Regulation,[1190] its changeable and situational nature might make it hard for parties and legal practitioners to predict which court will ultimately govern proceedings.

Another comment that can be made in view of the direct connections is that the place of celebration[1191] offers particular legal certainty for those in 'non-traditional' relationships, who can be assured, through this ground, of recognition of the effects of their relationship and an ability to safeguard their expectations.

4. Linking provisions, by their indirect nature, generally present less predictability than direct connections. However, this depends on the fixity of the ground with which the provision coordinates. For instance, Article 8(1)(c) and (d) of the Hague Maintenance Protocol presents a high level of predictability by requiring that a connection be made with a law which is already designated or in fact applies to the couple's property regime or their divorce or legal separation. On the other hand, the apparent possibility to make a pre-emptive agreement that designates the *lex fori* to apply to future proceedings under Rome III[1192] necessarily entails a much lower level of predictability at the time that the agreement is made.

   Article 7 of the Property Regulations presents a fairly high level of predictability in the linkage with either the applicable law that can be designated under the same instrument, or the place of marriage or registered partnership celebration. However, there is an evident lack of clarity with regard to the manner in which the relationship between Article 5[1193] and Article 7 of the Property Regulations is delineated. Whilst it is apparent that functionally the latter comes into play if the parties have not agreed to link jurisdiction to the court of dissolution under the former, this possibility is not made at all clear in the stated purpose of Article 7 in the texts of the respective Regulations or the accompanying documentation. Above all, it would appear that parties whose property relations primarily come within the scope of Article 5 cannot benefit from the advanced jurisdiction linkage that is permitted under Article 7 for property relations that occur outside of a succession or the dissolution of a relationship.

1190 Article 4(1)(a) and (c)(ii).

1191 Choice of court: Article 7 of the Property Regulations; Choice of law: Article 22(1)(c) of the Partnership Property Regulation.

1192 Article 5(1)(d) of Rome III.

1193 See Article 5(2) of the Matrimonial Property Regulation and Article 5(1) of the Partnership Property Regulation.

5. The mechanisms that involve a subsidiary regard for party autonomy entail the lowest level of legal certainty amongst the provisions examined here. This can be attributed to the fact that these mechanisms do not involve a regard for forward planning and focus instead upon securing other outcomes for the parties (primarily practical outcomes based on securing access to justice[1194]).
6. The temporal, formal and material requirements for a choice of court or choice of law within the present context provide much food for thought in terms of legal certainty. It is observed that the ability to capture a particular law or court in advance maximises legal certainty for parties, allowing them to move around the Union with a concrete notion of the legal system that will govern any proceedings that arise, and maintain expectations concerning their relationship on the basis of the rules that might ultimately apply. By contrast, the ability to make an advanced agreement in favour of an undetermined connection (e.g. under Article 4 of the Maintenance Regulation[1195]) clearly holds the propensity for legal uncertainty to arise from a shift in circumstances.
7. Due to its imprecise wording, the timing and manner of acceptance of jurisdiction under Article 12 of Brussels II bis presents a particular flashpoint with regard to legal (un)certainty. However, it should be noted that this provision has been the focal point of recent CJEU judgments that serve to clarify the manner in which it should be employed, albeit at times in a piecemeal fashion. Furthermore, the new Brussels IIa (Recast) Regulation demonstrates a considerably more prescribed process in this regard.[1196]
8. The variables that restrict the enforcement of a choice, by their essential function, have a negative impact upon legal certainty. On the basis of such rules or conditions, Member States or the relevant instruments themselves can limit the success of a choice, which in turn impinges upon the predictability of a designation and the expectations that the parties have pinned to this. Of particular risk in this regard is the refusal of certain Member States to recognise 'non-traditional' relationships that come within their jurisdiction and the participatory fragmentation that emerges from enhanced cooperation. Such situations might well result in the frustration of expectations that parties have fostered on the basis of choice of court or choice of law agreements that have been made within this present framework.

1194 See discussion in 11.4.

1195 See also Article 5 of the Property Regulations, Article 5(1)(d) of Rome III and Article 22 of the Succession Regulation.

1196 See Article 10 of the Brussels IIa Regulation.

On a positive note, it is observed that, at least in so far as the identification of overriding mandatory provisions and the usage of the public policy exception are concerned, such restrictions are required to be strictly interpreted in order to secure the objectives behind the EU's unification of private international law rules (including legal certainty). Furthermore, in view of the general stance towards the exclusivity of a jurisdictional choice, it can be argued that the relevant provisions are generally geared towards the enforceability of a specific choice of court agreement.

11.2.2. IMPACT OF THE INTERPLAY BETWEEN RELATED AREAS

In view of the coordination and cohesion between related areas, this evaluation has given rise to a number of observations with regard to the pursuit of legal certainty:

1. In view of the delineation of the subject matter covered by the respective instruments, it can be seen that there is a degree of overlap between property relations on the one hand, and maintenance or succession on the other. This holds the potential for legal uncertainty to arise concerning the question of which category a certain topic is deemed to fall within.

   It ought, however, to be taken into account that the CJEU has provided guidance as to how these subject areas are to be characterised in borderline situations.[1197] In particular, with regard to the relationship between property relations and maintenance, the court has provided a set of fairly comprehensive guidelines concentrating on the aim of an order. Although the same depth of examination has not been performed by the CJEU with regard to the delineation of property relations *vis-à-vis* succession,[1198] a recent judgment shed light on this distinction, again framing the *focus or aim* as pivotal to characterising the provision in question.

   Although there is also the potential for overlap between maintenance and succession, the latter instrument is fairly clear in demarcating the border between these two issues, stipulating that all maintenance obligations other than those that arise by reason of a death are excluded from the scope of the Succession Regulation.[1199]

1197 *De Cavel II* (Chapter 4, n.418).

1198 *Mahnkopf* (Chapter 4, n.326).

1199 Article 1(2)(e) of the Succession Regulation.

2. With regard to the coordinating provisions that determine jurisdiction through linkage with related areas, due to the fact that a choice of court is not permitted for matrimonial matters under the Brussels II bis Regulation, uncertainty can be seen to emerge under Article 5(2) of the Matrimonial Property Regulation, Article 4(1)(c)(i) of the Maintenance Regulation and Article 5(1)(d) of Rome III. Any prior agreement is indeterminate, and is only predictable in the sense that it would secure the applicability of an unsubstantiated connection in advance.

   An even lower level of legal certainty arises under Article 5(1) of the Partnership Property Regulation which links to the Member State court of the dissolution of the relationship. Since the EU has not unified private international law rules on this subject area, the level of clarity and predictability is in principal even less than that discussed above.
3. The employment of enhanced cooperation to bring about Rome III and the Property Regulations clearly impacts upon predictability in the process of attempting to achieve vertical and horizontal cohesion between related areas. Taking the example of coordination between the laws that apply to divorce, the dissolution of matrimonial property and maintenance, whilst the Hague Maintenance Protocol is participated in by all Member States apart from the United Kingdom and Denmark, only 17 Member States participate in Rome III, whilst 19 Member States have opted into the Property Regulations. In order to ensure the enforceability of a choice of law that achieves cohesion between the three related instruments, it would have to be ensured that the jurisdiction that is seised is one of the 13 that participate in all Regulations. This is complicated by the fact that no choice of court is permitted for divorce or legal separation under Brussels II bis, meaning that the parties cannot opt in advance for a participating jurisdiction.[1200]
4. In order to achieve consistency between the connections that govern related areas, parties need to be aware of the impact of differences in the temporal or formal requirements imposed by the respective instruments. The prime example is demonstrated with regard to a choice of law under Article 22 of both the Property Regulations and the Succession Regulation: to be assured with a high degree of predictability of the success of this coordination, parties should choose the law of their nationality at the moment of choice. It they opted instead for the law of nationality to be determined at the time of death, there is a risk that this might have shifted from the ground which

[1200] Furthermore, party autonomy is only partially permitted under Article 5(2) of the Matrimonial Property Regulation, and in any case generally leads to one of the grounds specified under Brussels II bis.

has already been determined according to the agreement made under the Property Regulation.

5. The potential for the refusal to recognise 'non-traditional' relationships in certain Member States poses an even greater challenge to predictability and the protection of expectations that arise through coordination of choice of law agreements. It might not be clear to the parties in advance whether their relationship (and thus their agreements) will be recognised by the forum. This is further perpetuated by the lack of a choice of court under Brussels II bis,[1201] and the jurisdictional limits imposed by enhanced cooperation that further restrict the number of suitable fori available.

11.2.3. GAPS TO BE ADDRESSED

Leading on from the in-depth discussion of the achievement of legal certainty in the preceding subsections, a number of gaps have been highlighted that would benefit from being addressed in the present context:

1. Firstly, it would be useful if the CJEU were to take steps to clarify the autonomous meaning to be attached to habitual residence in the EU private international law setting, particularly in the context of adult relationships or succession. Although this transient concept necessitates flexibility, the provision of guidelines as to its usage would increase uniformity in application and clarity for international parties and practitioners.
2. In view of the especially high level of predictability attached to the place of celebration as a connecting factor (particularly with regard to those parties who are in 'non-traditional' relationships), it is suggested here that its occurrence should be extended in the framework in both the jurisdictional and conflict of laws contexts. Most prominently, the place of celebration should be offered as a ground to be chosen under Article 22(1) of the Matrimonial Property Regulation in order to allow spouses to make a union between the law and court that will govern their proceedings under this particularly secure ground.
3. In contrast to the position of the EU legislator in drafting the Succession Regulation, it is argued here that the opportunity to designate the law of the deceased's habitual residence in advance would in fact serve to meet the expectations of the beneficiaries of the estate in some circumstances, such as when the deceased had recently moved to another Member State prior to death and retains ties with their original Member State.

[1201] Meaning that the parties cannot direct the proceedings that revolve around matrimonial matters towards a suitable jurisdiction.

4. It has been made clear from the above discussion that legislative gaps pose a major obstacle to the optimisation of legal certainty by restraining parties in the organisation of their legal relations through autonomy, and potentially leading to a frustration of their expectations. On this basis, it is strongly argued that a choice of court is an imperative addition in matrimonial matters, and that unified private international law rules should be introduced by the EU on the dissolution of registered partnerships (including the opportunity for a choice of court and choice of law in this setting). In the former regard, it is very unfortunate that a jurisdictional choice has not been included in the final draft of the new Brussels IIa (Recast) Regulation, which means the limiting *status quo* will continue for the foreseeable future.
5. Article 7 of the Property Regulations should be offered as an option on equal footing to Article 5 in determining jurisdiction in cases that arise in conjunction with the dissolution of a relationship. In view of the fragmented participation in enhanced cooperation in combination with the present lack of a choice of court provision under Brussels II bis and the lack of unified private international law rules on the dissolution of registered partnerships, the aforementioned opportunity under Article 7 would give parties an increased chance to safeguard the expectations pinned to a choice of law agreement made under the Property Regulations.
6. It is clear that the interests of international parties are jeopardised by the fragmentation brought forth by enhanced cooperation. It is not entirely clear how the EU legislator would go about providing a safeguard that protects the expectations of parties who make a choice of law agreement according to the rules of the Rome III or the Property Regulations, but it would appear appropriate to establish a provision that directs proceedings towards a participating jurisdiction in situations in which it is clear that the parties are acting under the law as determined by one of these instruments.
7. Finally, there are a number of diverse residual points that require clarification either by the CJEU or in EU documentation in order to improve usability and uniformity of application, such as the relations between the complex network of choice of court provisions contained in Articles 5, 6, 7, and 9 of the Succession Regulation,[1202] the question of whether a court could assume jurisdiction of its own motion under Article 12(3) of Brussels II bis[1203] and the breadth of scope permitted to the Member State in setting aside a law that offends its public policy in accordance with Article 13 of the Hague Maintenance Protocol.

[1202] In particular, there is a need to draw a distinction between the purposes of Article 7(c) and Article 9 of the Succession Regulation.

[1203] Although this issue appears to be clarified by the new Brussels IIa Regulation: see discussion at 8.2.1.

11.3. AFFINITY WITH THE APPLICABLE LAW

The second highlighted obstacle to be faced by parties who exercise their right to free movement in the Union involves a potential lack of affinity with the law that applies to their legal processes. In particular, the application of objective, 'one-size-fits-all' conflict-of-laws rules could give rise to the application of a law that does not reflect a party's life and/or relationships and the expectations that arise therefrom.

The existence of a legal connection in this regard is not the same as affinity, since this latter concept represents the actual ties that bind a party to a particular state's legal system. The considerations involved in forming such an affinity (*knowledge of the law*, *entrenched expectations*, *integration in society* and *shared values*) may be based on a particular state and its law – either the state in which their everyday life is situated, or where their culture and/or family origins are located. In addition to this *personal affinity*, there is another type of connection – *situational affinity* – that can be seen to link a particular relationship or property (rather than the parties themselves), to a certain legal system.

Given the strong link between the society within a country, its values, and the nature of its family or succession law, the existence of affinity can be seen as having a higher priority in the family or succession law setting than in other areas of private international law (e.g. contractual obligations). These are areas that often strike at the heart of personal values, and the law that applies to them ought to reflect these values accordingly.

11.3.1. GENERAL FINDINGS

A number of overall conclusions can be proposed in view of the scope for securing a law of close affinity within the present framework:

1. Habitual residence is a flexible ground that has risen to prominence in view of the need to cater to the increasing transience of populations across borders. Ascertained on the basis of a multitude of considerations,[1204] this is a social criterion that aims to reflect 'the life actually lived'[1205] by the parties. As a choice of law connection, habitual residence can be seen to provide a law that is integrated in the present circumstances of the parties and the expectations that arise from them, proving particularly useful where the application of the law gives rise to economic consequences

1204 For example, the duration of residence, intention to remain, nature of abode, employment or business ties, and the existence of family and social links.

1205 See the prioritisation of this in the Explanatory Memorandum accompanying the Property Regulations proposals (Chapter 2, n.179), at p.10, para.5.3.

(e.g. the calculation of maintenance). The disadvantage inherent in the flexibility of this criterion is that it is liable to become outdated in view of the long-running nature of family relationships and the shifting circumstances of internationally-active parties.

The opportunity to select the habitual residence of the parties is provided for in all the relevant instruments that establish a choice of law, with the exception of the Succession Regulation. One point of distinction which will be revisited later in this subsection is the fact that the Rome III Regulation requires the habitual residence to be connected to *both* parties,[1206] whilst under the Property Regulations and Hague Maintenance Protocol the habitual residence of *either* party can be designated.

2. In contrast to habitual residence, nationality relates to a fairly stable aspect of a person's status. Whilst internationally-active parties may change habitual residence a considerable number of times during the course of their lives, nationality is more difficult to lose or acquire, and is more much more likely to remain fixed during the course of a lifetime. As a question of official status, it is also much easier for a layperson to ascertain.

   Although, due to the increased global movements of persons across borders, nationality is no longer the guarantee of factual connectedness that it once was,[1207] it can nevertheless be asserted that parties tend to have at least some connection with the state of their nationality. With regard to its advantages in the choice of law context, nationality can be seen as a means of securing a law from a culture with which one is familiar.

   In contrast to the priority given to habitual residence in the objective conflict-of-laws rules in the present framework, nationality is the most prevalent choice of law connection in the context of party autonomy. It is accordingly provided for in all the relevant instruments that establish choice of law rules. In addition, it can be remarked that a connection to just one party is permitted in all areas.

3. The place where a relationship was created is a novel ground within the EU private international law framework, and is established as a choice of law under Article 22(1)(a) of the Partnership Property Regulation. The merits of applying this law to a legal process concerning a registered partnership centres on the fact that such relationships are neither uniformly recognised, nor do they entail the same consequences in each of the respective state laws in which they are provided for. By establishing a connection to the law of the state in which a relationship was created, the parties can maintain the expectations that arose from the original attainment of their status.

1206 See Article 5(1)(a) and (b) cumulatively: the (last) common habitual residence of the parties 'in so far as one of them still resides there at the time the agreement is concluded'.

1207 Fawcett / Carruthers (Chapter 6, n.626), at p.181 and McEleavy (Chapter 6, n.626), at pp.619–620.

4. In considering affinity with the applicable law, there are some additional barriers to connectedness that can be identified. Firstly, it is clear that the law does not have to be connected to both parties under the majority of the instruments concerning adult relationships. This is problematic in the sense that, at least in so far as the EU regulations are concerned, the recitals and accompanying documentation make it clear that the connection is to be made to the parties and their relationships. Allowing the habitual residence or the nationality of *either* party to be chosen does not equate to the understanding of affinity in this context.

   The detrimental impact of a law with which one party holds an affinity is particularly exemplified in the context of maintenance obligations. In order to obtain a calculation of maintenance that suits the circumstances of the creditor's life, circumstances or expectations, it is arguable that joint affinity to the applicable law is necessary. Whilst it could be argued that adults with decision-making capacity can be entrusted with agreeing to a designation which they perceive to meet their needs, this does not align with the constraints of close connection that govern this realm.[1208]

   Secondly, there is also the potential for a lapse in time or change in circumstances to give rise to a disconnect from the state whose law the party or parties have previously chosen. This is particularly likely to occur with habitual residence, especially in cases where the parties move frequently between different states. Whilst disconnect might also emerge between the parties and a chosen law of nationality, this is much less likely due to the entrenched nature of this status.
5. It is a foregone conclusion that the autonomy of the parties is restricted in this realm. However, there are nevertheless areas in which the EU legislator appears to be inconsistent or overly restrictive within these established confines. Most prominently, this is seen in the inability of a party to make a *professio juris* in favour of the law of their present habitual residence under the Succession Regulation. Even though the EU legislator justified this constraint on the basis of the need to balance party autonomy with the interests and expectations of the beneficiaries of the estate,[1209] it is argued here that permitting the selection of the party's habitual residence at the time of designation would actually, in some circumstances, cater to the interests of both of the deceased and his or her beneficiaries, such as where the deceased only recently retired abroad prior to their death and primarily retains links with a former habitual residence.

1208 See further discussion in the context of 'The manifestation of free will in the present framework' (11.5.).

1209 See Recital 38 of the Succession Regulation and the Explanatory Memorandum accompanying the Proposal for the Succession Regulation (Chapter 2, n.178), at p.6, para.4.3.

11.3.2. IMPACT OF THE INTERPLAY BETWEEN RELATED AREAS

A small number of observations can be made in view of the impact of the pursuit of cohesion upon the opportunity to select a law of affinity:

1. The generally high level of consistency between the applicable laws that are available to be chosen by the parties for related proceedings means that they will generally not have to sacrifice affinity in pursuit of the practical outcomes associated with cohesion. However, an exception to this is identified with regard to vertical cohesion under the Property Regulations in proceedings that occur in conjunction with a succession. Due to the automatic jurisdictional linkage with the court of succession under the Property Regulations, only the law of habitual residence or nationality will align with this jurisdiction, meaning that under the Partnership Property Regulations, the law of the place of creation cannot be selected if the parties wish to maintain this form of cohesion.
2. Notwithstanding the generally uniform provision of choice of law connections for related matters concerning adult relationships, there is inconsistency in the framework in terms of the requisite connectedness of both parties to a single habitual residence necessitated under the Rome III Regulation, which contrasts with the possibility for the habitual residence of only one of the spouses to be selected as a ground under the Matrimonial Property Regulation and the Hague Maintenance Protocol. This means that if the parties wish to secure horizontal cohesion, they are restricted to the law of their (last) common habitual residence as delineated under Rome III.
3. Parties might also have to prioritise certain grounds for determining the applicable law in order to ensure recognition of their 'non-traditional' relationship, or direct their proceedings towards a forum that participates in a regulation adopted under enhanced cooperation. An example of this can be identified under the Property Regulations, whereby the parties might have to eschew choosing a connection with a law with which they have a stronger affinity in order to secure a law of a participating Member State under Article 22 to which jurisdiction can be linked through Article 7.

11.3.3. GAPS TO BE ADDRESSED

A couple of gaps can be highlighted for further legislative scrutiny in view of the analysis of the parameters for selecting a law of affinity that have been discussed above:

1. In light of the argumentation proposed in the first subsection (11.3.1.), it is suggested that a possibility be introduced for a party to make a *professio*

juris in favour of their present habitual residence under the Succession Regulation. It is proposed that this would provide greater scope for a party to secure a law of close affinity whilst at the same time continuing to maintain an adequate level of protection for the expectations of the beneficiaries.

2. Given the ubiquitous trend of permitting the law of either party's habitual residence to be selected to apply to a process arising from a relationship under the relevant instruments that provide for a choice of law, it is not entirely clear how the EU legislator ought to proceed with regard to the highlighted issue of joint connection. However, the existence of this possibility clearly contrasts with the restrictive mandate that the EU legislator pursues in the field of cross-border family matters and succession. Thus, it is suggested here that this divergence between rhetoric and practice merits further consideration on the EU stage.

11.4. PRACTICAL CONSIDERATIONS IN ACCESSING JUSTICE

Action by the EU legislator to develop the area of freedom, security and justice has been justified by the goal to make everyday life simpler for those who exercise their right to free movement within the Union.[1210] In this regard, it was proposed in Chapter 3 that parties who are internationally active within the EU may come up against practical hindrances to accessing justice in legal proceedings concerning family matters and succession.

The practical obstacles referred to above have been framed as falling into three categories: (i) the need to travel to attend proceedings that are held outside a party's state of habitual residence and/or where related proceedings are held in different Member State jurisdictions; (ii) more complex and costly proceedings as a result of their cross-border character, for example, the possible unfamiliarity of the parties with the legal system and the necessity to hire additional expertise (e.g. translators or bi-lingual legal practitioners) to guide them through the process; and (iii) incompatible interactions, for instance if the applicable laws that concern related proceedings come from different countries and do not have a compensating effect upon one another. The above hindrances can be seen as obstacles to the right to access to justice, which forms part of the right to a fair trial under Article 6 ECHR and Article 47 of the EU Charter of Fundamental Rights.

1210 Tampere Conclusions (Chapter 1, n.2), at para.28 and the Hague Programme (Chapter 3, n.198), at para.3.4.1.

11.4.1. GENERAL FINDINGS

The conclusions regarding the practical outcomes relating to access to justice that have emerged from this evaluation of the present framework are summarised below:

1. The direct connections established in Chapter 5 primarily hold consequences in terms of the reflection of parties' free will and their ties of affinity, as well as the securing of legal certainty. On the other hand, the coordinating provisions (Chapter 6),[1211] and to an even greater extent, the subsidiary party autonomy provisions (Chapter 7) are aimed at eliciting practical outcomes for the parties. To employ the example of Articles 12(3) and 15 of Brussels II bis, both are principally designed to direct proceedings towards a more suitable jurisdiction, with particularly the latter *forum non conveniens* mechanism involving an comparative analysis of the practical merits of holding proceedings in the respective Member States (e.g. the availability of medical or social reports on the child and the language of the court[1212]). Other considerations, such as the exercise of the parties' free will, are given minimal regard in this setting.
2. Notwithstanding the assertion at the start of the first point above, direct selection of a present habitual residence as a jurisdictional choice also offers parties the opportunity to secure the most suitable forum in terms of access to justice. This relates not only to physical proximity, but also to the ease of coordination with national authorities in the enforcement of court orders. There are also practical benefits that are apparent in terms of applicable law: using the example of maintenance obligations, application of the law of habitual residence of the creditor may also cater to the calculation of an appropriate level maintenance on the basis of their present circumstances. However, the value of habitual residence is significantly diminished in both instances where this criterion is not common to both parties in an agreement (or, in the case of maintenance, at least associated with the creditor),[1213] and significantly more so when a choice based on this criterion becomes outdated over time (see discussion below).
3. The entrenched nature of nationality as a determinant of jurisdiction or applicable law can also be perceived to hold specific benefits in terms of access to justice, namely based on the notion that a basic familiarity with a culture of a certain country will permit a degree of accessibility to aspects

[1211] See further discussion with regard to interplay between related areas at 11.3.2. below.

[1212] AG Wathelet on *CAFA v. J.D.* (Chapter 8, n.819), at para.95.

[1213] See also for a critique of the potential for a lack of commonality in the connecting factors that apply: 11.3.1. and 11.5.1.

of its legal system[1214] (e.g. the language of the legislation and procedural paperwork, and familiarity with the values upon which the legal culture is based). However, it ought also to be recalled that it is possible to have no real connection to a party's nationality, thus this argument is by no means a foregone conclusion.

4. The examination of the temporal requirements for agreements has revealed a potential for an advanced choice of court to become, in itself, an obstacle to accessing justice. Due to the passage of time and the long-running nature of family relationships, a designation of a particular connection at the moment of choice (especially habitual residence) may well become outdated and no longer suitable as a determinant for the proceedings that will ultimately take place. Especially in the context of jurisdiction, the arising practical problems (e.g. a need to travel to a former habitual residence to attend proceedings) may be particularly harmful for creditors in maintenance proceedings in view of their already disadvantaged position. This problem would, however, be addressed in cases where the parties have made use of the possibility to form a non-exclusive choice of court agreement under Article 4(1) of the Maintenance Regulation, whereby the designated jurisdiction could be framed as simply an additional possibility through which to access justice.
5. The risk of orchestrated abuse on the basis of the *lis pendens* provision that is contained in all relevant instruments would appear to be low. Notwithstanding this, there however remains a residual possibility that this provision comes into play where one party wishes to seise another court in order to cause harmful delays to proceedings that sabotage the interests of a weaker party, or where the party no longer wishes to be bound by a prior agreement.
6. By mandating that parties are permitted to divorce and requiring that men and women can access divorce or legal separation on an equal basis, it is observed that Article 10 of Rome III serves to safeguard access to justice with regard to the effects of the applicable law. This provision can be seen to contribute towards an autonomous EU standard on the substance of the applicable law that may be applied according to its instrumentation.
7. On the other hand, access to justice may be completely obstructed where parties come up against a forum that does not recognise their form of relationship, or which does not participate in the exercise of enhanced cooperation under the Rome III Regulation or the Property Regulations. In certain situations, this is perpetuated by legislative gaps in the form of the lack of a choice of court under Brussels II bis and the complete absence

[1214] See outlined problems based on comprehension of unfamiliar proceedings at 3.5.2.2. and discussion of nationality as a means of tackling this at 6.5.1.

of unified private international law rules for the dissolution of registered partnerships.[1215] With regard to such circumstances, Article 9 of the Property Regulations can be seen to provide a well-prescribed route through which parties can attempt to access justice in an alternative jurisdiction.

11.4.2. IMPACT OF THE INTERPLAY BETWEEN RELATED AREAS

The interplay between related areas provides considerable scope for evaluation in terms of the practical considerations relating to access to justice:

1. Beginning with 'vertical cohesion'[1216] – the union between the court and applicable law – it is proposed that this possibility allows the parties to a proceeding to avoid the application of foreign law by the forum and the additional time and monetary costs that accompany this, as well as the possible inaccuracies in application that might arise at the hands of a foreign judge.[1217] Consulting the cumulative overview of the party autonomy provisions within the present framework (see Table 5 at 8.4.2.), it is observed that the possibility to unify the law and forum is provided for in matrimonial matters, maintenance obligations, property relations and succession.

   The routes to achieving this vary: according to Article 5(1)(d) of Rome III, the *lex fori* can be selected, whilst under Article 7(1) of the Property Regulations and Articles 5, 6, 7 and 9 of the Succession Regulation the court may be determined through linkage with the applicable law. It can be noted that, in line with the general remit of Article 7 of the Property Regulations, a union between the law and forum is not generally intended for cases concerning succession or the dissolution of marriage in this setting. With regard to maintenance obligations, parties can coordinate the law and court through either making direct choices under Article 4 of the Maintenance Regulation and Article 8 of the Hague Maintenance Protocol, or opting for the *lex fori* under Article 7 of the latter instrument.
2. The aspect of 'horizontal cohesion' involves consideration of the ability to select the same courts to govern related matters, namely those that arise out of the dissolution of a marriage or registered partnership (proceedings dissolving the relationship, in conjunction with the dissolution of the property regime, maintenance and / or parental responsibility), or upon the death of one of the spouses or partners (succession proceedings in

[1215] Whereby parties have fewer possibilities to direct a relationship towards a suitable forum.

[1216] See description of this term and sequential ones in 1.4.

[1217] See discussion at 3.5.2.2–3.5.2.3, 6.5.2.

conjunction with the dissolution of the couple's property regime). It has been argued that coordination in this regard reaps practical benefits such as removing the necessity to travel between jurisdictions to hear related proceedings, and eliminating the costly need to hire duplicate legal representation in separate jurisdictions.[1218]

The Brussels II bis Regulation is the lynchpin round which proceedings concerning matrimonial matters can be coordinated. The opportunity for linkage is provided in Article 5 of the Matrimonial Property Regulation, Article 4(1)(c)(i) of the Maintenance Regulation and Article 12(1) of Brussels II bis. These three provisions differ from one another in formulation: firstly, it is observed that the possibility for the parties to agree to extend jurisdiction to that determined through the grounds in Brussels II bis is only partially present in Article 5 of the Matrimonial Property Regulation; with regard to jurisdiction seised according to the first four indents of Brussels II bis, Article 3(1)(a) and Article 3(1)(b), linkage is automatic. Due to the lack of a choice of court opportunity under Brussels II bis, as well as the nature of linkage under Article 12(1) of this instrument, advanced planning does not appear to be facilitated in this setting.

It can be commented that the lack of a choice of court opportunity in this regard poses a specific obstacle to access to justice for same-sex spouses, since they cannot secure in advance a jurisdiction under Brussels II bis that will recognise their form of marriage. This situation is perpetuated if the forum seised under Brussels II bis is one with regard to which no agreement is required according to Article 5 of the Matrimonial Property Regulation; in such instances, the parties will not have the opportunity to consider the impact of non-recognition upon related proceedings.

It is also important to note that given the general blanket exclusion of party autonomy for maintenance obligations concerning minors under the Maintenance Regulation, it is not possible for the parties to agree to coordinate the jurisdiction that is competent for such matters with that which concerns related matrimonial matters or questions of parental responsibility.

The opportunity to coordinate with the courts that govern the dissolution of the registered partnership is only facilitated under Article 5 of the Partnership Property Regulation. Similarly to the situation for matrimonial matters, advance planning of the linkage is not possible, since there is currently a lack of unified private international law rules on the dissolution of registered partnerships. In view of the potential for non-recognition, it is interesting to note that in comparison to same-sex spouses, the lack of unified rules on the dissolution of registered

[1218] See discussion at 3.5.2.1.–3.5.2.2, and 7.6.1.

partnerships means that the parties might actually have more freedom to secure a jurisdiction that will recognise their relationship form.

Although it is technically outside the scope of this investigation, it can also be remarked that horizontal coordination between the court that is competent for succession and the court that makes decisions on matters concerning a couples' property regime in conjunction with this process is automatically facilitated according to Article 4 of the Property Regulations.

3. The other aspect of 'horizontal cohesion' that which exists between applicable laws on related matters – serves to avoid incompatible interactions between divergent applicable laws on related matters and to remove the need to hire duplicate or specialist legal representation with competence in both or all legal systems concerned.[1219]

This can be facilitated in matrimonial matters through the selection of the same connecting factors for the determination of applicable law. In overview of the grounds contained in Article 5 of Rome III, Article 22 of the Property Regulations and Article 8 of the Hague Maintenance Protocol, an agreement can be made under all three instruments designating the law of the (former) common habitual residence of the parties or the law of either of their nationalities.[1220]

Although there is no possibility for coordination on an EU level with the law that applies to the dissolution of a registered partnership, the applicable law that governs decision-making on the partners' property regime can be coordinated with that which applies to maintenance obligations in the same manner as for relations between spouses (Article 8(1)(c) of the Hague Maintenance Protocol).

Horizontal cohesion can be achieved between the law that is chosen to apply to a couples' property regime and that which is designated for each of their successions where the couple shares a common nationality and this is designated in advance under Article 22 of the Succession Regulation. If the parties do not share a nationality, the likelihood of cohesion is significantly less, since they will have to predict which party will predecease the other in order make a selection under Article 22(1)(b) of the Property Regulations. However, it should be noted that a solution to this problem has been proposed, whereby a clause providing for the application of the law of the nationality of the party who predeceases the other is inserted into the agreement on the choice of law that applies to the parties' property relations upon one of their deaths.[1221]

1219 See discussion at 3.5.2.2.–3.5.2.3, and 6.5.2.

1220 With Rome III being the obstacle to permitting designation of the law of the habitual residence of either party, since this is provided for under the other two instruments.

1221 See discussion in 6.5.2. in view of Villata / Valkova (Chapter 6, n.602), at pp.86–89, 95–99 and 124–128. However, see also the potential limitations of this solution discussed in 9.3.2.1.

4. Notwithstanding the particular functioning of Articles 6(a), 7(a) and Article 9 of the Succession Regulation and Article 8 of the Property Regulations,[1222] it can be remarked that the more open subsidiary party autonomy provisions do not, by their specific aims and limited remit, invite the achievement of cohesion between related areas.
5. Temporal limits and a possibility for an indeterminate choice to be made have been identified during this evaluation as holding the potential to impact upon the achievement of coordination. For instance, with regard to 'vertical cohesion' in maintenance obligations, whilst it appears to be possible to designate an undetermined jurisdictional connection in advance under Article 4 of the Maintenance Regulation, Articles 7 and 8 of the Hague Maintenance Protocol require that the connection be designated concretely at the moment of choice. Thus, in order to ensure cohesion, care should be taken to secure a particular court at the moment of choice.

   Another example arises with regard to 'horizontal cohesion' between applicable laws in the context of proceedings related to matrimonial matters. It is seen that whilst the Matrimonial Property Regulation permits a choice of law by future spouses prior to marriage, this does not appear to be a possibility under Rome III.[1223] The consequence of this is that if the parties make a choice of matrimonial property law in a prenuptial agreement and the chosen connection changes after marriage, they will have to amend this agreement in order to achieve coordination with a subsequent choice of law for a future divorce or legal separation under Rome III.
6. It is proposed that, in general, differences in formal or material requirements between related areas do not lead to a high degree of inconvenience for the parties involved beyond the need to adhere to different requisites when manifesting a choice.
7. Enhanced cooperation, in combination with legislative gaps, presents a barrier to the achievement of coordination between related areas. For instance, where a choice of law is made under the Rome III Regulation, the Matrimonial Property Regulation or the Hague Maintenance Protocol, the cohesion which is secured can be frustrated if the court which is seised according to Brussels II bis does not participate in either the Rome III Regulation and/or the Matrimonial Property Regulation.

1222 Which are specifically intended as alternative routes to securing vertical cohesion.

1223 Although Hague Maintenance Protocol has a wider personal scope, it is not stated whether the relationship between future spouses falls within the scope of this instrument for the purposes of making a choice of law. Prenuptial designation would, in any case, not appear to be appropriate.

11.4.3. GAPS TO BE ADDRESSED

In view of this evaluation in the context of the interaction between the party autonomy provisions in the present framework and the goal of removing practical obstacles to accessing justice, a number of areas for improvement can be highlighted:

1. The Property Regulations present a set of rules that, by their very complexity, hinder access to justice. It is thus useful to reiterate the need for a more direct route for spouses or partners to access the jurisdictional possibilities contained in Article 7 in cases involving the dissolution of the relationship in order to provide clearer pathways to navigating, in particular, the participatory fragmentation that exists within the framework.
2. This dimension of the evaluation has again highlighted the necessity for legislative gaps to be addressed, namely the provision of a choice of court under the Brussels II bis Regulation and the establishment of unified private international law rules (including jurisdictional choice) for the dissolution of registered partnerships. With particular regard to Brussels II bis, even a very limited choice of court (e.g. selection of the court of the law which applies to the divorce or legal separation) would bring significant practical benefits to the parties.[1224] However, given that the recast of this instrument has recently been introduced without any opportunity for party autonomy in matrimonial matters, a solution is not anticipated anytime soon.

   It is also proposed that the EU legislator revisit the possibility of allowing a degree of party autonomy in the jurisdictional context for maintenance obligations concerning minors. Although this is an area with specific sensitivities, it is argued that the present approach is inconsistent with the more permissive treatment of parental responsibility under Brussels II bis, and forms an obstacle to the coordination of related proceedings relating to the child and his or her family.
3. Although the interpersonal scope of the subject areas being discussed here means that orchestrated abuse of the *lis pendens* rule is unlikely to be pervasive, the widespread introduction of a similar provision to that contained in Article 31(2) of the Brussels I Recast would nevertheless remove the residual possibility for the harmful impact of such a rule upon a choice of court agreement. In this regard, it should be noted that the insertion of a provision that gives priority to party autonomy in Article 20(4) and (5) of the new Brussels IIa (Recast) Regulation demonstrates a step in the right direction.

1224 Particularly through coordination with the grounds in the Rome III Regulation. See for proposal of this approach: Viarengo / Marchetti (Chapter 3, n.313), at p.30.

4. The inclusion of a specific *forum necessitatis* rule[1225] or a provision that prescribes the route to an alternative jurisdiction in a similar manner to Article 9 of the Property Regulations would be a useful inclusion to other relevant instruments within the framework in order to direct a 'non-traditional' relationship towards a jurisdiction in which it will have access to justice.
5. In order to expand upon the establishment of an autonomous EU standard regarding the type of law that ought to be applied according to its instrumentation, it is suggested here that a similar provision to Article 10 of Rome III be established in other instruments (in particular, the Property Regulations and the Succession Regulation) in order to ensure baseline standards such as equality between men and women.

11.5. THE MANIFESTATION OF FREE WILL IN THE PRESENT FRAMEWORK

Having presented the findings of this analysis in light of the goals that lie behind the EU legislator's unification of the Member States' private international law rules, this final stage of the concluding synthesis brings the evaluation full circle by integrating its results into a (re-)consideration of the manifestation of free will within the present framework. Referring back to the baseline delineation of party autonomy that was presented in Chapter 2, this section will highlight the extent to which the manifestation of party autonomy, as represented during this examination, corresponds to this preliminary paradigm.

To recap on this principal stage of delineation, party autonomy in the EU's private international law rules on family matters and succession assumes a distinct, restrictive character that reflects the delicate balance between respect for an individual's free will, the juxtaposition of legal and societal interests in the family and succession law, and the need to protect the interests of specific parties in these fields.[1226] This book does not seek to challenge the present paradigm, but instead evaluates the manifestation of party autonomy within the purported confines in which it has been established. Particular attention will not only be paid to the extent of choice in this regard, but also the baseline foundations of free will – namely that a party's decision is authentic and sufficiently informed.

1225 That expressly addresses the denial of access to justice on the basis of the non-recognition of a relationship form.

1226 See establishment of these elements in 2.4.

11.5.1. GENERAL FINDINGS

The evaluation carried out here has revealed a network of conclusions regarding the breadth of choice that is permitted and the adherence to the standards established for the manifestation of free will within the EU's private international law rules on family matters and succession:

1. By firstly looking to the subject areas across which party autonomy can be exercised, it is apparent that parties are not offered the chance to exercise their free will fully in the realm of matrimonial matters, for which no choice of court is permitted. Furthermore, there is no opportunity for partners to organise the legal conditions to which the dissolution of their registered partnership is exposed. Finally, it is also clear that party autonomy is significantly curtailed with regard to maintenance obligations involving minors, in view of the general exclusion under the Maintenance Regulation (with the exception of Article 5), and the sole possibility to select the *lex fori* under Article 7 of the Hague Maintenance Protocol.
2. In view of the discussion at the start of this section, it is an accepted fact that party autonomy within the present framework is not unlimited. With a view to the breadth of choice within the constraints of close connection (see the cumulative overview in Table 5 at 8.4.2.), it is firstly observed that the relevant instruments concerning adult relationships generally provide for selection of the court and law of the habitual residence and nationality (or domicile) of either of the parties.[1227] Under the Succession Regulation, choice is limited to the court and law of nationality.

   As has been elaborated upon in previous sections,[1228] these two connections provide internationally-active parties with the option of designating either a flexible criterion that reflects their current situation, or one that offers the possibility of securing an entrenched, stable element that is representative of their culture. It can be seen that whilst such connections can be designated directly in the context of applicable law, selection through jurisdictional choice is generally[1229] determined on the basis of coordination.

[1227] See the exception to this assertion in Rome III, which only permits the selection of the law of the (last) common habitual residence of the parties in so far as one of the parties still resides there at the time the agreement is made (Article 5(1)(a) and (b)). Furthermore, jurisdictional choice in favour of the law of the parties' habitual residence or nationality can only generally be performed under Article 7 of the Property Regulations with regard to proceedings that occur outside of a succession or the dissolution of a relationship.

[1228] See 11.2.1. and 11.3.1.

[1229] With the exception of Article 4 of the Maintenance Regulation.

3. The place where a relationship was created is a novel ground within the EU private international law framework that has been introduced by the Property Regulations. In light of the potential for the frustration of expectations of those in 'non-traditional' relationships upon exercising their right to free movement, it is particularly useful for ensuring recognition across borders. It is both unfortunate and puzzling that it is only offered as a determinant of jurisdiction and applicable law under the Partnership Property Regulation (it is only a jurisdictional connection for property relations between spouses). Expansion of its presence within the relevant instruments would thus be a considerable attribute to the framework.
4. As mentioned in the context of considering parties' affinity with the applicable law,[1230] it can be highlighted that the Succession Regulation presents a particularly narrow parameter in which to exercise free will in the context of a choice of law, since only the law of nationality of a party at the time of designation or at their death can be selected through a *professio juris*. Although there is a need to strike a balance between the interests of the deceased and those of their beneficiaries, it has been argued that this should not have been an impediment to permitting the law of habitual residence at the time of choice to be selected.
5. Whilst a choice of law is generally determined on the basis of direct connection, jurisdictional choice is more likely to be indirect, exercised either through coordination or on a subsidiary basis. With regard to the latter-mentioned mechanisms (Chapter 8), the free will of the parties is not the underlying justification. Instead, practical considerations (e.g. the existence of a court which is better placed to hear proceedings concerning parental responsibility) are the guiding force behind such mechanisms.[1231]

   However, somewhat counter-intuitively, it can also be noted that the breadth of possible choice is, in fact, at its widest with regard to those provisions in which the free will of the parties is a subsidiary consideration. Most notably, under Articles 12(3) and 15 of Brussels II bis, as well as Article 5 of the Maintenance Regulation, any Member State court might possibly be prorogued or accepted by the participation of the parties.
6. In the specific context of the Property Regulations it is observed that the exercise of free will in the jurisdictional context is unequally established between the subject areas addressed by these instruments: whilst Article 5 appears to constrain the extent of choice to linkage with the court which is competent for the related dissolution of a relationship, Article 7 offers a comparatively wider range of options for a choice of court (generally) occurring outside of a succession or the dissolution of a relationship.

1230 See 11.3.1. and 11.3.3.

1231 See the discussion of practical considerations in accessing justice in 11.4.

7. In view of the recent Brussels IIa (Recast) Regulation, it can be highlighted that there are marked changes in terms of the tone and extent of party autonomy that the new instrument brings forth. In the context of Article 12 (recast: Article 10), the drafters appear to favour a more assertive tone that moves towards the choice of court agreement seen in other areas (albeit subject to ascertainment of substantial connection and the best interests criterion). At the same time, party autonomy within the *forum non conveniens* mechanism contained in Article 15 (recast: Articles 12 and 13) looks set to be scaled back, whereby acceptance by the parties will no longer be a necessity as an additional 'check and balance' in proceedings where the court has instigated this mechanism of its own motion or another Member State court has requested that a case be transferred to its jurisdiction.
8. Another matter that emerges from this evaluation relates to joint connectedness of the parties with a choice. In so far as the connection of habitual residence is concerned, the Rome III Regulation requires that this criterion be connected to both of the parties. Notwithstanding the criticism that can be levelled at this inconsistency within the framework, as has already been argued in the context of 'affinity with the applicable law',[1232] it is particularly troublesome that the EU legislator employs rhetoric based on a restrictive stance that indicates a preference for joint affinity or connection with the relationship in question, but does not act according to this mandate in establishing the grounds in the relevant instruments. Whilst this investigation is not aimed at challenging the constrained parameters of choice in this realm, the approach of the EU legislator can nevertheless be criticised as inconsistent with its established aims in this field.

   It is also highlighted that the issues which arise from the potential for disconnect are particularly pertinent in the context of maintenance obligations, whereby the governance of a jurisdiction that is difficult for the creditor to attend[1233] or the application of a law that does not reflect the social environment of the creditor might be especially detrimental to a claim for sustenance.[1234]
9. A choice in favour of an indeterminate connecting factor is permitted under the Maintenance Regulation, the Property Regulations, the Succession Regulation and, seemingly, Article 5(1)(d) of the Rome III Regulation. Whilst this possibility allows a choice to move with the circumstances of the parties, it potentially makes it harder to predict the ultimate law or forum that will govern a proceeding. In light of this, a choice in favour of

1232 See 11.3.1.

1233 See discussion at 11.4.1.

1234 See discussion at 11.5.1.

an undetermined connecting factor can be framed as an obstacle to the continuation of informed consent, since the parties cannot ascertain the precise content and consequences of their choice with certainty.

10. Where a choice can be made in advance and continues in perpetuity, it has been argued that a lapse in time can also be viewed as affecting the continuance of informed consent.[1235] This is particularly an issue with regard to areas in which a choice might govern subsequent proceedings that take place over a long period of time (e.g. maintenance obligations or property relations). There does not appear to be any specific regard for this scenario within the present framework.

    An additional point to make in the above regard particularly relates to the potentially detrimental impact of an advanced choice under Article 4 of the Maintenance Regulation. As has been discussed previously,[1236] the opportunity to exercise advanced party autonomy in this setting poses a particular risk of impeding access to justice for the creditor.

11. In view of the formal requirements established within the framework, at least with respect to a choice that is expressed in advance, it is seen that the relevant instruments impose requisites that serve to draw the parties' attention to what is being agreed and provide the primary element for evidencing material validity (tying in with the baseline requirements of informed and authentic consent respectively). Most of the instruments adhere to a high standard in this regard, requiring that a choice be written (or expressed electronically), dated and signed. However, it is notable that the Maintenance Regulation does not adhere to this high standard, simply requiring that an agreement be expressed in writing. This omission is all the more surprising given the inbuilt power inequality in the field of maintenance obligations.

12. There is a clear asymmetry with regard to the material requirements established in the provisions concerning choice of law compared to those that involve a jurisdictional choice. Apart from the Hague Maintenance Protocol,[1237] all the relevant instruments that provide for choice of law establish a route through which the law that applies to material (or substantive) validity can be ascertained. Rome III and the Property

---

1235 See this possibility in Article 5 of the Rome III Regulation, Articles 7 and 22 of the Property Regulations, Article 4 of the Maintenance Regulation, Article 8 of the Hague Maintenance Protocol and Article 22 of the Succession Regulation. It should be mentioned with regard to the primarily singular focus of divorce and succession that concerns regarding subsequent proceedings are of less concern here.

1236 See 11.4.1.

1237 Although guidance is nevertheless provided in this regard in the Explanatory Report: Bonomi (Chapter 4, n.400), at para.151.

Regulations also emphasise the importance of informed choice,[1238] and establish provisions designed to address material validity in situations in which the circumstances indicate that the consent of a party may have been compromised.[1239] The Hague Maintenance Protocol contains an even more extensive safety net that has the impact of setting aside a choice of law where its consequences are viewed as manifestly unfair or unreasonable, and it is ascertained that the parties were not fully informed or aware of such consequences at the time of choice.

13. In the jurisdictional context, with the exception of Article 8(2) of the Property Regulations (see discussion below), none of the instruments refers to the need to safeguard material validity at the time of choice. Although it could be argued that the impact of a choice of court is relatively easy for the parties to ascertain and does not hold the same substantive outcome as a choice of law, as has been discussed with regard to, in particular, the Maintenance Regulation, there are certainly situations in the jurisdictional context in which a party ought to be informed regarding the consequences of a choice of a potentially indeterminate connection.

    In addition to the above points, in view of the apparent possibility for minors to accept jurisdiction by entering an appearance under Article 5 of the Maintenance Regulation (see discussion below in this subsection), it is most concerning that there is no requirement for the defendant to be informed regarding their rights upon entering an appearance and the consequences that flow from it (as is established in Article 8(2) of the Property Regulations).

    It is also observed that the recent Brussels IIa (Recast) Regulation appears to raise both formal and material standards for jurisdictional choice in the context of Article 12 (new version: Article 10).[1240] This can be seen to signify a decisive shift in stance that would hopefully set a higher legislative bar for ensuring the fullness of the parties' autonomy in jurisdictional matters.

14. As mentioned in the introductory chapters, family matters and succession are areas that readily encompass relationships that involve emotional and/or financial interdependency. In view of this, there is a need to establish strong safeguards in order to ensure the fullness of parties' consent in this setting (i.e. the requirement that the exercise of free will be authentic

1238 See Recitals 18 and 19 of Rome III, Recital 46 of the Partnership Property Regulation and Recital 47 of the Matrimonial Property Regulation.

1239 See Article 6(2) of Rome III and Article 24(2) of the Property Regulations.

1240 See Recital 23 and Article 10(1)(b)(i) and (ii) of the Brussels IIa (Recast) Regulation.

and informed[1241]). In view of both general and specific propensities for a power imbalance to arise due to the interpersonal nature of relations in this realm, is especially important that the parties are sufficiently informed by an independent legal specialist regarding the content and consequences of their choice.

Despite sporadic references to the need for parties to be informed (e.g. see Recitals 18–19 of the Rome III Regulation) and certain provisions designed to cater to situations in which a party may have not been adequately informed (e.g. see Article 8(5) of the Hague Maintenance Protocol), it is striking that there is a lack of clear and consistent guidance as to the baseline standard to be imposed on this requirement.

15. As established in Chapter 2, there are a number of categories of party that, due to their inherent characteristics, are considered to be in a weaker position.[1242] Firstly, it can be seen – from the decisive influence of judicial discretion in the jurisdictional mechanisms established in Article 12 and 15 of the Brussels II bis Regulation, in combination with a mandated regard for consideration of the best interests of the child – that the interests of minors are in principle well protected within this instrument.

The well-delineated stance of the Brussels II bis Regulation contrasts with the inconsistent approach of the Maintenance Regulation. Whilst it is disputable – particularly in the absence of appropriate material safeguards – whether it is appropriate for minors (or their representatives) to accept jurisdiction by entering an appearance under Article 5 of the Maintenance Regulation, the general blanket exclusion of party autonomy under this instrument can be criticised as unduly constraining in view of the opportunities offered with regard to parental responsibility.

A divergence is also observed between the instruments concerning maintenance in their approach towards the category of vulnerable adults: whilst the Hague Maintenance Protocol restricts party autonomy for such parties on an equal basis to children, there is no parallel regard for the particular position of vulnerable adults under Article 4 of the Maintenance Regulation.

Remaining with the topic of maintenance obligations, it is seen that the Hague Maintenance Protocol establishes safeguarding provisions that are aimed at protecting the position of the creditor,[1243] and requires that an applicable law be identifiable at the moment of choice.[1244] In contrast, as has already been discussed in this subsection, the Maintenance Regulation

[1241] See 2.2.1.

[1242] See 2.4.2.

[1243] See Articles 8(5) and 14 of the Hague Maintenance Protocol.

[1244] A particular law must be chosen, meaning that the parties are at least aware at the moment of choice of the actual law that will ultimately apply.

does not appear to establish a well-defined approach that serves to protect the vulnerable position of the creditor in agreeing to a jurisdictional choice.

Moving on to the Succession Regulation, by allowing the beneficiaries and creditors of an estate to participate in a choice of court, as well as by restricting the breadth of choice for a *professio juris* in order to protect their expectations, this instrument demonstrates an extensive regard for the interests of potentially a large pool of parties. It might even be argued that the Succession Regulation goes too far in this regard: in addition to the aforementioned restrictions upon the deceased's choice of law, the influence that the 'parties concerned' have upon the jurisdiction that governs the dissolution of a couple's property regime can be strongly called into question.

It has been shown that the Property Regulations establish a carefully prescribed framework that provides rules which protect the interests of third parties from the adverse effects of a retroactive change in the applicable law.[1245] They also delineate the circumstances in which a third party can successfully request the non-applicability of a particular law to a dispute where they are ascertained not to have known[1246] that this law applied to the couple's property regime.

16. It has been established that Member States have the option to vary the application of a law that has been chosen by the parties on the basis of overriding mandatory rules and their own public policy. It is, however, emphasised that these restrictions upon free will are to be identified or employed very restrictively. More intrusive upon the exercise of party autonomy are the substantive provisions established in the relevant instruments that impose normative standards altering the impact of a choice of law, such as the requirement under Article 14 of the Hague Maintenance Protocol that, even if the applicable law provides otherwise, the needs of the creditor and the resources of the debtor should be taken into account in the determination of maintenance. Despite the restricting effect of their provisions upon party autonomy, it ought to be emphasised that such rules serve an important role in safeguarding fundamental standards or the interests of certain parties within the present framework.

17. The enhanced cooperation that has been employed to bring about the Property Regulations has had the effect of limiting the breadth of jurisdictional choice towards Member State courts that participate in such instruments. In order to ensure the enforceability of an agreement, the parties will have to give priority to a jurisdiction that participates in

1245 Article 22(3) of the Property Regulations.

1246 Article 28 of the Property Regulations: 'unless the third party knew or, in the exercise of due diligence, should have known of that law'.

the relevant regulation, regardless of other practical or affinity-based considerations.[1247] A similar line of argument can be made with regard to the recognition of a relationship, although this outcome might be even harder for the parties to ascertain in advance. In this situation, the parties would be constrained by the requirement that the jurisdiction that is chosen must recognise their relationship.

11.5.2. IMPACT OF THE INTERPLAY BETWEEN RELATED AREAS

A couple of different observations are made regarding the impact that the interplay between related areas has upon the manifestation of free will in the EU's private international law rules on family matters and succession:

1. As briefly discussed in the context of 'affinity with the applicable law',[1248] the pursuit of cohesion has the potential to constrain the breadth of choice. In addition to what has previously been established, it has also been shown that due to legislative gaps, the quest for horizontal cohesion could limit the breadth of choice in the jurisdictional context. For instance, if the parties to proceedings related to matrimonial matters wish to horizontally link the competent jurisdictions, the lack of a choice of court under the Brussels II bis Regulation would mean that the other choices are constrained by the court that is seised according to this instrument.[1249]
2. Turning specifically to the linking provisions contained in Article 5 of the Property Regulations, it is observed that since agreement is always required in order for a jurisdiction to be linked to that which is competent to dissolve a registered partnership under Article 5 of the Partnership Property Regulation, there is in fact more scope for party autonomy under this provision than under Article 5 of the Matrimonial Property Regulation (whereby extension to the first four indents of Article 3(1)(a) and Article 3(1)(b) is automatic).
3. In addition to restricting jurisdictional choice in a single process, enhanced cooperation and the possibility for the non-recognition of a relationship also hold the potential to constrain the breadth of choice available for achieving

[1247] Since a choice might have to be made in favour of the law of this jurisdiction, which can then be secured through Article 7 of the Property Regulations.

[1248] See 11.3.2.

[1249] Although linkage is usually directed to the court of matrimonial matters under Article 5 of the Matrimonial Property Regulation, under the Maintenance Regulation, the parties would otherwise have an option to choose from a broader range of jurisdictions.

horizontal cohesion in the jurisdictional context, since the parties will have to select a court in which an agreement can be enforced. For instance, partners would need to opt for a jurisdiction under the Article 7 of the Partnership Property Regulation that recognises this type of relationship and participates in this instrument; this would accordingly restrict a coordinating choice of court under the Article 4 of the Maintenance Regulation.

11.5.3. GAPS TO BE ADDRESSED

Several notable areas to be addressed, with a view to the manifestation of free will in the EU's private international law rules on family matters and succession, have emerged throughout this evaluation:

1. As has been made clear in this and prior sections,[1250] Article 7 of the Property Regulations is not generally intended to be used by parties in order to determine jurisdiction for proceedings concerning property relations upon the dissolution of their relationship. However, in view of the broader jurisdictional choice facilitated under this provision, it is suggested that its remit be extended to become an alternative option for decision-making concerning property relations upon the dissolution of a marriage or registered partnership.
2. The opportunity for parties to select the law of their habitual residence at a particular point in time would be a valuable addition to the Succession Regulation. It is argued that this inclusion would still maintain the delicate balance between the interests of parties in planning their estate and the expectations of the beneficiaries.
3. In view of the default connection between the jurisdiction that is competent for a succession and that which governs the resulting dissolution of a couple's property regime, the influence of all 'parties concerned' in a succession appears to be an inappropriate encroachment upon the free will of the surviving spouse or partner. It is argued that in such situations, the surviving spouse should be the only party who participates in jurisdictional choice under the mechanisms established in the Succession Regulation.
4. Legislative gaps (notably the absence of a choice of court under the Brussels II bis Regulation and the lack of unified private international law rules on the dissolution of registered partnerships) hold the potential to restrict the breadth of choice permitted in coordinating related choices. In light of this and of other areas of impact that have been discussed previously

[1250] See also 11.2.1. and 11.4.2.

in this chapter,[1251] addressing these gaps should be a priority for the EU legislator.[1252]

5. As highlighted in several areas of this analysis, it is unfortunate that the renewed Brussels IIa (Recast) Regulation has now been introduced without including a possibility for party autonomy in matrimonial matters. It can be commented that this omission is the result of, on the one hand, a strong reluctance by certain Member States to accept party autonomy in the sensitive realm of family matters (as arguably evidenced by the need to rely on enhanced cooperation with regard to Rome III and the Property Regulations) and, on the other hand, the desire of the EU legislator to achieve consensus amongst the Member States on this key instrument. In any event, it is now clear that this particular gap within the legislative framework will continue to exist for the foreseeable future.
6. Throughout this synthesis, it has been made clear that the exercise of party autonomy in maintenance obligations, particularly under the Maintenance Regulation, is not subject to sufficient safeguards. This is an area that is based on an inherent power imbalance, and steps ought to be taken to address this in order to ensure the fullness of consent. It has been argued that a discretionary approach, whereby jurisdiction is determined upon party agreement at the time of proceedings in a similar manner to Article 12 of Brussels II bis, would be appropriate given the problems that arise from party autonomy in the relational context.[1253] Whilst this method is particularly invasive, given the concerns that have been highlighted with regard to the impact of the present construction of jurisdictional party autonomy rules in the context of maintenance obligations (e.g. the challenge to informed consent in light of the possibility to make an indeterminate choice of court that continues in perpetuity under Article 4 of the Maintenance Regulation), it can be seen as a suitable option to be considered for remedying those problems.

   With specific regard to the possibility to accept jurisdiction by entering an appearance under Article 5 of the Maintenance Regulation, it can be commented that greater material safeguards should be in place in order to ensure that parties are adequately informed regarding their choice and its consequences in this setting (see example of material requisites under

1251 See 11.2.1.–11.2.2. and 11.4.1.–11.4.2.

1252 With regard to the dissolution of registered partnerships, see the suggestion in a recent EU-funded study that recommended the (at the time pending) recast of Brussels II bis should include such relationships within the scope of its rules through the introduction of a ground focused upon the Member State where the partnership was registered: Viarengo / Marchetti (Chapter 3, n.313), at p.26.

1253 Walker (Chapter 2, n.164), at pp.251–253, 255–257.

Article 8(2) of the Property Regulations), especially in view of the possibility for minors to be involved in this particular mechanism.

Notwithstanding the general need to strengthen the level of protection offered by the Maintenance Regulation, it has been observed that the blanket exclusion of the possibility to select a court in situations involving minors is unduly restrictive and unsuitable to cater to the variances of the child's best interests. It is thus suggested that the EU legislator examine the option of allowing a restricted form of party autonomy in such circumstances, subject to this aforementioned requirement.[1254]

Beyond the need to reconsider the possibility for party autonomy in the context of proceedings involving minors under the Maintenance Regulation, it is argued that future drafters should aim also to bring this instrument into line with the Hague Maintenance Protocol by establishing a parallel framework of safeguards designed to address the position of the vulnerable adult.

7. With reference to the issues of time lapse discussed in this and previous sections,[1255] there is an apparent absence of regard for the situation in which a chosen jurisdiction or applicable law has become disconnected from one or both of the parties through the passage of time. In order to tackle this problem, the discretionary approach outlined in the previous point (11.5.3. point 6) can be drawn upon. However, notwithstanding the specific merits of this method in the context of maintenance obligations, it is argued that there are less invasive means by which the EU legislator could generally deal with a time lapse in other areas of cross-border family law. For instance, this could be tackled by setting aside an agreement where one of the parties objects to it and there has been an appreciable change in circumstances (e.g. where neither party is habitually resident in the Member State which has been designated in a prior choice of court agreement for maintenance obligations).
8. It is proposed that the EU legislator re-examine its position in view of the comparative lack of material or substantive requirements imposed upon choice of court agreements within the present framework. It has been suggested that the drafters might take inspiration from Article 10 of the new Brussels IIa (Recast) Regulation or Article 25(1) of the Brussels I Recast as a starting point in this regard.
9. Although is evident that the EU has established substantive standards with regard to certain fundamental matters that it wishes to safeguard

---

1254 The format of such an approach would align with Walker's suggested involvement of judicial discretion for a general choice of court under the Maintenance Regulation. Walker (Chapter 2, n.164).

1255 See 11.4.1.

(e.g. Article 10 of Rome III), a well-defined stance on the importance of informed consent is not apparent in the relevant instruments. It is proposed that a rule requiring parties to seek independent legal advice before making a choice of court or law should be established within the relevant instruments, in order to provide a uniform safeguard in view of the general and specific power imbalances that foreseeably arise in family relationships.

11.6. CLOSING REMARKS

In coming to the end of this examination of party autonomy within the EU private international law framework relating to family matters and succession, a few closing observations can be made with a view to the coherence of these provisions with the parameters established in the Union setting. First and foremost, it is clear that party autonomy in this area holds immense potential as a means of tackling the obstacles faced by those who exercise their right to free movement within the European Union. Despite the constraints placed upon this freedom in cross-border family matters and succession, the provision of choice on a unified level allows parties the opportunity to cultivate their own legal conditions to fit their individual needs and circumstances.

At the same time, however, it is also obvious that party autonomy in this realm is an evolving project, a 'work in progress'. It presents a complicated and, at times, inconsistent, network of rules that necessitates further appraisal and development. To some extent this can be explained by the rapid but unsynchronised manner of the legislative action that has occurred during the past 20 years: it is thus suggested that the Union should move forward with the goal of creating a framework of rules that functions harmoniously as a whole (e.g. through consolidation of the relevant instruments into a single entity[1256]).

The restricted nature of choice in this realm is an acknowledgment of the fact that family and succession matters strike at the heart of the personal lives of individuals. However, it is apparent that the drafting of the current texts fails at times to reflect this position. In particular, there is a need to develop a uniformly high standard in both formal and material requirements in order to safeguard the fullness of consent in interactions that may readily involve

[1256] See analysis of the options in this regard in: X. Kramer, *European Private International Law: The way forward* in Policy Dept Citizens' Rights and Constitutional Affairs: Workshop on Upcoming Issues of EU Law (September 2014), PE 509.987, at pp.95–102. https://www.europarl.europa.eu/RegData/etudes/IDAN/2014/509987/IPOL_IDA%282014%29509987_EN.pdf.

financial and/or emotional dependency. Furthermore, the potential for disassociation from a prior choice, which is exacerbated by the long-running nature of relationships or processes in this realm, is a matter that requires deeper consideration.

Above and beyond the preceding discussion, it is the legislative and participatory gaps in this framework that appear to be the principal obstacles to achieving the full potential that party autonomy purports to offer in the context of cross-border family matters and succession. Recent history has demonstrated that in order to move forward and address these problem areas, legislative drive is not enough. The focus must be shifted to fostering a renewed desire amongst the Member States to achieve political consensus. It is hoped that this investigation, and other similar undertakings, will serve to contribute to this debate by providing a balanced evaluation of party autonomy within the present framework with a view to maximising the tangible opportunities that it offers EU citizens in the enjoyment of their fundamental freedoms.

BIBLIOGRAPHY

BOOKS

N.A. Baarsma, *The Europeanisation of International Family Law* (T.M.C. Asser Press, The Hague, 2011)

C. Barnard, *The Substantive Law of the EU: The Four Freedoms*, 3rd edn. (Oxford University Press, Oxford, 2010)

Bartolus, *Bartolus on the Conflict of Laws*, 3rd edn., J. Beale (trans.) (The Lawbook Exchange Ltd., Clark NJ, 2003)

J. Basedow, *The Law of Open Societies – Private Ordering and Public Regulation of International Relations* (Brill Nijhoff, Leiden, 2015)

J. Basedow et al. (eds.), *Encyclopedia of Private International Law* (Elgar, Cheltenham, 2017)

U. Bernitz et al., *General principles of EC law in a process of development* (Kluwer, Alphen aan den Rijn, 2008)

M. Brosch, *Rechtswahl und Gerichtsstandsvereinbarung im internationalen Familien- und Erbrecht der EU* (Mohr Siebeck, Heidelberg, 2019)

I. Brownlie, *The Rule of Law in International Affairs. International Law at the Fiftieth Anniversary of the United Nations* (Martinus Nijhoff Publishers, The Hague/London/Boston, 1998)

I. Curry-Sumner, *All's Well That Ends Registered?* (Intersentia, Antwerp, 2005)

A.V. Dicey, *Introduction to the Study of the Law and the Constitution* (Macmillan Press, London, 1959)

A.V. Dicey, *Conflict of Laws*. 5th edn. (Sweet and Maxwell, London, 1932)

J. Fawcett and J. Carruthers, *Cheshire, North and Fawcett: Private International Law*, 14th edn. (Oxford University Press, Oxford, 2008)

M. Harding, *Conflict of Laws*, 5th edn. (Routledge, Abingdon, 2013)

T.C. Hartley, *The Foundations of European Union Law*, 7th edn. (Oxford University Press, Oxford, 2010)

M. Hook, *The Choice of Law Contract* (Hart Publishing, Oxford, 2016)

D. van Iterson, *Ouderlijke Verantwoordelijkheid en Kinderbescherming* (Maklu, Apeldoorn/Antwerp, 2011)

I. Kant, *Groundwork on the Metaphysics of Morals*, M. Gregor (ed.) (Cambridge University Press, Cambridge, 1996)

K. Kroll, *Die Rolle der Parteiautonomie im europäischen Kollisionsrecht* (Mohr Siebeck, Heidelberg, 2013)

J.-J. Kuipers, *EU Law and Private International Law: The Interrelationship in Contractual Obligations* (Martinus, Nijhoff Publishers, Leiden/Boston MA, 2012)

J. Locke, *The Second Treatise of Civil Government*, 6th edn., T. Hollis, (ed.) (A. Millar et al., London, 1764)

E. McKendrick, *Contract Law: Text, Cases, and Materials*, 5th edn. (Oxford University Press, Oxford, 2012)

A. Mills, *Party Autonomy in Private International Law* (Cambridge University Press, Cambridge, 2018)

P. Nygh, Autonomy in International Contracts (Clarendon Press, Oxford, 1999)

A. Pillet, *Principes de Droit International Privé* (Perdone, Paris, 1903)

J. Raitio, *The Principle of Legal Certainty in EC Law* (Kluwer, Dordrecht, 2003)

M. Reimann and R. Zimmerman, *The Oxford Handbook of Comparative Law* (Oxford University Press, Oxford, 2006)

J.J. Rousseau, *The Social Contract*, 1st edn. D.G.H. Cole, (trans.) (J.M. Dent, London and Toronto / E.P. Dutton and Co, New York, 1913).

H. Schermers and D.F. Waelbroeck, *Judicial Protection in the European Union*, 6th edn. (Kluwer, The Hague, 2001)

J.M. Scherpe (ed.), *Marital Agreements and Party Autonomy in Comparative Perspective* (Hart Publishing, Oxford and Portland, 2012)

J. Schwarze, *European Administrative Law*, 1st revised edn. (Sweet and Maxwell, London, 2006)

M.N. Shúilleabháin, *Cross-Border Divorce Law: Brussels II bis* (Oxford University Press, Oxford, 2011)

T. Tridimas, *The General Principles of EC Law* (Oxford University Press, Oxford, 1999)

G. van Calster, *European Private International Law*, 2nd edn. (Hart Publishing, Oxford and Portland, 2016)

F.K. von Savigny, *Private International Law. A Treatise on the Conflict of Laws, and the Limits of Their Operation in Respect of Place and Time*, W. Guthrie (trans.), (T.&T. Clark, Edinburgh, Stevens and Sons, London, 1869)

L. Walker, *Maintenance and Child Support in Private International Law* (Hart Publishing, Oxford, 2015)

CHAPTERS IN EDITED VOLUMES

M. Abendroth, 'Choice of Court in Matters Relating to Maintenance Obligations' in P. Beaumont et al. (eds.), *The Recovery of Maintenance in the EU and Worldwide* (Hart Publishing, Oxford, 2014)

H.G. Beale, 'Duress and Undue Influence' in H.G. Beale (ed.), *Chitty on Contracts*, 30th edn. (Sweet and Maxwell, London, 2008)

R. Blauwhoff and L. Frohn 'International Commercial Surrogacy Arrangements: The Interests of the Child as a Concern of Both Human Rights and Private International Law' in C. Paulussen et al. (eds.), *Fundamental Rights in International and European Law* (T.M.C. Asser Press, the Hague, 2016)

M. Bodgan, 'Private International Law as Component of the Law of the Forum. General Course on Private International Law' in *Collected Courses of the Hague Academy of International Law, Volume 348* (Brill Nijhoff, Leiden, 2011)

K. Boele-Woelki, 'Unification and Harmonisation of Private International Law in Europe' in E. Hondius and F.W. Grosheide (eds.), *International Contract Law 2003: Articles on Various Aspects of Transnational Contract Law* (Intersentia, Antwerp, 2004)

A. Borrás, 'Chapter II – Jurisdiction, Section 1 – Divorce, Legal Separation and Marriage Annulment' in U. Magnus and P. Mankowski (eds.), *Brussels IIbis Regulation* (Sellier, Munich, 2012)

E. Castellanos Ruiz, 'Article 22: Choice of Law' in A. Calvo Caravaca et al. (eds.), *The EU Succession Regulation: A Commentary* (Cambridge University Press, Cambridge, 2016)

L. Collins et al. (eds.), *Dicey, Morris and Collins on the Conflict of Laws*, 14th edn. (Sweet and Maxwell, London, 2006)

G. Contaldi, 'Article 30: Special Rules Imposing Restrictions Concerning or Affecting the Succession in Respect of Certain Assets' in A. Calvo Caravaca et al. (eds.), *The EU Succession Regulation: A Commentary* (Cambridge University Press, Cambridge, 2016)

G. Contaldi and C. Grieco, 'Article 35: Public Policy (ordre public)' in A. Calvo Caravaca et al. (eds.), *The EU Succession Regulation: A Commentary* (Cambridge University Press, Cambridge, 2016)

A. Davì, 'Article 34: Renvoi' in A Calvo Caravaca et al. (eds.), *The EU Succession Regulation: A Commentary* (Cambridge University Press, Cambridge, 2016)

N. Dethloff, 'Arguments for the Unification and Harmonisation of Family law in Europe' in K. Boele-Woelki (ed.), *Perspectives for the Unification and Harmonisation of Family Law in Europe* (Intersentia, Antwerp, 2003)

N. Dethloff, 'Contracting in Family Law: A European perspective' in K. Boele-Woelki et al. (eds.), *The future of family property in Europe* (Intersentia, Antwerp, 2011)

M. Fallon, 'Constraints of Internal Market Law on Family Law' in J. Meeusen et al. (eds.), *International Family Law for the European Union* (Intersentia, Antwerp, 2007)

F. Ferrand, 'The Council Regulation (EC) No 4/2009 of 18 December 2008' in B. Campuzano Díaz et al. (eds.), *Latest Developments in EU Private International Law* (Intersentia, Antwerp, 2011)

P. Franzina 'Article 83: Transitional Provisions' in A. Calvo Caravaca et al. (eds.), *The EU Succession Regulation: A Commentary* (Cambridge University Press, Cambridge, 2016)

P. Franzina, 'The Evolving Role of Nationality in Private International Law' in A. Annoni and S. Forlati (eds.), *The Changing Role of Nationality in International Law* (Routledge, London, 2013)

R. Frimston, 'Chapter I: Scope and Definitions' in U. Bergquist et al. (eds.), *EU Regulation on Succession and Wills* (Otto Schmidt, Cologne, 2015)

R. Geimer, 'EG-VO Ehesachen, Verfahren betreffend die elterliche Verantwortung' in R. Zöller (ed.), *Zöller Zivilprozessordnung*, 29th edn. (Dr. Otto Schmidt, Köln, 2012)

E. Goossens, 'Different Regulatory Regimes for Registered Partnership and Marriage: Outdated or Indispensible? A European Perspective on the Belgian Model' in A. Verbeke et al (eds.), *Confronting the Frontiers of Family and Succession Law: Liber amicorum Walter Pintens* (Intersentia, Antwerp, 2012)

J. Halliday, 'Characterisation as Maintenance or Succession' in P. Beaumont et al. (eds.), *The Recovery of Maintenance in the EU and Worldwide* (Hart Publishing, Oxford, 2014)

M. Hellner, 'The Maintenance Regulation: A Critical Assessment of the Commission's Proposal' in K. Boele-Woelki and T. Sverdrup (eds.), *European Challenges in Contemporary Family Law* (Intensentia, Antwerp, 2008)

B. Hess and S. Spancken, 'Setting the Scene – the EU Maintenance Regulation' in P. Beaumont et al. (eds.), *The Recovery of Maintenance in the EU and Worldwide* (Hart Publishing, Oxford, 2014)

L. Hinchman, 'Autonomy, Individuality, and Self-determination' in J. Schmidt (ed.), *What is Enlightenment? Eighteenth-century Answers and Twentieth-century Questions* (University of California Press, Oakland CA, 1996)

E.A. Kramer and T. Probst, 'Defects in the Contracting Process' in A.T. von Mehran (ed.), *International Encyclopedia of Comparative Law* (Mohr Siebeck, Tübingen / Martinus Nijhoff, Leiden, 2008)

T. Kruger, 'The Quest for Legal Certainty in International Civil Cases' in *Collected Courses of the Hague Academy of International Law, Volume 380* (Brill Nijhoff, Leiden, 2016)

P. Lagarde, 'Chapter III: Applicable law' in U. Bergquist et al. (eds.), *EU Regulation on Succession and Wills* (Otto Schmidt, Cologne, 2015)

O. Lando, 'Contracts' in R. David et al. (eds.), *International Encyclopedia of Comparative Law (Private International Law: Volume 2)* (Mohr Siebeck, Tübingen / Martinus Nijhoff, Leiden, 2011)

J. Mair and E. Örücü (eds.), *The Place of Religion in Family Law: A Comparative Search* (Intersentia, Antwerp, 2011)

F. Marongiu Buonaiuti, 'Article 5: Choice-of-Court Agreement' in A. Calvo Caravaca et al. (eds.), *The EU Succession Regulation: A Commentary* (Cambridge University Press, Cambridge, 2016)

F. Marongiu Buonaiuti, 'Article 6: Declining of Jurisdiction in the Event of a Choice of Law' in A. Calvo Caravaca et al. (eds.), *The EU Succession Regulation: A Commentary* (Cambridge University Press, Cambridge, 2016)

F. Marongiu Buonaiuti, 'Article 7: Jurisdiction in the Event of a Choice of Law' in A. Calvo Caravaca et al. (eds.), *The EU Succession Regulation: A Commentary* (Cambridge University Press, Cambridge, 2016)

D. Martiny, 'Objectives and Values of EU Private International Law in Family Law' in J. Meeusen et al. (eds.), *International Family Law for the European Union* (Intersentia, Antwerp, 2007)

F. Odersky, 'Chapter II: Jurisdiction' in U. Bergquist et al. (eds.), *EU Regulation on Succession and Wills* (Otto Schmidt, Cologne, 2015)

E. Pataut, 'Chapter II – Jurisdiction, Section 2 – Parental Responsibility', in: U. Magnus and P. Mankowski (eds.), *Brussels IIbis Regulation* (Sellier, Munich, 2012)

W. Pintens, 'Chapter I: Scope and Definitions' in U. Magnus and P. Mankowski (eds.), *Brussels IIbis Regulation* (Sellier, Munich, 2012)

P. Quinzá Redondo, 'The EU Regulation of 24 June 2016 in Matters of Matrimonial Property Regimes: A General Overview' in A. Corella et. al. (eds.), *Legal Challenges of the XXI Century* (Tirant lo Blanch, Valencia, 2017)

P. Reuss, 'Art 4 EuUntVO' in R. Geimer and R. Schütze (eds.), *Internationaler Rechtsverkehr in Zivil- und Handelssachen*, 43rd edn. (Beck, Munich, 2012)

B. Reinhartz, 'Chapter VII: General and Final Provisions' in U. Bergquist et al. (eds.), *EU Regulation on Succession and Wills* (Otto Schmidt, Cologne, 2015)

J. Rodrigo Rodríguez, 'Article 24: Dispositions of Property Upon Death Other than Agreements as to Succession' in A. Calvo Caravaca et al. (eds.), *The EU Succession Regulation: A Commentary* (Cambridge University Press, Cambridge, 2016)

G. Rühl, 'Choice of Law by the Parties' in J. Basedow et al. (eds.), *Max Planck Encyclopedia of European Private Law* (Oxford University Press, Oxford, 2012)

S. Schmahl, 'Artikel 65 EGV' in A. Bardenhewer-Rating et al. (eds.), Kommentar zum Vertrag über die Europäische Union und zur Gründung der Europäischen Gemeinschaft (Nomos, Baden-Baden, 2003)

H.J. Snijders, 'Privacy of contract' in K. Ziegler (ed.), *Human Rights and Private Law: Privacy as Autonomy* (Hart Publishing, Oxford, 2007)

G. Straetmans, 'Non-economic Free Movement of EU Citizens and Family Law Matters' in J. Meeusen et al. (eds.), *International Family Law for the European Union* (Intersentia, Antwerp, 2007)

T. Szabados, 'Companies in EU Private International Law – An EU Law Perspective' in M. Király and T. Szabados (eds.), *Perspectives of Unification of Private International Law in the European Union* (Eötvös University Press, Budapest, 2018)

M. Torga, 'Drawing a Demarcating Line between Spousal Maintenance Obligations and Matrimonial Property in the Context of the New Instruments of European Union Private International Law' in P. Beaumont et al. (eds.), *The Recovery of Maintenance in the EU and Worldwide* (Hart Publishing, Oxford, 2014)

P. Wautelet, 'Party Autonomy in International Family Relationships: A Research Agenda' in C. Cauffman and J.M. Smits (eds.), *The Citizen in European Private Law* (Intersentia, Antwerp, 2016)

P. Wautelet, 'Private International Law Aspects of Same-sex Marriages and Partnerships in Europe' in K. Boele-Woelki and A. Fuchs (eds.), *Legal Recognition of Same-sex Relationships in Europe*, 2nd edn. (Intersentia, Antwerp, 2012)

M. Weller, 'Article 1: Scope' in A. Calvo Caravaca et al. (eds.), *The EU Succession Regulation: A Commentary* (Cambridge University Press, Cambridge, 2016)

M. Weller, 'Article 3: Definitions' in A. Calvo Caravaca et al. (eds.), *The EU Succession Regulation: A Commentary* (Cambridge University Press, Cambridge, 2016)

T. Wiedmann, 'Artikel 65 EGV' in J. Schwarze (ed.) *EU-Kommentar* (Nomos, Baden-Baden, 2007)

M. Župan, 'Innovations of the 2007 Hague Maintenance Protocol' in P. Beaumont et al. (eds.), *The Recovery of Maintenance in the EU and Worldwide* (Hart Publishing, Oxford, 2014)

JOURNAL ARTICLES

J. Basedow, 'The Communitarisation of the Conflict of Laws Under the Treaty of Amsterdam' (2000) 37 *Common Market Law Review* 687

S. Bariatti, 'Multiple nationalities and EU Private International Law' (2011) 13 *Yearbook of Private International Law* 1

A. Black, 'Window into Shariah Family Law: Part 2 – Aspects of Divorce' (2010) 16 *Family Relationships Quarterly* 2. (Newsletter of the Australian Family Relationships Clearinghouse).

K. Boele-Woelki, 'For Better or For Worse: The Europeanization of International Divorce Law' (2010) 12 *Yearbook of Private International Law* 1

K. Boele-Woelki, 'To Be, Or Not to Be: Enhanced Cooperation in International Divorce Law within the European Union' (2008) 39(4) *Victoria University Wellington Law Review* 779

A. Bonomi, 'Hague protocol on the law applicable to maintenance obligations' (2008) 10 *Yearbook of Private International Law* 333

A. Bonomi, 'Overriding mandatory provisions in the Rome I Regulation on the law applicable to contracts' (2008) 10 *Yearbook of Private International Law.*

L. Bracken, 'Assessing the Best Interests of the Child in Cases of Cross-border Surrogacy: Inconsistency in the Strasbourg Approach?' (2017) 39(3) *Journal of Social Welfare and Family Law* 368

J. Carrascosa González, 'La ley aplicable a la separación judicial y al divorcio en defecto de elección de ley por los cónyuges. Análisis del artículo 8 del Reglamento 1259/2010 de 20 de diciembre de 2010' (2011) 4(1) *Cuadernos de Derecho Transnacional* 52

J.M. Carruthers, 'Party Autonomy in the Legal Regulation of Adult Relationships: What Place for Party Choice in Private International Law?' (2012) 61(4) *International and Comparative Law Quarterly* 881

I. Curry-Sumner, 'Reactie op Artikel Alimentatieverordening 4/2009' (2013) 4(2) *Tijdschrift Relatierecht en Praktijk* 69

S. Darwall, 'The Value of Autonomy and Autonomy of the Will' (2006) 116(2) *Ethics* 263

Th. de Boer, 'The Purpose of Uniform Choice-of-law Rules' (2009) 56(3) *Netherlands International Law Review* 295

A. Fiorini, 'I. The Evolution of European Private International Law' (2008) 57(4) *International and Comparative Law Quarterly* 969.

S. Francq, 'Parental Responsibility under "Brussels II"' (2003) 4(1) *ERA-Forum* 54

V. Gaertner, 'European Choice of Law Rules in Divorce (Rome III): An Examination of the Possible Connecting Factors in Divorce Matters Against the Background of Private International Law Developments' (2006) 2(1) *Journal of Private International Law* 99

J. Gray, 'Identifying the Impetus behind the Europeanization of the Private International Law Rules on Family Matters and Succession' (2015) 17(2) *European Journal of Law Reform* 341

J. Gray and P. Quinzá Redondo, 'Stress-Testing the EU Proposal on Matrimonial Property Regimes: Co-operation between EU Private International Law Instruments on Family Matters and Succession', *Family and Law* (2013), available at: http://www.familyandlaw.eu/tijdschrift/fenr/2013/11/FENR-D-13-00008.

G.-R. de Groot and J.-J. Kuipers, 'The New Provisions on Private International Law in the Treaty of Lisbon' (2008) 15(1) *Maastricht Journal of International and Comparative Law* 109

S. Gössl, 'The Public Policy Exception in the European Civil Justice System' (2016) 4 *The European Legal Forum* 85

F. Ibili, '3.1 Tijdstip en wijze van aanvaarding bij: Verordening (EG) Nr. 2201/2003 betreffende de bevoegdheid en de erkenning en tenuitvoerlegging van beslissingen in huwelijkszaken en inzake de ouderlijke verantwoordelijkheid, en tot intrekking van Verordening (EG) nr. 1347/2000, Artikel 12', *Groene Serie Personen- en familierecht* (2017).

F. Ibili, '3.4.1 'onmogelijk' bij: Verordening (EG) Nr. 2201/2003 betreffende de bevoegdheid en de erkenning en tenuitvoerlegging van beslissingen in huwelijkszaken en inzake de ouderlijke verantwoordelijkheid, en tot intrekking van Verordening (EG) nr. 1347/2000, Artikel 12', *Groene Serie Personen- en familierecht* (2017)

J. Israel, 'Conflicts of Law and the EC after Amsterdam: A Change for the Worse?' (2000) 7(1) *Maastricht Journal of European and Comparative Law* 81

E. Jayme, 'Party Autonomy in International Family and Succession Law: New Tendencies' (2009) 11 *Yearbook of Private International Law* 1

E. Jayme, 'Rapport definitif' (1991) 64(1) *Annuaire de l'Institut de Droit International* 62

G. Kaeckenbeeck, 'The Protection of Vested Rights in International law' (1936) 17(1) *British Yearbook of International Law* 1

J.-J. Kuipers, 'Cartesio and Grunkin-Paul: Mutual Recognition as a Vested Rights Theory Based on Party Autonomy in Private Law' (2009) 2(2) *European Journal of Legal Studies* 66

T. Kruger and L. Samyn, 'Brussels II bis: Successes and Suggested Improvements' (2016) 12(1) *Journal of Private International Law* 132

T. Kruger 'Rome III and Parties' Choice', *Family and Law* (2014), available at: http://www.familyandlaw.eu/tijdschrift/fenr/2014/01/FENR-D-13-00010

T. Kruger and J. Verhellen, 'Dual Nationality = Double Trouble?' (2011) 7(3) *Journal of Private International Law* 601

V. Lazić, 'Procedural Justice for "Weaker Parties" in Cross-Border Litigation under the EU Regulatory Scheme' (2014) 10(4) *Utrecht Law Review* 100

M. Lehmann, 'Liberating the Individual from Battles Between States: Justifying Party Autonomy in Conflicts of Laws' (2008) 41(2) *Vanderbilt Journal of Transnational Law* 381

M. Lehmann, 'What's in a Name? Grunkin-Paul and Beyond' (2008) 10 *Yearbook of Private International Law* 135

E. Lein, 'The new Rome I / Rome II / Brussels I synergy' (2008) 10 *Yearbook of Private International Law* 177

P. Mancini, 'De l'Utilite de Rendre Obligatoires pour Tous les Etats …', (1874) 5(1) *Journal du Droit International Privé et de la Jurisprudence Comparée* 221

F. Maultzsch, 'Party Autonomy in European Private International Law: Uniform Principle or Context-Dependent Instrument' (2009) 12(3) *Journal of Private International Law* 466

P. McEleavy, 'The Communitarization of Divorce Rules: What Impact for English and Scottish Law?' (2004) 53(3) *International and Comparative Law Quarterly* 605

P. McEleavy, 'Current developments: I. Brussels II bis: Matrimonial Matters, Parental Responsibility and Mutual Recognition' (2004) 53(2) *International and Comparative Law Quarterly* 503

J. Mertens de Wilmars, 'The Case-law of the Court of Justice in Relation to the Review of the Legality of Economic Policy in Mixed-economy Systems' (1982) 9(1) *Legal Issues of European Integration* 1

J. Meeusen, '"What Has it Got to do Necessarily with the European Union?": International Family Law and European (Economic) Integration' (2006–2007) 9 *Cambridge Yearbook of European Legal Studies* 329

H. Muir-Watt, 'Party Autonomy in International Contracts: From the Makings of the Myth to the Requirements of Global Governance', (2010) 6(3) *European Review of Contract Law* 250

C.I. Nagy, 'What Functions May Party Autonomy Have in International Family and Succession Law? An EU Perspective' (2012) 4 *Nederlands Internationaal Privaatrecht* 576

M. Pauknerová, 'Mandatory Rules and Public Policy in International Contract Law' (2010) 11(1) *ERA Forum* 29

E. Paunio, 'Beyond Predictability – Reflections on Legal Certainty and the Discourse Theory of Law in the EU Legal Order' (2009) 10(11) *German Law Journal* 1469

S. Peari, 'The Choice-Based Perspective of Choice-of-Law' (2013) 23 *Duke Journal of Comparative & International Law* 477

S. Peari, 'Choice-of-law in Family Law: Kant, Savigny and the Parties' Autonomy Principle' (2012) 4 *Nederlands Internationaal Privaatrecht* 597

L. Rademacher, 'Changing the Past: Retroactive Choice of Law and the Protection of Third Parties in the European Regulations on Equity Consequences of Marriages and Registered Partnerships' (2018) 10(1) *Cuadernos de Derecho Transnacional* 7

T. Rauscher, 'Parental responsibility cases under the new Council Regulation "Brussels IIa"' (2005) 1 *The European Legal Forum* 31

P. Rogerson, 'Habitual Residence: The New Domicile?' (2000) 49(1) *International and Comparative Law Quarterly* 86

G. Rühl, 'Party Autonomy in the Private International Law of Contracts: Transatlantic Convergence and Economic Efficiency', 3 *CLPE Research Paper* 1 (2007)

A. Shapira, 'Territorialism, National Parochialism, Universalism and Party Autonomy: How Does One Square the Choice-of-law Circle?' (2000) 26 *Brooklyn Journal of International Law* 199

S. Symeonides, 'The Hague Principles on Choice of Law for International Contracts: Some Preliminary Comments' (2013) 61 *The American Journal of Comparative Law* 4

S. Symeonides 'Party Autonomy in Rome I and II: An Outsider's Perspective' (2010) 28(2) *Nederlands International Privaatrecht* 191

S. Verburgt, 'Bevoegdheid, Erkenning en Tenuitvoerlegging onder Alimentatieverordening 4/2009' (2012) 7 *Tijdschrift voor Relatierecht en Praktijk* 296

I. Viarengo, 'Choice of Law Agreements in Property Regimes, Divorce, and Succession: Stress-testing the New EU Regulations' (2016) 17(4) *ERA Forum* 543

I. Viarengo, 'The Rome III Regulation in Legal Practice: Case Law and comments' (2014) 15(4) *ERA Forum* 547

I. Viarengo, 'The EU Proposal on Matrimonial Property Regimes' (2012) 13 *Yearbook of Private International Law*

P. Vlas, '4. Exclusieve bevoegdheid bij: Verordening (EG) nr. 4/2009 betreffende de bevoegdheid, het toepasselijke recht, de erkenning en de tenuitvoerlegging van beslissingen, en de samenwerking op het gebied van onderhoudsverplichtingen, Artikel 4 Forumkeuze', *Groene Serie Burgerlijke Rechtsvordering* (2011)

L. Walker, 'Party autonomy, inconsistency and the specific characteristics of family law in the EU' (2018) 14(2) *Journal of Private International Law*

T. Yetano, The Constitutionalisation of Party Autonomy in European Family Law (2010) 6(1) *Journal of Private International Law* 155

M. Zhang, 'Party Autonomy and Beyond: An International Perspective of Contractual Choice of Law' (2006) 20 *Emory International Law Review* 511

OTHER RESOURCES

EU DOCUMENTATION

Action plan of the Council and the Commission on how best to implement the provisions of the Treaty of Amsterdam on an area of freedom, security and justice, [1999] OJ C 19

K. Boele-Woelki, European Parliament Note: *The Proposal for enhanced cooperation in the area of cross-border divorce* (Rome III) (2010), PE 432.730

A. Borrás, Explanatory Report on the Convention, drawn up on the basis of Article K.3 of the Treaty on European Union, on Jurisdiction and the Recognition and Enforcement of Judgments in Matrimonial Matters, approved by the Council on 28 May 1998 [1998] OJ C 221

C. Chateau, *European Parliament Briefing: Adoption: Cross-border legal issues and gaps in the European Union* (2015), PE 536.480

Commission Decision (EU) 2016/1366 of 10 August 2016 confirming the participation of Estonia in enhanced cooperation in the area of the law applicable to divorce and legal separation, OJ EU L 216

Communication from the Commission to the European Parliament, the Council, the European Economic and Social Committee and the Committee of the Regions, *Bringing legal clarity to property rights for international couples*, COM(2011) 125/3

Council of the European Union, *Press release: More effective rules to deal with cross border matrimonial matters and parental responsibility issues* (25 June 2019), available at: https://www.consilium.europa.eu/en/press/press-releases/2019/06/25/more-effective-rules-to-deal-with-cross-border-matrimonial-matters-and-parental-responsibility-issues/

Council of the European Union, *Interinstitutional File of the 30 November 2018: Proposal for a Council Regulation on jurisdiction, the recognition and enforcement of decisions in matrimonial matters and the matters of parental responsibility, and on international child abduction (recast) – General approach*, 10767/16 JUSTCIV 292

Council of the European Union, *Press release: 18 EU countries agree to clarify rules on property regimes for international couples* (9 June 2016), available at: http://www.consilium.europa.eu/en/press/press-releases/2016/06/09/property-regimes-for-international-couples/

European Commission, *Study on the assessment of Regulation (EC) No 2201/2003 and the policy options for its amendment: Final report, analytical annexes* (2018)

European Commission, Practice Guide for the application of the Brussels IIa Regulation (2014), available at: https://e-justice.europa.eu/fileDownload.do?id=b1f086c0-8d5b-4cb9-ad0e-85e38d528c7a

European Commission, *Communication from the Commission to the European Parliament, the Council, the European Economic and Social Committee and the Committee of the Regions: Bringing legal clarity to property rights for international couples*, COM(2011) 125/3

European Commission, *Commission staff working document accompanying the Proposal for a Regulation of the European Parliament and the Council on jurisdiction, applicable law, recognition and enforcement of decisions and authentic instruments in matters of succession on the introduction of a European Certificate of Inheritance: Impact Assessment*, SEC(2009) 153, available at: https://eur-lex.europa.eu/legal-content/EN/TXT/?uri=CELEX:52009SC0153

European Commission, *Commission staff working document – Annex to the proposal for a Council Regulation amending Regulation (EC) No 2201/2003 as regards jurisdiction and introducing rules concerning applicable law in matrimonial matters – Impact assessment*, COM(2006) 399 final

European Union, *Civil unions and registered partnerships* (30 April 2018), available at: https://europa.eu/youreurope/citizens/family/couple/registered-partners/index_en.htm

FRA, *Access to justice in Europe: an overview of challenges and opportunities* (2010)

Hague Programme: Strengthening Freedom, Security and Justice in the European Union, [2005] OJ C 53/1

X. Kramer, *European Private International Law: The way forward* (September 2014), PE 509.987, p.77

X. Kramer et al., European Parliament Study: *A European framework for private international law* (2012), PE 462.487, p.77

E. Pataut, European Parliament Note: *The public-policy exception and the Proposal for a Regulation of the European Parliament and of the Council on jurisdiction, applicable law, recognition and enforcement of decisions and authentic instruments in matters of succession and the creation of a European Certificate of Succession* (COM(2009)154) (2010), PE 432.741

Spanish Delegation to the Intergovernmental Conference on Political Union: The Road to European Citizenship (24 September 1990), unpublished Council document SN 3940/90

Stockholm Programme: An open and secure Europe, serving and protecting citizens, [2010] OJ C 115/1

Tampere European Council Conclusions 1999

HAGUE CONFERENCE DOCUMENTATION

A. Bonomi, Explanatory Report on the Hague Protocol of 23 November 2007 on the Law Applicable to Maintenance Obligations (HCCH Publications, the Hague, 2013)

M. Donovan and W.M. Waters, Explanatory report on the Law Applicable to Succession to the Estates of Deceased Persons (SDU Publishers, The Hague, 1990)

D. Waters, Explanatory Report on the 1989 Hague Succession Convention (HCCH Publications, the Hague 1990)

COUNCIL OF EUROPE DOCUMENTATION

Parliamentary Assembly of the Council of Europe, *Report: The Principle of the Rule of Law*, Doc.11343 (2007)

ELECTRONIC RESOURCES

T.M.C, Asser Institute et al., *Regulation Brussels IIbis Guide for Application* (2018), available at: http://www.asser.nl/projects-legal-advice/cross-border-proceedings-in-family-law-matters-before-national-courts-and-cjeu/guide-for-application-of-the-brussels-iibis-regulation

Couples in Europe, *Czech Republic: Is there a statutory matrimonial property regime and if so, what does it provide?* Available at: http://www.coupleseurope.eu/en/czech-republic/topics/2-is-there-a-statutory-matrimonial-property-regime-and-if-so-what-does-it-provide

Couples in Europe, *Czech Republic: What does the law provide for the property of registered and non-registered partners?* Available at: http://www.coupleseurope.eu/en/czech-republic/topics/8-what-does-the-law-provide-for-the-property-of-registered-and-non-registered-partners

Couples in Europe, *Republic of Ireland: Which law applies*? Available at: http://www.coupleseurope.eu/en/ireland/topics/1-which-law-applies

Couples in Europe, *Slovenia: what does the law provide for the property of registered and non-registered partners?* Available at: http://www.coupleseurope.eu/en/slovenia/topics/8-what-does-the-law-provide-for-the-property-of-registered-and-non-registered-partners

S. Daugule, *Brochure: Jurisdiction, applicable law, recognition and enforcement of decisions and cooperation in matters relating to maintenance obligations* (2012), at p.8, available at: https://www.tm.gov.lv/files/l1_aWVwaXJrdW1pL3Byb2pla3RpLzQwMDY1X1RNX2Jyb3N1cmFfRU4ucGRm/iepirkumi/projekti/40065_TM_brosura_EN.pdf

K. Boele-Woelki et al, *CEFL: Property relationship between spouses – The Netherlands* (September 2008), available at: http://ceflonline.net/wp-content/uploads/Netherlands-Property.pdf

European Commission, E-Justice Portal: Matters of matrimonial property regimes, available at: https://e-justice.europa.eu/content_matters_of_matrimonial_property_regimes-559-en.do

European Commission, E-Justice Portal: Matters of the property consequences of registered partnerships, available at: https://e-justice.europa.eu/content_matters_of_the_property_consequences_of_registered_partnerships-560-en.do

European Commission, *Property of international couples (marriages and registered partnerships)* available at: https://ec.europa.eu/info/policies/justice-and-fundamental-rights/civil-justice/family-law/property-international-couples-marriages-and-registered-partnerships_en#registeredpartnership

European Commission, *The information referring to Article 79 of Regulation (EU) No 650/2012 of the European Parliament and of the Council of 4 July 2012 on jurisdiction, applicable law, recognition and enforcement of decisions and acceptance and enforcement of authentic instruments in matters of succession and on the creation of a European Certificate of Succession*, available at: https://e-justice.europa.eu/fileDownload.do?id=92645e67-621a-486f-9907-f2b74fd6377a

R. Mańko, *Library of the European Parliament Briefing: "Habitual residence" as connecting factor in EU civil justice measures* (2013), available at: http://www.europarl.europa.eu/RegData/etudes/ATAG/2013/130427/LDM_BRI(2013)130427_REV1_EN.pdf

Notaries of Europe, *European couples are changing, but their need for legal certainty is not*, available at: http://www.notaries-of-europe.eu/index.php?pageID=226

Notaries of Europe, *The New EU Regulation 650/2012 on International Successions*, available at: http://www.notaries-of-europe.eu//index.php?pageID=9836

B. Rudevska, 'The "Coman" Case (C-673/16): Some reflections from the point of view of private international law' (2 July 2018), available at: http://conflictoflaws.net/2018/the-coman-case-c-673-16-some-reflections-from-the-point-of-view-of-private-international-law

W. Pintens et al, *CEFL: Property relationship between spouses – Belgium* (August 2008), available at: http://ceflonline.net/wp-content/uploads/Belgium-Property.pdf

I. Viarengo and F. Marchetti (eds.), 'EU FAM's Policy Guidelines', in: Università degli Studi di Milano et al. (eds.), *Planning the future of cross-border families: a path through coordination* (2017), available at: http://www.eufams.unimi.it/wp-content/uploads/2017/12/EUFAMS-Policy-Guidelines-v1.0.pdf

I. Viarengo and F.C. Villata (eds.), 'Final Study' in Università degli Studi di Milano et al., (eds.), *Planning the future of cross-border families: a path through coordination* (2017), available at: http://www.eufams.unimi.it/wp-content/uploads/2017/12/EUFams-Final-Study-v1.0.pdf

F.C. Villata and L. Valkova, 'Model Choice of Court and Choice of Law Clauses' in: Università degli Studi di Milano et al., (eds.), *Planning the future of cross-border families: a path through coordination* (2017), available at: http://www.eufams.unimi.it/wp-content/uploads/2017/12/EUFAMS-Model-Clauses-v1.0.pdf

MISCELLANEOUS REPORTS

EPEC, Impact Assessment on Community Instruments concerning matrimonial property regimes and property of unmarried couples with transnational elements (2009)

EPEC, Study to inform a subsequent Impact Assessment on the Commission proposal on jurisdiction and applicable law on divorce matters (2006)

Law Commission of England and Wales, Law Commission Report No.48 on jurisdiction in matrimonial causes (1972)

Swiss Institute of Comparative Law, The Application of foreign law in civil matters and its application for the future, JLS/2009/JCIV/PR/0005/E4

T.M.C. Asser Institute, Etude sur les regimes matrimoniaux des couples maries et sur le patrimoine des couples non maries dans le droit international prive et le droit interne des etats membres de l'Union Europeenne: Analyse comparative des rapports nationaux et propositions d'harmonisation (2003)

Utrecht University and University of Vienna, 'Moving to Another Country in the EU? This is what you need to know about the legal implications for your family', *Empowering European Families* (2019), available at: https://www.europeanlawinstitute.eu/fileadmin/user_upload/p_eli/Projects/EEF/EEF_Information_Sheet_for_Couples.pdf

Utrecht University and University of Vienna, 'Toolkit for advising European families: Married couples', *Empowering European Families* (2019), available at: https://backend.univie.ac.at/fileadmin/user_upload/p_eli/Projects/EEF/Toolkit_A_for_Advising_European_Families_Married_Couples.pdf

PRESENTATIONS

W. Grajdura 'Mandatory Rules and Public Policy', ERA Conference on Rome I & Rome II Applicable Law in International Contracts and Torts (Krakow, Poland, 3–4 November 2016)

N. Natov, 'Applicable law in matters relating to maintenance obligations – The 2007 Hague Protocol', EJTN seminar on Maintenance obligations in Europe (Sofia, Bulgaria, 5–6 December 2013)

INDEX

F

H

J

L

European Family Law Series

1. *Legal Recognition of Same-Sex Couples in Europe*, K. Boele-Woelki and A. Fuchs (eds.)
2. *European Family Law in Action Volume I: Grounds for Divorce*, K. Boele-Woelki, B. Braat and I. Sumner (eds.)
3. *European Family Law in Action Volume II: Maintenance Between Former Spouses*, K. Boele-Woelki, B. Braat and I. Sumner (eds.)
4. *Perspectives for the Unification and Harmonisation of Family Law in Europe*, K. Boele-Woelki (ed.)
5. *Family Law Legislation of the Netherlands*, I. Sumner and H. Warendorf
6. *Indépendance et interdépendance patrimoniales des époux dans le régime matrimonial légal des droits néerlandais, français et suisse*, B. Braat
7. *Principles of European Family Law Regarding Divorce and Maintenance Between Former Spouses*, K. Boele-Woelki, F. Ferrand, C. González Beilfuss, M. Jänterä-Jareborg, N. Lowe, D. Martiny and W. Pintens
8. *Inheritance Law Legislation of the Netherlands*, I. Sumner and H. Warendorf
9. *European Family Law in Action Volume III: Parental Responsibilities*, K. Boele-Woelki, B. Braat and I. Curry-Sumner (eds.)
10. *Common Core and Better Law in European Family Law*, K. Boele-Woelki (ed.)
11. *All's well that ends registered?*, I. Curry-Sumner
12. *Model Family Code – From a global perspective*, I. Schwenzer and M. Dimsey
13. *Harmonisation of Family Law in Europe. A Historical Perspective*, M. Antokolskaia
14. *Brussels II bis: Its Impact and Application in the Member States*, K. Boele-Woelki and C. González Beilfuss (eds.)
15. *Tensions between Legal, Biological and Social Conceptions of Parentage*, I. Schwenzer (ed.)
16. *Principles of European Family Law Regarding Parental Responsibilities*, K. Boele-Woelki, F. Ferrand, C. González Beilfuss, M. Jänterä-Jareborg, N. Lowe, D. Martiny and W. Pintens
17. *Juxtaposing Legal Systems and the Principles of European Family Law on Divorce and Maintenance*, E. Örücü and J. Mair (eds.)
18. *Convergence and Divergence of Family Law in Europe*, M. Antokolskaia (ed.)
19. *European Challenges in Contemporary Family Law*, K. Boele-Woelki and T. Sverdrup (eds.)
20. *Children and their parents*, M. Vonk
21. *La capacité de l'enfant dans les droits français, anglais et écossais*, L. Francoz Terminal
22. *Joint Parental Authority*, C.G. Jeppesen de Boer
23. *Debates in Family Law around the Globe at the Dawn of the 21st Century*, K. Boele-Woelki (ed.)
24. *European Family Law in Action Volume IV: Property Relations between Spouses*, K. Boele-Woelki, B. Braat and I. Curry-Sumner (eds.)

25. *Foundational Facts, Relative Truths. A Comparative Law Study on Children's Right to Know Their Genetic Origins*, R. Blauwhoff
26. *Imperative Inheritance Law in a Late-Modern Society. Five Perspectives*, C. Castelein, R. Foqué and A. Verbeke (eds.)
27. *Juxtaposing Legal Systems and the Principles of European Family Law on Parental Responsibilities*, E. Örücü and J. Mair (eds.)
28. *La justice des mineurs en Europe*, Y. Favier and F. Ferrand (eds.)
29. *The Future of Family Property in Europe*, K. Boele-Woelki, J. Miles and J. M. Scherpe (eds.)
30. *The Place of Religion in Family Law: A Comparative Search*, J. Mair and E. Örücü (eds.)
31. *Reconstructing Marriage. The Legal Status of Relationships in a Changing Society*, C. Sörgjerd
32. *Legal Recognition of Same-Sex Relationships in Europe*, K. Boele-Woelki and A. Fuchs (eds.)
33. *Principles of European Family Law Regarding Property Relations Between Spouses*, K. Boele-Woelki, F. Ferrand, C. González Beilfuss, M. Jänterä-Jareborg, N. Lowe, D. Martiny and W. Pintens
34. *Der nacheheliche Unterhalt: Grundlagen und Ausgestaltung im deutschen Unterhaltsrecht und in den Prinzipien der Commission on European Family Law*, P. Beuermann
35. *Family Law and Culture in Europe: Developments, Challenges and Opportunities*, K. Boele-Woelki, N. Dethloff and W. Gephart
36. *Children's Rights in Intercountry Adoption. A European Perspective*, C. Fenton-Glynn
37. *Nordic Cohabitation Law*, J. Asland, M. Brattström, G. Lind, I. Lund-Andersen, A. Singer and T. Sverdrup
38. *European Family Law in Action Volume V: Informal Relationships*, K. Boele-Woelki, C. Mol and E. van Gelder (eds.)
39. *Divided Parents, Shared Children. Legal Aspects of Residential Co-Parenting in England, the Netherlands and Belgium*, N. Nikolina
40. *Family Forms and Parenthood. Theory and Practice of Article 8 ECHR in Europe*, A. Büchler and H. Keller (eds.)
41. *The Child's Interests in Conflict. The Intersections between Society, Family, Faith and Culture*, M. Jänterä-Jareborg (ed.)
42. *Same-Sex Relationships and Beyond. Gender Matters in the EU*, K. Boele-Woelki and A. Fuchs (eds.)
43. *Nacheheliche Verantwortung in Frankreich und Deutschland*, K. Kaesling
44. *The Future of Registered Partnerships: Family Recognition Beyond Marriage?*, J.M. Scherpe and A. Hayward
45. *Plurality and Diversity of Family Relations in Europe*, K. Boele-Woelki and D. Martiny (eds.)
46. *Principles of European Family Law Regarding Property, Maintenance and Succession Rights of Couples in* de facto *Unions*, K. Boele-Woelki, F. Ferrand, C. González Beilfuss, M. Jänterä-Jareborg, N. Lowe, D. Martiny and V. Todorova
47. *Die Familienschiedsgerichtsbarkeit in Recht und Praxis: Eine Rechtsvergleichende Untersuchung des Deutschen und Englischen Rechts*, S.C. Zellerhoff
48. *Elderly Care and Upwards Solidarity*, Elisabeth Alofs and Wendy Schrama (eds.)